STATES OF TRANSITION

STATES OF TRANSITION

*Tackling Government's Toughest
Policy and Management Challenges*

William D. Eggers
Robert N. Campbell III

—————— EDITORS ——————

Deloitte.

A Deloitte Research Book

About Deloitte Research

Deloitte Research, a part of Deloitte Services LLP, identifies, analyzes and explains the major issues driving today's business and public sector dynamics and shaping tomorrow's global marketplace. From provocative points of view about strategy and organizational change to straight talk about economics, regulation and technology, Deloitte Research delivers innovative, practical insights organizations can use to improve their performance. Operating through a network of dedicated research professionals, senior consulting practitioners of the various member firms of Deloitte Touche Tohmatsu, academics and technology specialists, Deloitte Research exhibits deep industry knowledge, functional understanding and commitment to thought leadership. In boardrooms, government capitols and business journals, Deloitte Research is known for bringing new perspective to real-world concerns.

Disclaimer

This publication contains general information only, and Deloitte Development LLC is not, by means of this publication, rendering accounting, business, financial, investment, legal, tax or other professional advice or services. This publication is not a substitute for such professional advice or services, nor should it be used as a basis for any decision or action that may affect your business. Before making any decision or taking any action that may affect your business, you should consult a qualified professional advisor. Deloitte Services LLP, its affiliates and related entities shall not be responsible for any loss sustained by any person who relies on this publication.

Printed in Canada.

Copyright © 2006 Deloitte Development LLC. All rights reserved.

ISBN: 0-9790611-0-5
ISBN-13: 978-0-9790611-0-3

About Deloitte

Deloitte refers to one or more of Deloitte Touche Tohmatsu, a Swiss Verein, its member firms and their respective subsidiaries and affiliates. As a Swiss Verein (association), neither Deloitte Touche Tohmatsu nor any of its member firms has any liability for each other's acts or omissions. Each of the member firms is a separate and independent legal entity operating under the names "Deloitte", "Deloitte & Touche", "Deloitte Touche Tohmatsu" or other related names. Services are provided by the member firms or their subsidiaries or affiliates and not by the Deloitte Touche Tohmatsu Verein.

Deloitte & Touche USA LLP is the U.S. member firm of Deloitte Touche Tohmatsu. In the United States, services are provided by the subsidiaries of Deloitte & Touche USA LLP (Deloitte & Touche LLP, Deloitte Consulting LLP, Deloitte Financial Advisory Services LLP, Deloitte Tax LLP, and their subsidiaries), and not by Deloitte & Touche USA LLP.

CONTENTS

FOREWORD vii
by Governor Tom Ridge

CHAPTER ONE 1
Window of Opportunity

CHAPTER TWO 25
Serving the Aging Citizen

CHAPTER THREE 57
Bolstering Human Capital

CHAPTER FOUR 87
Solving the Pension Crisis

CHAPTER FIVE 115
Fixing Medicaid

CHAPTER SIX 147
Integrating Health and Human Services Delivery

CHAPTER SEVEN 173
Upgrading Emergency Preparedness and Response

CHAPTER EIGHT 207
Driving More Money into the Classroom

CHAPTER NINE 245
Closing the Infrastructure Gap

CHAPTER TEN 277
Transforming State Government

ENDNOTES 305

CONTRIBUTORS 327

ACKNOWLEDGMENTS 330

INDEX 333

{Foreword} *Governor Tom Ridge*

State policymakers hold some of the best political jobs in the nation. Governors and other state leaders wield unrivaled potential for improving Americans' lives and implementing positive change. Perhaps uniquely to U.S. politics, your state programs directly impact huge segments of society—and in many cases shape national policies. You enjoy wide latitude to innovate and have enough influence over state operations to translate your ideas into reality.

Taxpayers have placed immense responsibility in your hands. *States of Transition,* this new book from Deloitte Research, offers innovative and proven strategies for using that responsibility effectively.

This book delivers insights into solving some of the most vexing challenges facing state government leaders, including issues that already top your own to-do lists. You'll find strategies for improving public education by driving more money into classrooms. You'll find solutions for fixing a broken Medicaid system, which now consumes approximately one-quarter of total state budgets. And you'll find techniques for using technology to cut the cost of programs throughout government, while improving services to citizens whose expectations are higher than they ever have been.

For newly elected officials, this book offers advice that can help your administration get off to a quick and effective start. *States of Transition* will help you to face head-on the challenges of state governance—which soon will be landing on your desk at an overwhelming and intimidating pace. For those returning to office, these pages contain fresh ideas for implementing reforms that deliver lasting improvement. There is no simple recipe for transformation. Consider the concepts presented here and apply them in ways that fit the unique requirements of your constituents.

I also want to share a few lessons gleaned from my own experiences. These suggestions stem from advice I received upon entering office, as well as from hard-won experience, sometimes earned through painful mistakes. In passing these recommendations onto state policymakers—from governors to Cabinet secretaries to key staff members—I hope they will help you make the most of your leadership in these vital public service positions.

Here they are:

—*Take action.* Make the most of this fantastic opportunity. Tackle the issues that are most important to your state. Medicaid spending grew dramatically over the last five years, driven by a 40 percent increase in caseload. Be part of the solution that brings these costs under control, while improving services to the 53 million Americans who depend on the program for health care. Or, help reform an education system in danger of being overtaken by competitors abroad and imperiling America's traditional leadership in scientific innovation. Effective leaders are agents for positive change. You've worked incredibly hard to arrive where you are today. No doubt you've carefully considered your agenda. Now it's time to implement it.

—*Avoid complacency.* This is particularly true for administrations entering a second term. Voters rewarded your first-term results with another four years, so you're doing things right. But continue to push your agenda as aggressively as your first day in office. Build your legacy by doing all you can for your citizens every day.

—*Pick clear goals and stick with them.* There is plenty of work to do, but avoid the temptation to take on too many tasks at once. Identify six goals, state them clearly and see them through. Your success hinges on your ability to articulate these goals in a way that prompts others to share your vision.

—*Build a strong staff.* Seek out the best people you can find, wherever they are. Look for people who are committed to your agenda, but who aren't afraid to tell you the truth. And don't keep staff members who don't measure up. Be fair, **but act decisively**. The job is too big and the mission too important to settle for substandard performance.

A special note for governors: cast your net as wide as possible when forming your Cabinets. You'll be inundated with people who want to join your team. Unfortunately, some of the people who helped you win the election won't have the skills to help you govern. Deciding who's right for the task ahead is a delicate issue, but one you'll need to navigate. Create an effective organization to screen applicants—and do it early. This organization will help find the people you need, and just as importantly, it will serve as an invaluable buffer between you and the friends, relatives and supporters seeking employment with your administration.

—*Once you've built your team, empower them.* Give them your trust and support, and ensure they have the resources to succeed. Also, avoid the temptation to micromanage. You chose energetic people who share your vision: let them go to work.

—*Make increased efficiency a priority.* Follow your passion; tackle the issues most important to you and the citizens of your state. But also leave your mark on government's internal operations. Adopt technology that allows state agencies to deliver better programs at lower cost. Shake up old processes when they've outlived their usefulness. The more efficient you become internally, the more effective you'll be externally.

—*Take charge of your schedule.* Those of you starting a second term already know the importance of this. But for new governors and other top officials, we have a warning: competition for your attention will be fierce. Your time is immensely valuable, so spend it wisely. Focus on your goals and try to avoid distractions, of which there will be many. One final point here: build in time for your family. In the coming four years, it will be easy to become consumed with the activity around you. Don't ignore those who supported you on your journey to this office and who'll be with you when the ride is complete.

—*Deal with issues as they arise.* Senior state officials, particularly governors and Cabinet secretaries, can expect an emergency every day—sometimes it's a minor headache, sometimes an all-out migraine. The key is to confront these issues as they come up. Don't ignore them; they won't go away.

—*Use federal waivers to promote innovation.* A variety of waiver processes are available to relax the requirements of federally mandated programs, allowing states to experiment with ways of delivering health care, human services and other programs. Use these waivers to develop innovative new ways of funding, operating and delivering state programs. Be bold and aggressive and do not be afraid to do it.

—*Have fun.* As a governor, senior staff member or state legislator, you probably have spent much of your life working toward this goal. Now you have a chance to positively impact individuals, families and communities throughout your state. Few people reach this level of achievement. Enjoy it, embrace it and make the most of it.

Our nation is starved for problem solvers. History has demonstrated that solutions to many of the country's biggest challenges come from leadership at the state level.

Do all you can to give your citizens a chance to live in good neighborhoods, hold rewarding jobs and attend decent schools. Move decisively to make your state competitive in the global marketplace; partner your colleges and universities with local communities to make them engines of economic advancement. Push for sensible tax and regulatory structures that promote both equity and innovation. At the end of the day, wealth and talent flow toward opportunity. Governors and their administrations play an indispensable role in creating an environment of opportunity in their states, which translates directly into success and prosperity for their citizens.

At the same time, today's state government leaders shoulder unprecedented responsibility for constituent safety and security. Washington may set homeland security policies, but state leaders live at the intersection of policy and real-world implementation. Your actions have direct consequence on the safety of your citizens. Never forget that this vital duty rests on your shoulders.

Fortunately, today's state policy-makers hold office during a time of relative prosperity. After years of fiscal hardship and relentless budget cutting, conditions have rebounded. For the first time in recent memory, state leaders enjoy some financial breathing room, which affords them the ability to invest in reforms that bring dramatic improvement to government operations and to the lives of citizens.

All of you—governors, Cabinet secretaries, senior staff members and state legislators—face awesome responsibility, and yet you also have unlimited opportunity. It's all part of what makes your jobs among the most challenging and rewarding positions anywhere on Earth. Clearly, implementing meaningful changes carries significant risk, and it demands courage. Be confident. Think big. Much of this nation's history was written by state leaders. Now this opportunity is yours.

–The Honorable Tom Ridge
Former governor, Commonwealth of Pennsylvania;
Senior Advisor to Deloitte & Touche USA LLP

{1} *William D. Eggers and Robert N. Campbell III*

Window of Opportunity

The first decade of the 21st century has seen an onslaught of historic events and challenges: September 11th, the Iraq War, the War on Terrorism and the devastation of Hurricane Katrina. In the face of crisis and uncertainty, Americans understandably turn to the federal government. These events have demanded a national response, galvanizing our collective attention on Washington, DC—more so, in fact, than any other time for at least two decades.

These events have made the general public even more aware of government's importance—but also more skeptical of government's ability to effectively carry out its responsibilities as amply demonstrated by the '06 midterm elections when voters sent an unmistakable message to Washington: we want change. In short, Americans expect more from government in a post–9-11/Katrina world, but they trust it less.[1]

This credibility gap between government institutions and Americans presents a big challenge for today's leaders at the state level. States, after all, are directly responsible for many of the most important services and programs government provides directly to individual citizens. Often in partnership with local governments, states provide education, build and maintain the roads that enable commerce, enforce the law and house criminals, deliver social services, deliver Medicaid, organize disaster responses and undertake a host of other critical activities. Citizens see long-standing problems in some of these areas—runaway Medicaid costs, poor education, aged and under-maintained infrastructure—and wonder why improvement seems so slow in coming.

Low expectations, however, may set the stage for a great opportunity—

one that states are particularly well positioned to capitalize on. States are more agile than the federal government—in terms of their ability both to experiment with new solutions and to overcome partisan hurdles. As Tom Ridge (a former governor who also happened to have run one of the largest federal Cabinet agencies) has asserted, states remain the laboratories of democracy—the place where the boldest policy innovations occur. States are also the place where voters tend to put problem solving abilities ahead of partisanship and ideology—especially when they pick their governors (a phenomenon illustrated by the presence of many Democratic governors in red states and Republican governors in blue states).[2] States have also proven to be a fertile training ground for the presidency, with four of our last five presidents having been former governors.

In short, states are incubators for the great ideas and future leaders of American government at a time when citizens are seeking both—but are skeptical about whether government institutions can deliver either.

For these and other reasons we'll discuss in more depth later, we believe we are entering another significant period of state innovation—of daring policy experiments and fundamental reform of the structures and systems of state government. States today have a unique window of opportunity to regain public trust by tackling some of the toughest policy issues, those that have proven vexing for a generation, while also positioning themselves to address the new challenges of the 21st century—from an aging population to growing security concerns, to the challenges of global economic competitiveness.

This is a book about and for the states. It provides a roadmap for new and returning governors and their administrations to address sobering challenges and capitalize on the unparalleled opportunities before them.

Change Imperatives

Just a few short years ago state budgets were in free fall thanks to the post-Y2K recession and the bursting of the dot-com bubble. At the time, the only transformation most governors had the luxury of attending to was of the downsizing variety. The recession forced some across-the-board spending cuts (most of which were restored as soon as tax revenues began flowing back into government coffers), occasional accounting gimmickry and some raiding of rainy day funds—but not a lot of fundamental reform.

Since then, the economy and the budget picture have improved. Most states have found some breathing room, giving today's governors an opportunity that hasn't existed for at least a decade to strategically address some of the longer-term and structural issues they face and create a meaningful legacy for their own administration.

Why now? Several factors favor reform. First, the federal government in recent years has given states greater latitude to innovate and experiment. Governors today also have tools and technologies, unavailable in the past, to take advantage of these flexibilities, manage a state on an enterprise basis and approach citizen service in an integrated way. A large group of 11 freshmen governors is entering office, which history shows tends to bode well for reform. Finally, states today face a series of increasingly urgent challenges which require creative solutions, a subject we now turn to in more depth.

Autumn of Our Years: Demographics

State governments are about to feel the effects of a powerful force: the aging of their populations. This demographic transition will have far-reaching consequences for virtually everything: revenues, recruitment and the needs and expectations of citizens.

The private sector is already feeling the pinch. Baby Boomers are queuing up for retirement, with a much smaller population segment preparing to replace them. Businesses face a looming war for talent, as recruiters see a shrinking supply of skilled employees to fill various positions. To make matters worse, ever fewer Americans meet the educational standards demanded by leading companies, making for a talent pool even smaller than the census data suggest.

State governments are also likely to have difficulty meeting their workforce needs—likely even more so than the private sector. State agencies are not the employer of choice for most college graduates—or even for those with advanced degrees in public policy and administration.[3] Fewer of these graduates are going into government, and even fewer are choosing state government. The reasons for this disinterest vary, but the increased prominence of the federal government in a post–9/11 world, coupled with mission-oriented (and thus more appealing) jobs with federal agencies like the FBI or CIA, make state government less alluring to many top candidates. Moreover, private companies invest in their images and recruiting to attract the best— something state governments have never really tried. Given the emerging scarcity of talented workers, however, that will need to change.

Beyond the challenge of finding good workers, state governments face a less-than-promising revenue forecast. The demographic shift to an older population means that the most economically productive group—those aged 30–50 who provide the lion's share of tax revenues—will shrink in relative terms in many states, and in real terms in others. In 2000, about one-eighth of the U.S. population was 65 or older. By 2030 that group is expected to grow to almost one-fifth of the population.

Consider California. In 2004, roughly 3.8 million of the 36 million people living in California were 65 or older, representing about 11 percent of the state's overall population.[4] The state's older population is expected to double in 25 years and triple in 50 years. On the basis of current rates of labor force participation, the ratio of working-age Californians to those of retirement age will steadily worsen, moving from just over 5-to-1 in 2000 to less than 3-to-1 by 2030.

Beyond the numbers, the overall trend bodes poorly for the current approach to state taxation. In both absolute and per capita terms, seniors on average contribute less in nearly every category of tax receipts. The decline is especially pronounced in the case of income and payroll taxes, but a decline also occurs for sales and property taxes. Property taxes, of course, have been the traditional vehicle for financing schools. Yet these taxes are especially onerous for the elderly, who typically have limited incomes and much of their wealth tied up in their homes. Indeed, the two large groups that cost the most in terms of taxation and services—the old and the young—are growing, but the population that provides the most in tax revenue is shrinking. These challenges will force states to take a hard look at tax modernization.

Budget Busters

Whatever direction revenues take over the next decade or two, several line items in states' budgets are currently on unsustainable trajectories. In these areas costs are rising so dramatically that they already threaten to crowd out other essential services.

Number one on the list: Medicaid. The state-run public health insurance program for low-income individuals and families has recently nudged out elementary and secondary education spending to claim the No. 1 slot in state budgets. The federal Centers for Medicare and Medicaid Services predicts that annual growth in Medicaid spending will average 8.6 percent until 2014.[5] For some states, the outlook is even more dismal. Unless recent measures succeed, Florida's Medicaid program—which currently averages 13 percent annual growth—will consume nearly 60 percent of the state's budget by 2015. More than half of state Medicaid programs are equivalent in size to Fortune 500 companies, yet compared with their private counterparts, their management practices, technologies and business processes leave much to be desired. Successful transformation of Medicaid from a budgetary black hole into a sustainable, high-performing program will require, at a minimum, that states adopt commercial best practices.

Pensions and retiree health care present two other sobering examples. More than 87 percent of state pension systems are underfunded. And the bill for future medical benefits for retired state and local employees could top $1 trillion. These problems, if not addressed head on, will only get worse with the impending wave of Baby Boomer retirements.

Consider Illinois. In 2005, Governor Rod Blagojevich recognized the looming crisis in the state's retirement system, comprising five state-sponsored plans with unfunded pension liabilities totaling approximately $38 billion. "Unless we reform the way we fund our pensions," explained the governor, "we will never eliminate the structural deficit that takes money away from education, from health care, from law enforcement, from parks, and from everything else we care about." The Illinois system's assets covered only 60 percent of its future pension commitments, ranking it among the worst-funded state retirement systems in the nation. Illinois' pension debt amounted to an eye-popping $521 billion—including $220 billion in interest expenses.

Illinois' pension funding shortfalls were decades in the making. State payrolls—a key component of pension costs—grew rapidly throughout the 1980s. However, state contributions to public pension plans didn't keep pace. Strong investment returns helped bridge the gap for awhile, but the deficit began to widen by the end of the decade. Fortunately, Illinois has begun to address the problem with a series of reforms, discussed later in the book.

Budget busters deserve special attention because they represent a kind of test for states caught in the throes of the feast-or-famine budget cycle: they are structural problems that demand dramatic new approaches. Throwing a bit of this year's surplus at them is not an answer.

Rise in Uncertainty

Anyone who has been in a U.S. airport during the past five years will recognize the insignia of the Transportation Security Administration (TSA). This organization did not exist before 9/11, and if someone had proposed before the terrorist attacks that the federal government spend $5.6 billion annually to fund airport screeners, they would have been ridiculed.

Uncertainty is a given in today's world. Terrorism is no longer limited to the Middle East, and no one knows what form it will take next. The same goes for killer storms, biological threats and disease pandemics. They require federal and state governments to coordinate efforts to deal rapidly and effectively with threats that cannot be defined years in advance.

No matter how talented bureaucrats are, they aren't equipped to handle these challenges without a lot of help from other levels of government and the private sector. Yet citizens expect their state and federal governments to take the lead in orchestrating responses to the largest disasters and threats. Governments thus must prepare for potential disruptions and disasters by integrating a disparate array of organizations from each sector into functioning networks that share information, coordinate activities and synchronize responses to emergencies.

Beyond the uncertainties of terrorism and destructive natural events, it is by no means certain that state governments can count on continuing budget surpluses. The good old days may be slipping away as you read this; many economists rate the likelihood of a recession in 2007 much higher than they did in 2005 or 2006.[6] The challenges that state policy-makers face now could get a lot thornier in an economic downturn.

With few exceptions, state governments live by the budget cycle. When tax receipts are up, money is channeled to the most compelling agenda items; in downturns, states make frantic cuts, defer infrastructure maintenance and table plans. Although the spending decisions during "high tide" aren't necessarily bad ones, history shows that it is much easier to devise stopgap measures to address near-term requirements than it is to step back and approach things from a new perspective.

The current window of opportunity exists in part because states' coffers are relatively flush and the economy is performing respectably well. It will be harder to sell far-reaching, deliberate changes during the next low tide, when thoughts are again focused on cost cutting and near-term emergencies.

Evolving Federal-State Relationship

Today's somewhat schizophrenic federal-state relationship provides both challenges and opportunities for states. On the one hand, states increasingly have the opportunity to shape the debate in areas like health and human services and transportation where the federal government is giving them more freedom to innovate. The U.S. Department of Health and Human Services has approved more Medicaid waivers in the past four years than in all the years before then combined. Vermont, for example, struck a deal in which instead of paying a fee for each service provided, the federal government will give the state a lump sum payment for each person enrolled in its Medicaid program, thereby giving the state far more latitude to manage the program.

The federal government is also encouraging state experimentation in transportation—particularly with regard to innovative approaches such as congestion pricing and public-private partnerships. Moreover, the latest federal transportation bill promises that every state will get at least 92 cents of each dollar it contributes, resolving a contentious issue with some wealthier states, which had received a much smaller return on their contributions. In both areas, the federal push has strongly been in the direction of state innovation and flexibility.

On the other hand, you don't have to look far to see evidence of greater centralization or what some state policy-makers see as a return of the dreaded unfunded mandates. No Child Left Behind, the Bush administration's education accountability initiative, has engendered strong opposition at the state level for what some perceive as a huge underfunded mandate. Utah has been perhaps the most adamant in opposing the law. The state launched a legislative attack, authorizing its schools to ignore NCLB testing requirements that conflict with the state's own.

Another congressional measure viewed by many states as an unfunded mandate is the Real ID bill. This law requires states to issue tamperproof drivers' licenses that include biometric data by May 2008—an expensive proposition: $11 billion over five years according to the National Governors Association, which argues that the implementation deadline is unrealistic.

Real ID underscores how the war on terrorism and increased security concerns create more momentum toward a stronger federal role in certain areas. The very nature of technology like Real ID hinges on centralization and fail-safe implementation. But the Real ID project pushes the responsibility for implementation to the states. Likewise, the aftermath of Hurricane Katrina has put more political pressure on the Federal Emergency Management Agency to play a bigger role in the first stages of disaster response.

The delineation between federal and state roles, never black and white, is likely to get even more blurry in the future as citizens become increasingly intolerant of the poor service they receive as a result of the silos, overlapping boundaries and perverse incentives that go with a federal system of service delivery. Whether it's responding to a natural disaster like Hurricane Katrina or enhancing education, the general public doesn't care much about or understand the minutiae of how governments are structured. They just want performance and accountability. This, in turn, will put additional pressures on states to deliver results working across governmental boundaries.

Rising Citizen Expectations

Bill Gates calls this the "decade of velocity." Many of the world's largest companies didn't even exist in 1980. For governments, too, the rate of change is staggering. This is evident in the way services are provided and in the types of services governments are called upon to offer.

The unprecedented level of customization, ease and convenience that 21st century "on demand" consumers have grown used to in the private sector now also drives standards in the public sector, sending citizens' expectations of government to an all-time high. Today's consumer lives in a different world than the consumer of the 1980s. She is better informed, has 24-hour access to whatever she needs and is in constant communication with other consumers. She knows when a package will arrive, checks product availability online and does her banking at midnight. Businesses oblige gladly because the table stakes are too high *not* to; the same cannot always be said, however, for the public sector. Leading companies deliver customer service levels that most citizens feel exceed those of Uncle Sam. According to the American Customer Satisfaction Index, online giants Amazon and eBay, along with scores of other businesses, post customer satisfaction ratings more than 10 points higher than those given the federal government.[7]

No longer will citizens accept the bureaucratic maze that can make it hard to get the services they need. They don't want to provide the same information over and over again to different agencies. They get frustrated when they are forced to make multiple visits to multiple offices—and stand in multiple lines—especially for services that are closely related. As we discuss in chapter six, rising citizen expectations have made integrating services around the needs of citizens and businesses, instead of bureaucracies, a key objective in many states.

Today's "Netizens" also expect and demand not only that important public data be available online, but also that it be packaged in a user-friendly format that they can easily navigate. They want the full story, not the watered-down version that some public officials might want them to see. Few states have been more attentive to these demands for greater transparency than Virginia. The state's Results Web site gives citizens an easy way to keep tabs on government performance. Citizens can hop online and have

From the Bad Old Days and Back Again

In many states visiting a motor vehicles department sometimes feels like a trip to a Third World country, with long lines full of frustrated people. This is what it once felt like in Virginia. The roller coaster ride experienced over the past decade by the state's Department of Vehicles illustrates the phenomenon of rapidly expanding citizen expectations. For years the agency was considered the black sheep of Virginia state government. Back in the bad old days, Nadine Donofrio, the manager of Virginia DMV's Fairfax District, wouldn't even tell her friends where she worked.

Years later Donofrio cringes at the memory of standing behind that counter, day after day, avoiding eye contact with hundreds of furious citizens. "The line was very, very intimidating," she recalls with a shudder. "People would spend hours there. They spilled onto the sidewalk and around the building. When I'd have to go back to grab a form or something, people would get visibly angry. I could just feel them saying, 'What do you mean, you're taking a lunch?' It was just godawful."

Then in the mid-1990s, then-DMV commissioner Rick Holcomb set out to make the agency the most customer-friendly and technology-savvy in the state. Holcomb had experienced his share of DMV nightmares. "One time I just wanted to change my address on my driver's license and vehicle registration," he says. "They made me stand in separate lines to do each address change. I was there all day." Never again, he vowed, "would a Virginian have to endure such horrendous customer service."

Just a few short years and one philosophical and technological revolution later, the Virginia DMV was winning national acclaim for its high level of customer service. Before visiting one of the branches—that is, "customer service centers"—you could visit the agency website, www. DMVnow.com, and check the branch's current wait time, along with historical wait times for any month, day and time at any center in the state. Statewide wait times were down to six minutes

No, that's not a typo. The average time Virginians spent waiting in line at the DMV in 2001 was around six minutes, thanks to 30 new offices, new technologies like automated testing machines and electronic queuing systems and a new obsessive focus on customer service. The DMV became by far the most popular state agency in Virginia, enjoying satisfaction ratings (93 percent of respondents rated the agency's performance as excellent or good in one survey) that even Lexus would envy. "Every transaction with DMV used to be a guaranteed headache," read a typical survey comment. "This was quick and easy. Bravo!" Or: "Thank you very much for making your customers feel like VIPs."

A fairytale ending to the story? Not so fast. All was well until the state faced a massive budget deficit in 2002 and 2003. To reduce costs the state shut down 12 DMV branch offices, reduced office hours, eliminated service on Wednesdays and laid off 100 employees.

Soon the "new DMV" began to look a lot like the "old DMV." Motorists complained of long waits, sometimes of four hours or more. At the end of one 273-person line was Aina Santos, 48, of Vienna, Virginia, whose driver's license was expiring in a few hours. "This," she said, eyeing the slowly shuffling line of humanity before her, "is insane."

It didn't take long (in government time) for the budget cuts to be restored and branch offices reopened, but by then the damage was done. Years later, former Virginia governor Mark Warner recalls that some people are still mad over the DMV closures. The moral of the story? Customer expectations, once raised, can't be dialed back.

a live look at how an agency's actual performance stacks up against what the agency says it will achieve.

The bottom line is that addressing rising citizen expectations will require state governments to be more nimble, organized in a networked way so they can respond more quickly to changing conditions and offering personalized and multi-channel services.

Globalization

"In a world where technology has leveled the playing field, what happens in Mongolia affects us in Michigan, what happens in India affects us in Iowa," said Michigan governor Jennifer Granholm. "There is an inextricable link, and in a flat world the lines on the map just float off the page and we are left with a competition like we have never known."

On the up side, globalization leads to lower prices, a wider variety of goods and services, improved competitiveness and government policies that are tempered by market discipline. On the down side, lost manufacturing jobs have been a bitter pill to swallow for some advanced economies—a trend being repeated in the service sector through offshoring.[19]

Michigan has been hit harder than most. Since 2000, it has lost 282,000 jobs, 180,000 in production alone and another 60,000 in professional and business services.[8] Most of the state's woes stem from upheavals in the auto industry, which has been buffeted by globalization and difficulties navigating evolving labor markets. Between 2000 and September of 2006, the combined market share of Ford and General Motors fell nearly 10 percentage points (from 51.1 to 41.3 percent). Both companies are highly concentrated in Michigan, including their global headquarters, research facilities and 12 of their 34 U.S. assembly plants.[9]

The Global Knowledge Economy

The global transformation to a knowledge-based, idea-driven economy has put new demands on states to educate more of their citizens to higher levels than ever before or risk losing jobs and lowering quality of life. Ninety percent of the fastest-growing jobs in the new information and service economy require some postsecondary education while the number of jobs that require only on-the-job training is expected to decline rapidly. The greatest demand will occur in the so-called STEM fields (science, technology, engineering and mathematics). The Department of Labor projects that by 2014 there will be almost 5 million new job openings combined in health care, education, and computer and mathematical science.

The key factor generating prosperity has become knowledge itself, yet other countries are educating more of their citizens to more advanced levels than the United States. We spend more on primary and secondary education than most developed countries, yet we have larger classes, lower test scores and higher dropout rates.

Institutions of higher education are also falling short of meeting the nation's needs. A recent report by the federal Commission on the Future of Higher Education concluded that U.S. colleges and universities are not well prepared for the challenges of a more competitive global economy and an increasingly diverse student population. The report said that "too many Americans just aren't getting the education that they need" and that "there are disturbing signs that many students who do earn degrees have not actually mastered the reading, writing and thinking skills we expect of college graduates." The panel recommended a series of far-reaching reforms to improve student preparation and learning, make colleges more affordable, provide parents better information on colleges' costs and performance and strengthen institutional accountability.

The bottom line: absent dramatic and rapid improvement, for the first time in the history of the United States, the next generation of Americans could be less educated than its predecessors.

Globalization has wreaked havoc on Michigan's economic base. It has cast shadows on the futures of millions of auto industry employees and their families. Meanwhile, the state has been thrust into the position of helping displaced workers develop new skills and identify new sources of economic growth.

Alabama offers a contrasting example of the impact of globalization. In 1993, when Mercedes-Benz announced plans to set up its first manufacturing plant in Vance, Alabama, investors and the public were caught off guard.[10] But this was not some random decision. Alabama, which had been losing jobs in its textile and paper industries, had made a studied and strategic decision to target the automotive industry. It saw an opportunity to replace lost jobs with high-paying ones.

Moreover, seeing that a new automotive corridor was opening up in the region, Alabama also aggressively promoted the advantages of a clustering effect, which it saw leading to additional investment from component manufacturers and suppliers. It advertised its non-unionized environment, recognizing that even some European companies with long-standing traditions of union recognition and collective bargaining tend to establish non-unionized factories when undertaking greenfield investments.

Furthermore, the state entered into agreements with Mercedes-Benz to buy its products for the state motor pool. The results have been stunning: Mercedes started with an investment of $300 million and soon followed with a $600 million expansion.[11] Hyundai followed suit with its first U.S. manufacturing plant, an investment expected to bring $1 billion and 2,000 jobs to Alabama. This follows a $440 million Honda vehicle assembly plant, a $220 million Toyota engine plant and a $350 million International Diesel plant in the state.[12] Honda subsequently doubled its production capacity, bringing its total investment in Alabama to $1 billion.[13] The automotive industry now employs nearly 45,000 people in the state.[14]

Globalization exerts tremendous pressure on existing business models and wrings inefficiencies from industry. Michigan shows how the effects are sometimes disheartening, but Alabama on the other hand illustrates the fertile opportunities globalization also affords.

Beyond Legacy Thinking

As state governments struggle to respond to these imperatives for change, many find themselves shackled by the old ways of governing: hierarchical organizational structures that use a narrow, siloed approach to tackle complex problems; personnel practices and pension systems designed for an age when lifetime employment was the rule, not the exception; service models driven by government bureaucracy, instead of citizen needs and preferences; budgets that measure results based on how much is spent, not what is achieved; and tax systems and trade policies designed around manufacturing, physical goods and localized markets—rather than services, information and a seamless global economy. Some of these legacy problems are systemic, reflecting the failure to update Industrial Age processes and business models. Others are structural—rooted in statutes and state constitutions from a bygone era.

The exorbitantly high costs embedded in our education system, as an example, are a product of both. In many states at least 40 cents of every dollar spent on schools never makes it into the classroom and teachers make up a little more than half of all school district staff. (In Europe, by contrast, teachers account for between 60 and 80 percent of all school staffing.) One culprit? Thousands of tiny school districts, each operating its own transportation, human resources, food services, information technology, building maintenance, administration and other largely support functions. This business model is an anachronism in a world in which most corporations share services for these and other non-core functions across the enterprise. Shifting just a quarter of the tax dollars spent by school districts on non-instructional operations to shared services, for example, could potentially yield savings in the range of $9 billion to the nation's school districts. (We discuss this in more detail in chapter eight.)

The same kind of huge administrative inefficiencies can be observed in the duplication and overlap between many county and city governments and between each of them and the thousands of special districts that have mushroomed the last three decades in states across the country. In some cases, the answer is the same as with school districts: intergovernmental service sharing. But a more fundamental question must be asked of many of these units: are they simply relics of a different era and no longer needed? (No one has yet accused our governments of dismantling bureaucracies prematurely.)

Legacy Issues	Emerging Issues
Medicaid cost management	Advancing health care outcomes
High education administrative costs	Improving education performance
Outmoded hiring practices	Attracting Gen Y to state government
Underfunded pension systems	Protecting the homeland
Infrastructure gap	Boosting emergency response capabilities
Service delivery maze	Tax system modernization
Management of state as a loose-knit confederation of agencies, boards, commissions and programs	Restructuring services to serve an aging population

Legacy thinking also permeates the ways many states still hire, fire, pay and promote their employees. Survey after survey demonstrates that many highly skilled job candidates who say they would like to work in public service end up not working in government. Why? For one thing, many state personnel and pension systems still reflect a time when most employees came to work for the state right out of school and never left. This is not a model of employment likely to appeal to today's "free agent" Generation X and Y workers. Equally unappealing are outmoded state hiring practices, which often require multiple levels of clearances and approvals. This vetting can chew up months before the candidate knows whether she has the job. To become a choice employer among the emerging workforce, the public sector must appeal to these young workers' expectation of a sociable, flexible, purposeful and technologically savvy work environment.

Given the huge gap between past practices and current and future needs, incremental change won't be enough. Obsolete, century-old systems need to be replaced with new models that better address the needs of the 21st century. This transformation will require new ways of doing business for every aspect of government, from organizational structures and operating practices to personnel systems and service delivery models. These changes won't be easy, but they are necessary. Moreover, they are now possible—states have new tools and, for the time being, a favorable environment for change.

Clean Slate

Getting urban schools to work is an issue that has vexed policymakers for years. Despite decades of reform, many large school districts are still plagued by high dropout rates, low test scores, poorly trained teachers and stultifying bureaucracies. The poster child for these woes has long been the New Orleans school system, where nearly three-quarters of eighth graders are not proficient in math or English.[15] Fully 63 percent of New Orleans schools were deemed academically unacceptable during the 2004–05 school year.

In the wake of Hurricane Katrina, the Louisiana Department of Education took over almost all New Orleans public schools and realized it had been given a rare opportunity to start over in a district infamous for an immovable bureaucracy that had become "a morass of incompetence, indifference and outright corruption."[16] According to Leslie Jacobs, vice president of the state Board of Elementary and Secondary Education, the state had been given the chance to "hit a restart button."[17]

The Louisiana Department of Education decided to open up the school system, creating over 30 new charter schools—community schools that receive public funding and must meet public academic standards, but have much greater freedom to hire and fire teachers, set salaries, choose curriculum and manage daily operations. Although there are over 3,600 charter schools across the United States, no city has done anything approaching the scale of the New Orleans experiment: making charter schools the de facto norm, not the exception, as the organizational model for schools.

Advocates claim charter schools promote innovation and accountability by giving principals and teachers more freedom and authority and getting parents more involved. For New Orleans, charter schools offer new hope in a city known for its poorly managed and poorly performing schools.[18] Now more than half the schools in New Orleans will be given broad new powers and parents unprecedented freedom of choice. "We have the most extraordinary opportunity ever in the modern history of dealing with public education," said Paul Pastorek, a New Orleans lawyer and former chair of the state board of education. "We have a clean slate."[19]

Building New Foundations

One of the world's foremost experimenters, Albert Einstein, was fond of the saying, "Out of difficulty, find opportunity." It would be hard to imagine a more difficult set of circumstances than those left by Katrina's flood waters, but New Orleans has snatched opportunity from desperation, and its schools may be poised to provide a better education to the city's schoolchildren.

Most states are now confronted with opportunity amid calmer seas: relatively healthy state budgets, recently elected governors, a political climate tolerant of innovation and the technology that enables unprecedented levels of service delivery and personal choice. The tide is high. State governments can make substantive changes—changes that strategically address issues from spiraling Medicaid costs to underfunded public pensions that have accrued over the last generation.

Experimentation is hard, however. It requires first that problems be understood in a different context; only then can officials try new ways of doing business to find out what works and what doesn't. Even more important, experimentation requires commitment—keeping at it until you get it right. That's a tall order.

To get started, governors need to put in place the infrastructure for 21st century governance and understand the full portfolio of state assets that can be brought to bear in connecting *the what* to *the how*. No longer can a state be effectively managed as a loose-knit confederation of agencies, boards, commissions and programs. Instead governors must begin to think of state governance as a single enterprise—one in which employees, technology, business processes and resources are networked across agencies to provide the state's residents with effective and efficient services. Statewide strategy planning, performance goals and outcome targets and enterprise-wide technologies, business processes and performance reporting are key attributes of this new approach. But all of this demands strong, consistent and focused leadership.

Historically, the amount of cash in public coffers has served as the limit on the services government can provide. However, in the face of a declining tax base, looming pension obligations and economic uncertainty, governors must also think more creatively about how to produce new public value—value that can be applied to address the new challenges of the 21st century. Examining the value of a state's assets provides a starting point. It serves to highlight those assets that are currently underutilized and thus can be leveraged to tackle higher priority problems. Land is a prime example, but the evaluation shouldn't stop at physical assets.

Another example is intellectual property. State university systems invest billions in research and development annually. The commercialization of leading research breakthroughs is another area for potential public value creation.

With philanthropy on the rise and the nonprofit sector poised to expand its reach, understanding the value that nonprofit organizations can bring to bear on societal problems can help a state leverage its own resources to a greater degree than would otherwise be possible. Evaluating the landscape of potential partners—public, private and nonprofit—allows states to take advantage of resources that lie outside the purview of the state budget.

A few states have already begun experimenting with innovative approaches to governing and service delivery. These big experiments involve fundamentally new ways of thinking about challenges, much as welfare reform in the mid-1990s represented a radically new way of looking at that problem. Instead of simply dispensing cash benefits to welfare recipients, governments began to help families achieve economic self-sufficiency. Administrative entitlements were out; work requirements, job training, transit assistance and time limits were in. Far-reaching, albeit less publicized, management changes complemented this shift in mission. States and counties adopted a fundamentally different delivery model—an outcomes-based, networked model of service delivery involving public, private and nonprofit organizations.

While experimentation is rarely the easy path, emerging examples show how state governments can break new ground. As you might expect, some of the greatest challenges are in areas such as education and, in view of an aging population, health care. However, even seemingly innovation-proof areas such as infrastructure—roads are roads, right?—have benefited from new approaches to expensive problems. Some of the more provocative experimentation opportunities include education, health care and transportation.

Education

For states whose prospects depend on new generations of talented citizens, education has been a source of incredible frustration. Despite numerous reforms tried over the last decade—reducing school class sizes, increasing overall funding, providing better training for teachers, enhancing local control—the academic achievement levels of the average 17-year-old have not improved since 1970, according to the National Assessment of Educational Progress. While 9- and 13-year-olds have shown progress in reading and mathematics, most of the gains seem to be lost by the time they graduate high school.[20] Frustrated by the lack of progress, state leaders are looking for bolder and more comprehensive solutions that address the entire educational system.

High school reform is now the hottest issue for many state leaders, policy-makers and nonprofit groups. The Bill and Melinda Gates Foundation is leading the way on many innovative reform efforts. Transformation has come in many guises: creating smaller high schools; establishing early college programs; strengthening the core curriculum; and empowering more charter schools. Because a high school degree no longer means much in the workplace, states are seeking to make the last year of high school a transition point to college rather than the often wasted year it has become.

The most dominant state-level strategy today is standards-driven accountability. This strategy, built on explicit performance standards, systematic testing and consequences for results, is being expanded throughout the education enterprise. Policy-makers are now applying it to their higher education systems.

Some innovative schools are also showing the way to a brighter future. The KIPP Academy Charter Schools, now being expanded nationwide, cater almost exclusively to minority and low-income families (98 percent of its students come from a low-income background). Studies of the program show above-average gains in reading, language and mathematics from 2003 to 2004 and very high levels of college enrollment.

Another innovative high school receiving recognition is TechBoston Academy, created in 2001 to provide low-income students with a technology-based, college-preparatory curriculum for work in the high-tech industry by offering industry certifications in IT essentials, as well as access to advanced technology courses.

On the opposite coast, students at San Diego's Tech High School study in labs instead of classrooms, have access to workstations with Internet-ready computers and work on long-term projects that promote in-depth learning. After only four years, Tech High is in the top 10 percent of all California public schools based on Academic Performance Index scores. Every one of its 2004 seniors applied to college and all were accepted; 80 percent of these students enrolled in four-year institutions.

Early college programs are also receiving a lot of attention. A number of these small schools, designed so that students can earn both a high school diploma and an Associate's degree or up to two years of credit toward a Bachelor's degree, are springing up. Ohio had one of the earliest. They have the advantage of saving families money and giving kids a challenging, relevant curriculum.

Health Care

The demographic shift toward an older population, in tandem with health care costs that can hardly be mentioned without some allusion to "soaring," "skyrocketing" or "spiraling out of control," puts health care front and center among the challenges confronting states. These costs have come to haunt states, largely because their health care systems were designed long ago when medicine was less pervasive and expensive—in other words, their systems were never really intended to control or even consider costs. Several states have set forth on the path to reform.

South Carolina's Medicaid reform plan, in which the state is establishing personal health accounts for most of its 850,000 Medicaid recipients, aims to sensitize beneficiaries to the costs of their health care and remove the economic incentive for patients to overuse services. This represents a watershed for Medicaid reform: an effort to install incentives or otherwise include Medicaid recipients in the effort to improve the quality of care they receive.

MASSACHUSETTS' EXPERIMENT WITH COMPREHENSIVE HEALTH CARE REFORM. South Carolina is not the only state fundamentally rethinking its legacy health insurance system. Massachusetts has made a serious commitment to addressing the problem of the uninsured, enacting a comprehensive health reform package that aims for universal coverage. Governor Mitt Romney summed up the problem confronting the state: "Some 20 percent of the state's uninsured population qualified for Medicaid but had never signed up. Another 40 percent of the uninsured were earning enough to buy insurance but had chosen not to do so. Another group of uninsured citizens…[made] too much to qualify for Medicaid, but not enough to afford health-care insurance."[21]

Massachusetts' reform plan addresses some of the legacy elements of the 40 year-old program in a comprehensive fashion. The plan also experiments with innovative new approaches to broaden access to private health care. To increase Medicaid access for citizens that qualified for the program but were not enrolled, the state developed Virtual Gateway. The Web portal allows hospital staff and clinicians to enroll patients who qualify for the program directly into the system when they seek care.

For those who don't qualify for Medicaid, the state's new "connector" model allows individuals to purchase private health insurance coverage at more affordable rates through a state-sponsored exchange. By relaxing some of the state's insurance regulations, Massachusetts enabled private insurers to offer consumers more choices in health insurance products, including less expensive options such as health savings accounts. In cases where affordability is still an issue, the state will provide subsidies based on an individual's ability to pay. Because the insurance is not tied to a particular employer, it is portable, and thus more convenient for today's workforce.

Infrastructure

Crowded schools, traffic-choked roads and deteriorating bridges are eroding the quality of American life. An American Society of Civil Engineers (ASCE) survey gave the nation's infrastructure an overall grade of D for 2005 and offered a sobering estimate of $1.6 trillion as the cost to bring the U.S. infrastructure to acceptable standards over the next five years. Couple that estimate with the aftermath of Hurricane Katrina, and other natural disasters, as well as unexpected costs for increased security, and it becomes alarmingly clear that states are facing unprecedented challenges. What's more, they're relying on gas tax revenues that fail to generate sufficient funds to maintain the current infrastructure, let alone make the needed improvements.

TEXAS INFRASTRUCTURE PUBLIC-PRIVATE PARTNERSHIPS. The ASCE survey gave Texas' roads, bridges, transit systems, aviation facilities, schools, drinking water systems, wastewater systems, and other infrastructure a cumulative grade of C-, indicating a below-average condition in most infrastructure categories. Although the state has made significant investments and improvements in some areas, many other areas still need substantial investments for repairs, rehabilitation and expansion in order to provide quality service to the growing state population.[22] The 2004 Texas Transportation Institute (TTI) Urban Mobility Study ranked Dallas/Ft. Worth fourth worst and Houston sixth worst nationally in traffic congestion.

A lackluster highway system and a grim morning traffic report hurt, but the real wake-up call for Texas was PC maker Dell's decision to locate its next expansion in Nashville rather than in Austin, because Austin's roads were inadequate. This represented a loss of 10,000 jobs for Texas. Fearing further loss of business and jobs, the state broke with tradition and turned to private financing and tolls to solve Austin's mobility crisis. It is now applying the same financing model to the rest of the state.[23]

Recent legislation and new agency policies have prompted a dramatic change in the way Texas pays for highways. Toll roads, now rarely encountered outside the state's largest metropolitan areas, may soon become commonplace in cities large and small as the Texas Department of Transportation (TxDOT) incorporates tolling elements into virtually all of its planning for new road construction and the expansion or extension of existing highways. This new policy, combined with TxDOT's recently approved bonding authority, represents a fundamental departure from the state's longstanding approach to highway financing.[24]

Recognizing the real economic cost of inadequate roads, Texas has emerged as something of a role model in applying public-private partnerships (PPPs) to transportation infrastructure, remaking the processes used to finance, build and operate major highways.[25] Ten major projects are already under PPP contract or in progress, and the list is expected to grow.

The Trans Texas Corridor is probably the best-known PPP. In March 2005, TxDOT and Cintra-Zachry, an international consortium of engineering, construction and financial firms, signed an agreement to develop highway TTC-35. Cintra-Zachry proposes investing as much as $7.2 billion to develop the approximately 600-mile, Oklahoma-to-Mexico portion of the Trans Texas Corridor. The consortium, using private resources, will operate the toll road for 50 years and then return it to the state.

Texas' program has drawn praise globally for its ambition, sophistication and size. They don't do things small in Texas: the state's public-private transportation initiative is among the largest in the world.

The Execution Challenge

As the New Orleans, Massachusetts, South Carolina and Texas examples demonstrate, states out of necessity have recently entered another age of big policy experiments. These developments are good news. We need more BHAGs (big, hairy audacious goals) to meet today's complex challenges. Big, bold ideas can alter the course of history. That's especially true when those ideas come in response to tremendous problems. Unemployment insurance, the GI Bill, the student lunch program, deregulation of industry and welfare reform all emerged from attempts to solve the major challenges of their day.[26]

But good ideas alone carry you only so far.

"Unless you translate big thoughts into concrete steps for action, they're pointless," wrote Larry Bossidy and Ram Charan, the authors of *Execution: The Discipline of Getting Things Done.* "Without execution, the breakthrough thinking breaks down, learning adds no value, people don't meet their stretch goals, and the revolution stops dead in its tracks. What you get is change for the worse...."[27]

The policy world, after all, is littered with big ideas, badly executed. Think of the urban renewal policies of the 1960s, which were designed to rejuvenate cities but which, in practice, destroyed many neighborhoods and helped trigger the flight of the middle class to the suburbs. It was a big, bold idea—albeit a flawed one, and poorly implemented.

Or consider the introduction of citizen choice in services ranging from education to health care. Recent history teaches that choice without proper guidance can create confusion and frustration. Some of the people needing assistance can't make rational choices about which service providers are best for them. Others may find that having too many choices is overwhelming and confusing.

That is what happened, to some extent, with the rollout of the Medicare Prescription Drug Plan, which required elderly Americans to choose among dozens of different plans, each covering a different list of medications and carrying different costs. Trying to sort through the complex menu to settle on the plans that best met their needs, many seniors and their caregivers became hopelessly mired in the fine print. Telephone lines set up to answer questions about the new program were temporarily overwhelmed and unable to provide service to all callers as crucial enrollment deadlines approached. People grew frustrated and scared. Although the program is now running much more smoothly, these early perceptions persist.

Government agencies must tread carefully when introducing programs offering choices. Without good navigation support, lots of consumer choice can easily lead to confusion and disillusionment. This is especially true among the elderly, whose appetite for change is often limited.

Or take education reform. Urban school districts across the United States debut education reform plans nearly every school year, but few yield tangible, long-term results. Parents, educators, community members, private businesses, higher education partners and other stakeholders want their local school systems to succeed. Change-minded mayors have taken control of numerous urban school districts. Governors have invested a huge amount of their time and political capital into reforming urban schools. Yet, despite all this, the last decade was plagued with failed education reform initiatives in some of the country's largest school districts.

As governors work to improve the way state governments do business—integrating services around the citizen, offering people more choices, providing multiple channels into government, giving citizens a greater say in government and making other admirable reforms—they need to think hard about execution.

This means heeding certain lessons that emerge time and again: Understand your customers intimately—what services they need and how they prefer to receive them. Use strategies drawn from the private sector, but tailor them to government's particular needs. Don't try to do everything yourself—collaborate with partners in other jurisdictions, in the nonprofit world and in the private sector. Tackle the easy parts of the problem first, and then apply what you learn to the tougher challenges. Spend a lavish amount of time on managing change—stakeholders must understand the real costs, benefits and rationale.

Big ideas define where we want to be. A detailed strategy for execution ensures that we get there. This book aims to provide both—to bridge theory and practice. And by doing so, we offer a roadmap for state leaders as they grapple with how to tackle some of their toughest challenges and develop solutions based on proven best practices.

Chapter 1: The Final Word

THE CHALLENGE
• *Credibility gap*. Americans expect more from government in a post-9-11/Katrina world, but trust it less.
• *Aging populations* will impact state spending, revenues, the mix of services and the way state agencies deliver services to citizens.
• *Budget busters*. Several line items in state budgets, from spiraling Medicaid costs to underfunded pension systems, are currently on unsustainable trajectories.
• *Industrial Age structures*. At a time when citizen expectations are rising and states face increasingly complex challenges, many state governments find themselves shackled by the old ways of governing.

REFORM STRATEGIES
• *New delivery models*. State governments have a host of innovative delivery models at their disposal to help meet 21st century challenges including tailoring and integrating services to citizen needs and offering the public more channels, more choices and more influence over critical decisions.
• *New governance models*. A growing number of state agencies are "governing by network," in which executives' core responsibilities center on organizing resources, often belonging to others, in order to produce public value.
• *Measure performance by results and outcomes*—not by how much money gets thrown at the problem.

EXAMPLES
• *Massachusetts'* comprehensive new health reform package provides access to private insurance coverage to all state residents through a quasi-governmental insurance brokerage agency.
• *New Orleans school system*. The state department of education has opened up the school system, creating over 30 new charter schools, thereby making charters the de facto norm, not the exception, as the organizational model for the city's schools.

NEXT STEPS
• *Tackle long-term, structural issues*. Runaway Medicaid costs, poor education, inadequate and under-maintained infrastructure have built up over a generation.
• *Build for the future*. Address the emerging issues of the next generation, such as advancing better healthcare outcomes.
• *Focus on execution*. The policy world is littered with bold ideas, badly executed. Avoid the same thing happening to your policy initiatives.

{2} *William D. Eggers and Greg Pellegrino**

Serving the Aging Citizen

As the Baby Boom generation begins to reach retirement age in the next five years, state and local governments in the United States will face important challenges.[1] Before 1995 elderly residents exceeded 15 percent of the population in only five states; by 2025, the elderly share will exceed 15 percent in every state but Alaska and California (as well as the District of Columbia). The number of Americans 65 and older will more than double in at least 20 states and then continue to grow for decades to come (see figures 1 and 2).

The consequences of this demographic sea change will be far reaching. Not only will it force state governments to examine existing benefit programs as they relate to the elderly, it will also push them to rethink how to address the full range of elderly needs with the resources they have and other resources they can mobilize.

Pennsylvania, a state that has already experienced "premature graying," provides a case in point. The state ranks second for the percentage of population 65 and older, is experiencing out-migration (that is, more younger residents are moving out than moving into the state) and has a low fertility rate. Thanks to these demographics, it is the nation's third slowest-growing state in terms of population, behind North Dakota and West Virginia.

Pennsylvania's aging began in the 1970s, when the collapse of the traditional industrial job base forced many young adults to migrate to other states in search of career opportunities.[2] To address service demands for the

---

* Shalabh Singh of Deloitte Services LLP contributed substantially to the research and writing of this chapter.

Figure 1: Graying States

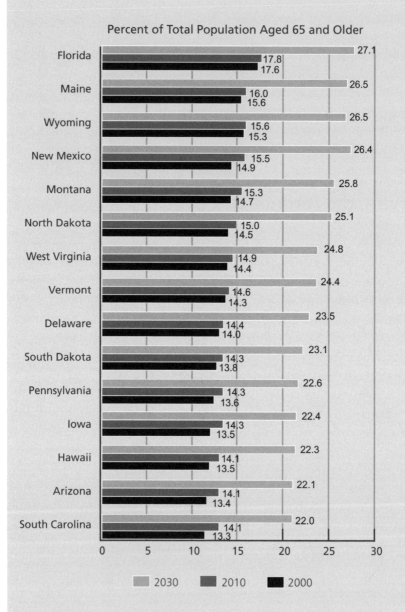

Percent of Total Population Aged 65 and Older

Florida — 27.1 / 17.8 / 17.6
Maine — 26.5 / 16.0 / 15.6
Wyoming — 26.5 / 15.6 / 15.3
New Mexico — 26.4 / 15.5 / 14.9
Montana — 25.8 / 15.3 / 14.7
North Dakota — 25.1 / 15.0 / 14.5
West Virginia — 24.8 / 14.9 / 14.4
Vermont — 24.4 / 14.6 / 14.3
Delaware — 23.5 / 14.4 / 14.0
South Dakota — 23.1 / 14.3 / 13.8
Pennsylvania — 22.6 / 14.3 / 13.6
Iowa — 22.4 / 14.3 / 13.5
Hawaii — 22.3 / 14.1 / 13.5
Arizona — 22.1 / 14.1 / 13.4
South Carolina — 22.0 / 14.1 / 13.3

2030   2010   2000

Source: U.S. Census Bureau, State Interim Population Projections 2004-2030

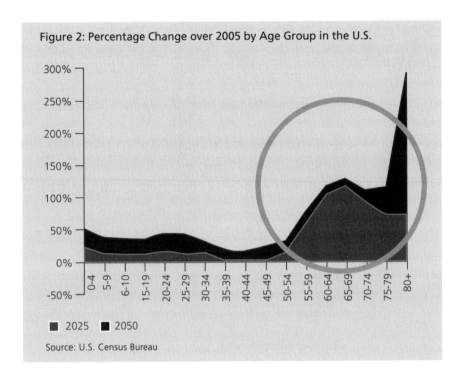

Figure 2: Percentage Change over 2005 by Age Group in the U.S.

■ 2025   ■ 2050

Source: U.S. Census Bureau

growing and substantial senior population, the state in 1972 implemented the first and, to date, only state lottery that dedicates all proceeds to senior programs (in most states, lottery proceeds go to education). Since then, it has spent nearly $15 billion on elderly assistance programs, ranging from providing subsidized prescription drugs and transportation to assistance in rent and property tax.

The United States, of course, is not the only country facing the challenges of an aging population. Throughout the developed world, birth rates are declining, life expectancies increasing and populations aging. The birth rate in the United States, at 2.04 per woman, is higher than in most other Western countries (Germany's rate is 1.4, Japan's 1.3 and Italy's 1.2), yet it still remains just below the replacement rate—the rate necessary to maintain a steady population level in the absence of immigration. Among other implications, this means fewer workers will be available to support the elderly.

As the population and workforce ages in America, governments at all levels will have to address the challenge of how to deliver retirement and medical benefits to a surging number of aging citizens. Many of the key issues—including extending retirement ages and reducing benefits—have been probed in depth. A less thoroughly explored but equally critical issue is how the growing ranks of the elderly will affect the way government agencies are organized and the services they deliver: the design and mix of services they offer; the delivery channels they use; the funding sources they rely upon; and the way aging citizens will affect civic participation.

For example, the growing elderly population may give states compelling reasons to move traditional office-based services online as a way to expand their reach and reduce costs. State and local government agencies may also want to consider new types of service collaborations with business or philanthropic partners. And they may need to pursue ways to reduce dependency on general taxes through greater reliance on user fees and other funding models. Moreover, state government will need to reach beyond their traditional role as service providers to become more aggressive in orchestrating service delivered by others.

There is little doubt that states will face trade-offs, including how to provide services to both the very young and the very old without further straining limited coffers. To do so, governments will need to anticipate the changing needs and preferences of their citizens. Elderly people have different needs from those in other age groups, and they expect to access services easily.

This chapter highlights options available to governments for dealing with the challenges associated with population aging. As a first step, states need to thoroughly understand how they will be affected by certain demographic trends and the factors likely to shape these trends.

Key Demographic Trends Affecting States

Before exploring how government services and service delivery will need to change in response to the aging citizenry, it's important to understand the major demographic trends directly or indirectly related to the aging population that will occur in the coming decades. Decisions made today can have potentially large effects on the future.

Old-Age Dependency on the Rise

One statistic that summarizes the problem of the aging population is the dependency ratio: the ratio of working-age people (15–65 years) to everyone else—children (0–14 years) and the elderly (65+).

As the number of elderly people increases, dependency ratios are projected to rise in most developed countries.[3] In practical terms, this means there will be far fewer taxpayers to support recipients of government ser-

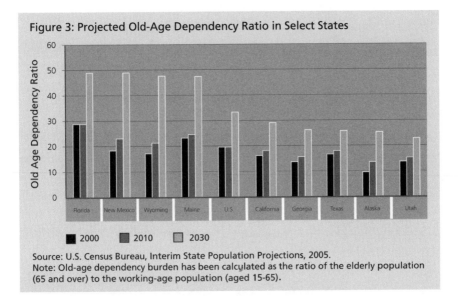

Figure 3: Projected Old-Age Dependency Ratio in Select States

■ 2000 ■ 2010 ☐ 2030

Source: U.S. Census Bureau, Interim State Population Projections, 2005.
Note: Old-age dependency burden has been calculated as the ratio of the elderly population
(65 and over) to the working-age population (aged 15-65).

vices in the future.

In the United States, dependency burdens will begin climbing within a decade. The four states with the highest percentages of elderly residents (Florida, Maine, Wyoming and New Mexico) will see their old-age dependency ratios go from nearly one elderly person for every four working-age persons in 2000 to one for every two in 2030 (see figure 3). North Dakota, Montana, and Arizona all too face escalating old-age dependency rates, which are likely to drive steep increases in total dependency. All in all, many states by 2030 will look demographically more like Florida, Pennsylvania and West Virginia look today.

WHY DOES THE DEPENDENCY RATIO MATTER? What does a rise in dependency—and in particular old-age dependency—imply? Among other things, it potentially means a reduced labor supply, less consumption, slower economic growth and increased government spending but declining revenues, more regional disparities and new fiscal pressures. Consider just two of these impacts:

- **Reduced Labor Supply.** A rising old-age dependency ratio corresponds to a relative decline in the labor force as a percentage of population but also in absolute numbers in some states like Maine, Iowa, Ohio and Pennsylvania, which in turn would lead to a decline in GDP.[4]

Figure 4: Current Per Capita Cost of Benefits by Program and Age

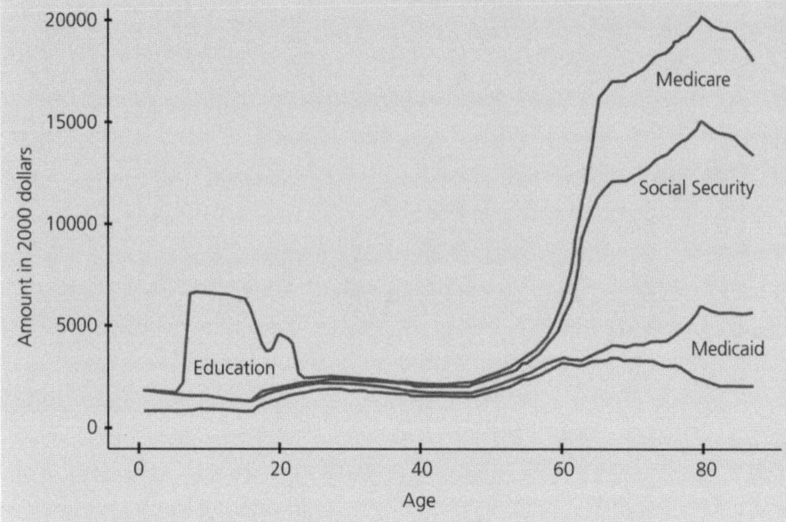

Source: Ronald Lee and Ryan Edwards, "The Fiscal Effects of Population Aging in the U.S.: Assessing the Uncertainties," in James M. Poterba, ed., *Tax Policy and Economy*, Volume 16, MIT Press for NBER, June 2002, pp. 141-81.

• **Fiscal Pressure.** A key challenge is how to cover increased expenditures for Social Security, Medicaid and Medicare as revenues fall with a shrinking workforce as a percent of the population.[5] Typically, benefits for the elderly tend to cost substantially more on a per capita basis than benefits for children (see figure 4).[6] Some regions will likely see a rapid growth in population at both ends of the age spectrum and be hard pressed to balance the needs of the elderly and the young. In California, for example, the population of the group aged 0-17 will rise by almost 30 percent between 2000 and 2020, while the 65-and-over population is expected to grow by a staggering 70 percent.[7] This rapid growth at both ends of the demographic spectrum contrasts sharply with an antici- pated slight decline in the age 30–49 population. California is thus likely to face a growing service burden at both ends of the spectrum, with the demand for schools and universities increasing at the same time as the demand for elderly services is on the rise. Meanwhile, the number of taxpayers in a key high-earning demographic group will be declining.

Three main factors influence the size of the old-age dependency ratios:

- The level of immigration
- The fertility rate
- The workforce participation rate among the elderly.

The specific roles these factors will play in the future will depend on public policy and on a variety of economic, social, and political considerations.

Changing Patterns of Immigration and Domestic Migration

The leading destination for foreign migrants has been North America, which received 1.3 million (legal) immigrants (and millions more illegal immigrants) from 1990–2000 and is likely to continue attracting immigrants on a similar scale.[8] In the United States, the immigration rate (immigrants as a percent of total population) has increased from 0.16 percent in the 1950s to 0.37 percent in the 1990s.[9] China, India and Mexico have been the leading countries of origin.

Like immigration, domestic migration (both in-migration and out-migration) can be a major factor in the makeup of regional populations and in turn can have a significant impact on the level of demand for benefits and services. During the 1990s, for example, the population in the Sunbelt States increased by nearly 25 percent. More than one-third of that increase came from U.S. residents moving into the Sunbelt from other states; less than 7 percent of the increase was attributable to foreign immigration. In melting pot states, however, such as New York, Illinois and California, where the population rose by nearly 15 percent, almost 40 percent of the increase resulted from foreign immigration (an increase that was partially offset by net domestic migration out of the melting pot states of nearly 24 percent).[10]

Until fairly recently, foreign immigrants tended to settle in "gateway" states such as California and New York while the domestic population out-migrated to states like Georgia, Arizona and North Carolina. In the last 10–15 years, however, increasing numbers of immigrants have moved to other areas after a brief stay in the gateway states or have bypassed the gateways altogether to settle in areas that traditionally did not attract large numbers of immigrants.[11] Overall, the U.S. population is shifting from the Northeast to the South and West.[12]

So what are the implications of the data on domestic migration for state governments? We see two main implications. First, the elderly tend to stay put. Elderly populations are likely to stay where they are and age in place.[13] And rather than relocating to institutional settings, many would prefer to receive services at their doorsteps. This will require thinking beyond the confines of health issues and developing new long-term care options for living in communities, aging in place, social support, transportation, and entertainment.[14]

Second, some regions will feel the effects of migration more than others. Regions that are neither gateways for immigrants nor attractive areas for domestic migrants will age much faster than others. These regions could potentially have more difficulty delivering services to the elderly. States with large numbers of younger immigrants about to enter childbearing age may fare better. It must be recognized, however, the dynamic nature of these demographic trends. Immigrants have always followed jobs and family connections. As the demand for jobs to serve the elderly increases in "aging-in-place" states such as Maine, Ohio, Pennsylvania and West Virginia, immigration levels could rise in these states. In fact, immigrants from Mexico have already begun to bypass traditional gateway states and are migrating to states such as Delaware, Indiana, Michigan, New Hampshire, South Dakota and other states that have not traditionally seen large influxes of immigrants.[15]

Immigration and domestic migration offer only partial solutions to the problem of aging populations. Therefore, it is important to understand other potentially critical factors: fertility rates and the age of retirement.

Fertility Rates

In the developed world, fertility rates (measured by the average number of children born to a woman of reproductive age) have fallen to dramatically low levels (see table 1). A fertility rate of 2.1 is needed to maintain the population at a constant level in the absence of net immigration. In most developed countries, total fertility rates are far below this, with the exception of the United States where the rate is just a tad shy of the replacement level.[16]

Fertility is declining for several reasons. The social and economic costs of raising children are increasing while the returns from childbearing are declining. As more and more people have moved away from farming and rural areas to urban centers, children have become more of an economic cost than asset. In addition, as opportunities in the workplace have improved for women, they have chosen to devote less of their time to child-rearing and more to work. Many knowledge-age parents also want to invest more resources in each child, thus limiting in many cases the number of children they can

Table 1: Estimated Fertility Rates in Selected Developing Countries

Country	Total Fertility Rate
France	1.87
Germany	1.32
Italy	1.28
Japan	1.37
United States	2.04

Source: United Nations Population Division, "World Population Prospects: 2004 Revision (http://esa.un.org/unpp/index.asp?panel=2).

support.[17] And although the responsibilities of parenting are considerable, parental authority and the social prestige associated with parenting have declined in recent years, creating less societal incentives to have children.[18]

Average Retirement Ages

Another way to influence old-age dependency rates is to encourage seniors to stay in the workforce longer. In the early 1960s, male workers in the industrialized countries typically remained in the workforce past age 65. [19] Over the next three decades, the average retirement age—the youngest age at which at least half the working population leaves the labor force—fell steadily. In the United States, the average fell to about age 62, while in Canada and many European countries, it dropped even lower.

Only recently has the retirement age in some countries begun to increase.[20] For example, the U.S. average recently edged up from age 62 to 63, putting it in a slightly better fiscal position compared with some countries in the European Union, where average retirement ages are still in the high 50s in some cases.[21] Additionally about 53 percent of American men in the age group 60–64 are in the workforce, compared with 51 percent for Canada and 39 percent for the European Union.[22]

Longer life expectancies make the financial implications of extending retirement ages even more important. The longer seniors can be encouraged to remain in the workforce even as part-time workers, the more taxes they pay to contribute to the revenues needed to meet the burgeoning expenditures for Social Security and health care systems.

Realistically, however, an increase in the average retirement age can provide only part of the solution to the revenue problem that governments face from aging. What's more, there are several complicating factors. First, rising life expectancies will increase the time spent in retirement beyond the additional time spent working.[23] Even given a higher average retirement age, government expenditures may still outstrip new revenues.

Second, increasing the average retirement age cannot be accomplished with changes on the supply side alone. To have a meaningful impact, a rise in the supply of elderly workers requires that businesses increase their demand for older workers.[24]

Lastly, for many people involved in physical labor, an increase in the retirement age may be unrealistic.

Philanthropy and Civic Engagement on the Rise

A large intergenerational wealth transfer from the World War II generation to the Baby Boomers will occur in the United States over the next decades. This transfer—estimated to be anywhere from $7.2 trillion to $13.7 trillion—could influence the average retirement age (enabling some Baby Boomers to accelerate their retirements) and also have a large impact on some government services, for example by accelerating the shift to nonprofit organizations delivering social services and being engaged as partners in tackling big public policy issues.[25] The total intergenerational transfer, including that from the Baby Boomers to the successive generations, over the period 1990–2044 is expected to be a minimum of $41 trillion at 1998 prices.

The anticipated wealth transfer from the World War II generation to the Baby Boomers is attracting a lot of attention from the media. Together with the recent multibillion dollar gift announcements by wealthy individuals such as Bill Gates and Warren Buffett, the projected surge in philanthropy is feeding expectations that private donors may play an increasingly influential role in how public services are organized and delivered. Overall, only a tiny percentage of Baby Boomers (less than 2 percent) will inherit enough money to reduce or eliminate their need for continued earned income. The big difference, both in the next few years and beyond, will be in the amount of wealth earmarked for charity.[26]

Baby Boomers already give more to charity than their parents' generation did, and they plan to increase their giving in the next five years.[27] By one estimate, the flow of assets into charity could be as high as $3 trillion from 2001 to 2010, almost double the $1.6 trillion donated during the 1990s.[28]

Major new donors have already indicated they will follow priorities and strategies different from many established charities. For example, the Bill and Melinda Gates Foundation identified disease eradication in poor countries as one of its primary focuses. To the extent that the new wave of philanthropists directs some of their funds to programs for the elderly, there is the prospect that their approach to program management will be more corporate. In addition to providing the resources, they are apt to get more deeply involved in program design, implementation and evaluation.

A rise in philanthropy isn't the only way the aging of the Baby Boomers will affect civic engagement. Across nearly every measure of civic participation—voting, attending town hall meetings, volunteering, contacting government officials—the elderly have higher participation rates than nearly every other demographic group. Consider the following:

VOTING. As people age their propensity to vote goes up. The voting rate of citizens ages 55 and older in the 2004 U.S. presidential election was 72 percent, compared with 47 percent among those aged 18–24 years. Similarly, in the 2001 United Kingdom general election, 70 percent of the elderly voted, compared with 50 percent of the population as a whole.[29] With the expected rise in the proportion of the elderly in the population, and given their higher voting rates, the issues that affect senior citizens will gain greater importance.

PARTICIPATION IN DEMOCRACY. Those over age 65 are much more likely to contact the government to express an opinion—33 percent, compared with the 19 percent average.[30]

VOLUNTEERING. A large percentage of retirees spend at least part of their time volunteering, and all indications are that Baby Boomers will ratchet up their volunteer activity as they retire.[31] In just two years, from 2002 to 2004, the percentage of retired boomers who volunteered rose from 25 to 30 percent.[32]

The volunteer activity of the Baby Boom and younger generations is more focused on education and youth services than on the elderly today who tend to be very involved in church-related volunteer activities. This reflects changes that governments may expect in the future. Overall, as boomers age, volunteer activity in nearly all sectors will likely increase.

Volunteer organizations are gearing up to exploit this tremendous potential. For example, Civic Ventures, a California-based think tank, is promoting volunteerism among Baby Boomers through one of its biggest initiatives,

The Next Chapter, designed to mobilize older citizens. The National Council on Aging has launched "RespectAbility" to help nonprofit organizations make effective use of older Americans to renew communities.[33] State and local governments can leverage this trend toward rising civic engagement and philanthropy to meet the mounting responsibilities in the face of declining resources as a ratio of government expenditure.[34] Already, initiatives such as Citizen Corps, Community Emergency Response Teams, Volunteers in Police Service, and the Medical Reserve Corps exemplify how governments can leverage the greater community to tackle new challenges.[35]

Financing Services

The aging population will have a major impact on state and local finances. Revenue could become a significant issue as the number of elderly increases and a declining percentage of individuals assume the bulk of the tax burden. In many cases, states are likely to consider modifications to their tax structures and alternative approaches to funding services. Several trends are likely to become more prominent in the next few decades as states grapple with the challenges of funding services and programs in the face of an aging population:

- Modernization of the tax system

- Increase in retirement age

- Greater emphasis on user fees

- Growth in public-private partnerships (particularly involving the nonprofit sector)

Tax System Restructuring and Modernization

Once the Baby Boomers begin to retire and the proportion of working-age citizens shrinks, growth rates in personal income tax revenues could slow significantly.[36] This slowdown will have a serious impact on the United States and other countries heavily dependent on the personal income tax. Many state and local governments provide preferential income tax treatment to retirement income and preferential property tax treatment to the elderly, and the cost of these tax preferences will rise as retirement income grows as the population ages. Moreover, tax receipts on purchased goods as a ratio of total personal consumption expenditure are likely to decline as well since the elderly tend to spend less than younger people on goods and

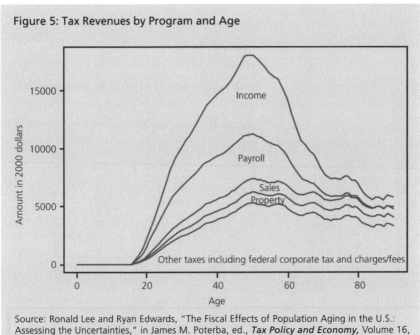

Figure 5: Tax Revenues by Program and Age

Source: Ronald Lee and Ryan Edwards, "The Fiscal Effects of Population Aging in the U.S.: Assessing the Uncertainties," in James M. Poterba, ed., *Tax Policy and Economy,* Volume 16, MIT Press for NBER, June 2002, pp. 141-81.

more on services (which are taxed less if at all under state sales taxes).

In both absolute and per capita terms, seniors on average contribute less in each category of tax receipts. The drop with age is especially pronounced in the case of income and payroll taxes, but a decline also occurs for sales and property taxes (see figure 5).

To meet their funding requirements, governments will have to modernize their tax systems—retain their existing tax base while extending it into new areas. Key features of modernized tax systems are likely to include:

- **Fewer tax preferences.** Governments at all levels will likely look to reexamine tax preferences. Seniors in particular benefit from such preferences. A review of Minnesota's tax system, for example, shows that only about 46 percent of the gross income of seniors is taxable compared with 67 percent for younger taxpayers.[37]

- **Taxes on services.** Many state tax systems are designed for an Industrial Age economy (see figure 6). Manufactured goods tend to be heavily taxed, while services are lightly taxed—or not taxed at all. Given both the growth of a more service-

Figure 6: The Mismatch between Tax and Output Structure in Minnesota

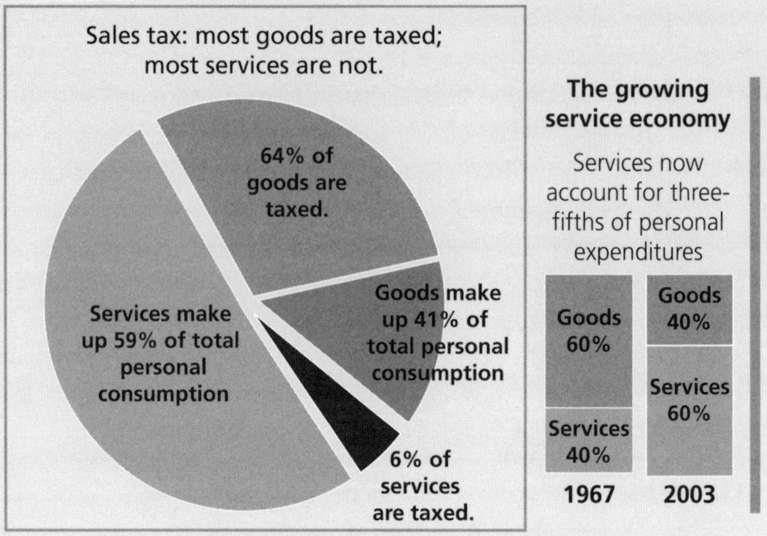

Sales tax: most goods are taxed; most services are not.

64% of goods are taxed.

Goods make up 41% of total personal consumption

Services make up 59% of total personal consumption

6% of services are taxed.

The growing service economy

Services now account for three-fifths of personal expenditures

	1967	2003
Goods	60%	40%
Services	40%	60%

Source: "Minnesota's State and Local Tax System," Minnesota Revenue, January 2005 (http://www.taxes.mn.us/legal_policy/other_supporting_content/tax_sytem/overview.pdf).

based economy and the fact that the elderly spend relatively less on goods and more on services than younger people do, such tax structures may not be sustainable over the long term. Despite the political difficulties of doing so, services are likely to be more heavily taxed in the future.

• **A balanced-basket tax approach.** The aging of the population will mean that idiosyncratic tax structures that rely on narrow tax bases will prove increasingly untenable. States will need more diversified and broad-based revenue sources in the future. The same goes for local governments, which now depend heavily on property taxes as the funding source for education. This approach will come under tremendous political pressure from an aging population in many places. As many as 20 states have recently seen revolts against property tax increases.[38] In addition to being less able to pay rising property taxes out of fixed incomes, the elderly, having no children in local schools, tend to place comparatively less priority on education spending than do parents of school-age children. In short, the property tax will likely increasingly need to be supplemented with other revenues sources to fund education.

State and local governments have also favored narrower sales taxes, which are weighted heavily toward goods. However, there is a limit to how much further governments can go with this approach—both politically and in terms of overall effectiveness—because sales tax rates approaching 10 percent begin to push a lot of economic activity to the black market and damper economic growth. To avoid these problems, states will likely shift to broader, more diversified tax regimes.

Increase in the retirement age

After age 60, most Americans pay significantly less income tax than they did previously, meaning potentially less revenue from income taxes for states and the federal government. One way to stem this potential erosion of the income tax base is by extending the average retirement age to better reflect increased life expectancies. The older Americans are when they retire, the less they will draw on Social Security, Medicare and Medicaid and the more tax revenues they will pay into the government coffers. In fact, every year a person eligible for Social Security defers drawing the benefits, saves the system 7 percent.[39]

Raising the retirement age by just a few years may not be enough, however. Professor Jeremy J. Siegel of the Wharton School warns that the retirement age will have to increase much faster than the increase in life expectancy to narrow the dependency gap in a meaningful way.[40] Otherwise, living standards will fall and taxes will increase to unpalatable levels to fund Social Security and Medicare, he says.[41]

Some foreign governments have begun to understand the depth of this problem and have become more aggressive in their response. The United Kingdom has proposed shifting the retirement age to 68 over the next 40 years in response to an increase in life expectancy.[42] In the United States, if the planned increase in the retirement age to 67 were accelerated and completed in 2015, then rose to 70 by 2030 and the increase slowed to one month each two years thereafter, Social Security outlays would actually fall by 12 percent by 2050.[43]

Efforts to get people to postpone retirement can go only so far, however, without significant changes on the demand side. Currently, companies face a host of disincentives for retaining or hiring older workers. Tax, pension and age discrimination laws often discourage employers from implementing phased retirement. For instance, many workers cannot afford to reduce their work hours without receiving a part of their pension, but rules prohibit employers from making payments from defined benefit plans.[44] To affect real changes, these kinds of obstacles will need to be removed.

Increased reliance on user fees

Instead of raising more general taxes, governments have been relying more and more on user fees in recent decades to finance services in areas such as roads, urban parking, locally owned utilities (including Internet access through Wi-Fi), parks, and health care.[45] This method of finance, which entails charging fees directly to the users of public services, will likely continue to gain popularity in the future. If current trends continue, county governments in the United States could receive nearly as much revenue from user fees as from property taxes within a few decades.[46] User fees hold several advantages over general taxes:

- **They promote efficiency.** User fees help ration scarce resources by forcing users to pay the cost of the services they consume.

- **They align the costs of services with the benefits.** Those who use the services are the ones who pay. This discourages people from asking the government to provide ever-higher service levels in the expectation that other groups of voters will bear the cost of those services.

- **They are flexible.** User fees are a more flexible source of funding than taxes because the amount charged can vary with demand and the costs associated with providing the service.

Growth of nonprofit role

The emergence of a vastly bigger and more sophisticated nonprofit sector will create new opportunities for partnering and for leveraging private dollars for public causes. Already, the rise of the nonprofit sector means that governments in the United States now deliver less than half the social services they finance; in most communities, three-fifths or more of health and social services are now delivered by either nonprofit or for-profit providers. Similar changes have occurred in other countries. In 1980 government agencies in Great Britain delivered the overwhelming majority of social services in that country: only 14 percent were provided by private firms or voluntary organizations. Less than two decades later, that number had jumped to 40 percent.[47]

As the population ages and demands for many social services increase, the continued growth of the nonprofit sector will allow governments to engage this sector's innovative spirit and creativity in efforts to solve major social problems.[48] Moreover it will enable government officials to discharge government's important role in solving social problems by better supporting functioning elements of civil society.

Changing Service Mix

In addition to changes in government funding, the growth of the elderly population will drive changes in the composition of government services. In absolute terms 19 states are expected to see a decline in the number of persons under age 18 in 2030 compared with 2000. This will cause the demand for many services catering to the elderly to rise while, with fewer school-age children in many states, the demand for education and youth and child welfare services will fall.

Florida, the grayest of the states with close to 18 percent of the population age 65 and over, offers a glimpse into what the future might look like in many states. Florida has invested considerable resources into offering better transportation services and aggressively screening older drivers to make sure they can safely operate motor vehicles. The Florida Commission for the Transportation-Disadvantaged, for example, offers cost-effective transportation services to older people who cannot drive.

Meanwhile, the Florida Senior Community Service Employment Program offers training for older workers to enable them to continue working or find a new job. CVS Pharmacy and Home Depot have partnered with the agency and hired older workers with experience and a willingness to work flexible hours as part-time or seasonal workers.[49]

Law enforcement is another area likely to see major adjustments, such as increased attention to preventing and investigating crimes and frauds against the elderly. In Florida, the Administration on Aging has funded more than 300 education sessions on consumer fraud for more than 9,000 seniors, their families and law professionals.[50]

Furthermore, given the fact that increasing age generally leads to a reduced propensity to commit crimes, the prison population, and therefore the demand for new prisons, will likely fall. Another likely impact of the

Table 2: Changing Mix of Services at a Glance

Increased Demand	Reduced Demand
Home-based health care	K-12 education
Public transportation	Youth services
Adult education	Playgrounds
Job retraining	Child welfare
	Prisons

Source: Deloitte Research

aging population upon law enforcement will be changes in sentencing and imprisonment. Some states are already beginning to provide alternatives to incarceration for elderly criminals, both as a way of saving money and making the last years of their lives more humane. Florida, for instance, has a chapter of Projects for Older Prisoners that identifies low-risk older prisoners for alternative forms of incarceration or for special release. The state has also created special geriatric units for high-risk older prisoners and instituted a special unit for elderly female prisoners.

Programs that promote healthy lifestyles through preventive public health care measures, wellness centers and health clubs, and education on low-cost, healthy, easy-to-prepare meals are also likely to increase in popularity as a result of the aging population.

Closely examining two sectors the government is heavily involved in—health care and transportation—sheds more light on the kinds of changes we can expect in government services in response to the aging citizen.

Elder Care

A profound shift has occurred over the past few decades in how society cares for the elderly. Just a generation or two ago, adult children cared for the majority of the elderly in their own homes; as more women entered the workface, families turned more to nursing home care for their elderly. But the once-strong demand for nursing home care has fallen steadily over the past two decades.[51] Meanwhile, the demand for home health care grew dramatically in the early 1990s, tapering off just slightly toward the end of the decade.[52]

Healthier living habits, technological and service innovations, cost considerations and deep-seated preferences of the elderly to live at home rather than in institutional care have driven the growth of home health care and assisted-living facilities over that of nursing homes. Home health care costs much less than nursing home or hospital care, and technological advances have made it as effective as hospital care for many treatments. The continued rise in the elderly population will cause the demand for home-based health care to increase at an even faster clip in the future.[53]

The savings from home-based health care costs over nursing home care costs are no longer a subject of dispute. Not only is the average Medicare home health service expenditure lower, but it also increased at a much slower rate than nursing home care between 1992 and 2002.[54] Governments can save considerable money by encouraging home-based health care, more so because the morbidity pattern is shifting toward chronic diseases (such as cardiovascular disease) that require long-term treatments. Technology can shrink costs further. By employing customized wearable devices, electronic patient records, wireless Internet-linked systems and "smart devices" that can monitor a patient's vital signs and automatically transmit the information to the relevant health care staff, providers can deliver relatively inexpensive but convenient, user-friendly and customized health care in the home.[55] By one estimate, the yearly equipment cost is equivalent to just two weeks of residential care.[56]

Home health care for the elderly depends on a complex set of linkages between the government, families and the health care industry. Governments play an important role by creating, through funding, policies and regulation, the overall framework for interactions among institutions serving the low-income elderly.

Given the tremendous cost savings to be had, state governments are beginning to take steps to accelerate the trend toward home-based health care for the elderly. For example, governments are examining how they can help support families who care for their older members. Families now provide approximately 80 percent of the care needed for ill and disabled family members living at home. In the United States, about 20 million adults care for their aging parents, according to the Family Caregiver Alliance, a San Francisco–based social service organization.[57] Because of changing demographics, however, the number of available caregivers will decline in relation to the number of people who need care.[58]

A number of policies can strengthen needed support: vouchers, greater flexibility in working hours, phased retirement programs, and information to navigate the managed-care system. In Massachusetts, for example, low-income families receive $1,500 a month to take care of seniors who need help

Snapshot: South Dakota

A big challenge faced by many Heartland states is the impending huge increase in demand for long-term care that will occur at the same time the number of younger workers will be falling. In addition to presenting broader economic challenges, this dynamic is likely to make it difficult simply to meet the rising demand for long-term care workers. Take South Dakota: By 2010, a third of the state's population will be over 50, a percentage that will grow to 42 percent by 2025.[60] Thanks to these trends, the South Dakota Department of Labor forecasts that health care and social assistance will be the fastest-growing industry in the states by 2012. However, the population of nurses age 25–55 is dropping. About 80 percent of the 110 nursing homes in South Dakota are understaffed, a percentage expected to grow as younger people continue to leave the state.[61] Around 11,000 additional health care workers will be needed to meet the demand.

with everyday tasks.[59] Since treatment costs are usually lower when there is early diagnosis, family members also need better education about diagnosis, prevention and treatment of health problems associated with old age. The channels of communication between families and the home health care industry also need be strengthened, with increased emphasis on coping with caregivers' emotional stress and respite needs.

As the demand for home-based health care continues to rise, governments will face increasing pressure to regulate the industry more heavily. Home health care providers often employ low-wage, temporary homecare workers who frequently aren't trained adequately to provide skilled services. This leads to high attrition, shortages of personnel to meet the rising health care needs of the elderly, and potential safety problems. To avoid more extensive government regulation, the home health care industry will likely need to take active steps to self-regulate staff training, improve working conditions, reduce attrition, and create a safe environment for the elderly. Safety is a growing concern because home health care workers are frequently called upon to provide relatively skilled services, such as helping the elderly take medications.[62]

Improved Transit Options

Instrumental to a well-functioning home-based health care system is a public transit system that addresses the mobility needs of both the elderly and home health care workers. The elderly also desire access to entertainment, shopping and the ability to get together with friends and relatives. Aging in place will

Veterans Administration Tele-Health Program

Tele-health offers a powerful clicks-and-mortar approach to reduce spiraling health care costs. In Florida, for example, the number of elderly veterans is escalating, and many veterans are rural residents. The distance from medical facilities can deter patients from seeking care until their condition has deteriorated to the point where expensive hospital stays, surgeries and other intensive treatments are necessary.

To address these issues, the Sunshine Network Veterans Health Administration, which encompasses VA hospitals in Florida, Puerto Rico and the Virgin Islands, is deploying high-tech, user-friendly tele-health computer devices to allow many elderly veterans to lead more independent lives. Patients can solicit advice from health professionals in remote medical centers; keep tabs on their own disease progression and measure their blood pressure, blood sugar, blood oxygen, temperature and weight; record their peak flow and stethoscope sounds; and take electrocardiograms—all from the comfort and convenience of their own home. "We are addressing health concerns before they worsen," explains Patricia Ryan, from VHA's Office of Care Coordination. "Diabetics, for example, need to be concerned about getting eye exams, so we are using special cameras that can take a picture of the eye with a tele-retinal camera. We used this technology to transmit the images over an hour away to get read by an expert."

Traditional rounds have been replaced by control centers that monitor patients through real-time videoconferencing. The patient's home is equipped with various electronic monitoring devices, and a schedule for check-in calls is established. Each device is customized to individual patient needs and designed to increase patient compliance by reminding them to take their medications and asking them questions to assess their well-being.

Currently 20,000 patients are enrolled in the tele-health program nationwide, with a goal of 100,000 patients by 2009. In addition to the home tele-health program, MyHealthyVet, which provides interactive access to veterans' electronic medical records, is available online to all veterans in the VHA system.

increase the demand for mobility choices so that older people can remain independent and in control of their lives as they age.

Senior citizens in the United States tend to associate mobility with driving one's own vehicle rather than public transportation. The next generation of elderly—the Baby Boomers—is even more likely to do so.[63] The elderly are by and large unprepared for the transition to the stage where they can no longer drive. As a result, they can become isolated, vulnerable, and dependent on others. One in five Americans age 65 and older does not drive, and more than half of these non-drivers stay at home on any given day.[64]

Aging populations will require inexpensive and easy-to-use public transportation.[65] But mobility for the elderly will need to extend beyond introducing more rail and bus services to include:

- Convenient location of grocery stores

- Well-planned developments that reduce dependence on cars

- Coordinated delivery of human and social services so that hours of service coincide with those of public transit

- Revamped highway systems, with clear and legible signs, well-marked roads, and bright lighting

- Improved safety for pedestrians and cyclists

Important issues in transport are the need for policies and regulations that promote safety, and vehicles and infrastructure that are old-age friendly. Older drivers tend to have somewhat better driving records than commonly believed. But they are also more vulnerable to injuries and death from auto accidents.[66] These crashes are often caused by age-related physical and cognitive frailties.[67] According to the U.S. Department of Transportation:

> *Crash involvement of aging drivers often stems from lack of attention or errors in comprehension. Failure to yield the right of way, misunderstanding of signs and signals, and inaccurate judgments of speed are typical mistakes.*[68]

Making roads safer is crucial to promoting elderly independence and quality of life, and it can also go a long way toward reducing accident-related health expenditure costs. To do so, governments need to improve pavements and roads (lines, lights, and signs), develop better methods for testing driving ability and, with help from the private sector, create more parking spaces reserved specifically for seniors. Governments can also encourage automakers to develop safety features designed to compensate for age-related declines in motor functions and other physical abilities.[69]

In this vein, New York Department of Motor Vehicles commissioner Nancy Naples believes that the next decade will see an increase in reexaminations, refresher courses and defensive driving instruction for elderly drivers.[70] Her agency encourages senior drivers to self-assess their driving ability by providing information that draws attention to the impact of age on driving skills. Visual acuity, motor skills and response-time awareness are just some of the visible indicators affecting driving capabilities that are highlighted.[71]

Families also need to be more involved in the process of determining whether an elderly person can still safely drive. The New York DMV will also educate doctors on what to look for in evaluating whether an elderly person should be reexamined or take a refresher course.[72]

Future trends will also force governments to rethink their spending allocations across various services, paying particular attention to how they balance services for the young and elderly. To do so, government agencies will have to figure out the future demand patterns for their services. They will also have to reevaluate the channels for delivering services to avoid burgeoning costs at a time when their revenues may be flat or declining.

Service Innovations for the Aging Citizen

The private sector is responding to the aging of the Baby Boomers and the rise of the elderly population by undertaking fundamental changes in the way services are delivered and products are brought to the market. Home Depot, the home improvement retail chain, has shifted from the "do-it-yourself" to the "do-it-for-you" approach by offering home improvement installation services.[73] Meanwhile, Oxo International introduced the Good Grips line of kitchen tools to cater to the senior cohort. Fidelity Investments redesigned its new Web site to make it easier for aging customers to navigate. Increasingly, customer-centered private companies are focused on understanding their aging customers and learning how their needs change as they get older. That knowledge helps them redesign their products and services to meet the critical needs of this important customer segment.[74]

What about government? How will the aging citizen affect government delivery of services and programs? How can governments simultaneously meet the very different service channel preferences of aging citizens and the younger digital generation—without heaping huge new costs on a shrinking number of taxpayers?

These are the kinds of questions facing government agencies of all shapes and sizes. Agricultural departments wrestle with how to shift farmers to low-cost, online channels for reporting and obtaining information without alienating older farmers. Veterans departments try to figure out how to deal with the very different preferences younger and older veterans have for interacting with the government. Social Security agencies ponder whether they will need their extensive networks of physical offices a decade from now—and whether they can even afford them. Motor vehicle agencies struggle with how to advance both safety and mobility in the face of rapidly increasing numbers of much older drivers.

No matter what types of services or programs a government agency is responsible for, they all have a common concern: how to shift to the most cost-efficient channels of service delivery without upsetting current customers or compromising citizen expectations. In tackling this issue, governments are pressed to meet two often-conflicting objectives—provide value to taxpayers by reducing cost, and provide value to customers by addressing individual preferences. Which objective should receive priority? Both. Businesses don't try to cut costs irrespective of customer preferences. They would end up losing customers. Governments, for their part, could face a political uproar. Therefore they will need to find a way to strike a balance between demand and cost considerations as the population ages. To do so, government agencies will need to acquire a deeper understanding of three critical areas:

- **Customer segments.** Who are the agency's customers now, and how might they change in the future?

- **Customer preferences.** What do different customer segments need and desire, and what types of solutions are they looking for?

- **Delivery channels.** What is the full range of service delivery channels—both high- and low-cost—available to agencies? Can customer preferences for delivery channels be changed over time, and how can they be influenced?

These questions, in turn, can't be addressed in isolation—they are closely intertwined. Together, the answers form the core of a holistic customer strategy for the aging citizen.

Segmenting Customers

Governments have long looked at their "customer" base as a homogeneous group. The result has been a tendency to provide one-size-fits-all services. The problem with this approach is it fails to meet the rising expectations of citizens accustomed to more personalized and convenient services in the private sector. It is bound to become even less acceptable as the base of the demographic pyramid becomes increasingly elderly. Not only do the young and the old have different service needs that must be managed, but increasingly, each different age group—and segments within these groups—have their own preferences for how they want services provided. Moreover, these preferences may continue to change in the future. Segmenting customer citizens according to needs and means of delivery allows governments to rethink their options for allocating resources. The goal: aligning services with customer needs and service preferences.

Such customer segmentation is standard practice at consumer-oriented businesses. They use demographic data and interviews to formulate customer profiles (for example, age, income and geography) and to determine what kinds of products and services different customer groups want. Governments have the opportunity to do the same.

The starting point is building a hypothesis about customer needs that is closely tied to the characteristics of the particular segment (for example, the need for elderly transportation or health care). By understanding customer characteristics today and how those characteristics are likely to change over time, governments can anticipate how customer preferences may evolve and adjust service channels accordingly.

Take the issue of transportation for the elderly, particularly during the evening hours. Currently, the accident rate for elderly people shoots up after dark. To address this problem, one response could be to provide cheap, safe public transportation after 5 p.m. But first the public transit authorities should assess who the potential customers are and how likely they are to use the service. A public transit agency would begin by gathering core data about the elderly population: the number of elderly drivers, the number of accidents (by hour of the day), and elderly usage of public transportation. It would be important to know the age and income characteristics of elderly bus riders and what encourages and discourages ridership. If buses were easier to board and more comfortable, drivers friendlier, and service better publicized, would demand for the service increase? And how might usage change in 5 or 10 years, as the number of elderly grows and targeted customers age?

Understanding Customer Preferences

Understanding customer needs and preferences is a many-tiered process. In addition to age, other factors such as education, wealth, health, geographic location and experience with technology come into play. In thinking about how to design or reorganize services, governments should recognize that different groups have different needs and may be more comfortable doing business one way (say, face-to-face or by phone) than another (on the Internet or by e-mail). Before inducing customers to change channels, governments need to understand the underlying preferences of different customer segments and the corresponding cost implications.

Consider the case of veterans. Mark Sullivan, the secretary of Australia's Department of Veteran Affairs, notes that service delivery in his department is geared heavily toward World War II veterans, who prefer high-contact, in-person service. As a result, these customers are extremely satisfied with the service they currently get. But many younger veterans think the service is too slow and cumbersome. They don't like having to fill out multiple forms, and prefer 24/7 one-stop shopping online. So what should the department do? How can Veterans Affairs simultaneously cater to the needs of both customer segments? In this case, age is a dominant variable in channel preference—in-person services are "entrenched" within the department's World War II customer segment. The size of this customer segment is declining, however, because members of this generation are dying of old age and various illnesses. This means that eventually some of the more expensive physical channels can be phased out.

Health care provides other examples. We have already noted that demand for home-based health care will increase significantly with the aging of the population. But governments have to recognize that the needs of the elderly poor will be significantly greater than those of people with resources. Those with resources, for example, may require little or no government assistance at all in arranging for in-home services and paying for them. Others, particularly those who can't rely on family members to provide daily help, may need significant support in getting information about benefit eligibility and access to services. As the recent rollout of the Medicare Prescription Drug Plan illustrates, government agencies need to be careful about introducing programs that offer too many choices. Without good navigational support, lots of consumer choice can easily lead to confusion and disillusionment.

Surveys can provide helpful information about customer preferences, as can demographic modeling and testing ideas with focus groups.[75]

Managing Delivery Channels

Increasingly, citizens want to access public services through different channels. Providing services through multiple channels, however, can be expensive to government agencies.

If cost were the only consideration, governments would quickly shift as many citizen customers as possible to the lowest-cost channel (usually the Internet) and eliminate some of the old physical and paper channels. But the fact that many seniors may prefer in-person visits or phone calls to online channels adds a serious wrinkle to this strategy.[76] Many of today's elderly are not comfortable enough with technology to access government services through the Internet. For some, it's a matter of age-related disabilities: diminished vision, decline in motor and muscular control, and reduced response to stimuli. However, there are two other important factors. First, the complexity of many citizen-government interactions increases with age.[77] This makes it harder for people to be satisfied with simple answers. Second, many older people have a desire for social interaction, which causes many of them to prefer in-person visits. (This equation may change over time. The Baby Boomers are far more comfortable with technology than the generation that preceded them. As they age, they will be far more comfortable using the Internet than today's elderly.)

Given these considerations, how can governments accelerate customer shifts to lower-cost channels and improve overall efficiency without alienating the elderly and near elderly? Four strategies can help to balance the trade-offs.

Do the easy things first

Age-related disabilities (vision loss, hearing loss, memory problems and mobility loss) are common among elderly citizens. Therefore, it is important to pay special attention to user design interfaces. For documents, this means making sure that they are clearly written and printed in easy-to-see type. For online information, it means making sure that material is visually and substantively coherent and easy to navigate.[78] Making online services age-friendly will help not only the elderly, but others as well, and may encourage customers using other channels to go online.

For face-to-face interactions, improving user interfaces means training front-office employees and customer service representatives in responding to the unique needs of aging citizens. For example, employees at department of motor vehicle offices will need to be specially trained to interact with seniors from a customer service perspective, by recognizing their unique needs and communicating with them in the best way to help them solve their problems. Road safety inspectors will likewise need advanced training in understanding the driving implications that come with changes in visual acuity, motor skills, and response times as people age.

Develop ways to handle complex needs online

Governments need to find better ways for e-government initiatives to address complex needs, which will only grow in number as the elderly population increases. The conventional wisdom is that online services may work well for simple tasks but are unfit for helping people with more complex issues. This is not completely true. Technologies using various forms of artificial intelligence, now widely available, can be used to answer complex questions that previously could only be answered by humans.

Online expert assistance tools developed by the U.S. Department of Labor and the Occupational Safety and Health Agency, for example, offer potential models. These agencies promulgate thousands of new rules and regulations that businesses must comply with each year. To help small businesses, the agencies have built more than 30 expert advisor programs, which provide customized assistance for complying with various DOL and OSHA regulations. The expert systems capture and organize facts and knowledge by "cloning" expert experience, which can be used to solve tricky but routine problems. Based on answers to dynamic questions, the computerized expert advisors can lay out precisely what people need to do to comply with particular regulations. For example, in 10 to 15 minutes, the Hazard Awareness Advisor can interview a restaurant owner, analyze her workplace based on answers she provides, and write a customized 5- to 20-page report on probable hazards. Typically a knowledgeable professional would need two to three days to conduct the interview and complete the report. OSHA estimates that this advisor alone will save small businesses between $40 million and $83 million a year.[79]

Expert systems and other technology tools could be employed in a similar manner to help make electronic channels more appealing to seniors. Through interactive question-and-answer formats, they can enable seniors with only the most rudimentary computer literacy skills to navigate their way through complex online government programs.

These self-service Web tools also provide the ability to do real-time customer segmentation. Based on the answers to the questions, agencies can discern various patterns in their customers. This in turn allows them to better tailor their service offerings and channels to customer preferences.

Develop clicks and mortars solutions

Governments can also use technology to transform traditional physical channels into "clicks and mortars" services that offer some of the personal interaction many seniors want while using technology to reduce costs. Airline check-in kiosks that are now prevalent at many airports offer a good private sector example. The kiosks reduce queues and allow the airlines to serve customers with fewer front-counter employees, while providing for in-person support where necessary.

Government agencies that rely on direct interactions with customers have opportunities to provide similar services. By setting up a network of kiosks, New York's DMV will allow motorists to receive services that previously required direct staff assistance.[80] In addition to placing kiosks in DMV offices, the department intends to put them in other locations, such as convenience stores. Kiosks already provide a channel for conducting banking and utility bill payments. For some motor vehicle-related transactions—for example, printing car registrations and other documents—the kiosks could be an alternative to the Internet, providing documents on the spot.[81] The DMV hopes that, in addition to reducing postage and handling costs, the kiosks will reduce wait times for elderly people and others who require over-the-counter services.[82]

One of the problems with phasing out physical offices is the perception that customer service will decline, especially for customer segments that prefer face-to-face interaction. Mobile offices offer one way to continue face-to-face service while reducing the overhead costs of physical infrastructure.

Establish public-private "channel" partnerships

Governments don't own all the channels of delivery. Nor can they meet all the service needs of customers on their own without driving up costs. In some cases, it will make sense to "piggyback" on the investments others have made in service lines and delivery channels to meet the needs and preferences of aging citizens. Governments can do this by establishing "channel partnerships" with private firms, associations and nonprofit organizations that would conduct transactions on behalf of government agencies in the same way that retail stores act as a distribution channel for manufacturers. In most states, for example, auto dealerships can handle motor vehicle registrations. Similarly, sporting goods stores often serve as outlets for fishing licenses. The opportunities for governments to provide services to the elderly through partners are both broad and deep.

The essential idea is to leverage the investments private sector organizations—for example, the American Association of Retired Persons (AARP) or health care companies—are already making in the elderly market by partnering with them to create robust channels for distributing information and handling a variety of important transactions. A model for this kind of partnership is Earth911.org, a nonprofit organization that offers community-specific resources in a variety of environmental areas including recycling. People looking for information about their communities can simply enter their zip code and learn about solving their own specific problems—everything from how and when to get rid of used oil and tires to where to charge electric vehicles.[83]

Internet portals catering to the elderly could gather together community-specific elderly resources in one place. (In addition to having information about health care, the sites could offer updates on transportation options, home care resources, and upcoming events.) But there is also an opportunity to coordinate the various interactions people have with the government. Most elderly people have a variety of different transactions with the government including filing tax forms and receiving retirement benefits. As more and more seniors remain active and continue to work part time, the number of transactions will grow.

Today, these transactions happen in silos. A more efficient system would treat the discrete transactions as part of a more integrated relationship, which could be cheaper and less cumbersome for both individuals and governments to manage. This is particularly true of low-value transactions, which are costly to administer. To deal with these inefficiencies, for example, the Australian government allows families to reconcile their government benefits with their tax returns, reducing the amount of paperwork and costs associated with multiple transactions.

Conclusion

The population in the developed world is aging, and some countries face declining populations. These changes will lead to an increasing problem of old-age dependency and, in many countries, a wide gap between government expenditure and revenue. Three factors—openness to immigration, higher fertility rates, and increases in average retirement ages—will somewhat mitigate the potential problems in the United States, compared with Japan and much of Europe.

Nevertheless, the aging population will still prove quite challenging for state governments to serve. Among other concerns, governments will need to look at the expenditure side of their budgets and either reallocate funds or identify ways to reduce the cost of delivering service. This will force governments to change the way they deliver services, particularly to senior citizens.

As a first step toward gaining a better understanding of the myriad ways the aging citizen will affect their state, governors can follow the lead of the state of New York, which in 2002 required every state agency to produce a plan detailing how they were preparing to cope with the impact of the state's aging and increasingly diverse population. Such planning will be crucial to avoid being swamped by the coming demographic tidal wave.

Chapter 2: The Final Word

THE CHALLENGE
- The number of Americans 65 and older will more than double in at least 20 states by 2030 and then continue to grow for decades to come.
- Revenue could become a significant issue as the number of elderly increases and a declining percentage of individuals assumes the bulk of the tax burden.
- Government agencies will need to determine how to allocate scarce resources across competing demands from various age groups.

REFORM STRATEGIES
- *Explore alternative revenue models.* User fees, public-private partnerships and other models can help to finance new and existing services.
- *Develop clicks and mortars solutions.* Governments can use technology to transform traditional physical channels into "clicks and mortars" services that offer some of the personal interaction many seniors want while using technology to reduce costs.
- *Establish "channel" partnerships.* In some cases, it will make sense for governments to "piggyback" on the investments private firms and nonprofit organizations have made in service lines and delivery channels to meet the needs and preferences of aging citizens.

EXAMPLES
- *Pennsylvania*, faced with the problem of "premature graying," implemented in 1972 the only state lottery to date that dedicates all proceeds to senior programs. The state has spent nearly $15 billion on elderly assistance programs.
- *The Sunshine Network Veterans Health Administration* in Florida deploys high-tech, user-friendly tele-health computer devices to allow many elderly citizens to lead more independent lives.

NEXT STEPS
- *Understand how the aging population will impact your state.* Require state agencies to produce a plan detailing how they will cope with the impact of the aging population.
- *Do the easy things first.* Pay special attention to the design of information prepared for older users. Age-related disabilities (vision loss, hearing loss, memory problems and mobility loss) are common among elderly citizens. For online information, this means making sure that material is visually and substantively coherent and easy to navigate.
- *Segment customers* to predict changes in customer characteristics, needs and desires and use the information to allocate resources across services and delivery channels.

{3} *William D. Eggers, Mike Phelan and Tim Phoenix*

Bolstering Human Capital
How the Public Sector Can Beat the Coming Talent Crisis

In the next 10 to 15 years, the United States' population profile will change dramatically as the Baby Boom generation ages and begins to retire.

New York State is living proof of the effect this will have on the public sector. As of Jan. 1, 2005, 26 percent of a critical segment of the state's workforce hit 55 years of age, putting their retirement right around the corner, and 72 percent of that same segment—the managerial/confidential (M/C) job classification—was 45 years old or older. Chief executive officers of New York state government find themselves fighting a two-front war: Not only is the state facing the retirement of a quarter of these key personnel, the very group groomed to replace them will be retiring at practically the same time.

Unfortunately for the state, this group of executives includes occupations that perform some of the most crucial state government functions from senior law enforcement and emergency response officials to the people running the human service programs. By 2010, more than 33 percent of the M/C classification will be eligible for retirement, and by 2015, another 34 percent will be ready to hang up their white collars.[1] Although the particulars differ, most state governments face a similar human capital crunch, and it's up to governors to give life to innovative strategies to keep the government enterprise running smoothly.

The Boomer generation, often called the "pig in the python" of U.S. demographics because it moves along the United States' age-distribution

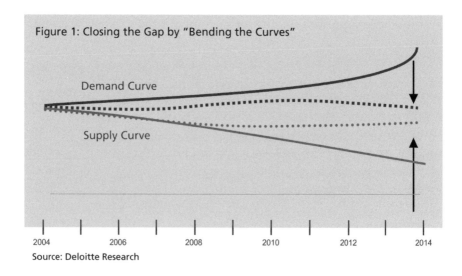

Figure 1: Closing the Gap by "Bending the Curves"

Demand Curve

Supply Curve

2004   2006   2008   2010   2012   2014

Source: Deloitte Research

line as a huge, pronounced bulge, profoundly influenced American society as it began to come of age in the 1960s. Baby Boomers will exert a similarly significant impact in the 21st century as their retirement leaves a significant void in both the private and the public workforces. Three major trends affecting the public sector connected to the Boomers' march to retirement—an aging government workforce, a shrinking pool of talent and the need for a new set of skills—will soon create a gap between the supply of skilled state government workers and the demand for them. With that said, the gap also creates a significant opportunity to fundamentally change the way government employees perform their mission. The most vivid way to portray the talent gap barreling toward the public sector is to plot the rising demand for public sector employees against the declining supply (see figure 1). The result is two curves bending away from each other, leaving a gap that will grow ever wider over the next decade and a half unless states take immediate steps to develop strategies and programs to "bend the curves" to help close this gap.

Closing this gap is among the most critical challenges most state and local governments will confront over the next five years. Governors and state legislators will have to take a hard look at state government's work culture, especially at ways to reinvent that culture to attract a new generation of workers.

Still, state and local governments have always been in the vanguard of public management. Their smaller size than the federal government gives them the ability to make operational changes quickly to match society's evolution. Government's coming human capital crisis will put that ability to the test.

Looming Talent Shortage

Government agencies today face sobering facts: the Baby Boom generation (those born between 1946 and 1964) will begin to reach senior citizen status in 2011, and from 2010 to 2030, the share of the population age 65 and over will increase from 39.4 million people to 69.4 million. The Boomers' departure from the workforce will send shock waves throughout the private and public sectors as organizations of all types struggle to replace them.

There is hope. Generation Y (Gen Y, for short)—the generational cohort born between 1977 and 1997—is nearly the same size as the Baby Boom generation. This means the public sector can count on another major wave of workers emerging to replace the Boomers, but the problem is one of timing. By 2014, nearly 20 percent of the total U.S. workforce will be eligible for retirement. In the same year, 50 percent of Gen Y will still be under 25 years of age. As Gen Y comes of age, employers will face a period of transition as its senior level employees retire to be replaced by a generation with minimal work experience. The looming talent shortage, already showing its effects in some parts of the public sector, will hit hardest in the next 10 to 15 years.

Widening gaps both in the quantity and quality of workers is driving this talent shortage. The U.S. Bureau of Labor Statistics projects that by 2010 there will be 168 million skilled jobs to fill in the United States but only 158 million people in the workforce. A shortage of three million workers is expected in the manufacturing sector alone. Meanwhile, NASA projected that 2 million science and engineering workers would retire between 1998 and 2008, yet only 198,000 students would graduate in these specialized fields to fill vacancies. Similarly, the Information Technology Association of America advises that the number of science, technology, math and engineering graduates must double from 430,000 to 860,000 annually to satisfy increasing labor demands in the United States and for the nation to remain globally competitive.[2] The public sector will be forced to compete fiercely with the private sector for the limited supply of qualified computer systems analysts, engineers, nurses, skilled managers, accountants, scientists and other professions.[3]

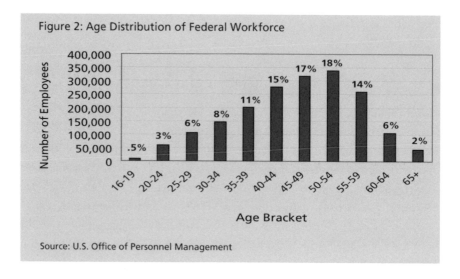

Figure 2: Age Distribution of Federal Workforce

Source: U.S. Office of Personnel Management

Federal Government Retirement Picture

In the face of such competition, the public sector faces particular difficulties filling employment vacancies from both a quantity and quality perspective. Downsizing and reduced hiring of federal employees during the late 1990s increased an already widening supply gap between private and public sector employment in the United States and opened the door for third-party contractors to compete for public sector services.[4] Concurrently, the average age of federal employees has risen. About 57 percent of the federal civil service is currently over 45, nearly double the 31 percent in the private sector. Further, only 3.5 percent of the federal workforce is less than 25 years old (see figure 2).

The Partnership for Public Service estimates that 58 percent of supervisory federal employees will be eligible for retirement by 2010.[5] Slightly more than half of federal civil servants are eligible to retire in the next five years, and 71 percent of those are in the Senior Executive Service, meaning the biggest recruiting challenges will be for more senior-level positions where competition for top talent is particularly fierce.

State Government Retirement Picture

In most states, the average employee age in the public sector also far exceeds that in the private sector. In Michigan, Texas and Wisconsin, for example, 60 percent or more of the state government workforce is over age 40 (see figure 3). New York faces a similar problem—57 percent of the state gov-

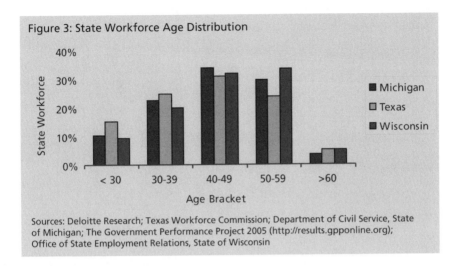

Figure 3: State Workforce Age Distribution

Sources: Deloitte Research; Texas Workforce Commission; Department of Civil Service, State of Michigan; The Government Performance Project 2005 (http://results.gpponline.org); Office of State Employment Relations, State of Wisconsin

ernment workforce is between the ages of 45 and 64, while only 29 percent lies between the ages of 35 and 44.

One thing these statistics clearly demonstrate is the dearth of "30- some-things" working today in many state capitals. One of the most entrepreneurial generations in American history, Generation X's aversion to large bureaucratic organizations and its tendency to change employers frequently has made this generation particularly challenging for government from a recruiting and retention standpoint. Also contributing to this problem is the fact that many state governments had hiring freezes in place during parts of the 1980s and 1990s when this generation was entering the workforce. This has created a gap of relatively "new" talent at the mid-manager levels.

Like the federal government, states, too, face large waves of retirement over the next decade or so. The California State Personnel Board reports that 70,000 state government employees—34 percent of the state's workforce—will be eligible to retire in the next five years. (Some independent studies estimate the number eligible for retirement at 100,000 California state employees, or 49 percent of California's state workforce). More than 50 percent of Pennsylvania's state workforce will be eligible to retire over the next 10 years, while more than 40 percent of Minnesota's workforce will reach retirement eligibility (see table 1).

The bottom line is that absent very aggressive recruiting and development efforts, state workforces, already significantly older than those in most private companies, will continue to age in the near future. The relatively small numbers of employees in their thirties and early forties ready to move up into leadership positions, combined with the concurrent retirement eli-

Table 1: Retirement Eligibility in Selected States

State	Average age of workforce	Eligibility for retirement	
		In 5 years	In 10 years
Michigan	44.3	28.8%	55.9%
Minnesota	45.0	20.7%	40.4%
New York	46.2	13.5%	28.3%
Pennsylvania	46.0	33.0%	54.0%
Wisconsin	45.5	18%	36.0%

Sources: Deloitte Research; Department of Civil Service, State of Michigan: The Government Performance Project 2005 (http://results.gpponline.org); "New York State Workforce Management Report 2004," Department of Civil Service, New York State (http://www.cs.state.ny.us/hr/docs/2004.pdf); "Pennsylvania's 2005 Governor's Annual Work Force Report," Commonwealth of Pennsylvania (http://www.hrm.state.pa.us/oahrm/2005-GAWFR.pdf); Office of State Employment Relations, State of Wisconsin

gibility of state agencies' upper-level management, will present significant management and succession challenges.

Beyond the Numbers: Generational Convergence

State government workforce challenges go well beyond these demographic numbers. Many state agencies are behind the curve in cultivating a work culture that will entice a new generation of employees as Gen Y's prepare to embark on their professional careers. To become a choice employer among this emerging workforce, the public sector must appeal to a population insistent upon a sociable, flexible, purposeful and technologically savvy work environment.

For members of the Baby Boom, job satisfaction is often tied to time and schedule flexibility, retirement benefits, and financial security, among other things. Those from Gen X value a very different set of benefits, such as mortgage assistance, career planning, infertility/adoption assistance, stock options, and alternative work hours. Gen Y reports that benefits such as career coaching, continuing education, access to health clubs, and social lives tied more to work—through functions such as happy hours—matter most when evaluating job satisfaction (see table 2).

Table 2: Most Important Benefits Contributing to Job Satisfaction

Generation Y (1977–1997)	Training Promotion/career coaching Continuing education Auto insurance Lease review	Extra work hours Extra vacation Gym memberships Social functions (work happy hours, etc.)
Generation X (1965–1976)	Mortgage assistance Career planning Infertility/adoption assistance Education savings plans	Stock options Extra work hours Extra vacation Gym facilities
Baby Boomers (1946–1964)	Aging parent/child care Schedule flexibility Retirement benefits Savings plan College tuition Retirement planning	Financial planning Investment counseling Significant time off Travel planning Life insurance priorities Extra disability
Silent Generation (1922–1945)	Social interactions sponsored by work Reverse life insurance Extra major medical insurance	Reverse mortgages Drivers/shuttle service Flexible hours/part-time work

Source: Deloitte Research

Several factors contribute to these generational differences. Having grown up with both parents in the workforce, Gen X and Gen Y appear to shy away from overly work-centric lifestyles, resulting in an emphasis on additional vacation hours and social events. Further, as children of the "downsized generation," many members of Gen Y have witnessed a parent lose a job. The shift from job security to employment at will, the uncertainty of the labor force in the 1990s, the burst of the dot-com bubble and recent economic turbulence have all changed employer-employee dynamics. Members of Gen Y and Gen X assume responsibility for their own employability, creating an increased demand for professional development, long-term career planning and continued education.[6] Mentoring and career coaching alleviate concerns about an unstable job market, while social networking serves as an informal career resource, elevating the value of each to the Y generation.[7]

Walking the halls of many government agencies, one is struck by the dearth of workers in their thirties. How can government agencies avoid a similar fate with Gen Y?

First, the good news. Many of the workplace values most important to Gen Y align quite well with public sector work (see figure 3). For example, Gen Y demonstrates a notable preference for job mobility within a single organization as opposed to the open market.[8] This, too, may be a result of the

Courting Gen Y: Secrets of a Successful Suitor

Among federal agencies, the Government Accountability Office (GAO) has established a reputation for its innovative and effective recruiting strategies.[a] Successfully courting Gen Y, however, requires demonstrating interest beyond the initial pursuit. In addition to its marketing-branding strategy and campus outreach initiative, the GAO uses a well-developed internship program, competitive compensation packages and ongoing professional development opportunities to attract and retain top talent.

To dispel the lackluster perception of public sector employment, the GAO developed a branding strategy to portray itself as a high-impact, global consulting organization. Operating under the slogan, "At GAO you make a real difference in American life," the agency works alongside academic institutions to recruit top talent from undergraduate and graduate programs. Often, GAO employees serve as adjunct professors at target universities to cultivate relationships with administrators and students.

In addition to campus outreach programs, the GAO has a formal internship program designed to fill 50 percent of entry level positions annually. The internship includes presentations on Capitol Hill, networking opportunities with senior GAO officials, brown-bag presentations and live viewings of CNN's Crossfire. In addition, interns are assigned a supervisor to facilitate formal networking and a "buddy" to help with informal networking and socializing.

Networking opportunities continue after recruits have accepted a position with GAO. Among its retention strategies, the GAO created a "First Day" policy to impress new hires—an employee's work space, laptop and phone are ready for business on day one. New hires are eligible for pay increases every six months for the first two years, receive ongoing feedback and evaluations and enjoy mentoring and career advancement opportunities.

The GAO also offers ongoing career advancement through its Professional Development Program. Over a two-year period, the program augments on-the-job experience with classroom training and offers continual coaching and mentoring. Participants gain exposure to various management styles, partake in speaker series, attend congressional hearings and shadow senior staff members.

GAO's success in attracting and retaining talent has created a demand for the organization to serve as a consultant for a number of government agencies, offering guidance and sharing secrets of its successful courtship of Gen Y.

a. More information can be found at http://www.gao.gov/new.items/d05164.pdf.

Table 3: Attracting and Engaging Generation Y

Gen Y Workplace Needs	Public Sector Strengths	Public Sector Weaknesses	Strategies for the Public Sector
Flexibility	Breadth of opportunities within public sector	Absence of career planning; slow advancement	Provide long-term career planning; cultivate learning opportunities; promote mobility
Balance/ Sociability	Good work/life balance	Lack of social activities, mentoring, networking opportunities	Host social events; develop formal/informal networking programs; enable flexible schedules
Sense of Meaning/ Purpose	History of public service	Poor public perception due to bureaucratic inefficiencies	Highlight core values; prioritize social responsibility; initiate branding campaign and campus outreach
Access to Technology	Significant funding on technology	Sub-par technology hinders flexibility, sociability, training	Offer online recruiting; provide flexibility around media choice; develop electronic learning tools

Source: Deloitte Research

downsizing and economic uncertainty of recent decades.[9] The public sector can capitalize on this preference and highlight the variety of opportunities available within public sector employment to recruit top talent within Gen Y. State employers should also implement professional development initiatives to promote flexibility in career advancement.

A strong interest in public service and the pursuit of meaningful work are two additional Gen Y characteristics that bode well for government recruiting efforts. Seventy-four percent of university students interested in working for the federal government cite "the opportunity to make a difference" as a major reason for their interest.[10]

The bad news is that certain perceptions of government work, if not reversed, provide powerful deterrents to attracting Gen Y into state government. The image of the public sector as a slow-moving, bureaucratic monolith, juxtaposed against a fast-moving, anti-bureaucratic Gen Y, poses one significant challenge. The perception that government is several years behind the private sector in utilizing the latest technologies also hurts the public sector's appeal to Gen Y.

The public sector also must compete with the nonprofit sector for the affections of a socially conscious Gen Y. In numerous surveys, today's college students interested in public service say they favor working for nonprofit organizations over the public sector.[11] Sixty percent of college students identify the nonprofit sector as better at spending money wisely, compared with 6 percent who identify government as a smart spender. Moreover, 76 percent cite the nonprofit sector as better at helping people; only 16 percent say the government is better.[12]

Pennsylvania state officials have run up against these image problems in trying to lure new talent to the public sector workforce. Workforce planning officials discovered that there is no story to tell about working for the public sector that stirs the interest of prospective employees from younger generations. If there's no story, there's no message about what it means to work for the public sector to entice bright young graduates to the public service.

That's not good for Pennsylvania, but the state certainly isn't alone. State and local governments struggle with articulating the unique opportunity for personal and professional growth that working in the public sector presents. Plenty of young and energetic graduates carry the instinct to work for government. But if they don't get the message that the public sector wants them, they'll look elsewhere.

Government executives have no time to waste in learning how to deliver a coherent, comprehensive and understandable story about what it means to work in the public sector. A human capital crisis is in the making, and the time to say, "Come work for us" is now.

In the private sector, the oil and gas industry has faced similarly challenging public image issues with the environmentally conscious Gen Y. Several Fortune 500 companies in the industry have implemented successful branding programs to revamp their image among the emerging Gen Y population, including campus outreach engagements and increased environmental efforts.[13]

This initiative speaks to an article published nearly 10 years ago on the need for a shift in the general perception of the public sector professional career. The article cited the British senior service as an exemplar of three qualities central to senior government employees' successful careers: "initiative, characterized by a willingness to exercise discretionary authority and a preference for autonomy as a work style; strong intellectual abilities, shaped by a broad liberal education and strong technical skills; and a spirited desire to serve the public."[14]

Until they tap these qualities, government leaders won't be capable of reversing the all-too-common negative perceptions of public sector jobs.

Other Human Capital Challenges Facing Government

With a clearer picture of the generational shift taking place in the workforce, it's apparent that governments must adapt to build the public workforce of the future. The convergence of these generations in the coming years takes place against the backdrop of additional changes within the labor environment. State governments must also devise strategies to counter the following challenges.

MANAGING THE SUCCESSION GAP. The number of people nearing retirement age is larger than ever before, causing the government workforce—particularly at the senior executive level—to shrink rapidly. Even as new employees enter the workforce, public sector agencies must plan appropriately to ensure that existing staff develop the experience and knowledge necessary to take on increasing levels of responsibility as senior staff retire. Beyond attraction and retention, public sector agencies must give employees the skills and resources to develop their talents, assigning them to well-matched positions and helping them build social networks that ensure they establish relationships that foster their professional development and advance their careers. Strategies to address succession planning and knowledge transfer are critical to navigating the succession gap.

REDUCED EDUCATION LEVELS. Today, 85 percent of jobs require education beyond high school, compared with 61 percent in 1991. It is estimated that 60 percent of future jobs will require training that only 20 percent of the current workforce possesses. According to the Bureau of Labor Statistics' 2004 employment projections, Hispanics are currently the fastest-growing population segment.[15] Further, Hispanics represent the demographic most interested in government careers, with 51 percent of surveyed university students reporting that they are "very" or "extremely" interested in working for the federal government. However, while 72 percent of white students enrolled in 9th grade graduated from high school on schedule in 2001, just over half of the same group of black and Hispanic students did so. State governments would be wise to target this growing segment and foster these students' interest in public sector employment and continue to work to enhance education performance levels.[16]

NEW SKILL SETS. With the dramatic increase in public-private partnerships, outsourcing and intergovernmental collaboration occurring in recent years, state governments now need many more people who possess not only traditional planning and budgeting skills, but also a contemporary skill set. Today's employees need proficiency in project management, mediation, negotiation, the ability to collaborate across sectors and agencies, contract management, risk analysis and other complex skills. The changes to the public sector workforce raise important human capital questions every agency must address: What is the best way to attract this sort of person to the public sector? What level of pay is necessary? What aspects of the culture of the public sector workforce and job specifications must be altered to lure people with the necessary skill sets?

FOCUSING ON CRITICAL TALENT. In response to widening gaps within the workforce, shifting demographics and evolving skill sets, the public sector must improve its ability to identify critical talent. Within every organization, a subset of the staff exerts a disproportionate amount of influence because it possesses a higher level of relevant skills and abilities. These individuals represent the organization's critical talent, and efforts to increase workforce supply—particularly in a tight labor market—should focus on identifying and seeking out critical talent. Private sector organizations have a long record of successfully identifying and focusing on critical talent. Couriers at FedEx, for example, have regular and direct contact with customers and take responsibility for decisions that affect the performance of the supply chain as they determine their delivery routes. As a result, couriers may be considered more critical than other staff, such as cargo pilots or warehouse staff.[17]

These four challenges, together with those presented by the generational differences between Gen Y and its predecessors, pose a threat, but they also present an opportunity to rethink many of the ossified cultural and organizational relics of the early 21st century preventing government from attracting the workforce it needs in the future. Unless these challenges are met head on, government agencies will be unable to attract and retain the talent they require, particularly in the face of stiff competition from the for-profit and nonprofit sectors.

Governments must learn new tricks to bend the supply and demand curves toward one another, even as the distance between them widens. Public agencies that stick with the status quo will fall behind, finding themselves on the wrong side of the gap.

Bending the Supply Curve Up

The traditional "Let the HR Department take care of it" approach usually separates an agency's strategy for finding talent from broader aims, like its mission and strategic goals. Traditional approaches also often focus too narrowly on metrics and outcomes. As a result, those approaches don't allow

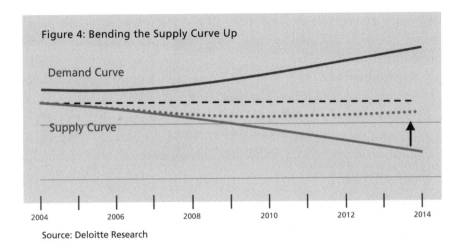

Figure 4: Bending the Supply Curve Up

Demand Curve

Supply Curve

2004   2006   2008   2010   2012   2014

Source: Deloitte Research

individuals or organizations the flexibility needed to grow, and they often fail to provide people with work that engages them over time as their skills change.

Bending the supply curve up requires, first and foremost, a shift in mindset (see figure 4). Instead of making the talent gap a human resources (HR) problem focused solely on acquiring and retaining talent, the public sector needs to develop integrated strategies around issues that matter most to its critical talent. In particular, agencies must recognize that talented people care about how their work promotes their development or growth. Training is just a small part of that.

Talented employees want to work in jobs or on projects that engage them. They want jobs that will give them connections to other employees who will be important to their future, such as mentors, advisers and networks of colleagues. The most valuable employees want the chance to constantly learn how to do their jobs better. This means organizations must create the roles—and the environmental and cultural conditions— that tap employees' greatest potential, while providing them with fresh challenges. In the private sector, where recruiting and managing talent has been a way of life for some time, companies have learned a valuable lesson—successful recruitment and retention depend on a desirable organizational culture that nurtures employees' talent.

Talent management is also critical for the public sector, particularly as the values and expectations of the future workforce shift. Opportunities for development, meaningful work and social connectedness have become the most important factors in career choices. Today's approach to talent management is shifting to a model predicated on development, deployment and connection as the differentiators that will attract employees and make them stick with an organization.

Governments must implement an integrated talent management strategy that narrows the talent gap by putting equal energy into solving both the workforce supply problem and the workforce demand problem. Most immediately, the imminent human capital shortage created by the Boomers' retirement requires a critical examination of government's current recruitment and hiring practices.

You're Hired. When Can You Start?

All too frequently, government takes a passive approach to recruitment, depending on potential job candidates to conduct extensive research on their own to find available job openings and to assess their qualifications for those jobs. According to a recent report by the Partnership for Public Service, 42 percent of college students are "very" or "extremely" interested in working for the federal government, while only 13 percent are "very" or "extremely knowledgeable" about job opportunities.[18] This passive approach must change, and the public sector has a good deal of ground to cover in the race to attract and retain a supply of skilled and knowledgeable workers to offset the coming workforce gap as the Baby Boomers retire.

THE FIRST STEP. Step one involves modernizing outmoded hiring practices. Why do many highly skilled candidates who cite a desire to do public service end up not working in government? Fifty-three percent of interested candidates cite "too much bureaucracy" as a major reason for forgoing the pubic sector. In extreme cases, the hiring process for public sector agencies requires multiple levels of clearances, and approvals chew up many months before the candidate knows whether she has the job.

Timing is a critical component of the job-selection process, particularly for highly skilled, highly educated and highly experienced candidates. Private firms gain a significant competitive advantage in recruiting over government agencies by quickly making formal offers to the nation's brightest students and most qualified candidates—often before public agencies even reach the interview stage. In many cases, graduates of top public policy schools must chose between a clear-cut job offer from a private firm and the vague impression of a possible offer from a government agency. Often burdened with significant debt from six or more years of higher education, the idea of turning down a firm offer from the private or nonprofit sector in favor of months of agonizing uncertainty is often enough to dissuade graduates from a career in public service.

New York University professor Paul Light reports that 67 percent of college students with more than $20,000 in student loans consider the ability to repay college loans a very important part of their job selection process. With 63 percent of the same population describing the government hiring process as confusing, and an overwhelming 78 percent describing it as slow, it's little wonder candidates often prefer the private and nonprofit sectors. By comparison, the nonprofit sector resonates with college students as both simple (69 percent) and fast (56 percent) from a hiring perspective.[19]

The challenges in public sector hiring practices extend beyond timeliness. A recent report by the Partnership for Public Service highlights the ineffectiveness of government's assessment practices in predicting job performance. According to the study, only 39 percent of federal employees believe their work unit is hiring people with the right skills.[20] Further, the method most frequently employed by federal, state and local governments in selecting employees, a point system that evaluates self-reported prior experience, is among the least predictive assessment practices.[21] This approach favors experience over talent and fails to account for performance and achievement. The consequences of this flawed recruiting method include increased turnover, low productivity and absenteeism, none of which government can afford in the wake of an impending talent crisis. To reverse this trend of poor selection, public sector entities must develop effective assessment tools to identify, target and aggressively recruit the best candidates.[22]

Contrary to conventional wisdom, government is capable of radically improving hiring practices. Several government agencies have taken great pains to strengthen their ability to compete for the best and brightest talent by streamlining the application, selection, clearance and approval processes. For example, by using technology, the U.S. Census Bureau was able to reduce the time required to hire staff in several critical positions from six months to as little as three days.[23]

DECENTRALIZING HIRING. Some states have made progress in speeding hiring and expanding applicant pools, by, for example, devolving more authority for hiring decisions from central personnel offices to the agency or department level. Arizona, Kansas, South Carolina, Washington and Wisconsin have all decentralized hiring practices, entrusting departments with greater flexibility in filling vacancies. This move away from the traditional gateway, "one

The U.S. Army Increases Recruiting Efforts and Expands its Talent Pool

To combat waning enlistment numbers, the Department of Defense (DOD) has increased its recruitment efforts. In the past few years, the Army has used video games to promote service in the Armed Forces. "America's Army," for example, has been downloaded 16 million times. Army Recruiting Command and the Naval Postgraduate School (MOVES division) collaborated to provide potential recruits with a game experience it considers both realistic and educational.

The Army has also started offering shorter enlistment options to appeal to recruits who do not want to commit to the full enlistment period. The new Reserve program allows recruits to spend three years in a Selected Reserve Troop Program Unit (TPU), instead of the traditional six years. Similarly the National Call to Service Enlistment Option, which promotes and facilitates military enlistment in support of national duty, lasts only 15 months (not including training).

In March 2005, the Army Reserve implemented a test program to raise the age limit for first-time enlistees by five years to 40 years, expanding the Army's pool of potential candidates. The Army plans to focus more on recruits' level of fitness instead of age.

size fits all" approach common to state personnel hiring allows departments to conduct their own recruitment efforts, assist with the design of eligibility exams and administer supplemental questionnaires to screen candidates who meet minimum qualifications. Wisconsin's Entry Professional Program combines on-site interviewing and immediate job offers.

To meet tough labor market competition, some public sector agencies are conducting interviews at job fairs and on college campuses. Candidates are quickly screened to determine if they are qualified, and qualified applicants are then interviewed by line managers who have the authority to make immediate job offers. Usually, these job offers are contingent on reference or other background checks.

Additionally, some states have eliminated arbitrary restrictions on the number of qualified candidates who can be interviewed. Wisconsin and Idaho now use flexible certification guidelines rather than more traditional rules that require the top three or five candidates to be interviewed for a job before others can be considered.

Fast Tracking Critical Talent

Fixing recruiting problems is only half the battle. Once the best and bright-

Speeding the Hiring Process Through Position-Based Hiring

In 2003, the San Jose, California, Employment Services Department (ESD) eliminated most centralized civil service eligibility lists in favor of a de-centralized, position-based hiring process. Instead of testing each new applicant on a standardized classification exam, the ESD now works with each department to develop position-specific minimum and desired qual-ifications. ESD then screens applicants based on these pre-established criteria and forwards the five most-qualified candidates to the appointing authority for interviews and selection.

As a result of implementing online job applications and the new posi-tion-based hiring system, the average time to hire a new employee (non-public safety) in San Jose has been cut nearly in half, from an average of 130 days to 68 days. This compares with an average of 113 days to establish an eligible list in San Francisco, plus the time to get a requisi-tion approved and then to fill a vacancy, a process that varies greatly by department.

San Jose's model is similar to that used by the city of Indianapolis, Indiana, which does not have a civil service system but can hire a new employee in an average of just 30–45 days. Like its counterpart in San Jose, the Indianapolis Human Resources Department reviews the qualifi-cations of applicants and forwards the most qualified to the appointing department. Once that department selects a candidate to hire, human resources conducts a background check and provides orientation to the new employee.

est get hired, public sector agencies must pay particular attention to putting those employees on a fast track to positions of increased responsibility. In part, fast tracking is a supply-side approach that makes the public sector at-tractive to the critical talent of the future because it matches the values and expectations of potential Gen X and Gen Y employees, who want to know that opportunity beckons. They seek personal and professional challenges, and fast tracking maps out those challenges.

The public sector must work hard to change the perception that once hired into government a person faces an interminable wait to move into a position where he or she can have an impact. Graduates of top public-policy schools are often unaware of the variety of public sector jobs available be-cause public sector recruiters do not make a strong effort to sell those stu-dents on the promise of a career in government.[24]

Perhaps more important, fast tracking helps government agencies ad-dress the looming critical talent shortage by accelerating the development of staff to replace the coming wave of retiring workers. It's akin to a human-capital savings account—agency directors can rest easier knowing that new employees are being groomed for high-level positions and responsibilities as Baby Boomers retire.

Every state government should have direct conduits to the state's graduate schools of public policy and administration; launching fast-track programs is one way to aggressively target such graduates, as well as other highly desired candidates. Private sector firms take full advantage of career fairs at colleges and universities to tell graduates what they can expect if they join their firm.

One successful public sector fast-track program is the Presidential Management Fellows (PMF) program, a two-year program sponsored by the Office of Personnel Management. The program introduces men and women from various academic disciplines and career paths to the public sector, and it's an integral component of the federal government's succession planning strategies for future human capital needs.

Applicants who complete their graduate degree (master's, juris doctorate, or other doctoral-level degree) are eligible to apply for the following year's PMF class. Applicants must be nominated by their university or college to be considered. The 2005 PMF class consisted of 643 fellows from 200 different colleges and universities.[25]

Once accepted into the program, participants must determine which federal agency appeals to them and apply to that agency. Fellows develop a two-year strategic plan to help focus their learning, development and career advancement by leading people, change or projects within that agency. Fellows must also take 80 hours of additional training a year, focusing on gaining skills to help them achieve their goals and objectives.

State governments now lag behind both the federal government and the private sector in adopting fast-track strategies for current and prospective employees.

The Develop-Deploy-Connect Cycle

To deal with the coming talent shortage, governments must let go of outdated and ineffective recruitment and retention strategies and instead opt for talent-management models that nurture, inspire and reward employees in new ways. This shift enables forward-looking public sector organizations to develop an integrated talent-management strategy based on what we call the develop-deploy-connect cycle (see figure 5).

In the "develop" part of the cycle, public sector organizations seek to ensure that employees have the opportunities, experiences and guidance they need to be successfully positioned and connected to their work. The support, resources, information and learning opportunities the organization provides to management and employees are targeted on improving their performance. South Australia's Graduate Development Program, for example, targets new graduates within one to six months of their employment with the public sector. The six-to-eight month program includes information sessions, workshops, career planning, mentoring and competency assessments. The training package seeks to impart practical skills for public sector employment, develop insight about public sector issues and processes, encourage networking, provide a supportive work environment and expand professional competencies and options.

The "deploy" part of the cycle is meant to ensure that the correct candidate is matched to a critical job. The organization stays focused on its critical talent to ensure employees' skills, interests and capabilities evolve in line with strategic objectives. The essential elements of this part of the cycle are proper experiences, support and connections that will help employees master roles for which they were not originally trained.

One of the best examples in the public sector is the United Kingdom's Civil Service Fast Stream Development Program. Fast Stream is a service within the Cabinet Office that focuses on attracting and retaining top talent for Senior Civil Service careers. Those who join Fast Stream are exposed to a series of intensive job placements designed to prepare them for senior managerial positions. Not only are Fast Streamers heavily engaged in high-profile projects within their departments, they also are eligible for priority hiring in other departments and agencies, as well as endorsed among European and international partners. Civil servants displaying strong performance must be nominated by their department and are exempt from qualifying tests.[26]

Similarly, the State of Illinois' Upward Mobility program, a partnership with the American Federation of State, County and Municipal Employees, provides state employees personalized guidance and training to advance to new and more challenging positions.[27] So if a road crew supervisor wanted to eventually be a regional supervisor, the program would lay out a plan for how to get from here to there while also offering individual counseling, training and the possibility of some tuition reimbursement. Almost 13,000 state employees have been through the program. "You have to say to employees that you want them to grow, and if you're not willing to do that, then the message is that we want you to stay stagnant because we don't

Figure 5: The Develop-Deploy-Connect Model

"Develop" means providing the real-life learning employees need to master a job. This doesn't mean just traditional classroom or online education. As important are the "trial-by-fire" experiences that stretch their capabilities and the lessons they learn from peers, mentors and others.

"Deploy" means working with key individuals to identify their deep-rooted skills, interests and knowledge; find their best fit in the organization; and craft the job design and conditions that help them to perform.

"Connect" means providing critical employees with the tools and guidance they need to build networks that enhance individual and organizational performance and improve the quality of their interactions with others.

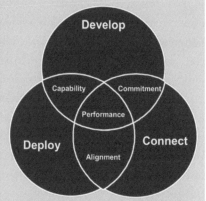

The Develop-Deploy-Connect model should be at the core of an organization's talent strategy. By focusing on these three elements, organizations can generate capability, commitment and alignment in key workforce segments, which in turn improve performance. When this happens, the attraction and retention of skilled talent largely take care of themselves.

Source: Deloitte Research; For more details on this model, please refer to the 2004 Deloitte Research Study, "It's 2008: Do You Know Where Your Talent Is?"

value you," explains Paul Campbell, the director of the Illinois Department of Central Management.[28]

The "connect" part of the cycle seeks to ensure that employees make the kind of connections within the organization that will give them access to useful information, help them solve problems and attain their goals. The result is employees who are more engaged and effective. At the World Bank, for example, more than 100 active Communities of Practice (CoPs) link bank employees and their many constituencies around the globe, allowing, for example, a staff member assisting the Nepalese Ministry of Education to easily engage colleagues in Hungary and Turkey involved in similar projects. In the past, the World Bank had no way to facilitate this level of knowledge sharing.

An Integrated Talent Management Strategy

The develop-deploy-connect approach elevates talent management to a new level of importance within an organization. It enables public agencies to implement an integrated talent-management strategy that will put them in a far more competitive position when the coming human-capital crisis hits the government workforce. There are four stages in this integrated strategy.

IDENTIFY ORGANIZATIONAL PRIORITIES. This is especially important for public sector organizations, whose near-term goals are often pulled in different directions by changing budgets or political shifts. To thrive during the coming talent shortage, an organization must identify and stay focused on its core mission and long-term priorities so it can identify the kinds of talent it will need to reach its objectives.

In particular, government organizations should identify the current and future challenges they face and map their talent strengths and gaps against these challenges. To do so, it is useful for organizations to conduct executive and key stakeholder interviews to understand the organization's mission, vision, strategic goals and plans, and to assess its high-level talent capabilities. With those interviews in hand, organizations can analyze current and future challenges.

After comparing talent strengths and gaps with challenges, organizations can analyze the current and future external drivers and internal requirements, including likely economic and demographic changes as well as possible political shifts. Identifying priorities and then mapping talent strengths and gaps against them will underline the fact that public sector organizations cannot manage the gap between talent supply and demand by human resources programs alone. Closing the gap will take productivity, automation and sourcing solutions, as well as fine-tuning the HR program to bend the supply and demand curves toward one another.

DEFINE CRITICAL WORKFORCE SEGMENTS. Identifying priorities and mapping them against talent strengths and gaps will enable government organizations to identify the segments of the workforce that disproportionately contribute to their success. Forward-looking government organizations isolate the unit cost of labor per segment, based on historical data and project future unit costs.

They also understand supply and demand pressures affecting workforce segments, while analyzing cost-per-hire metrics specific to the segments of the workforce most important to organizations. Officials with Health Canada, for example, recognized that to ensure the availability of critical talent in the future, they needed to understand how supply and demand will change. The agency developed complex forecasting and planning models to assist in quantifying future supply and demand. By manipulating these models, Health Canada officials can develop a real sense of how different management and policy levers will influence the government workforce in the future.[29] For example, they can estimate how certain changes in health care policy might affect the supply and demand for health care workers.

In addition, government organizations should review process work flows, matching specific processes and activities to determine common skills and experiences. Once critical segments are identified, employers must also gauge the depth of the talent pool. The shrinking number of science and engineering degree candidates, for example, should prompt the public sector to devise strategies to recruit those segments aggressively.[30] Additionally, public sector employers must pay attention to the other parties at the watering hole. The private sector is enjoying significantly more success attracting engineers, with 71 percent expressing interest in private sector work and only 29 percent in public sector employment.[31]

VALIDATE CRITICAL WORKFORCE TRENDS. With priorities identified and critical workforce segments defined, public sector organizations can isolate specific workforce trends likely to have the most impact on the supply of needed talent. By understanding which roles and skills are critical to an organization's performance, recruiting efforts can be precisely tailored to candidates with those skills.

The key to success in validating critical workforce trends is for public sector leaders to avoid trying to "boil the ocean." When examining workforce trends, many public sector organizations look at themselves as a whole. The most successful organizations focus first on positions that require scarce skills or skills that are in high demand, then focus on positions requiring "commodity" skills. For example, from 2002 to 2005, the number of undergraduate and graduate computer science degree candidates declined 33 and 25 percent, respectively.[32] Monitoring this trend and increasing efforts to aggressively recruit this critical and increasingly scarce pool of candidates should be a top priority for federal and state governments.

The process to replenish the public sector's skilled workforce will likely take years. Public agencies must simultaneously engage several fronts to reform hiring practices, succession planning, workforce planning, and retention practices to acquire the workforce necessary to survive the Boomers' retirement. The most successful public sector organizations will start with a low-disruption, low-cost, quick-time-to-results approach, developing a prioritized set of strategic and tactical actions to manage the gap between the supply of and demand for talent.[33]

Succession Planning and Capability Transfer

As government leaders consider strategies to bend the supply curve up,

Targeting Your Critical Workforce: The U.S. Government's IT Workforce Initiative

The federal government's IT Workforce Initiative seeks to attract and retain information technology professionals through improved hiring practices and competitive compensation scales. One component of this initiative was the launch of a job fair Web site in 2002. Making extensive use of Web technology to screen and assess applicants, the job fair site received 2.3 million hits and processed thousands of applications for 270 job openings. The assessment tools worked successfully and screened out half of the applicants. Ultimately, 113 positions were filled with a single recruiting event. The Virtual Job Fair demonstrates that it is possible to hire competent IT workers within a few weeks, as opposed to a few months under former practices.

In addition, the Office of Personnel Management made a new pay classification system for IT positions, creating 10 specialty titles under the 2210 IT management series of workers, and updated an inflexible classification system. The result was not an increase in pay for all IT workers, but rather a targeted approach geared to entry- and developmental-level federal IT workers with the latest skills. The special salary rates cover computer specialists, computer engineers, computer scientists and the information technology occupational series, and produced overall net pay increases of 7 percent to 33 percent for IT workers.

Under the Workforce Initiative, IT specialists are also eligible for retention allowances, which are paid at the rate of 5, 10, or 15 percent, depending on the educational degrees and certifications earned by the employee. The initiative allows the government to cover employees' student loan repayments and payments toward professional certification. Before the initiative, such incentives were not allowed.

it's important to understand that the problem is more complicated than simply replacing x number of retirees with y number of entering workers. What is in the heads of those retirees can play a significant role in helping bend the supply curve up. Any enterprise looking at large numbers of people retiring is also looking at a severe case of "brain drain" as years of accumulated knowledge walk out the door. For the public sector, which often relies on older IT systems or home-grown software written by agency IT staff to solve idiosyncratic agency-specific problems, brain drain can paralyze government agencies. One consequence of an older government workforce is that when senior-level government managers begin to retire, many staff in the level immediately below them will also retire, creating a huge gap in knowledge and skills.

Strategic Workforce Planning: An Example from Seattle

As part of its 2006–07 Strategic Plan, Seattle Public Utilities identified a need for stronger employee development programs, proactive succession planning and workforce data analysis as key initiatives for the fiscal year. Through efforts such as reengineering delivery of workforce training, capturing institutional knowledge of staff and analyzing relevant workforce data to focus on local and national trends, the utilities agency believes it can stay ahead of the rapidly changing workforce. Another initiative is one that looks to forge a strong and cooperative partnership with organized labor. The agency plans to initiate joint efforts between labor and management to explore, evaluate and design new alternatives for an efficient and flexible workforce.

Stopping that knowledge drain is a critical issue facing public sector leaders. Most public sector organizations do not compare favorably to the private sector in succession planning and capability transfer. Private sector leaders take full advantage of strategies to transfer knowledge from departing staff to incoming staff. One such strategy is mentoring programs, in which senior-level staff work closely with new employees over a period of months or years to pass knowledge and capabilities on to the next generation. This satisfies the older generations' desire for creating a lasting impact and meets the younger generations' desire for training and coaching.

Bending the Demand Curve Down

More than ever, the quality of the public sector workforce becomes a key factor in meeting public expectations and public needs. Providing better services to more citizens with less money is challenging enough, but in an environment of ever-decreasing workforce stability, the challenge appears more daunting. But if the public sector takes steps to bend the demand curve down, agencies can mitigate the potentially dire impacts of the coming workforce shortage (see figure 6). The public sector can manipulate the demand curve through technological advances, organizational restructuring, sourcing strategies and performance management initiatives.

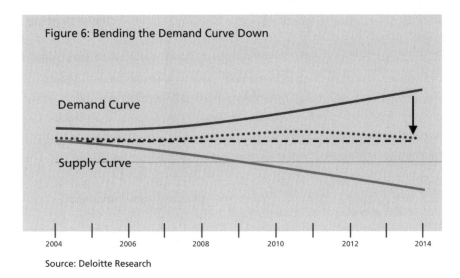

Figure 6: Bending the Demand Curve Down

Demand Curve

Supply Curve

2004   2006   2008   2010   2012   2014

Source: Deloitte Research

Technological Advances to Improve Efficiency

Technology can increase the productivity of existing staff levels in several ways, but in an increasingly tight labor market, one of technology's greatest benefits is in reducing the need for high numbers of personnel in any given government agency. This is particularly the case for lower-skilled workers who conduct highly routine activities day in and day out, such as entering data or processing paper-based forms and mailings, where automation and Web-enabled transactions can take up much of the burden of these routine tasks.

E-GOVERNMENT SELF-SERVICE. Public sector agencies can shift the demand curve for new workers by turning to self-service initiatives targeting external service requests from constituents and internal service requests from employees or other government agencies.

Private corporations have long sought to bend their workforce demand curves down by using technology. Private sector success stories show compelling promise. For example, leading companies derive huge cost savings from shifting millions of customer calls to self-service Web transactions. By moving 35 million customer-service calls to such a self-service environment, IBM saved between 70 and 90 percent on the cost of a service call handled by a customer representative.[34] The automation, which was part of a $9 billion cost savings initiative that took place between 1995 and 1998, saved the company $750 million, led to increased productivity and reduced unnecessary headcount.[35]

Online self-service initiatives have been somewhat slower to catch on in the public sector. Still, the moves of some states to drive efficiency in government through self-service technology initiatives show that public sector executives aren't afraid to shake their risk-averse label. California's Franchise Tax Board (FTB) first offered its ReadyReturn pilot for the 2004 tax year. Under the pilot, the FTB selected 50,000 California residents who file as single persons, claim no dependents, take the standard deduction, have only one employer and have wages as their only source of income. The FTB provided ReadyReturn participants with a completed tax return, based on information collected from their employer, and the participants then reviewed the completed tax return, signed it and sent it back to the FTB. An online option of e-filing the ReadyReturn was also available. Due to positive response from taxpayers who used ReadyReturn, the FTB continued the e-program in tax year 2005.

Increasing efficiency through self-service technology is not only about external customers. Public sector agencies can also automate internal service requests to drive down workforce demand. Automating functions such as human resource management, finance and training can provide the greatest potential benefit in the short term. Minnesota's Transformation Roadmap developed under Governor Tim Pawlenty's Drive to Excellence program recommends creating a shared services center for processing staff payroll and benefits. The approach will reduce costs, increase employee self-service and establish centers of excellence to provide specialized HR functions for all public agencies in the state.

PROCESS AUTOMATION. Routine business processes consume a disproportionately large share of government's resources. Printing, sorting, stuffing and mailing materials require significant time and expense. By automating these and other processes, government can free up significant resources to focus on critical activities. The cost of processing tax returns in many states, for example, is huge, often in the tens of millions of dollars a year. A consulting report commissioned by the Texas Comptroller's office several years ago found that between $10 and $20 million of these costs could eventually disappear with Internet tax filing. Whole activities can be eliminated with Web filing, including opening the returns, data entry, error correction, and postage. The report estimated that eventually the agency could cut the number of employees needed to process taxes in half.

At the federal level, the Department of Homeland Security's Customs and Border Protection Bureau has aggressively pursued process automation.

To apply for many managerial jobs, candidates fill out applications online, listing their education and experience and answering a series of questions to determine their qualifications.[36]

Automated decision-making systems, or technologies that use computer processing to make decisions and implement programmed decision processes, could also potentially help to bend the demand curve down. Decision automation systems exist because information technologies can make some decisions better, faster and at a lower cost than a human decision-maker. Such systems are now used by airlines in their yield management systems, by hotel chains to optimize hotel room rates and by insurance companies to underwrite and evaluate home equity loan applications. In the public sector, such systems could potentially be used for a host of areas from traffic management (where they are already beginning to be deployed) to human services to education. Through data-based decision-making, for example, state education departments have started to tie together the thousands of different data elements collected by school districts and states into a centralized computer depository educators can use to look for patterns in the data that could help improve educational performance.

GREATER PRODUCTIVITY. One benefit of an increasingly technological government is that staff at all levels see immediate gains in productivity and become key contributors to the government's success. At the U.S. Department of Education, one of the greatest benefits of recent technology projects is reducing the burden of routine, trivial reporting processes.

The department's Performance-Based Data Management Initiative brought together federal and state education agencies and industry partners to improve the quality and timeliness of education information. The goal is an education data exchange network that gives all the partners the capacity to transfer information about education programs more smoothly and to better analyze available data.

State education agencies are expected to use the system to submit required performance information to department staff, who will be able to spend more time analyzing the data, instead of collecting it. The reduced reporting burden achieved by the system will also help redirect state and local resources from responding to data-collection requests to addressing core mission objectives.[37]

REDUCING PAPERWORK. Many IT systems also seek to increase productivity by reducing paperwork. Government agencies have long interacted as disparate silos of information, often requiring laborious layers of paper-work to execute routine transactions. Techniques such as simplifying work flows, reducing paperwork and streamlining organizational interfaces have proved successful in generating productivity in public and private sector organizations.

The U.S. Office of Disaster Assistance developed the Disaster Credit Man-agement System to streamline the processes for reviewing and granting or denying Small Business Administration disaster loans. The system employs such technologies as electronic processing, scanning and imaging, automatic interfaces and workflow management to allow agents to process loans in the field. With this system the agency has the opportunity to meet its outcome and performance goals more quickly while using fewer resources.[38]

Organizational Restructuring to Streamline Operations

Applying technology and streamlining business processes can help meet a growing public demand for government services while simultaneously re-ducing the demand for workers' time and effort. Another effective step to bend the demand curve down is to restructure the ways individual agencies work and the overall enterprise operates. Government leaders have turned to consolidation, enterprise-wide technology solutions, business process re-engineering, sourcing strategies and employee performance management to help trim the number of staff needed to handle the day-in-and-day-out duties of the public sector. Governments are moving away from the rigid, hierarchical model to better meet increasing public expectations of govern-ment accountability and performance. To meet the growing demand for better service delivery even as workforce shortages increase, agencies must continue to pursue a more streamlined structure.[39]

CONSOLIDATION. State and local governments have used consolidation to at-tack the workforce demand curve. Many states, including Delaware, Minne-sota and Virginia, have created statewide technology offices and staffed the centralized office with IT employees pulled from state agencies.

With one office in control of the technology that supports common busi-ness tools, such as e-mail, telephone and Internet access, state governments control IT spending and reduce the number of employees needed to man-age the technology infrastructure. Centralized IT offices also can provide shared technology services, such as payroll, accounting and procurement, to state agencies, thus eliminating duplicated functions throughout the government enterprise; agencies can turn to one source for these services, rather than hiring their own staff.

Conclusion

When asked to name the top challenges facing states few observers would put forward the public workforce. It's just not a subject that gets much attention—even amongst state capitol insiders. Yet without people who have the requisite skill sets to manage multi-billion dollar programs and tackle complex public policy challenges, state government transformation has little chance of success. Moreover, whether favoring a smaller or bigger role for government in society, most citizens want a government that is effective, efficient and responsive. This too requires a cadre of skilled state managers and front-line employees.

Unfortunately many states today face a looming crisis meeting these human capital needs. State workforces are getting older and preparing for retirement. In many states the average state employee is more than 10 years older than in the private sector. Meanwhile, a shrinking talent pool overall means states will face increasingly stiff competition for talented workers from the private and nonprofit sectors at the same time that the skill sets needed by state governments are changing—becoming both more sophisticated and more expensive. Add to this the fact that state government is the employer of choice for a smaller and smaller number of university graduates, even for those students graduating with masters' degrees in public policy and public administration.

This situation won't be turned around by just tweaking hiring policies or investing a few more dollars into recruiting. Bolstering the state workforce and beating the coming talent crisis requires far reaching changes to how governments attract, develop and deploy employees. Outdated hiring and firing policies will need to be modernized. To attract and retain Gen Y, workforce environments will need to be made more flexible, dynamic and technology savvy. But most of all, human capital issues will have to go from being a back office concern to a gubernatorial priority.

Chapter 3: The Final Word

THE CHALLENGE

• The U.S. workforce demographic will change considerably in the next 10 to 15 years with the retirement of the Baby Boom generation (those born between 1946 and 1964). State governments will face significant challenges because their workforces are significantly older on average than the private sector workforce.
• While Generation Y (those born between 1977 and 1997) is comparable in size to the Baby Boom generation, its members lack the experience necessary to replace senior-level employees, creating serious succession challenges.

REFORM STRATEGIES

• *Bend the curve.* State governments need to evaluate the future demand for skilled state employees against the likely supply and aim to bend the supply and demand curves toward each other.
• *Fast-track critical talent.* Once critical talent has been successfully hired, organizations must work to ensure that top talent is on a fast track, with increasing responsibility and opportunities for professional development. By fast-tracking top talent, states can address gaps in succession planning and capability transfer.
• *Use the "develop-deploy-connect" model.* This model represents an integrated talent management strategy in which employees receive relevant experience and guidance, are aligned in the appropriate position for their skills and interests and develop the proper connections to advance within the organization.

EXAMPLES

• The *San Jose, California,* Employment Services Department adopted a decentralized, position-based hiring process, which cut hiring time nearly in half, from an average of 130 days to just 68 days.
• *The Presidential Management Fellows Program,* sponsored by the federal Office of Personnel Management, targets students who are completing graduate degrees. Once accepted, fellows develop a two-year strategic plan to help focus their learning, development and career advancement.
• *Illinois*'s Upward Mobility program provides state employees personalized guidance and training to advance to new and more challenging positions. Almost 13,000 state employees have been through the program.

NEXT STEPS

• *Modernize outdated hiring practices.* States must update hiring practices so that the process is faster and more efficient.
• *Identify and target critical workforce segments.* State agencies should determine segments of their workforce that contribute disproportionately to the success of their organizations. And then use campus recruiting initiatives, outreach programs and internships to find potential employees for those segments.
• *Adopt innovative recruiting strategies.* States should develop relationships with local graduate programs and offer competitive, Gen Y–tailored employment packages.
• *Assess organizational structure.* States should review their organizational structures for consolidation or sourcing opportunities.

Solving the Pension Crisis
Practical Strategies for Tackling the Public Pension Crisis

In April 2005, San Diego mayor Dick Murphy stepped before a hastily assembled crowd of news reporters and announced his resignation. Murphy, elected to office just five months earlier, had become the focal point of public backlash over a city pension deficit of nearly $2 billion. Not only were San Diego's pension troubles a key factor in Murphy's resignation, they also hindered the city's effort to complete capital projects. San Diego's credit rating fell in 2004, hobbling the city's ability to sell bonds to finance initiatives such as water and sewer improvements, the *Los Angeles Times* reported.[1]

Murphy's resignation may be the most visible fallout yet from unfunded public pension liabilities. But he's certainly not the only public official feeling heat from this festering issue.

- In Texas, the state Pension Review Board placed an unprecedented 18 public retirement plans on its watch list, a warning that the plans have insufficient funds to meet future obligations. Among them are the state's largest pension systems—the Teacher Retirement System of Texas and the Employees Retirement System of Texas—with combined assets in the hundreds of billions of dollars.[2] The list also includes retirement plans for the cities of Austin, Dallas, El Paso, Fort Worth, and Houston.

- In New Jersey, where newly elected governor Jon Corzine

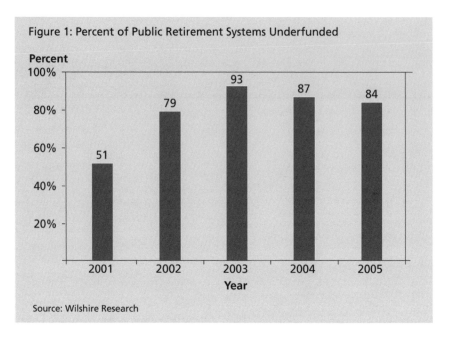

Figure 1: Percent of Public Retirement Systems Underfunded

Source: Wilshire Research

made public pension reform a campaign issue during his race, taxpayers may need to come up with nearly $400 million in 2006 to cover skyrocketing pension costs for municipal workers, police and firefighters. New Jersey's state and local public retirement systems are underfunded by as much as $35 billion—a shortfall that must be filled either by investment gains or taxpayer contributions over the next three decades. Those growing pension costs are set to broadside local government budgets, potentially forcing city and county leaders to contemplate an unsavory mix of tax increases and service cuts. Newark, for example, saw its bill for public pensions jump from $9.6 million in 2005 to $20.2 million in 2006, according to the *New Jersey Star-Ledger*.[3]

• Cities and counties in New York saw their pension contributions grow by as much as 248 percent in 2004.[4] For example, the pension bill for Binghamton jumped from $1.6 million to $4.2 million in a year, prompting Mayor Richard Bucci to brand the increase a "fiscal atom bomb." The city hiked property taxes by 7 percent in 2004—half of which went to cover pension costs—and by another 7 percent in 2005 for the same reason.[5]

Figure 2: Funded Status of State and Local Public Pensions

Funded Ratio	Number of Plans	Percent of Plans	Unfunded Liability (in $000)
<70%	20	17.1	111,933,655
70 – 79%	19	16.2	76,182,085
80 – 89%	38	32.5	137,909,272
90 – 99%	29	24.8	23,908,976
100% +	11	9.4	(13,598,723)
Total	117	100.0	$336,335,265

Sources: National Association of State Retirement Administrators and the National Council on Teacher Retirement

The news is similar across the nation, as states and localities confront the widening gap between the amount of money collected by pension plans through employee contributions and investments and the amount of money these plans are committed to paying out in the form of benefits to government retirees.

A 2006 survey of 125 state retirement systems by Wilshire Research shows the breadth and magnitude of the problem. Of the 58 plans that provided actuarial data for 2005, 84 percent of them were underfunded. For those providing data for 2004, the number was even higher at 87 percent. This is up from 79 percent in 2002 and 51 percent in 2001 (see figure 1).[6] On average, the underfunded plans had enough assets to cover only 80 percent of their future pension commitments.

Another report from the Reason Foundation warned that the current price tag for unfunded pension obligations dwarfs the federal government's bailout of the savings and loan industry in the late 1980s, which cost taxpayers $124 billion.[7] Today, taxpayers may be exposed to more than five times that amount in unfunded pension obligations across the public and private sectors.

That said, not all state and local retirement plans are in trouble. A recent survey sponsored by the National Association of State Retirement Administrators and the National Council on Teacher Retirement, found results similar to those of the Wilshire Research survey. Of the 117 public retirement plans included in the survey (with complete funded status data), 91 percent were underfunded. However, it is important to understand that a plan is considered underfunded if its assets are less than its liabilities—even by one dollar. Therefore, not all underfunded plans are in crisis.

Four Myths of Public Pension Reform

Myth #1: Defined contribution plans will fix the problem sometime soon. Though it might be the right thing to do in the long run, transitioning to defined contribution plans that do not promise a specific amount of benefits at retirement likely will do little to resolve near- or medium-term pension fiscal problems. Governments must phase in defined contribution pension plans gradually as new workers enter the system, meaning they may not see significant relief for 20 to 30 years.

Myth #2: Plans just need to invest more in equities to get their returns up. Investment policies must balance profit potential with risk. Plans opting for higher-yield investment strategies must understand the higher risks involved and ensure they can afford the potential losses.

Myth #3: All employees cost the same. Defined benefit pension costs for younger workers are typically significantly less from an actuarial standpoint than pension costs for older workers who have spent long careers in the public sector.

Myth #4: Deferring costs can lessen the fiscal pressures. Deferring pension costs may offer a quick fix for spiraling pension expenses, but the practice usually results in serious, long-term consequences.

In fact, only 17 percent of the 117 had a funded ratio below 70 percent and only 33 percent had a funded ratio below 80 percent. The remaining 67 percent had funding ratios ranging from 80 percent to 112 percent. Florida is a good example of a state that has historically met its annual funding obligations—the Florida Retirement System is 107 percent funded, with assets of $112 billion and liabilities of $104 billion. In addition to Florida, 10 other retirement plans also had funded ratios in excess of 100 percent.

The real problem is with the 33 percent of plans that had a funded ratio below 80 percent. Unfortunately these plans have a total unfunded liability of $188 billion. Even worse, the unfunded liability of plans with a funded ratio below 90 percent totals $326 billion (see figure 2).

The bottom line is that public sector retirement costs pose a serious threat to many state and local governments—making pension reform a key factor in future economic success of communities and quality of life for constituents. Pension costs consume resources that could be directed elsewhere. For example, spending more budget dollars to fund pension commitments potentially means fewer resources for public safety, education, transportation, health care and other vital needs.

In a special report, *Business Week* magazine highlighted the impact of

Even Bigger Time Bomb:
Retiree Health Care Costs

As if the pension issues were not challenging enough, state and local governments also face the daunting task of figuring out how to pay for huge unfunded retiree health care liabilities that soon could approach $1 trillion.[10]

States and localities generally fund retiree health care benefits on a "pay-as-you-go" basis, instead of through the prefunding model that at least in theory is used to fund pension benefits. Thus, while states and local governments set aside $2.5 trillion to help pay for pension benefits, they generally set aside nothing to pay for retiree health benefits. The result: governments have piled up huge unfunded health care liabilities, the dimensions of which are just now being realized thanks to a pending accounting standard (Governmental Accounting Standards Board Statement 45) that requires estimating these unfunded liabilities. Pay-as-you-go expensing will no longer be permitted; instead accrual-based accounting for expenses is required as well as measurement and disclosure of the plan's funded status.

Consider school districts. In many districts, very generous retiree health benefits were negotiated over the past decade or two. Rising costs and Boomer retirees mean the bill for these is now coming due.[11] "It is the single most important issue facing districts nationwide," says Tom Henry of California's Fiscal Crisis and Management Assistance Team.[12]

States and localities also routinely added perks to public sector retirement plans to attract qualified workers. For instance, the state of Hawaii pays the full cost of medical, prescription drug, dental and vision insurance for life for retirees with 25 years of service. Ironically, such measures sometimes have the unintended effect of prompting many to retire in their early 50s.[17]

Little by little, states and local governments have begun to address

Table 1: Sample State and Local Retiree Health Care Liabilities

Jurisdiction	Unfunded Liability
State of California	$70B[13]
State of Maryland	$30B[14]
Los Angeles School District	$6.9B[15]
City of New York	$50B[16]

Sources: Various and Deloitte Research

this issue.[18] New York City mayor Michael Bloomberg has pledged to set aside $1 billion for retiree health care benefits.[19] Hawaii plans to redefine the eligibility criteria for full benefits, switch to defined contribution plans and require future employees to make contributions toward their retirement costs. Moreover, workers hired after June 30, 2001, will not receive health coverage for their dependents when they retire.[20] Michigan meanwhile is contemplating legislation that would require teachers retiring after 20 years to pay 40 percent of their health insurance premiums as well as co-payments and deductibles.[21]

As with the pension issue, there is no simple solution to this looming crisis. Governments have to rearrange budgets, raise funds through taxes or bonds, or cut down on retirement health benefits.

exploding pension costs on several communities.[8] One of these is Jenison, Michigan, where contributions to pensions and retiree health care are the fastest-growing expense for the public school system. The bill came to $1 million in 2005 and jumped to $1.5 million in 2006. With state school funds frozen for the past three years, the district coped with growing pension expenses by eliminating teaching positions and instituting fees for after-school sports and field trips.

As these impacts become more pronounced, public officials will face growing taxpayer concern over the spiraling expense of government retirement programs. The problem will only get worse when the huge wave of Baby Boomers begins to retire, starting in 2008. The programs must be proactively managed to maintain a cost-benefit balance. As U.S. representative John Kline of Minnesota put it, "[T]he looming crisis is real, and without action, on some level, it will not go away."[9]

This chapter examines the causes of the current dilemma and presents a framework for addressing this increasingly pressing challenge. We also set straight some of the common misperceptions about the pension problems.

The Top Ten Causes of the Public Pension Crisis

The current pension crisis stems from a mix of historical policy decisions and lack of planning—all of which were exposed by the stock market slide of the early part of the decade. Ten factors contributing to the crisis are discussed here.

1. Lack of Prefunding Requirements

There are generally no requirements forcing public retirement plans to fund their pension liabilities. As a result these plans are funded to varying degrees, including some that are completely unfunded and operate on a "pay-as-you-go" basis. Paying less than the actuarially determined contribution each year increases the unfunded liability. This may adversely affect debt ratings for state and local governments and cause future required contributions to be even higher.

In contrast, private sector organizations must comply with the Employee Retirement Income Security Act of 1974 (ERISA), which sets minimum funding standards for company-sponsored retirement plans. Therefore, these plans tend to be better funded, on average, than their public-sector counterparts—despite the well-publicized private pension problems of recent years.

2. Benefit Expansions

Flush with earnings from a bull market that lasted through much of the 1990s, government retirement plans opted not only to expand benefits for retirees, but also to make those benefits easier to get. States and localities routinely added perks to public sector retirement plans, often justifying the increases as necessary to retain qualified workers. In some cases, the benefit expansions were given in lieu of politically more difficult pay raises. For example, Texas state lawmakers approved $14 billion in benefit enhancements for public school employees over the past 10 years.[22] Benefit enhancements added in Illinois between 1995 and 2003 boosted liabilities by approximately $6 billion.

3. Growth of Supplemental Benefits

Retirement plans also greatly expanded supplemental benefits over the past 10 years, which in turn significantly increased pension costs. For instance, an ever-growing number of public employees were classified as public safety workers, thus qualifying them for higher retirement benefits because of the hazardous nature of their jobs. In Illinois, special benefits once reserved for police officers now go to approximately one-third of all state workers.[23] Likewise, one in three California government workers now receives a public safety pension, up from one in twenty during the 1960s.[24]

In addition, generous rules on selling back unused sick leave and vaca-

Public Pension Funding 101

Benefits Paid
+ Administrative Expenses
- Investment Return on Plan Assets
_____

= Ultimate Pension Plan Cost

- Benefits paid are determined by negotiated and legislated plan provisions.

- Administrative expenses are determined by investment, funding and system policies.

- Investment return is determined by investment and funding policies.

- Ultimate plan cost is generally shared by employees and employer.

- Annual employee and employer contributions represent a systematic means of prefunding the ultimate system costs.

- Annual contributions for public employees and employers are generally set by statute.

Source: Deloitte Research

tion time caused artificial hikes in final year earnings. Since retirement benefits usually are based on how much workers earn during their last several years of employment, these income spikes resulted in bigger lifetime pension amounts for retirees and permanently higher costs for taxpayers. These sell-back benefits will cost New Jersey taxpayers nearly $1.5 billion in the coming years.[25]

4. Smaller Employee Contribution Share

Most public retirement plans require participants and their employers to contribute to the plan. But as plan costs have risen, employee contributions generally have not kept pace. This has a multiplying effect on pension expenses for public entities.

For example, a retirement plan may have an estimated long-term cost of 10 percent of a worker's pay. The employee contributes 5 percent and the employer matches that amount. But that equation falls apart when questionable policy decisions to increase benefits in "good times" or poor investment returns increase the retirement plan's total cost to 15 percent of pay. The employee's share typically remains at 5 percent, but the employer's share inflates to 10 percent. So, even though the plan costs grew by a third, the burden on taxpayers doubled and the employee's cost remained the same.

In Illinois, for example, state employees contribute 8 percent of pay to their pension plan while teachers contribute 9.4 percent. The state's contribution rate is projected to increase to more than double those rates—reaching 21.3 percent by 2010 and remaining at approximately that rate for the next 35 years.

5. Lucrative Early Retirement Packages

Not only were benefit amounts rising in the 1990s, but public retirement systems were paying out fatter pension amounts for longer periods of time. Lucrative "unreduced" early retirement benefit provisions had the effect of actually encouraging many employees to retire in their early 50s. Such early retirement adds significantly to the costs of these plans because earlier benefit commencement coupled with constant improvements in health care (resulting in retirees living longer) mean that retirees now draw benefits longer than ever before.

Second, special early retirement windows programs, implemented to reduce the size of the workforce, are often designed without sufficient consideration given to how to provide the underlying services with a much smaller workforce or to the costs of the window. The result is that these programs often cost more money in the long run than they save. For example, the state of Illinois implemented an early retirement incentive program in 2003. The program was expected to cost $622 million, based on initial estimates of the number of participants who would take advantage of the program. The state significantly expanded eligibility for the early retirement program, however, as well as the retirement incentives offered under the program. Those changes pushed the actual cost of the program to more than $2.5 billion.

The drive to cut costs by encouraging early retirements also is often done without regard to the skills that may be lost and the impact of those retirements on critical government services.

6. Higher Risks of Defined Benefit Programs

All of the issues already discussed are magnified by the fact that government retirement plans tend to be much more expensive to support than those offered by private employers. Unlike the private sector today, the vast majority of government retirement systems still offer defined benefit plans, which guarantee retirees a predetermined benefit amount based on the number of years they work and their final or highest average compensation amount.

Public employees typically contribute a fixed portion of their paychecks into a pension fund, which is invested to produce revenue to pay for a portion of their retirement benefits. Because retirees are guaranteed a certain benefit amount, the government must make up any shortfall resulting from actual investment returns that are less than anticipated.

By contrast, most private companies have shifted to defined contribution plans, which are less risky from the sponsor's perspective. Under these plans, retirement benefits fluctuate with the investment performance of an employee's pension assets. Because employees shoulder the investment risk in a defined contribution plan, rather than taxpayers, there is never a shortfall for taxpayers to make up.

7. Structural Weaknesses Masked by 1990s Stock Market Boom

The increasing cost of government pensions (and the failure of many public pension sponsors to fund their plans adequately) was masked by a booming stock market in the 1990s. Thanks to historic market gains during the dot-com era, pension fund investment revenue easily kept pace with expanding retirement perks.

Investment returns were so good, in fact, that many governments made no contribution at all to their retirement funds during that period. Before 2005 local governments in New Jersey had gone six years without paying anything toward public employee retirement plans, the *Star-Ledger* reported.[26] Some retirement systems even gave away extra earnings to plan participants in the form of bonus "13th" pension checks—meaning an extra month's worth of payments—instead of saving the money to offset shortfalls when the market inevitably cooled off.

Although many states underfunded their public retirement systems for years, thanks to the hot investment market, their pension plans remained reasonably well funded. When the dot-com bubble burst, retirement systems accustomed to earning a handsome return on their investments abruptly found themselves in a financial bind. As investment markets cooled, lucrative benefit packages approved during the boom years began pushing retirement expenses much higher than expected.

Salary growth, of course, directly affects pension costs. Missing revenue or cost estimates even by a few percentage points can have a devastating

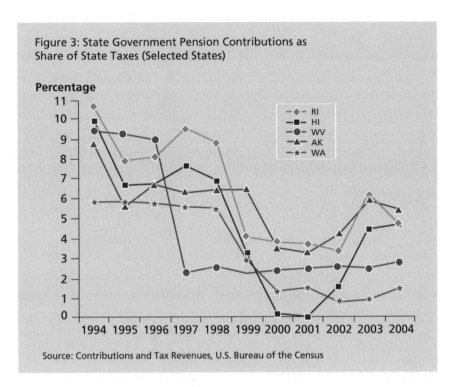

Figure 3: State Government Pension Contributions as Share of State Taxes (Selected States)

Source: Contributions and Tax Revenues, U.S. Bureau of the Census

impact on public retirement systems, potentially leaving them seriously un-derfunded and requiring a significant infusion of taxpayer dollars. For exam-ple, Wilshire Associates forecasts a long-term return on state pension assets equal to 7.2 percent a year, which is 0.8 percent below the average actuarial interest rate assumption of 8.0 percent. If correct, this asset performance shortfall alone will increase total unfunded liabilities for state pension plans by an additional $40 billion a year.

8. Deferring Pension Contributions to Balance Budgets

Dwindling investment returns and growing pension costs would seem to demand bigger government contributions to prop up the ailing retirement funds. But, in fact, the opposite actually occurred over the past few years (see figure 3). The faltering economy crimped general government reve-nues, leading jurisdictions to divert retirement fund contributions to other priorities. States such as New Jersey and North Carolina reduced retire-ment fund payments to help balance their books. Now they are struggling to reduce unfunded pension liabilities——and the credit rating agencies are taking notice.

9. Little Incentive or Urgency to Fix Problem

Public pension policy often suffers from an "It won't be my problem after I am out of office" mentality. Although public pension costs are huge in many states and poised to grow even larger, policy leaders have little incentive to exercise fiscal restraint. Instead they typically reap political rewards for creating new benefits for public employees or underfunding retirement systems and using the "saved" money to fund short-term goals.[27] The bill for increasing unfunded pension liabilities is left for future administrations and generations.

10. Difficulty of Modifying Retirement Plans

Pension costs are outpacing contributions, but it is extremely difficult to increase the amount employees pay into their plans or reduce the benefit amounts they receive. Retirement benefits are often the product of collective bargaining agreements, and these benefits are fiercely guarded by employee groups. Politics also plays a very large part in the decision-making process.

Public pensions also are not like pension plans at private companies. To be sure, it's seldom easy to change private pension plans—particularly for employers subject to collective bargaining agreements and union opposition. Nevertheless, private sector employers can scale back future benefit accruals, freeze benefits, or if they are at or near bankruptcy, shed their insolvent pension plans entirely, turning them over to the Pension Benefit Guaranty Corp., a quasi-governmental insurance agency.

Public pension rights, however, typically are considered part of a contract between the employer and employee. That makes it much harder to modify a public pension plan's terms. Furthermore, public employee pension benefits, once approved, have constitutional protection in some states.

Experts generally agree that governments can change or reduce benefits for employees who have not yet been hired, but they cannot change them for retired employees. The gray area is whether benefits can be reduced for the employees in between—workers who are hired, but not yet retired. The answer may come soon, as some states have signaled a desire to reduce pension benefits for this group of employees.

Roadmap to Recovery

How can governments escape the fiscal black hole some already have entered and others are on the verge of falling into? Unfortunately, there is no silver bullet—no single strategy fits all situations. Several options exist, and states and localities must choose approaches that best fit their fiscal situation, political climate and future goals.

Setting and meeting funding goals are crucial steps, but real pension reform ultimately also means reducing the costs of public employee pension programs for governments. There are really only four ways to do that:

- Restructure employee benefits

- Increase investment returns

- Reduce administrative costs

- Find alternative funding sources

The next section first explores techniques for producing immediate savings. We then address the needed medium- and long-term reforms to put public sector retirement plans on firmer financial footing. Individual circumstances will vary greatly as some states' pension programs are in solid financial shape; what we offer is a general guide to recovery.

Six Immediate Fixes

For states and localities facing large unfunded pension obligations, it is vital to stop—or at least slow—the financial bleeding. This means first making sure that current contributions at least cover current liabilities.

Ultimately, public retirement plans must reduce the cost of public pension benefits or dedicate more funds toward paying for pension obligations. More than likely, states and localities will need to implement a combination of cost-cutting and revenue-enhancing changes to bring their public pension systems back into balance.

As mentioned earlier, pension benefits are difficult to modify for existing public employees and nearly impossible for retirees. Therefore, more fundamental reforms often can be applied only to new employees entering the public workforce, so the impact of these changes may not be felt for many years.

The six cost-cutting and revenue-boosting options listed here generally can be applied to current public workers, however, depending upon specific contract and legal provisions of the pension plan. These strategies are designed to deliver relatively quick improvements for underfunded public pension systems.

1. CLOSE LOOPHOLES. A plan sponsor may not be able to change basic benefit formulas for existing workers, but it may be possible to modify ancillary plan provisions, some of which are extremely costly. Options for reform include:

- **Tightening the practice of granting large pay raises in the years immediately before retirement,** which can allow employees to spike final earnings amounts.[28]

- **Tightening overly generous sick-leave policies,** which also can allow employees to spike final earnings amounts affecting benefit computations.

- **Narrowing eligibility for high-cost public-safety pension benefits.**

The state of Illinois sought to close these loopholes through legislation designed to limit the impact of end-of-career raises on state pension plans. The act targets the common practice by local school districts of granting large pay raises to school employees a year or two before they retire. The school district pays the higher salary briefly until the employee retires, but the state absorbs the long-term expense of fatter pension benefits triggered by the salary increase.

The Illinois law shifts the long-term cost of these salary increases back to the local school districts, which now pay the pension liability for raises exceeding 6 percent during a worker's final four years of government employment. State officials believe the reform will save Illinois billions of dollars over the next 40 years. The Illinois law also requires agencies to pay the pension costs generated by granting public employees extra sick leave.

These reforms don't necessarily shrink overall pension plan costs—although they may prompt more fiscal responsibility among local agencies, since those employers will feel long-term pain from practices that trigger higher pension payments. The reforms do cut the states' share of the public retirement burden, however.

Numerous states also have begun to target growth of special public-safety pension benefits by limiting the categories of eligible workers.

2. ADJUST BENEFIT FORMULAS. Some pension plans offer special benefit formulas that increase plan costs. For example, the State University Retirement System in Illinois had a basic benefit formula and a special money purchase formula. University employees automatically got the most lucrative of the two benefit calculations.

The Illinois pension reform law eliminated the money purchase formula for Illinois state university employees hired after June 30, 2005, and changed the way interest rates are set for current employees who remain eligible for the money purchase formula calculation. Previously, those rates were set by the retirement system. Now the state controller sets them. Although the changes don't reduce benefit accruals already earned by university employees, they do limit interest rates (and costs) going forward.

3. RAISE EMPLOYEE CONTRIBUTIONS. States and localities can consider raising the amount that employees contribute to public retirement plans. As noted earlier, employee pension contributions generally have held steady as plan costs have increased. Instead, contribution amounts could be tied to actual plan costs. So, for example, if total pension plan costs increase by 10 percent, employee contributions would increase by the same percentage or at least by some amount.

These adjustments are common for employee health plans. But instituting similar practices for pension contributions would depend on potentially difficult negotiations with public employee unions and consideration of state constitutional provisions.

Another cautionary note: in the private sector, it is rare for employees to contribute to a defined benefit plan. Employees do, however, contribute to Social Security, which they do not do in many public plans.

4. FIND NEW REVENUE SOURCES. State and local governments may have untapped revenue sources that could be used to fund pension obligations. Finding these dollars will require innovative thinking, however. Illinois, for example, is exploring selling or leasing its state tollway system. Proceeds from the sale would be funneled into the state pension system. Public infrastructure also represents an increasingly popular investment alternative for pension funds. Other revenue sources might include sales of unused public properties with the proceeds dedicated to pension funding.

Another tactic used to pump more revenue into retirement plans is pension obligation bonds. This approach requires governments to issue bonds at low interest rates and then reinvest the bond proceeds into higher-yielding taxable financial investments. The difference between the cost of debt service on the bonds and revenue created by investing the bond proceeds generates income that is used to prop up pension funds.

A caution, however: this strategy is highly risky because it depends on careful market timing. The state of New Jersey discovered this when it sold

The Dangers of Deferring Costs

Governments often seek relief from growing pension expenses by deferring the costs to future years. Unfortunately, that merely shifts the pension burden to a new generation of taxpayers. Common cost deferral strategies include:

- Changing funding policy
- Changing actuarial assumptions
- Altering actuarial funding methods
- Adopting new asset valuation methods

Deferring pension costs may offer a quick, short-term fix for spiraling pension expenses, but the practice usually has serious, long-term consequences. Bond rating agencies are increasingly concerned about underfunded pension liabilities. These liabilities can lead to higher borrowing costs, which in turn can hamstring government's ability to undertake capital improvement projects and other important initiatives. And deferring pension costs simply means that future contributions will have to be higher.

Furthermore, if pension debt continues to mount, states and localities will eventually be forced to increase taxes to cover the tab. Needless to say, this could have dire consequences for elected officials in office when the bill comes due.

$2.7 billion in pension obligation bonds in 1997 and invested most of the proceeds in equities. The investment paid off handsomely for several years, but the stock market crash in 2000 wreaked havoc with the strategy. Invested proceeds from New Jersey's pension obligation bonds have averaged an annual return well below the 7.6 percent the state owes in interest.[29]

Another problem with pension obligation bonds is that the state is converting a soft liability (the pension funding) into a hard liability (the required bond payments). Moreover, voters may balk at the prospect of approving new long-term debt. West Virginia governor Joseph Manchin III convinced state lawmakers to sell as much as $5.5 billion in bonds to help cover unfunded pension liabilities. But voters rejected the bond measure in June 2005, leaving state officials—who are under a state Supreme Court order to close West Virginia's pension gap by 2034—searching for other solutions.

To be sure, this risky strategy sometimes pays off. Illinois used the technique successfully in 2004, selling $10 billion in pension obligation bonds when interest rates in the bond market had nearly hit bottom. The move allowed the state to, in effect, refinance $10 billion of pension debt at approximately a 5 percent interest rate instead of an 8.5 percent interest rate. The bulk of the bond proceeds went directly into the state retirement fund, increasing the funding status by more than 10 percent overnight. Despite Illinois's success, as a general rule pension obligation bonds are a highly risky strategy.

5. REVIEW AND REFINE INVESTMENT POLICIES. If risky, high-yield investment policies are imprudent, overly cautious investment strategies needlessly reduce income potential. They also often do not offer the flexibility that is needed to manage the portfolio and manage risk. For example, conservative investment policies often place a ceiling on equities and don't allow hedging or alternative investments. Yet limiting the types of investments and investment mix can actually create greater risks under certain market conditions.

Therefore, investment policies must balance earnings potential with risk. Plans opting for higher-yield investment strategies must understand the risks involved and ensure they can afford the potential losses. Achieving the right balance of risk and reward maximizes investment income and limits the chance of devastating losses. Plan managers should undertake a review and analysis of their investments policies to determine if they are appropriate for the particular plans. States and localities can analyze the risk-reward relationship by conducting an asset and liability projection study. Finally, investment advisors need to be given enough latitude to manage the investments prudently but should fully understand all potential investments.

6. CUT ADMINISTRATIVE COSTS. Reducing administrative expenses won't solve the pension crisis—not by a long shot. Nevertheless, cutting plan overhead should be a component of any comprehensive solution.

The biggest opportunity lies with consolidating multiple pension plans. There are more than 2,600 public employee retirement systems nationwide, according to the U.S. Census Bureau. In Texas, for example, dozens of state and local public retirement plans cover government workers, teachers, police and firefighters. Similarly, the state of Illinois has five separate retirement boards, each with its own workforce and infrastructure.

Combining these plans where sensible would eliminate redundant administrative staffs and functions, producing lower operating costs and leaving more dollars available for pension payments. Consolidating pension plans could be politically difficult, but it's a commonsense reform that deserves consideration.

Outsourcing certain administrative tasks or automating processes represents another opportunity to trim overhead expenses. Jurisdictions can also benefit from a thorough review of vendors and service providers involved in their public pension systems. Analyzing pricing and services provided by third parties—and renegotiating contracts when appropriate—can deliver savings. California, New Mexico and New York are among a growing number of states deploying information technology designed to boost efficiency in their public employee retirement systems.

Reforms for the Medium and Long Term

Beyond the short-term measures outlined above, fundamental pension changes are needed to protect the long-term viability of public retirement programs—and to prevent shifting a mountain of pension debt to future taxpayers. The impact of these reforms often won't be felt until a new generation of public workers is hired and younger current workers begin to retire.

1. IMPOSE DISCIPLINE—DEVELOP A PENSION FUNDING POLICY AND STICK TO IT. Jurisdictions must develop sound funding policies for their public pension systems and then have the discipline to follow them. For more than 30 years, ERISA has spelled out requirements and responsibilities for funding private sector pension and health plans. In the absence of similar laws for public sector plans, funding decisions must be guided by sound fiscal policy. States should consider crafting laws that require minimum funding levels for public retirement systems.

There is no magic number for pension plan prefunding requirements—funding targets may range from 80 percent to 100 percent. Policy-makers need to decide on a level of pension funding that balances short-term needs with long-term goals.

Jurisdictions with seriously underfunded plans also will need to map out practical repayment strategies. Once these policies are set, they should be reviewed periodically to ensure they are still appropriate.

Careful design is vital to the success of repayment strategies. Some repayment plans have proven to be unaffordable once they were put into practice. Illinois set a goal of repaying the bulk of its unfunded pension liabilities over a period of 50 years. The plan was designed to increase the funding ratio for the state's five pension systems to 90 percent by the year 2045. But the payments required for reaching that goal are rapidly becoming unmanageable for the state.

Furthermore, pension funding policies have little impact if no one follows them. Officials must make the minimum required pension contributions when times are tough. Just as important, they must resist politically expedient pension giveaways when times are good.

Public sector pension plans differ from private sector plans in many ways. One particular example is that upside potential—that is, funded ratios in excess of the targeted goal, often times 100 percent—can be nearly as bad as downside risk in the public sector. This sounds counterintuitive. However, when public pension plans are more than 100 percent funded (even if only in the relative short term), politicians may be very tempted to pay out that reserve by increasing benefits or diverting it to other needs. Then when the investment market turns sour and assets drop below liabilities, there are fewer assets remaining and the effect on costs is exacerbated.

2. RESTRUCTURE PENSION BENEFITS. Governments have several options to restructure employee benefits. The most obvious method is to reduce them. There are two basic methods to accomplish this:

- Reduce future benefit accruals for current employees as well as for future employees.[30] Of the two methods, this approach will have the greater impact on costs. But it likely will be politically difficult and may also result in legal challenges.

- Reduce benefit accruals for future employees only. It will take many years for this two-tiered approach to reduce costs significantly.

Because of the difficulty of reducing benefits for current employees, the most practical option for cutting overall costs is to scale back retirement packages for newly hired workers. Such two-tier retirement programs, extremely common nowadays in the private sector, reduce retirement and health benefits for employees hired after a specific date, while maintaining agreed-upon benefit packages for existing workers.

Implementing two-tier benefit programs for public workers could prove politically difficult. Although such programs don't affect current employees, employee groups have opposed these ideas in the past.

Another risk of a two-tiered approach is that simply by proposing benefit cutbacks for younger workers, older workers might ask "Am I next?" This slippery slope may lead many employees eligible for retirement to retire earlier than they may have otherwise in order to "lock in" their pensions.

The Promise and Limits of Switching to Defined Contribution Systems

Governors of five states proposed strategies in 2005 that would move state workers into defined contribution, 401(k)-style retirement programs.[31]

Of the five, Alaska governor Frank Murkowski was the only one to win legislative approval for his reforms. All Alaska state workers hired after July 1, 2006, will be covered under a mandatory 401(k)-style retirement program, where the state contributes a set amount each month into an employee's investment fund. Employees receive the money in these funds when they retire.

California governor Arnold Schwarzenegger floated a similar proposal but dropped it after running into a buzz saw of opposition from teachers, firefighters and other members of public employee unions. Governors Mitt Romney of Massachusetts, Donald Carcieri of Rhode Island and Mark Sanford of South Carolina also proposed switching to 401(k)-style retirement plans in 2005.

These reform efforts struggled in 2005 and 2006, but it seems likely that over time defined contribution plans will become more common for government workers. Defined benefit plans—once the norm for both private and public employees—continue to disappear from the private sector as employers seek less costly and less volatile pension alternatives. Just 24 percent of private sector employees now enjoy defined benefit plans with guaranteed payouts, compared with 90 percent of public sector workers.[32]

The impact of defined benefit plans on public sector compensation costs is substantial. In September 2004, benefit costs for private sector employees were $6.80 for every employee hour worked, or 28.6 percent of their total compensation, according to the Employee Benefits Research Institute (EBRI).[33] That represents an increase of slightly less than 2 percentage points over 17 years. Conversely, benefit costs for public sector employees were $10.89 an hour (31.4 percent of their total compensation) in September 2004—up from $6.79 an hour in March 1991, EBRI said. These figures indicate states and localities could save significantly over the long term by shifting workers from traditional pensions to 401(k)-style plans

But defined contribution plans are no silver bullet for managing near-term runaway retirement costs. Laws and court rulings make it difficult, if not impossible, to modify existing pension agreements for public employees. So governments must phase in lower-cost retirement plans gradually as new workers enter the system, meaning they may not see significant relief for decades.

Indeed, switching new employees to defined contribution plans can actually increase costs in the near term. When Illinois officials studied shifting new hires to a defined contribution plan for one of its pension systems, they found that total costs would be higher over the next 30 years. The reason: transition costs. Putting new hires into a different plan means their contributions stop flowing into the existing underfunded defined benefit plan, so other revenue would be needed to make up the difference.

Jurisdictions with large underfunded pension liabilities may find the cost of paying off defined benefit plans while creating new defined contribution plans for new, younger workers too painful to bear. Therefore, switching to defined contribution plans is more practical for jurisdictions with reasonably funded retirement plans; these jurisdictions may be able to tolerate higher short-term costs in exchange for minimizing future costs.

Governments have two principal options for implementing two-tier programs. Probably the most common two-tier pension program strategy is to shift newly hired public employees from traditional defined benefit plans to less risky defined contribution plans. Defined contribution plans do not necessarily reduce employee retirement benefits, but they limit employer and taxpayer exposure to investment risk because ultimate retirement benefits under a defined contribution plan are determined by the performance of an employee's retirement investments. By contrast, defined benefit plans pay a set pension amount regardless of a fund's investment performance, with taxpayers picking up the tab for any deficiency. However, transitioning to defined contribution plans likely will do little to resolve near-term pension fiscal problems.

The second option is to provide a defined contribution benefit to new workers, but with a guaranteed minimum retirement income (or floor) provided through a defined benefit plan to reduce the investment risk to the employee. This approach is typically more expensive than simply providing a defined contribution benefit alone to newly hired workers, but it may be more politically palatable.

3. ADJUST COST-OF-LIVING INCREASES. Automatic cost-of-living increases tied to increases in average salaries are common in public sector retirement programs. By contrast, these provisions have become rare in the private sector because they are extremely costly.

Contractual issues will make it hard to eliminate cost-of-living provisions for public sector retirees in many jurisdictions. Indeed, public retirement systems replace Social Security benefits in many states. So it is politically difficult and perhaps unfair to abolish cost-of-living increases for

Confronting Illinois' Pension Challenges

When Rod Blagojevich began his first term as governor of the State of Illinois in January 2003, he had a host of priorities he wanted to address: improving schools, investing in the state's underfunded infrastructure, increasing access to health care and so on. There was only one problem: after a few months in office, he learned that the state's public employee retirement system was staring at an unfunded liability of $43.1 billion (with a funding ratio of under 50 percent).

If things continued on their present path, annual state payments into the system would have to jump from $1 billion in 2006 to $4 billion in 2013 and $16 billion in 2045. "Unless we reform the way we fund our pensions," explained the governor, "we will never eliminate the structural deficit that takes money away from education, from health care, from law enforcement, from parks, and from everything else we care about."

Illinois' pension funding shortfalls were more than 30 years in the making. State payrolls—a key component of pension costs—grew rapidly throughout the 1980s and 1990s. But state contributions to public pension plans stayed relatively flat. Strong investment returns temporarily helped bridge the gap, but the deficit had begun to widen by the end of the century.

Facing one of the most underfunded public pension plans in the country, resulting from decisions made long before he took office, Blagojevich went about taking out costs and liabilities from Illinois' five state retirement systems.

The first step was to give the state pension systems a cash infusion and reduce the state's pension debt. In June 2003, the state issued $10 billion worth of pension obligation bonds. Of this total, $7.3 billion was disbursed to the pension systems as an additional state contribution over and above any annual contribution requirements. This additional cash infusion on July 3, 2003, immediately reduced the pension system's unfunded liability from $43 billion to approximately $36 billion and increased the system's funded ratio from 49 percent to 57 percent literally overnight. (With investment earnings, the funded ratio actually improved to slightly more than 60 percent by June 30, 2005.)

Loopholes and abuses have been curtailed. School districts, for example, had routinely approved generous salary increases for teachers in their final years of employment, producing inflated pension amounts that became the responsibility of state taxpayers when teachers retired. No more. School districts must now pick up the tab for pension increases triggered by pay raises in excess of 6 percent.

Another big cost driver in Illinois was expensive special benefits once reserved for police officers for risking their lives in the line of duty. Over the years, one-third of all state workers had become eligible for these benefits. Under Blagojevich, eligibility for these benefits was cut back to those they were originally intended for: public safety workers.

To avoid making the same kinds of mistakes that got Illinois into trouble in the first place, the governor convinced the legislature to stipulate that all future benefit enhancements would expire after five years unless they are renewed by the governor and the state legislature. In addition, every future benefit increase is required to have a dedicated revenue source.

These changes not only produced immediate cost savings but will also move Illinois toward long-term improvement in its public pension funding.

Illinois offers important lessons for other states and localities embarking on fixing their pension systems. The first lesson is to gain a firm understanding of your current pension situation. What are the real pension costs? How big is the problem? If the public pension fund is only 65 percent funded, say, you'll first have to stop the bleeding. Once that is accomplished, you can focus attention on longer-term reforms.

Illinois also shows that few of the pension reform options are painless. Indeed all of them demand strong political leadership and the willingness to confront entrenched interests.

public sector plans when private sector workers receive them through Social Security benefits.

But some public retirement plans offer extremely generous automatic increases—as high as 5 percent, regardless of inflation. Tying cost-of-living increases to actual inflation rates could produce significant savings, while still protecting retirees from rising living expenses.

4. SCALE BACK EARLY RETIREMENT PROGRAMS. Generous early retirement provisions often allow public sector workers to retire with full benefits as early as age 55 or 60, instead of 65, which is the typical retirement age in the private sector. In some cases, state and local officials also have viewed early retirement programs as cost-cutting measures to reduce the size of government workforces with delayed cash implications.

As a huge number of Baby Boomers near retirement age, these provisions often prove to be extremely expensive and poorly designed. In some states, nearly half of the public workforce will be eligible for early retirement within 10 years. Some jurisdictions already have been forced to offer older workers additional incentives not to take early retirement benefits. Restructuring early retirement provisions would save money and encourage valuable workers to stay on the job. Several options are available to reinvent early retirement programs. One set of options is known as the Deferred Retirement Option Plans (DROP). Developed to keep experienced workers in the public workforce, these plans typically allow senior employees to collect their full pension benefits and their standard paycheck for a certain number of years beyond retirement age. Pension payments are deposited into an interest-bearing account, and employees collect the money once they actually retire.

Though well-intentioned, DROPs have often proven to be terrifically expensive for state retirement systems and ineffective at retaining workers. In many instances, DROP benefits are so lucrative that they actually entice senior employees to leave the workforce earlier than they would have otherwise.

Phased Retirement Programs are another option. These programs may be a better option than deferred retirement option plans. They are designed to keep older employees in the workforce longer and therefore delay the onset of full pension benefits. North Carolina kicked off a program in 2006 under which state employees can start receiving partial pension benefits at age 59—and continue working flexible hours. The goal is to keep many of these workers from fully retiring, thereby reducing both the amount of pension they draw and the period of time over which they will draw full benefits.

Similar ideas are under consideration in the federal government; however, it remains to be seen whether this strategy reduces the number of public employees who take a complete early retirement or instead entices workers who would have remained full-time employees into partial retirement at an earlier age.

Getting from Here to There

As governments embark on the road to pension reform, heeding five implementation guidelines will help to make the experience a successful one.

1. Assess the Problem

What are the root causes of the pension crisis? Are investments performing poorly? Are benefits overly generous? Is the plan underfunded? Is it being abused? Answering these questions requires an in-depth analysis of current pension funds and public retirement benefits. The information revealed by this process will guide the design of pension reforms and avoid repeating similar problems in the future.

2. Involve the Stakeholders

Pension reform often involves difficult and politically sensitive changes. Involving political officials, business leaders, labor unions and other stakeholders helps build support and buy-in for these initiatives. Some states, for example, have appointed independent advisory commissions to develop pension reform recommendations. Giving key players a voice in this process can deliver crucial support for implementing changes.

3. Educate the Stakeholders and Public

Once reform proposals are developed, a broad education campaign is required to explain their value to constituents. In Illinois, for example, state officials launched an extensive communications campaign to promote the governor's pension reform plan. Officials met with most members of the state legislature and with union representatives. They also met with almost every major newspaper in the state and sent letters to teachers and other retirement plan participants. These efforts were designed to explain the magnitude and urgency of the problem and to show how the suggested reforms could fix it.

4. Manage Expectations

Pension problems are complex. They took years to develop and stem from multiple causes. It's unrealistic to believe pension challenges can be solved overnight. Therefore, it is crucial to manage expectations for quick results from pension changes.

Certainly, some of the strategies proposed here will deliver relatively quick savings—and it's important to publicize those results in order to show progress. But curing large-scale pension ills is a long-term, multistep process. And political officials, plan participants and taxpayers need to be aware of this reality.

5. Don't Separate Pension and Retiree Health Reform from Broader Human Capital Issues

The pension funding crisis—not to mention the looming and equally daunting retiree health care cost crisis—tends to be viewed as a financially driven problem that needs to be addressed with options that will resolve the financial problems facing plan performance, costs and funding. Even though the pension crisis is financially driven, it should not be viewed purely through a financial prism. The underlying plans are after all "employee benefit" plans that were designed, even if flawed, to attract, retain and motivate talented individuals to seek and remain in employment.

To overlook or underemphasize the impact on the workforce of plan changes may have unintended consequences on the organization's ability to achieve its mission and serve its constituents. While this has always been an important issue, in today's environment the public and private sectors collectively are facing the largest demographic shift from active workers to retirees in the nation's history. The retirement of the Baby Boom generation is a certainty—but the timing is not. Therefore all financial decisions regarding pensions are also human resource decisions that may have significant workforce consequences.

When the state of Pennsylvania reviewed its health care plan for retirees, it made several changes for employees retiring after December 31, 2003. By most measures these changes were relatively minor, but they did shift some costs to retirees. Between the announcement and the end of the year, hundreds of unexpected additional employees chose to retire before the plan change deadline. Did the small cost changes drive employee decisions? Most likely.

Many employees are very concerned about the amount and security of their retirement benefits (especially in the last few years of employment when an employee is already "retirement eligible" under plan provisions). Any proposed changes may create employee nervousness. The value to an employee of one or two years of additional salary to stay employed versus perhaps 30 years of retirement benefits is hard for some employees to really grasp and measure. Employees who ask why they should risk lower future benefits may opt to retire while the benefits are still generous.

On the other side of the coin, pension benefits geared to employees who want to work for the public sector for decades can be a disincentive to recruiting younger workers who might not want to make a long career in government.

Either way, the point is that pension issues cannot be divorced from their impact on talent acquisition and management. Clear, understandable and repeated employee communication is critical throughout the period of change.

Time for Action

Clearly, public leaders risk voter backlash as runaway pension costs hit taxpayers in the pocketbook and cripple economic competitiveness. As tax increases or service cuts become more commonplace to address this issue, citizens will demand that public policy-makers implement reforms to control the price of public employee pension programs. What's more, without corrective action, the pension crisis is likely to worsen as Baby Boomers start reaching retirement age in the near future.

Interviewed in *Business Week*, Professor Stephen D'Arcy, warned that states could pay a significant price for failing to lower retirement expenses. D'Arcy, a professor at the University of Illinois at Urbana-Champaign's College of Business, said tax hikes implemented to fund pension liabilities could drive employers and residents to other states that are in better financial shape.[33]

Few of the pension reform options mentioned here are painless. Indeed all of them demand strong political leadership and the willingness to confront entrenched interests. Yet the stakes are too high to ignore—and the time for action is now.

Chapter 4: The Final Word

THE CHALLENGE
• More than one-third of state and local pension plans have a funded ratio below 80 percent; their total unfunded liability: $188 billion.
• Unfunded state and local retiree health care liabilities soon could approach $1 trillion.
• The problem will only get worse when the first cohort of Baby Boomers begins to retire from their public jobs in 2008.

REFORM STRATEGIES
• *Close loopholes.* Options for reform include tightening the practice of granting large pay raises in the years immediately before retirement (which can allow employees to spike final earnings amounts) and narrowing eligibility for high-cost public safety pension benefits.
• *Two-tier retirement programs.* These programs reduce retirement and health benefits for employees hired after a specific date, while maintaining agreed-upon benefit packages for existing workers.
• *Phase in retirement.* This strategy is designed to keep older employees in the workforce longer and therefore delay the onset of full pension benefits. North Carolina's program allows state employees to start receiving partial pension benefits at age 59 while they continue working flexible hours.

EXAMPLES
• *New Jersey's* state and local public retirement systems are underfunded by as much as $35 billion.
• The *Texas* Pension Review Board placed an unprecedented 18 public retirement plans on its watch list, a warning that the plans have insufficient funds to meet future obligations. Among them are some of the state's largest pension systems.
• *Illinois* has initiated a series of strategies to reduce its unfunded liability including curtailing loopholes and abuses; mandating that all future benefit enhancements will expire after five years (unless they are renewed by the governor and the state legislature); and requiring every future benefit increase to have a dedicated revenue source.

NEXT STEPS
• *Assess the problem.* Conduct an in-depth analysis of current public pension funds and retirement benefits to ascertain the size of the problem and its causes.
• *Stop the financial bleeding.* Ensure that current contributions at least cover current liabilities. This step entails a combination of cost-cutting and revenue-enhancing changes.
• *Scale back generous early retirement programs.* These provisions are proving to be extremely expensive and poorly designed as a huge number of aging Baby-Boomers nears retirement age.
• *Involve stakeholders.* Involving political officials, business leaders, labor unions and other stakeholders helps build support for these initiatives.

{5} *Matt Kouri and Tiffany Dovey*

Fixing Medicaid

Fortune favors the bold.

At least that's what more and more state officials are betting on these days, offering up innovative ways to reign in health care costs—costs that have ballooned to nearly one-third of the annual budget in many states.[1] As it stands Medicaid costs alone account for about 20 percent of total state expenditures, making it the largest line item in most state budgets—recently surpassing elementary and secondary education spending.[2] While Medicaid spending growth slowed to just under 3 percent in FY2006, rising health care costs, coupled with reductions in employer-sponsored health insurance, continue to exert upward pressure on program spending. As former Idaho governor Dirk Kempthorne explained, unless something is done "to cure the systemic problems and rein in the escalating costs [of Medicaid]...we'll be forcing the care of our grandparents to be in direct conflict with the education of their grandchildren."[3]

Across the country state governments are rethinking their Medicaid programs. Restructuring benefits. Letting market forces exert downward pressure on costs. Giving beneficiaries and health care providers incentives to use and deliver health care more efficiently. Moving away from the old model of developing benefits packages within prescribed federal options to a new defined contribution model where a state sets a limit on the annual amount spent on health care for individual Medicaid beneficiaries and lets individuals choose how to best spend their allocated dollars. Establishing new state-sponsored "connector" models to broker better private health insurance rates for uninsured individuals. Once the exception, innovation is now the rule.

Years of state officials pleading with the federal government for more state control over how to run their Medicaid programs have finally paid off. The federal Deficit Reduction Act of 2005 allows for unprecedented flexibility in how states structure and manage their Medicaid programs. States now have greater flexibility to alter benefits, charge patients for services, and expand the role of private insurers.

The U.S. Department of Health and Human Services (HHS) is also doing its part to increase the latitude states have to tailor their programs to their own needs. HHS, led by Secretary Tommy G. Thompson (2001–2005), approved more Medicaid waivers in four years than the total of all waivers ever granted previously—a trend that has continued under Thompson's successor, Michael Leavitt. By taking advantage of this new flexibility in the basic Medicaid law and the way it is applied, states have the opportunity to take the reins and shape the debate on real Medicaid reform.

But every silver lining has a cloud. While it appears that some states are headed in the right direction with their new policy reforms, it is worth remembering that earlier attempted reforms (such as Medicaid managed care) have not gotten states to where they need to be. A solution to controlling health care costs while concurrently *maintaining and improving health outcomes* has so far eluded the best health care minds.

Solving the health care cost riddle will require significant investment in new approaches and a commitment to learning from both the successes *and* failures that experimentation yields. That means the current mindset has to change—dramatically. States have to stop chasing the latest initiative du jour and start putting in place structural mechanisms that will set them on a sustainable long-term path to fiscally responsible management of Medicaid. Move beyond complying with minimum federal requirements for Medicaid information systems to investing in management tools that will allow greater insight into what is now a black box of data in most states. Stop thinking health care and start thinking health outcomes. That means seeing health care more holistically—focusing more on prevention, not just treatment. It also means giving individuals a greater role in managing their own health care.

Also required is a reality check on the management half of the reform equation. While the principles of good management aren't nearly as sexy as innovative policy proposals, the truth is that the two must go hand in

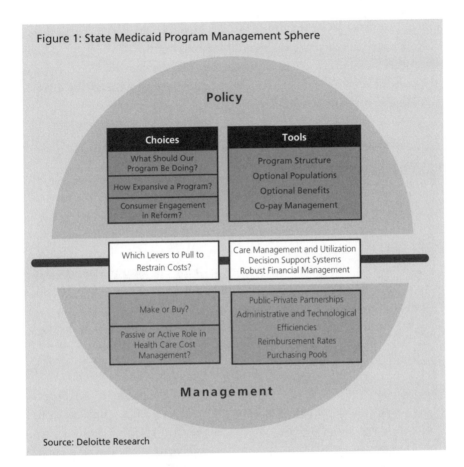

Figure 1: State Medicaid Program Management Sphere

Policy

Choices	Tools
What Should Our Program Be Doing?	Program Structure
How Expansive a Program?	Optional Populations
Consumer Engagement in Reform?	Optional Benefits
	Co-pay Management

Which Levers to Pull to Restrain Costs?	Care Management and Utilization Decision Support Systems Robust Financial Management

Make or Buy?	Public-Private Partnerships
Passive or Active Role in Health Care Cost Management?	Administrative and Technological Efficiencies
	Reimbursement Rates
	Purchasing Pools

Management

Source: Deloitte Research

hand. Regardless of which policy or cost saving innovation is selected, if it is not *implemented and managed effectively,* the benefits won't be realized. It is disheartening to compare the management resources, technology, tools and decision support systems available to the major corporations to those available to state Medicaid directors charged with managing budgets of greater size. States have traditionally under-resourced these areas because Medicaid is seen as such a massive cost drain on state budgets. Why would legislatures want to appropriate $30 million more to a program that they've been trying to cut $300 million out of? What is poorly understood is that the $30 million technology appropriation might result in hundreds of millions of dollars in savings because of better information about how to run the program. It's exactly that kind of myopic thinking that must change if Medicaid is to be transformed into a high-performing, cost-effective program.

In this chapter, we put forward a new approach for thinking about reform, one framed around a set of critical policy and management choices states must make about the future of their Medicaid programs. These choices are unavoidable if states are to get Medicaid costs under control and salvage other state priorities. In addition, we offer a framework states can use to assess the current state of their Medicaid program, followed by a set of guidelines for moving forward with reform.

Learning from Earlier Cost Control Strategies

Since Medicaid's inception in 1965, significant changes have occurred in the health care marketplace, in technology and in the population the program serves. It is clear that trying to address the health care needs of today's low-income uninsured with a solution legislated in a completely different era is a failed strategy. If reform is to be effective, fundamental structural flaws in the program must be addressed. Before jumping ahead to the choices states must make today, it is worth taking a step back to understand why previous reform strategies failed to deliver the cost savings promised and how states are adapting their approaches to take account of the earlier lessons learned.

The Medicaid Balloon

One way to think about Medicaid is to envision the program as a balloon. Many previous cost containment strategies failed to achieve lasting savings because cutting costs in one area simply shifted costs elsewhere in the system. The strategies just pushed around air; they did little to address in a holistic manner the rising cost of the program. As Dr. Bernadine Healy, chairwoman of Ohio's Commission to Reform Medicaid, observes, "Decades of reform have failed and attempts to reform will continue to fail until we change the system." A move to reduce the rolls, for example, may increase cost as uninsured patients seek out "free" emergency room care.[4] Drug formularies may have the effect of restricting the use of beneficial drugs, which in turn can impede preventive care and lead to increased hospital stays. How then can states achieve lasting cost reduction? Reduce the overall volume of the balloon. This can be accomplished by redesigning the program, stamping out inefficiencies, reducing overutilization and fraud, eliminating perverse state funding incentives and aggressively managing costs, among other things—and achieving better health outcomes. Healthy people, after all, are the cheapest patients.

There is no silver bullet solution to such deflation; rather, cost containment first requires the recognition that many states fail to actively manage their Medicaid programs. Instead they tend to be reactive: forecasting numbers of eligibles and the cost of the program, then loosely *tracking the program's progress rather than aggressively managing it*. States need to focus on the major policy decisions driving costs: who gets served, what services do they receive based on what conditions, and what frequency and duration of care gets covered. These decisions need to be rooted in substantive analysis of what works and what doesn't.

To be sure, a handful of states are investing in new ways of managing. However, too many program administrators still do not consistently manage their programs to an expenditure budget. Many state legislatures do not pursue consistent policies, with a long-term focus on health outcomes and cost effectiveness; instead they expand and contract coverage and services with the ups and downs of the state's economy. Numerous health and human services agencies—frequently the administrative home of Medicaid programs—continue to experience technological, contractual and budget crises involving the Medicaid program and have difficulty managing through those crises. And there's nothing quite like a crisis to impede long-term planning.

Moving from Tactical to Strategic Thinking

Just as all cost control measures should not be treated equally, lumping the vastly different groups that make up the Medicaid population together into a one-size-fits-all program tailored to the "average" patient makes little sense either. Good management goes beyond putting out routine fires and implementing broad cost control measures. It means understanding your program's major cost drivers and applying a strategic approach toward dealing with them. In 2001, high-cost enrollees—those with annual Medicaid spending in excess of $25,000—made up just 3.6 percent of the total Medicaid population but accounted for nearly half of all spending.[5] Focusing attention on a small percentage of high-cost patients is imminently possible and can go a long way toward stabilizing costs. Nearly half of those in the high-cost category are elderly, making this category vulnerable to demographic pressures with the aging of the baby boomer generation, and thus, very costly to ignore. Recognizing this, several states are taking advantage of new provisions in the DRA that allow for unprecedented flexibility for states to choose how they structure and manage their programs.

Pioneering the way, states including Florida, Idaho, Kentucky, Massachusetts, and West Virginia are developing tiered benefits packages to reflect the very different coverage needs of various groupings of individual beneficiaries. Kentucky is offering four different packages customized to the age and the health status of the state's Medicaid recipients. Beneficiaries with chronic diseases are rewarded with "Get Healthy" benefits for successful participation in Kentucky's disease management programs. For example, an individual with diabetes who signs up for a disease management program can earn credits toward extra benefits such as dental benefits or nutritional counseling. West Virginia's plan assigns individuals to benefit tiers based on their behavior rather than on anticipated health needs. In order to enroll in enhanced benefits programs, individuals must pledge to comply with the plan's requirements—failure to do so results in a downgrade to a more limited plan. Florida's plan departs from the others because individuals *choose* their benefit package with guidance from a counselor rather than being assigned to a particular tier.

Changing Skewed Incentives

The problem of Medicaid cost management is also inextricably tied to 40-year old federal matching formulas. With about 57 percent of state Medicaid funding coming from the federal government, states have a strong but perverse incentive to drive any and all state costs into the program in order to secure greater federal participation. This is beginning to change, with Vermont leading the way. The state struck a deal with the federal government to get out of the traditional financial arrangement where the state is required to report minute details of what it is spending so the federal government can come back and match those dollars at the approved federal match rate on a line-item-by-line-item basis. Now, instead of paying a fee for each service provided, the federal government will give the state a lump sum payment for each person enrolled in Vermont's Medicaid program and more freedom to the state to manage the program. Under the global commitment waiver, the state is required to cap costs at $4.7 billion over a five-year period. If Vermont spends more than that, then the state is responsible for making up the difference. If, on the other hand, the state can deliver care for less, then it can put those savings toward other innovative state health initiatives.[6]

Tough Choices States Must Confront

States can overcome the challenges of reforming Medicaid—provided they have the right approach, the right incentives, the right priorities and a commitment to actively managing the transformation process. Currently, however, many Medicaid programs are not managed to attain specific goals or

The Many Plagues of Medicaid

Before addressing the tough choices each state must confront, policy-makers must first fully understand the most pressing challenges their programs now face. Soaring costs and fickle legislative funding top the trouble lists confronting many state officials, but state Medicaid programs face a variety of other challenges that often threaten the very stability of state governments.

1. RISING PROGRAM COSTS
Almost every state has reported some degree of fiscal crisis related to Medicaid costs. Rising Medicaid costs, which have far exceeded inflation rates, are attributable to a number of causes, including an expanding safety net; an aging population; increased immigration; rising drug prices; waste (overuse, underuse, and misuse); consumer demand for more services, more drugs, and more advanced treatments; salary pressures resulting from shortages of qualified health workers; and the increasing prevalence of chronic illnesses and the high cost of treating those illnesses.[7]

2. THE MANY-HEADED MONSTER: PROGRAM COMPLEXITY
Medicaid is one of the most complicated programs in government today. What does that mean? According to one state Medicaid official, it would take two trucks to haul all of the program's rules and regulations from the Medicaid office over to the state legislature. As a joint federal-state program, it has the structural overhead of two levels of government oversight (three in the instance of county-administered states). The costs of the program, variety of care-delivery models, extensive relationships between Medicaid and other state programs and diverse set of stakeholders contribute to this complexity.[8] Medicaid, for example, has an immense network of private and politically active providers, many of whose entire livelihood is built on revenues that come from the program. Further contributing to this complexity is the diversity of its beneficiaries. These are distinct and separate groups of individuals with fundamentally different needs and characteristics: people with disabilities, the poor—most typically young women and their children—and the elderly poor.[9]

3. TOO MANY COOKS IN THE KITCHEN
The size of the Medicaid program, both in terms of budget and its footprint on society, makes for a very large number of very interested stakeholders, most of whom demand to be involved in any potential program change. Not only are program directors attempting to steer the organizational equivalent of an ocean liner, but they are doing it with multiple hands tugging at the wheel.[10]

4. OBSOLETE TECHNOLOGY
Data, and the technology that provides it, may be both the bane of Medicaid and one of the keys to its longer-term survival. The systems that run

Medicaid are huge, complicated, expensive and in most cases outdated. The short-term issues are the high costs and even higher risks associated with upgrading Medicaid management information systems and enhanced data analytical capabilities. If a state is not in the process of reprocuring or rebuilding a system, it has likely either done so recently or is currently in the process of an upgrade. The situation is exacerbated by the small oligopoly of private firms with state Medicaid technology experience and high cost of entering the market.

5. MEDICAID 24x7
From banking to travel to shopping for just about anything, consumers have much higher expectations now when it comes to accessibility and convenience. As Medicaid providers and recipients become increasingly technologically savvy, Medicaid programs will have to invest in new Web-based technologies to meet citizen and stakeholder needs. The old days of providers submitting boxes of paper claims to a state for payment are slowly coming to an end, and both providers and recipients expect ready Internet access to claims and eligibility information, benefits and related program information.[11] Such expectations are not met today.

6. BOULDER IN A SWIMMING POOL: MEDICAID'S LARGE RIPPLE EFFECT
While Medicaid officially accounts for 20 to 30 percent of a typical state budget, it actually drives a much larger chunk of a state's allocation of limited resources. Because many other state programs receive their funding in large part from Medicaid, those programs, suffer whenever Medicaid costs exceed their budget. Whether school-based health care, community clinics, local mental health/mental retardation services or university-based teaching programs, Medicaid touches many other areas of state government. This ripple effect, which magnifies Medicaid's financial impact, increases the need to manage Medicaid differently and more closely.

to meet meaningful performance measures. And when goals are established, they're often not guided by a clearly articulated overall strategy.

This is not particularly surprising. Strategy implies a long-term perspective. With the aforementioned complexity, dizzying amounts of data, changing administrations, uncertainty about federal program changes and the constraints of a politicized annual budgeting process, it's a challenge to set out a strategy and work toward it over time. There are enough urgent initiatives, budget pressures and piles of inconsistent data to dissuade any leader from willingly plunging into strategic planning.

Historically, states have simply been so focused on solving short-term fiscal problems and managing a backlog of claims that they have not been

Tough Choices: A Summary

- **WHAT SHOULD WE BE DOING—AND NOT DOING?** What should be the core functions of our Medicaid program?

- **HOW EXPANSIVE?** How expansive should our program be?

- **CONSUMER ENGAGEMENT IN REFORM?** To what degree should Medicaid recipients share the state's burden of cost reduction and quality enhancement?

- **WHICH LEVERS TO PULL TO RESTRAIN COSTS?** Which policy and management levers will we use to reduce, or at a minimum contain, the costs of our program?

- **MAKE OR BUY?** Will we directly manage the services in our program or will we contract for them?

- **PASSIVE OR ACTIVIST ROLE IN INFLUENCING HEALTH CARE COSTS?** Will we move past simple program administration and use our Medicaid program to actively control the cost outcomes and overall quality of health care in our state?

either able or willing to step back, think through their strategy and address the underlying issues of Medicaid reform. Finally, recognizing the shortcomings of such a reactive approach, many states have begun to examine the more fundamental issues and commit to finding real solutions that will move them toward their long-term goals. Lasting reform requires first confronting a set of difficult choices that go to the very heart of what kind of Medicaid program each state wants to have. By fully addressing them, states can focus on a long-term strategy that will take their program in the direction they want it to go *without* breaking the bank or losing site of the program's mandate to serve individuals in need.

Policy Choices

Once the exception, policy innovation is becoming the rule. States that haven't yet considered large-scale innovation in their Medicaid programs are behind the curve. Before diving head first into a massive overhaul, however, states need to understand fully what reforms other states are undertaking and *what their own state needs to be doing*. This understanding begins by answering a few fundamental questions on a state-specific basis.

What Should We Be Doing—and Not Doing?

Many state Medicaid programs have an identity crisis. Some are primarily claims processors; others are health providers. Some are primarily financial stewards; others are contract administrators. Most of them, however, are a confusing combination of various roles. The underlying problem: Medicaid programs typically never ask the fundamental question: "What are we really here to do?"

Ignoring this question can cause inconsistency, inefficiencies and an inability to adapt to changing workforce and technological trends that can help a program reduce costs and improve care.

Florida provides an example of a state that has rethought its role in Medicaid and is moving from claims processor to a policy and contract management role. On its current trajectory, with expenditure growth averaging 13 percent annually, by 2015 Florida will spend nearly 60 percent of its budget on Medicaid.[12] Florida's $14 billion program provides care to 2.2 million Floridians a year by using about 80,000 different fee-for-service providers, in addition to multiple managed care providers.

Against this backdrop, Florida has decided to reinvent its Medicaid program. Until recently the state's Medicaid program has essentially operated as a claims-processing outfit, structuring the health benefit coverage Medicaid beneficiaries receive and then processing the claims submitted by various providers of that coverage. Florida's new Medicaid initiative, Empowered Care, allows health care networks to develop their own health care plans to compete for Medicaid patients. Provider networks receive a set premium every month for each Medicaid beneficiary covered, with the amount varying to reflect each beneficiary's individual risk, thereby shifting the burden of cost control and fraud reduction to participating networks.

Since gaining approval from HHS and subsequently the Florida Legislature, the state's Medicaid program is on track for fundamental change. Starting with pilots in Duval and Broward counties, the Medicaid program is being transformed into an organization focused largely on performance management and provider oversight. In its new role, the state will be charged with counseling beneficiaries about which program best matches their individual health care needs, monitoring Medicaid providers to ensure they properly deliver services and setting the spending level for Medicaid, thus stabilizing out-of-control expenditures. This means that the state will no longer establish benefit packages and reimburse individual health providers on a fee-for-service basis. The state will instead leave it up to managed care plans to figure out the best way to control costs, while the state turns its attention to helping beneficiaries navigate the wide array of care options available to them and to monitoring the providers of that care.

How Expansive?

Medicaid, with its appealing federal cost match, has been the preferred vehicle for states to expand their health care offerings to a broader population. It is easy to understand why. Besides the prospect of persuading the federal government to cover a significant portion of the costs, many state Medicaid programs have already-established provider networks, technology infrastructure, and an established administrative foundation on which to build.

A critical decision facing state Medicaid policy-makers, however, is just how expansive the program should be. Basic Medicaid, with its labyrinthine qualification processes and numerous restrictions, often cannot move the state toward its broader health care goals. And while universal coverage underpinned by Medicaid can be appealing, it can also lead a state down an unsustainable fiscal path, one most dramatically illustrated by the TennCare program. Tennessee's rendition of Medicaid has emerged as an example of the kind of financial problems that can result if a state does not understand program costs or does not have the systems and processes in place to understand and control utilization in a managed care environment.

In 1994 TennCare was heralded as a national model for its unprecedented generosity and broad reach; it provided health care for the uninsured and uninsurable who wouldn't typically qualify for Medicaid benefits. TennCare benefits exceeded even those of many private health plans. For example, the state elected to forgo limits on hospital stays and the number of prescriptions it would cover for any one patient (TennCare picked up the tab for an average of 30 prescriptions per beneficiary annually).[13] The predictable result: massive overuse. Making matters worse, many private employers used the advent of TennCare as an excuse to drop health coverage for their employees.

More than a decade later, legal battles and bankruptcies of managed care plans forced the state to assume the financial risks associated with its Medicaid program and essentially brought Tennessee's experiment with near-universal health care for Tennesseans to an end. TennCare costs were consuming nearly a third of the state budget in 2004 and, barring a change in course, would require hundreds of millions in additional state revenue to sustain current spending levels.[14] Given the dim fiscal outlook, Tennessee Governor

Phil Bredesen pushed forward with major reforms, essentially bringing the TennCare story full circle and restoring the program back to a more traditional one. Full coverage will remain in force for children, but coverage and enrollment for adults has been reduced.

Still, many states are forging ahead with programs to expand health care coverage—with the hope that they can avoid many of the unintended consequences that befell TennCare. The most ambitious initiative is in Massachusetts. The state has made a serious commitment to addressing the problem of the uninsured, enacting a comprehensive health reform package that aims for universal coverage within Massachusetts.

Beginning July 1, 2007, every resident in Massachusetts is required to have health insurance. For residents with incomes well above the poverty line, insurance ("Commonwealth Care") can be purchased through a new Commonwealth Care Exchange, which facilitates the pretax payment of premiums by working individuals, resulting in a 15 to 30 percent savings off their insurance bill depending on their income. (This is just one way the Massachusetts plan differs from TennCare.) The reform plan also offers a program for those under the 300 percent federal poverty level: Safety Net Care. The plan, enabled through a Medicaid waiver, is to deliver private health insurance to these lower-income residents with the same benefit levels as Commonwealth Care, but with lower co-pays and no deductibles (see Key Elements of Massachusetts Plan box).

The issue of how to reduce the number of uninsured—which in turn should reduce costly emergency room visits—is being debated in nearly every state. Several states are considering a "connector" model similar to Massachusetts' through which uninsured individuals purchase insurance from a state-sponsored exchange at more affordable group rates. As policy-makers examine their options, they must seriously consider whether their state's climate is right for more aggressive, often quite creative and no-doubt risky Medicaid-based program expansions. Broad-based support is critical, including from providers, member advocates and even the business community, which often bears some of the increased financial burden (and some of the benefit as well) for such expansions. Rigorous financial planning and control is also key, and most state programs lack much of the financial and actuarial analysis talent required to effectively design and manage these creative programs. Finally, the right political support and timing are also important, as such programs often require complicated legislation and multiple years (and therefore multiple legislative cycles) for full implementation.

The Key Elements of Massachusetts Plan

- **"Connector" model:** Individuals and workers in businesses with 50 or fewer employees may purchase private health insurance coverage at more affordable rates through a state-sponsored exchange; premium payments by both employers and workers are paid on a pretax basis.

- **Subsidies for low-income residents:** Low-income residents (with incomes up to 300 percent of the federal poverty level) receive subsidies to off-set the cost of health insurance.

- **Individual mandate:** Individuals are required to buy health insurance cov-erage or pay a fine; options include Health Savings Accounts with high deductibles, inexpensive policies for younger populations, and a wide array of coverage options purchased through the Connector or from the marketplace.

- **Employer mandate:** Businesses with more than 10 employees that do not offer health insurance coverage face a maximum penalty of $295 per worker to subsidize the cost of coverage.

- **Increased health plan flexibility:** Providers are given increased latitude to structure their health plans (higher deductibles, more restrictions on how patients access care, for example), with the added benefit of a state moratorium on new legislative mandates that dictate the benefits that must be offered.

Consumer Engagement in Reform?

An increasingly important decision to be made in designing or reforming a Medicaid program is how it will apportion the burdens of cost and quality control between the state, on one end of the spectrum, and the consumer on the other end (with various potential combinations in between). If the state assumes all of the burden, the result is the all-too-common situation in which consumers are oblivious to the costs of services and state budgets are held hostage to fluctuations (historically upward) in health care usage and cost. Conversely, Medicaid recipients—by definition—cannot shoulder the costs involved in a large deductible model, where an initial outlay of several thousand dollars might be required before insurance kicks in.

Most states have tried to offload some of the burden of cost contain-ment, often through increasing member co-payments for certain services or prescription drugs, or both. The results have been mixed. Few states have gone so far as to directly include Medicaid recipients in the effort to improve the quality of care they receive. Private sector insurers are moving strongly toward consumer-directed models of insurance and care management where more financial and decision-making responsibility is placed on the shoulders of consumers. However, the jury is largely still out on their success. And while most states haven't fully mastered client burden-sharing in a way that results in cost savings and improved care, the tide may be turning. Consider South Carolina.

Until now, South Carolina's Medicaid program has operated in a typical fee-for-service fashion, with residents who meet certain eligibility requirements entitled to receive approved health care services regardless of the associated cost. South Carolina's new Medicaid choice initiative aims to sensitize beneficiaries to the costs of their health care and remove the economic incentive for patients to overuse services.

Under South Carolina's Medicaid reform plan, the state would establish personal health accounts for most of South Carolina's 850,000 Medicaid recipients, helping to control the total amount spent on the program. South Carolina would opt out of assuming unlimited financial risk, mirroring what the federal government is doing with the Medicare program.

Under the plan, the $4 billion spent annually in South Carolina on Medicaid reimbursements to providers would be diverted to personal health accounts funded with an actuarially determined amount that would be used to buy private health insurance or pay for care directly. Beneficiaries would also receive catastrophic and preventative benefit coverage, in addition to enrollment counseling, so that patients understand which plans best meet their needs.

Management Choices

When it comes to Medicaid reform, the tail is frequently wagging the dog. Management and technology initiatives are underfunded while program policy decisions drive up total costs in an irregular manner. For reform to be successful, you can't have one without the other. The manner in which Medicaid is administered significantly affects its performance—how state resources are deployed, how policies are implemented and enforced, how cost savings are identified and realized, and how critical day-to-day decisions affect health and financial outcomes. The majority of state Medicaid programs are run by a small staff—often lacking the right skills—using outdated technology, with antiquated management and organizational structures.

While it's common knowledge that each year Medicaid consumes a big-

Medicaid 500: State Medicaid Programs Equivalent in Size to Fortune 500 Companies

Rank	Company	Revenues ($ millions)	Rank	Company	Revenues ($ millions)
1	Wal-Mart Stores	288,189.00	355	Massachusetts	5,816.00
2	Exxon Mobil	270,772.00	358	Estee Lauder	5,790.40
3	General Motors	193,517.00	359	Missouri	5,745.00
4	Ford Motor	172,233.00	368	KeyCorp	5,564.00
5	General Electric	152,363.00	369	CMS Energy	5,483.00
59	Goldman Sachs Group	29,839.00	370	Connecticut	5,479.00
60	California	29,486.00	371	Monsanto	5,478.00
63	American Express	29,115.00	373	Black & Decker	5,464.60
67	DuPont	27,995.00	375	Georgia	5,438.00
68	New York	27,562.00	394	Kerr-McGee	5,178.70
69	Sprint	27,428.00	395	Minnesota	5,172.00
71	Viacom	27,054.80	396	Washington	5,170.00
86	Merck	22,938.60	397	Ameren	5,160.00
136	Emerson Electric	15,615.00	415	Qualcomm	4,916.00
137	Texas	15,442.00	416	Louisiana	4,878.00
140	Express Scripts	15,114.70	417	RadioShack	4,841.20
141	Pennsylvania	15,048.00	419	Caesars Entertainment	4,805.00
142	Delta Air Lines	15,002.00	420	Wisconsin	4,797.00
166	Humana	13,104.30	442	Jacobs Engineering Grp.	4,594.20
167	Florida	13,079.00	443	Maryland	4,574.00
168	FirstEnergy	12,949.00	444	Mirant	4,572.00
174	Tenet Healthcare	12,496.00	467	Indiana	4,307.00
175	Ohio	12,494.00	468	Molson Coors Brewing	4,305.80
220	Lennar	10,504.90	479	Universal Health Svcs.	4,157.90
221	Illinois	10,500.00	480	Kentucky	4,120.00
222	Gillette	10,477.00	481	Omnicare	4,119.90
270	Apple Computer	8,279.00	490	United Stationers	3,991.20
272	Michigan	8,255.00	491	South Carolina	3,957.00
273	Alltel	8,246.10	503	Corning	3,854.00
289	Tennessee	7,631.00	504	Virginia	3,826.00
290	New Jersey	7,629.00	505	Arizona	3,814.00
291	Air Products & Chem.	7,411.40	512	Alabama	3,773.00
294	North Carolina	7,381.00			
295	BJ's Wholesale Club	7,375.30			
354	Unisys	5,820.70			

Despite the size of their programs, most Medicaid administrators lack the management tools available to their private sector counterparts. While there's no shortage of program data available, administrators often lack the sophisticated decision support tools needed to transform that sea of data into useful information to inform decision-making. Also lacking is accurate, regularly updated financial information to track budget to actual expenditure on an incurred basis by service and category of beneficiary—most administrators are lucky if they get good numbers on an annual basis. The same goes for fraud detection. It's estimated that about 10 percent of all health care spending—whether by a Medicaid plan or a private health plan—is fraudulent. Absent advanced analytics tools, most states don't get anywhere near identifying even 1 percent of fraudulent or abusive activity. Furthermore, there are significant disparities between disease management programs in the public and private spheres. Private sector health plans employ disease managers to actively seek out ways to save costs and improve the health outcomes of their members; most Medicaid programs are still in the infancy of their disease management programs.

Sources: Deloitte Research, "Fortune 500 2006: Our Annual Ranking of America's Largest Corporations," Fortune, April 17, 2006 (http://money.cnn.com/magazines/fortune/fortune500/full_list/); "2004 State Expenditure Report," National Association of State Budget Officers, January 2006 (http://www.hasbo.org/Publications/PDFs/2004ExpendReport.pdf); Steven Malanga, "Hot to Stop Medicaid Fraud: For Starters, States Should Try," City Journal, Spring 2006

ger percentage of the state budget, few realize the enormity of the actual size of the program. To put this in perspective, consider this: if state Medicaid programs were included in *Fortune* Magazine's Fortune 500 List of the largest companies in America, *nearly half the country's Medicaid programs would make the list.* If included in the Fortune 100, both California and New York, because of the size of their Medicaid programs, would beat out companies like media powerhouse Viacom and pharmaceutical giant Merck (see sidebar). Yet state Medicaid programs have a comparatively small portion of the management talent, investment capacity, and technology wherewithal of their private sector counterparts.

Aggressive state Medicaid directors and administrators don't have to sit back and wait for legislative directives to transform their programs. They are already in a position to do so, but first they must address the following tough choices:

Which Levers to Pull to Restrain Costs?

The common assertion that the "Medicaid problem" is the inevitable result of rising and seemingly fixed costs can serve as an excuse to treat the program as a hopelessly complex black box—thriving on funding stakeholders in exchange for their support of the program in ways that defeat the original intent. A lot of this "inevitability" is the product of the current design and management of Medicaid, and some of the "fixed" costs simply reflect the difficulty in making and sustaining tough policy changes rather than costs that cannot be controlled.

Our analysis of each state's Medicaid cost per member and cost growth rates over the last four years shows, for example, that the specific policy choices states make do in fact significantly affect Medicaid costs (see figure 2). The chart demonstrates which states' Medicaid programs are growing faster and spending more per capita compared to the average, and which are not. The factors that would be expected to drive average cost per enrollee or cost growth rates—a state's size, geography, cost of living, and level of poverty—appear to have little impact on program cost. More important in explaining the dramatic state-to-state variation in program costs is the individual program structure and the policy decisions made by each state.

Some states, for instance, have changed policies to allow for some cost sharing by Medicaid recipients, particularly in program areas with more lenient income requirements (such as the Katie Beckett program, which covers certain children under age 18 who have disabling conditions and live at

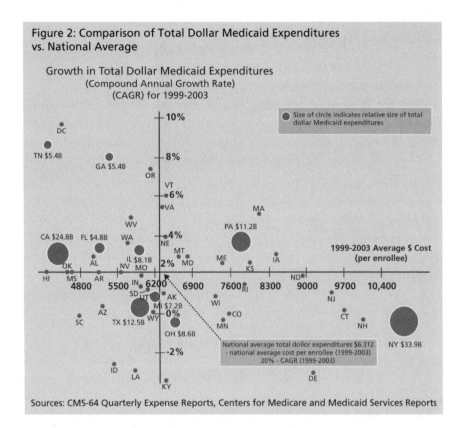

Figure 2: Comparison of Total Dollar Medicaid Expenditures vs. National Average

Growth in Total Dollar Medicaid Expenditures
(Compound Annual Growth Rate)
(CAGR) for 1999-2003

Sources: CMS-64 Quarterly Expense Reports, Centers for Medicare and Medicaid Services Reports

home); other states haven't. Similar decisions—all of which are admittedly difficult and sometimes politically risky—include whether to limit quantities of certain benefits (such as prescription drugs and certain doctor visits) and whether to require reverification of eligibility on a more frequent basis (such as every six months, as Texas has considered for certain groups).

States that are willing to use policy decisions to aggressively manage program costs will likely find that, given a better understanding of their program's performance data, they have a number of levers available to pull—at both the policy and management level.

Effective policy management can go a long way toward better controlling the various cost drivers of the program, but setting and managing Medicaid program policy is no easy task. Medicaid policy is often shared across multiple entities (including the state legislature, the governor's policy staff, and the Medicaid agency's policy staff). This can sometimes create confusion and less-than-ideal levels of coordination. Policy decisions are also often inadequately informed and forced to rely on insufficient and often inaccurate data on program performance and costs. While a few states

Cost Savings Levers

1. Choosing the most cost-optimal **program structure** for the state.

2. Managing the **optional populations** served by the program.

3. Managing the **optional benefits** provided by the program.

4. Implementing consumer choice and related mechanisms to secure quality and reduce unnecessary **utilization of care.**

5. Using **management tools** (for example, decision support systems, robust financial management) to enable more informed decision-making.

6. Developing **public-private partnerships** to address health care needs in a less fragmented manner and to facilitate the development and implementation of health information technology infrastructure.

7. Identifying and implementing **administrative and technological efficiencies**. For example, Florida has successfully used e-prescribing to check medication side effects and patient prescription histories to track costs. The state gave personal digital assistants to doctors with the highest volume of Medicaid patients, allowing for real-time data on current medication history. Physicians working with this new information dropped severe drug reactions by 4–7 percent. Officials expect the program to save $4 million in 2006.[15]

8. Structuring **reimbursement rates** to provide cost-savings incentives and control provider costs.

9. Leveraging **purchasing pools** to extract deeper discounts on prescription drugs.

use advanced decision support systems (data warehouses) and related actuarial analysis to mine claims and tease out data to identify key cost drivers in their program, most states do not.

To be truly effective at understanding and better controlling the costs of their programs, states must first put the tools and processes in place, such as better delineation of policy-making roles and responsibilities, and enhanced decision support tools, to better manage policy. Only then can they begin to make hard, micro-level policy decisions that can have significant impacts on program costs and health outcomes.

Recent experience reveals that not having these tools and processes can turn good intentions to manage costs into money losers. For example, a state can spend more on administration of a prior authorization program than it saves in health care dollars if the services on the prior authorization list are inappropriate. At a minimum, using decision support technology and care management expertise, states should annually prepare and analyze costs and benefits of their prior authorization programs and make decisions based on the previous year's results and identified opportunities. One recent such medical cost review in a New England state revealed that for every dollar spent on administering the state's prior authorization program, the state recouped only about 50 cents—not a good return on limited "investment" resources.

Closer cost scrutiny doesn't stop at the state level. As more of the cost-bearing burden gets shifted to individuals, states must assume responsibility for improving health literacy so that beneficiaries are in a position to make wise health care decisions. Using a broad scope of educational tools and methods, states need to educate patients on the basics of benefit selection, prevention and prudent use of health care services.

Make or Buy?

For years, many states have largely taken for granted the operating model of their program. Some states, though, have embraced a more strategic view of their program and how they administer it and are asking whether some functions can be better performed by partnering with private organizations.

Texas stands out among the states that have moved away from directly running major components of their program. Texas outsources most of the operations of its Medicaid program, including claims processing, Medicaid Management Information Systems (MMIS) administration, provider and client relations, third-party liability and recovery, drug program management, client enrollment, client outreach and education and even eligibility determination (currently in the pilot phase). Accordingly, most of the state staff within the Texas administering agency are essentially contract managers, working to monitor contractor performance. While the Texas model is not suitable for every state, many lessons can be gleaned from the state about how to leverage external expertise to deliver traditional government services.

Following Texas's lead, more and more states are slowly getting out of the business of health care program administration and moving toward a contract management role. Claims administration has been historically administered by contractual fiscal agents in many states—states are now moving to contract other Medicaid administrative services. Because of the increased level of outsourcing in many Medicaid programs and the sheer size and inherent complexity of the services being outsourced, states have had to manage significantly more contract arrangements—in the process cultivat-

Table 1: Medicaid Management Information System

Primarily state operated	Primarily contracted out	
Arizona	Alabama	Nevada
Hawaii	Alaska	New Hampshire
Illinois	Arkansas	New Jersey
Iowa	California	New Mexico
Maine	Colorado	New York
Maryland	Connecticut	North Carolina
Massachusetts	Delaware	Oklahoma
Michigan	District of Columbia	Pennsylvania
Minnesota	Florida	Rhode Island
Nebraska	Georgia	South Carolina
North Dakota	Idaho	Tennessee
Ohio	Indiana	Texas
Oregon	Kansas	Vermont
South Dakota	Kentucky	Virginia
Utah	Louisiana	Washington
	Mississippi	West Virginia
	Missouri	Wisconsin
	Montana	Wyoming

Source: "MMIS Fiscal Agent Contract Status Report," Centers for Medicare and Medicaid Services, February 15, 2006

ing a skill that hasn't always come easily. State leaders also need to clearly understand that administrative delegation does not abrogate the need for qualified state staff to oversee contracted services.

Making this shift is an enormous adjustment for Medicaid employees who are far more likely to possess "old model" Medicaid administration skills (such as social services, member and provider relations, policy analysis and claims adjudication) and fewer of the "new model" skills (namely, contract, financial management, actuarial analysis and project management). The adjustment is made even more difficult as Medicaid tries to compete for the same talent pool in demand by the private sector—a pool that only will become shallower with the impending retirement of the Baby Boom generation. High-profile contract failures, many of which have cost Medicaid programs a lot of money, have exacerbated the political challenges and risks of outsourcing.[16]

Given these challenges, states need to take into consideration several factors in assessing when and if it makes sense to outsource certain Medicaid functions to the private sector. First, they should measure performance and output of particular functions and compare those results to benchmarks from other state programs and the private sector. This comparison can sometimes be difficult, given differences in how performance is defined and calculated, but it is imminently possible. Second, states should assess whether the state agencies involved in administering the program have, or can readily acquire, the workforce skills and technology necessary to stay on the cutting edge of a particular function. Finally, states should develop a formal business case (often using formal Requests for Information, or RFIs) to aid in evaluating the cost-benefit effectiveness of partnering with outside organizations. The state division or unit currently responsible for administering the function in question should have equal ability to present a proposal and "compete" for the work.

In cases where states choose to outsource "medical management" activities such as disease management and case management, states should also take care not to disrupt the continuity and coordination of care. Outsourcing strategies should focus on implementing a concerted strategy that can merge what are often fragmented medical management initiatives spread across multiple state departments and on avoiding further fragmentation by not contracting with too many disassociated vendors.

Passive or Activist Role in Influencing Health Care Costs?

Medicaid's role in health care provision in many states is as big as, or bigger than, that of many states' largest private insurers. Medicaid's immensity can make it hard to manage, but it also provides a unique opportunity to use the program's purchasing power to move beyond complaining about high cost and poor outcomes to actually doing something about those problems. States must decide whether to invest in innovative arrangements (such as pooled purchasing deals) and more advanced contracting models to manage health care costs and outcomes more systematically. Such decisions, however, should not be made without careful consideration of the risks and costs associated with each choice.

As states battle to hold down one of Medicaid's top cost drivers—rising prescription drug costs—some new alliances already are emerging. States are pooling their purchasing power to negotiate better deals with pharmaceutical companies. Georgia is one of the states beginning to do just that.

Realizing that prescription drug costs were quickly rising across state health plans, Georgia established the Department of Community Health to oversee health benefits for state employee health plans, Medicaid, the State Children's Health Insurance Program, and the Board of Regents of the university system. Multiagency purchasing and the resulting volume has enabled the state-contracted pharmacy benefit manager to negotiate deeper discounts and has generated significant savings. The reorganization has successfully brought down state Medicaid costs, slowing pharmaceutical expenditure growth by about 15 percent over a two-year period.[17]

Georgia is not alone. Interstate purchasing pools are sprouting up across the country. Alaska, Hawaii, Kentucky, Michigan, Minnesota, Montana, Nevada, New Hampshire, New York and Tennessee are all part of the National Medicaid Pooling Initiative, which allows them to pool their collective purchasing power to extract better rebates from pharmaceutical companies. Kansas is teaming up with its small businesses to significantly increase its bargaining power with insurers.

States can also use their purchasing leverage to enhance health care quality. Several states hold their Medicaid managed care organizations contractually accountable for meeting certain health care performance measures. Texas, for example, is working to provide contractual incentives for health maintenance organizations that can measure and demonstrate progress on certain "proxies" for care quality, such as the number of mammography screenings conducted as a proxy for breast cancer reduction. The idea is to move toward a point where care coordinators and providers receive extra money from the state if they meet certain quality-of-care targets. If they don't meet the targets, they receive no bonus.

Before embarking on such bold initiatives, states must take care to evaluate potential risks and costs. For example, pooled purchasing with other states would make a state partially dependent on other states for the success of its efforts, a dependency that in volatile political times can be hazardous. From a cost point of view, states must weigh the additional investments in time and resources needed to perform both the up-front due diligence and the ongoing monitoring required to ensure the integrity and performance of the initiatives against the benefits.

How Well Do You Really Know Your Medicaid Program?

Before making these difficult choices, states first need to articulate the specific issues they are seeking to address and consider viable alternatives. This requires that states conduct a thorough assessment of their current Medicaid program. Because Medicaid programs are so complex, no individual has a handle on everything that goes on in the program. An assessment of current Medicaid outcomes, technology and administration can provide this broader view and give policy-makers and program administrators enough informa-

Figure 3: Recent Medicaid Reforms Across the Country

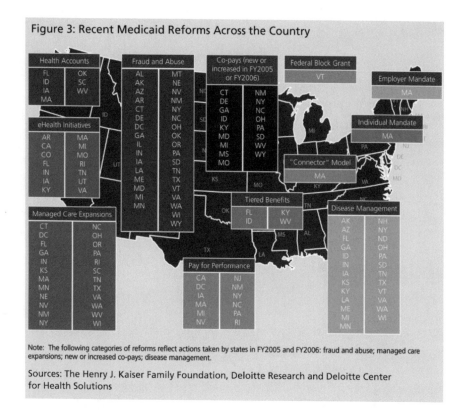

Note: The following categories of reforms reflect actions taken by states in FY2005 and FY2006: fraud and abuse; managed care expansions; new or increased co-pays; disease management.

Sources: The Henry J. Kaiser Family Foundation, Deloitte Research and Deloitte Center for Health Solutions

tion about the program and the way it is administered to be able to make informed decisions about the program's strategy and the necessary reforms (see figure 3).

Outcomes Assessment

Is the program maximizing health outcomes while minimizing client service costs?

The Medicaid program should be assessed against two broad sets of outcomes: client-focused outcomes and financial outcomes. The traditional focus on client outcomes has been, "How many dollars do we have?" or "How many clients are in our program?" The emphasis instead should shift to, "What are the outcomes that we should buy?" One barrier is that most states don't have adequate outcomes data. Medicaid officials have traditionally measured only the provision of care and not necessarily the quality of the care or the ultimate outcome. The situation is analogous to education several years ago when inputs could be measured pretty well but capabilities to measure the outcomes were weak, so instead schools used outcome

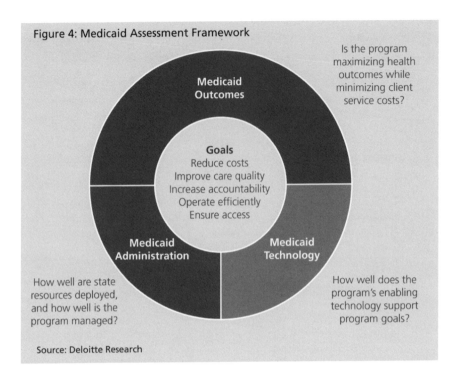

Figure 4: Medicaid Assessment Framework

Is the program maximizing health outcomes while minimizing client service costs?

Medicaid Outcomes

Goals
Reduce costs
Improve care quality
Increase accountability
Operate efficiently
Ensure access

Medicaid Administration

Medicaid Technology

How well are state resources deployed, and how well is the program managed?

How well does the program's enabling technology support program goals?

Source: Deloitte Research

surrogates, like evaluations of faculty or number of graduations or awards. The outcome focus has since changed in education through No Child Left Behind and can also change in Medicaid.

Financial outcomes also present a challenge because meaningful measurement demands the sorts of information systems and management processes used by well-run private sector businesses. Medicaid programs are large enough to wield power over vendors, and their expenditures are large enough that they ought to be scrutinized through the eyes of business managers set on delivering the best services available at an advantageous cost. The opportunities are significant and, for the most part, untapped.

Technology Assessment

How well does the enabling technology support program goals?

Technology is a critical lever in Medicaid modernization. The difficulties measuring outcomes are partly the result of the baffling complexity of Medicaid services and beneficiaries and an absence of advanced information systems that would enable this kind of decision-making. Disjointed legacy information systems, and a reactive approach to modernizing them, contribute to the fog.

Quality Over Quantity

Throughout the past 40 years, Medicaid's reimbursement system has centered on rewarding the quantity of services provided. Cal Ludeman, acting commissioner of the Minnesota Department of Human Services and chair of the governor's Health Cabinet, explains, "Purchasing health care based on volume, as we do now, does not provide incentives to increase quality. Improving quality will save lives, improve the quality of life for people living with chronic illness, and help to keep health care affordable."[18]

Ludeman's statement underscores the importance of establishing a measurable focus on the quality of outcomes and on rewarding states for their ability to improve outcomes, which can lower the current and future cost of care. For instance, treating hospital-acquired infections, which can be prevented through the use of best practices, on average cost $52,600 per infection.[19]

Improving the quality of care depends upon two factors. The first is the ability to track quality and to define what it means to provide quality care. According to the National Committee for Quality Assurance, the widespread variation in clinical practice outcomes contributes to tens of thousands of preventable deaths every year and an estimated $2.8 billion to $4.2 billion in avoidable medical costs.[20] The second factor in improving quality is a reward system that encourages providers with thin profit margins to invest quality of care improvements. The potential for adding 1 or 2 percent to a provider's margin can prompt them to invest in higher quality care.

The Centers for Medicare and Medicaid Services, through the Medicare program, has begun to take the lead in tracking quality measures on a pilot basis and using financial incentives to encourage quality improvements. The test provided a 1–2 percent financial incentive for those performing in the top 20 percent of any of the measured categories.[21] The results showed a 6.6 percent increase in quality across those measures.

It is important to make the reward a financially viable one that offsets the costs of change in a cash-strapped system rather than a mere system of penalties for not reporting or reaching quality indicators. Both the tracking of best practices and the tracking of errors allow for a more value-based reimbursement.

There is also a continuing cloud over the Medicaid Management Information Systems required by the federal government, caused by the perception that the promised cost savings from these systems never really seem to materialize. Technology has improved business processes in almost any industry you can name, but MMIS has been something of a black hole of mandatory upgrades with no apparent payback.[22] In part, this is because states have continued to refine aged legacy systems and then implemented

Outcomes Checklist

Clients

❏ Are the clients being served by the program truly experiencing **quality health care**?

❏ Are prevention messages and **preventative services** available and utilized?

❏ Is client **care improving** as a result of being a part of a Medicaid program?

❏ How are we performing in comparison with **performance metrics** of other states and private health care?

❏ Are clients and providers satisfied with the level and quality of **customer service** they receive?

Financial

❏ Are we actually **saving money** on cost-reduction initiatives?

❏ Is our financial management of the program comparable to financial management of **private sector programs**?

❏ Do we have access to timely, **meaningful information and reports** that inform programmatic decision-making?

❏ Are our vendors **sharing risks** appropriately, creating the correct **incentives for cost savings**?

❏ Are we accurately pricing our **capitated services**?

❏ Are we experiencing **adverse selection** because vendors are bidding on, or carving out, only certain services?

minimally compliant systems without pushing for advanced technology that would enable them to identify potential cost savings, thus resulting in more of a band-aid solution than a real fix.

At one level, Medicaid program directors must ensure that their information systems comply with the Health Insurance Portability and Accountability Act and other federal reporting requirements. But the business questions of adapting advanced technology, technology-driven cost savings and continual process improvement ought not to be far behind.

Technology Checklist

❑ Are we efficiently using all of our **IT resources** (people, hardware, and software)?

❑ Are our systems enabling the **timely and accurate** delivery of services to stakeholders?

❑ Can we comply with changing **federal reporting requirements** and technical standards?

❑ Are we using new technologies to **reduce the net cost** of our program?

❑ Are our systems providing the level of management reporting needed to inform better **decision-making?**

Administration Assessment

How well are state resources deployed, and how skillfully is the program managed?

Another important aspect of Medicaid reform planning involves assessing how well each program is operating against the benchmarks of an optimized program. Do the program's operations fit its stated strategy? The mantle of success for Medicaid programs rests, to a greater degree than is often appreciated, with the administrators and policy developers who manage the state's Medicaid agency and program. The manner in which a Medicaid program is administered—how cost savings are identified and realized, how state resources are most efficiently deployed, how policies are implemented and enforced, and how critical day-to-day decisions affect health and financial outcomes—significantly affects the relative success of each program. Even the most well-crafted and well-intentioned legislation and statewide health policies will fail without effective program management and administration.

Next Generation Medicaid

Once state leaders understand the building blocks of their Medicaid program and have answered a set of key strategic questions about what they want their Medicaid program to be, they must follow through with decisions and actions that move them toward the next generation of Medicaid. Some initial questions to answer include:

Administration Assessment Checklist

❏ Are we effectively evaluating the performance of our program overall, our staff, and our contractors?

❏ Does our program's performance across key benchmarks of a well-run program (such as claims payment accuracy and timeliness, customer service timeliness and satisfaction, and achievement of projected cost savings) measure up to industry best practices?

❏ What is our overall program strategy, and are our operations aligned with that strategy?

❏ What business processes do we manage, and how well do we manage them?

❏ Is our program structured in the most effective and efficient manner possible?

❏ What are our staff resources, skill sets, and organization, and do they support our business processes well?

❏ Are state resources effectively deployed to provide the right level of services for the lowest cost?

❏ What is the culture in our organization, and is it aligned with our program strategy?

- What priority initiatives do we need to implement?

- What external assistance do we need to help guide implementation?

- What organizational, staff and business process changes do we need to implement?

- What training does our staff need to be able to manage the transformed program?

The overarching issue administrators need to address is: How do we build a performance-based program that has efficient business processes, is organized correctly, sets measurable goals and does the right things according to a broader strategy? Keeping in mind the following principles can help to ensure that Medicaid changes are successful implemented:

OPERATE MEDICAID LESS LIKE A TRADITIONAL GOVERNMENT BUREAUCRACY AND MORE ACCORDING TO PROVEN BUSINESS PRINCIPLES. Long regarded as just one in a family of health and human services programs, Medicaid can no longer be managed in a bureaucratic fashion. The cost pressures and need for informed management, based on sophisticated analysis of real data, are beyond the capabilities of Medicaid in its current incarnation. Many states are realizing that to be effective, Medicaid needs to be run with the same financial and managerial disciplines used to operate a modern insurance or health care company. With this in mind, states should focus more intently on enhanced financial management, improved forecasts and managing against a budget.

FOCUS ON THE CORE COMPETENCIES REQUIRED TO RUN A MODERN MEDICAID PROGRAM. This step entails securing and fostering staff with skills in project management, contract management (necessitated by an increasingly heavy reliance on third-party contractors) and financial management (required by the sheer cost of the programs and their impact on a state budget).

ASSESS, UPGRADE AND REDIRECT RESOURCES TO THEIR BEST USE. States have a tendency to resist resource reallocation until a serious problem exists. The cost of making no changes is the mismatch in skills mentioned previously and a tendency to contract for specialized work—and then to contract with contractors to watch other contractors, all of which creates a riddle when it comes to management. State programs should continuously reevaluate and deploy human and financial resources to their Medicaid programs.

ARM MANAGERS WITH THE INFORMATION THEY NEED. The amount of information and data flowing through a typical Medicaid program is immense, but most states do not tap that information in a way that program managers can use to inform key decisions. Medicaid generates an ocean of data, making it something of a case study on the importance of control and reporting. The immense volume of information that flows through Medicaid and its information systems related to patient care, program costs, provider participation, and countless other program elements often serves to hamstring a state's ability to process and make use of such information.

This glut of information, coupled with the focus on the technology itself, has shifted attention away from a deeper problem: the shortage of useful management information. Many states struggle to get complete and useful managed care information. That, in conjunction with too little useful comparative data across states, makes the information pool much shallower than is desirable for decision-makers.

In addition to inadequate technological and managerial data, most states also lack the kind of sophisticated, easily accessible financial information that would help them manage Medicaid more proactively. The problem: the information systems are so huge, expensive, and time- and resource-consuming that by the time the minimum requirements to get one up and running have been met, most states are exhausted or out of money and not ready to think about enhancing the system to the point where it can actually be useful from a management information perspective.

Many states, among them Pennsylvania and New York, have invested in new, state-of-the-art decision support systems (commonly referred to as "data warehouses") to help them make sense of the multiple terabytes (that's a lot) of data. These systems are growing more and more important as program administrators are increasingly expected to extract information (not just data) from their programs to support difficult policy decisions and to ensure that those decisions are made using all available and accurate information. The New York data warehousing system saved an estimated $12 million in Medicaid fraud prevention in 2002.

RIGOROUSLY SET PERFORMANCE EXPECTATIONS, MEASURE PERFORMANCE AND HOLD PROGRAMS ACCOUNTABLE. Clear performance expectations and measurement abilities are critical to promoting program success, but they require dedicated effort to develop and even more effort to evaluate continuously—investments that are typically worth making.

Innovative reform strategies, be they managerial, process-based, or technology or people-centric, are key to enacting real change in the Medicaid program. Case studies incorporating personal health care spending accounts and purchasing pools, for example, have shown considerable promise for reducing costs and enhancing quality of care. Program innovation coupled with strategic management can dramatically improve the state of Medicaid as it now exists.

Conclusion

There's nothing easy or obvious about fixing Medicaid.

From an outcome perspective, broad-brush, across the board cost-cutting is counterproductive for society and its most vulnerable citizens—simply lopping off part of the eligible population is a temporary budget fix but hardly a solution consistent with Medicaid's charter. With regard to management, it is clear that fashionable initiatives and firefighting have not worked over the longer term. Medicaid policy has been as much a product of politics and budgets as it is of rational strategic planning based on real, comprehensive data. Technology has been more an albatross than a solution, yet it is apparent that Medicaid could be run much more efficiently by going beyond compliance and implementing information systems that enable decision-making—and not simply administration.

Traditional reforms have not resulted in long-term cost savings, and it is hard to assert that the massive increase in costs has brought a superior health care program to Medicaid's customers. With the new federal funding flexibility and significant latitude from HHS, states have an unprecedented window of opportunity to take the lead and shape the debate on Medicaid reform. By making the tough choices, using improved management techniques and, most important, adopting an entrepreneurial approach to reform—trying new things to figure out what works and what doesn't—Medicaid can be transformed into a sustainable, high-performing program.

Chapter 5: The Final Word

THE CHALLENGE

• Medicaid costs have ballooned to nearly one-third of the annual budget in many states, making it the largest line item in state budgets. The current fiscal path, if left unchanged, will crowd out other state priorities.

• Medicaid has so far defied states' attempts to control its costs while maintaining and improving the health outcomes of the citizens it serves.

• While nearly half of the country's Medicaid programs have budgets the size of Fortune 500 companies, most Medicaid administrators lack the management tools needed to transform the sea of program data into useful information to inform decision making.

REFORM STRATEGIES

• *Choice-based reform.* Personal health accounts and the ability to choose health benefits packages allows health care to be tailored to the specific health care needs of an individual. Establishing a fixed benefit amount allows the state to control its Medicaid costs, while giving individuals the power to decide how those limited dollars are best spent.

• *"Connector" model.* A "connector" allows individuals to purchase private health insurance coverage at more affordable rates through a state-sponsored exchange.

• *Tiered benefits.* Customized benefits packages allow health care to be targeted to specific populations with different health care needs.

EXAMPLES

• Under the *Florida Choice* program, the state's role has shifted from claims-processing to policy and contract management, which has in turn shifted the risk of cost control to managed care plans.

• Under *Vermont's new global commitment waiver,* the federal government gives the state a lump sum payment for each person enrolled in the state's Medicaid program, leaving the state with greater freedom to manage its program and full responsibility for controlling costs.

NEXT STEPS

• *Assess the program.* An assessment of current Medicaid outcomes, technology and administration will give policy-makers and program administrators enough information about the program and the way it is administered to be able to make informed decisions about the program's strategy and the necessary reforms.

• *Ask the tough questions.* States must make difficult choices that go to the very heart of what kind of Medicaid program each state wants to have, such as which policy and management levers will be used to reduce, or at a minimum contain, program costs.

• *Give managers the information they need.* States need to give program managers the management tools they need to turn the immense volume of information that flows through Medicaid and its information systems into meaningful data to inform key decisions.

{6} *Kara Harris and Tiffany Dovey*

Integrating Health and Human Services Delivery

Shortly after Hurricane Katrina made landfall, states across the country opened their doors to storm victims trying to get back on their feet after the disaster. Michelle Kelly of Pass Christian, Mississippi, summed up the challenge faced by those displaced by Katrina: "I'm going to try to find a house by this weekend, get the kids in school by Monday, and then look for a job. That's the plan. I don't know how it's gonna work out, but that's the plan."[1]

In the ordinary world of social services, such a timetable would have been met with the same sentiment of impossibility. But something happened in Minnesota. Recognizing the need to help survivors swiftly restore a sense of normalcy to their lives, representatives from state and federal government agencies, nonprofit organizations and religious groups all convened under one roof with the single goal of meeting victims' needs—comprehensively and expeditiously. On September 15, 2006, the Minnesota State Aid Center in St. Paul, dubbed the Northern Comfort General Store, opened its doors to those who had fled from Hurricane Katrina. Families received assistance with identification, driver's licenses, Social Security, housing, legal aid, medical care, social services, school enrollments, and jobs—all in one stop.

The result? The State Aid Center was an overwhelming success. Major Rebecca Sjögren, in charge of the Salvation Army's Northern Division Women's Ministries, observed, "People are extremely appreciative of what they are receiving here. Many of them never expected or thought they would receive so much assistance in one place. They never thought they would receive new clothing, personal care items, diapers, towels, strollers, job assistance, legal aid, social services, and more, all in one center in one day."[2]

The center shut down when the flow of hurricane evacuees started to dwindle. After witnessing the level of coordination between all the various actors and the integration of service delivery that was possible, some Minnesotans wanted to know why the same level of service and convenience wasn't readily available to needy citizens on a routine basis.

They are not the only ones asking that question.

Service integration is a hot topic in state government these days, especially in business transactions and health and human services (HHS). In 2006, nearly every governor highlighted HHS in their state of the state address.[3] With Medicaid costs recently surpassing elementary and secondary education spending—accounting for 22.3 percent of total state expenditures—and case loads rising, states are pressed to find ways to uncover greater efficiencies. There is no indication that the pressure will let up in the near-term. The federal Centers for Medicare and Medicaid Services predicts that Medicaid spending will average annual growth of 8.6 percent until 2014.[4] Over the next three years states will spend an estimated $1.3 billion on integrated eligibility projects that tie multiple health and human services programs together to reduce costs and streamline service delivery mechanisms.[5]

Governors and state and local HHS officials are under tremendous pressure from politicians and the public to deliver integrated services. As Pennsylvania governor Edward Rendell explains, "Government 'of the people and by the people' also needs to be accessible."[6] While everyone agrees that integrating siloed HHS agencies offers an opportunity to save money and improve service delivery systems for citizens who rely on these benefits, there is a huge disconnect between what service integration means conceptually and how it actually is put into operation.

Most people are not sure what "service integration" even means. Some define it as combining related service offerings—for example, combining all state health care programs like Medicaid, the Children's Health Insurance Program (CHIP), and disability services—into a single offering. Others see it as grouping different departments and agencies under one umbrella organization, that is, integrating health care, nutrition, and public health services as part of health and human services delivery. To many, service integration can be as simple as a common Web portal with links to various agency websites.

The truth is service integration is all of those things—and more. To do it right, three critical elements must be addressed: service offerings, technology and workforce management. Focusing on just one is like getting new tires for your car without filling up the gas tank. It might improve the ride, but in the end you probably won't get very far.

The most effective combination of these elements depends on the particular agencies, programs and people involved. But states can't wait for the federal government to prescribe a solution; they must choose their own course of action—then make it happen themselves.

This chapter describes what service integration is and lays out the benefits that come with moving to an integrated service delivery model. It offers a new way to look at service integration in health and human services that will help government officials understand where they are now on the continuum of service integration and where they want to go. Finally, it offers guidance on how to overcome the most common challenges states encounter in moving from the conceptual to the operational level.

What Is Service Integration?

Health and human services are supposed to make life better for people. Yet many traditional methods for accessing and using those services are anything but easy to navigate.

Citizens in need of social services face a number of challenges, including a bureaucratic maze that can make it hard to get the services they need. Typically, a citizen will access various income support programs (for example, Temporary Assistance for Needy Families, or TANF, Medicaid and food stamps) at a local human services office. Job training and other state employment services are housed separately, while county- administered child welfare services are in yet another location—to say nothing of the mental health and substance abuse programs that are run out of another office, and housing and education services, among others, still elsewhere. With little coordination and information sharing between different departments and agencies, citizens are required to provide the same information over and over again. They end up getting the runaround and are forced to make multiple visits to multiple offices—and stand in multiple lines—even for services that are closely related. For example, someone on public assistance might need a variety of related services, including job training and placement, child care, food stamps and drug rehabilitation. Navigating the maze places a tremendous time burden on individuals in need—time that could be better spent working toward independence.

Advocacy groups and community partners generally face the same issues as the citizens they represent. In addition, they must rely on various agencies to interpret and clarify government programs and policies, often with conflicting direction. These inefficiencies waste tax dollars and create new problems for the very people the services are supposed to help.

Third-party providers, including community partners, encounter a similarly wide range of problems, including redundant forms, hard-to-track cases and applications, lack of a single view of the client across providers and different procedures for working with different agencies. They also face the challenge of getting paid for their services, which often requires jumping through multiple hoops to submit an invoice, mastering complicated coding and adjudication systems, and then trying to determine what the problem is when an invoice or claim is rejected.

On the other side of the desk, agency workers have their own set of issues. Recent trends in business and technology, like the widespread use of the Internet, have raised the public's expectations for responsiveness, service quality and 24/7 convenience—performance standards that agencies are challenged to meet. A recent survey of more than 1,000 social services clients in Texas found that around 80 percent of those surveyed would like the convenience and privacy of applying for benefits over the phone or on the Internet rather than having to apply in person. Four out of every five surveyed wanted flexibility to apply outside the traditional hours of 8 am to 5 pm.[7] Frontline workers bear the brunt of the public's disappointment, yet generally lack the authority, productivity tools and training to respond effectively.

Service integration addresses these problems. For citizens, their advocates and service providers, service integration means less guesswork and frustration trying to figure out the maze of fragmented government programs. Employees benefit from reduced paperwork and a closer link between programs and outcomes for families. Consider Pennsylvania's efforts.

Pennsylvania's new Web-based portal, COMPASS, puts a number of health and human services under one umbrella, regardless of where the program physically resides. The single mom who needs transportation assistance, job training, child health care and day care assistance doesn't have to travel to several different physical locations, find the transportation to

Before Service Integration

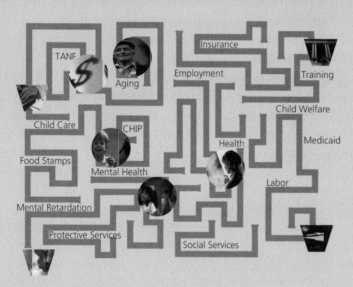

Source: Deloitte Research

Government organizations often appear to be a maze and are complex for outside customers to understand. Before services are integrated, health and human service delivery is often characterized by:

• Inconsistent business processes;

• Stovepipe applications all performing similar functions because of funding streams;

• Multiple points of contact for clients and providers;

• Clients and providers registered differently on different systems;

• Requirements for the same information to be provided to different agencies at different times;

• Duplication across the technical infrastructure leading to expensive maintenance costs; and

• Subjectively defined standards that are not enforced and monitored effectively.

do so and the energy and will to cover all bases. She is able to go to one place with all her needs and receive an integrated services plan customized just for her.

The result is a holistic approach to human services—versus something more fragmented. And for those agencies that are trying to help that single mom, integration lessens redundancy and enables a single point of contact to see that all needs are being met. The ability for those in human services to identify needs across a range of areas, put solutions in place more quickly, and save someone from filling out endless paperwork and standing in six different lines at four different locations is empowering.

Pennsylvania is not alone in its pursuit of a better model for delivering health and human services. Across the country there are efforts under way in more than half the states to better integrate service delivery, giving citizens a single point of entry for problems that require responses from multiple government units.

The Case for Integrated Services

Service integration brings related services together in a way that makes them more convenient, more accessible and more effective. Resources are focused on the real problems citizens face—not just those a particular agency is set up to address. Activities are better coordinated. And tax dollars are used more efficiently, with fewer resources wasted on redundant activities, unnecessary services and partial solutions.

Service integration also helps eliminate the walls—both real and artificial, between organizations, thus improving visibility and transparency. Workers are able to deliver services more efficiently and effectively. Agencies are able to identify fraud, waste and other avoidable costs that might otherwise slip through the cracks. And government leaders are able to allocate resources where they will do the most good.

The result? More help for more people—and more positive outcomes. A closer look at the benefits of service integration follows.

Bridging the Customer Service Gap

Compare the experience of planning a vacation using an online Web service such as Orbitz to applying for benefits through state health and human services agencies. With Orbitz, everything you need is consolidated in one place, user-friendly and can be done in one sitting (plane tickets, hotel, rental car, even vacation activities) at the user's convenience. Applying for health and human services benefits, in contrast, requires navigating a complex maze of different agencies—each operating independently with its own systems and processes—filling out multiple paper forms, often with duplicative information and only during office hours. It is not obvious why there should be such an enormous disconnect in customer service. With an increasing number of states embracing service integration, that gap is narrowing. Case in point: Massachusetts.

Recognizing that Massachusetts health and human services agencies had been left behind by the 21st century technological revolution, the state officials orchestrated the most significant reorganization of HHS in the state's history. A critical component of the effort is Virtual Gateway, an online Web portal that serves as a single front door for HHS services. Explained governor Mitt Romney, "As technology advances, we need to make sure state agencies are prepared to provide solutions in a modern, savvy way. The use of cutting-edge technology will make our programs more accessible to those who need our help the most."[8]

With the new gateway, citizens can log on to find out about the programs offered by HHS agencies and complete an anonymous online survey to determine what services they are eligible for. The hope is that by making it easier for citizens to figure out what services exist and what programs they are eligible for, families in need will take advantage of the support available to them. With Virtual Gateway, citizens can now apply for food stamps online. Explains John Wagner, the commissioner of the Massachusetts Department of Transitional Assistance: "By making the food stamp applications available online, we wish to encourage more people to apply for this important nutrition program."[9]

Third-party providers, community partners and client advocates benefit as well. Registered providers no longer have to fill out multiple forms for different programs and services. Rather, they can submit a single online application for up to 17 programs, including Medicaid, food stamps, and the Special Supplemental Nutrition Program for Women, Infants, and Children (WIC). Registered community partners can log on and see on one screen all the applications they have personally entered as well as all the ones colleagues in their organization have initiated to avoid duplication of effort. When low-income patients turn up in the emergency room, hospital staff can check to find out if the patient has any insurance. If the answer is no, they can immediately enter Medicaid application data into the system. The time it takes to complete eligibility applications for MassHealth and Uncompensated Care has plummeted from 42 minutes to only 9.[10] As of September 1, 2006, more than 277,000 applications have been processed through the gateway since it went live in 2004. Fully 90 percent of the frontline users surveyed by Community Partners report that Virtual Gateway made their jobs either somewhat or much easier.[11]

Focus on Outcomes

Integrating services can also make work more meaningful for agency workers. Service integration means a greater focus on client outcomes, and that, in turn, makes for a more rewarding work experience for those actually delivering the services. With client information available in a single system, work becomes less of a paperwork exercise and more about helping clients more toward self-sufficiency. Consider the effect Oregon's service integration had on its workforce.

In Jackson and Coos counties, health and human services—once delivered in piecemeal fashion by an array of different programs and providers—have been integrated. Employees from state, county, private and nonprofit programs work together in the same office space, under the direction of a single manager. The staff is organized into multifunctional teams that focus on families with multiple needs. A family needing food stamps, child health care and employment-related services can drop into the Ashland Family Center in Jackson County and get all its needs met by a team working toward a common goal of helping the family become self-sufficient.

After visiting health and human services offices in a dozen states in various stages of service integration, including offices in Jackson and Coos counties, Mark Ragan, a former official with the Federal Administration for Children and Families, observes: "While it was clear during discussions with hundreds of human service professionals that service integration is challenging, they were universally excited about their work. Staff and managers believe that they have seen a better way of doing business. They say that they would never go back."[12] It is not surprising that caseworkers find the holistic approach much more satisfying. By co-locating staff from multiple health and human services programs in a single office and having them work as a team, caseworkers can see the bigger picture, rather than just a bunch of disjointed parts.

Improving Value for Money

Integrating multiple health and human services programs offers an opportunity to save money and improve services to citizens who depend on these benefits. Government entities currently spend huge amounts of tax dollars determining eligibility for and operating stand-alone programs that provide food stamps, assistance payments, health care and other social services. Integrating eligibility processes and other functions for social services programs can cut the cost of delivering these services. Consider the following:

- *Florida.* The state turned to Web-based technology in 2002 as part of a "big bang" strategy to integrate its public benefit eligibility determination process. As a result, it was able to reduce the Department of Children and Families workforce by approximately 43 percent as of June 2006. During the same time period, the number of public assistance clients rose from 1.9 million to 2.3 million—a 20 percent increase in only four years.[13] By successfully leveraging technology and community partnerships, Florida has created an integrated, versatile service delivery model that has saved taxpayers over $83 million since its inception.[14]

- *California.* According to the California Performance Review (CPR), eligibility processes cost an average of $77 per person for Healthy Families, the state's Children's Health Insurance Program, compared with an average of $337 per person for Medi-Cal, CalWORKs and Food Stamps. Statewide integration would reduce the average costs for administering the three programs to $111 per recipient, saving the state $4 billion over five years according to the performance review.[15]

From the client perspective, the savings in time and travel could also be significant. The Texas Health and Human Services Commission estimates that if a third of human services applicants saved just two hours of lost time from a minimum wage job, the savings would total almost $12 million annually. Eliminating just one trip every year to the local HHS office could add up to another $4.5 million if just half of clients decided to access help over the phone, on the Internet, by mail or by fax instead of making the trip into the nearest agency office.[16]

For citizens, service integration can also mean greater stewardship of their tax dollars. A recent audit of the Colorado Department of Human Services revealed that improper welfare payments totaled $90 million in 2005.[17] Uncovering greater efficiencies and rooting out fraud and abuse— certainly not unique to Colorado—means that tax dollars go further and reach their intended destination.

Table 1: Summary of Benefits from Service Integration	
Benefits to Citizens	**Benefits to Advocacy Groups**
• Services that are easier to locate and use • Complete solutions to real problems • Less runaround • Less paperwork • Services available 24/7 • Greater stewardship of tax dollars	• Improved convenience and service for citizens • Consistent guidance from agencies • Less time required to navigate bureaucracy on behalf of citizens
Benefits to Agencies, Agency Workers	**Benefits to Third-party providers, community partners**
• Improved efficiency and reduced transaction costs • Improved effectiveness and outcomes • Ability to resolve problems completely and permanently, reducing the overall workload • Improved ability to identify and eliminate fraud, errors, overlap and waste • Easier and cheaper to develop and maintain systems • Client information consolidated in a single system • Improved job satisfaction, making it easier to attract and retain talent	• Easier to do business with agencies (enrolling, registering, getting paid) • Easier to connect with the citizens who need help • One system to work with • Streamlined processes

Source: Deloitte Research

Roadmap for Service Integration

After defining service integration and understanding the benefits that it offers, the next step for government agencies is to draw up their roadmap for service integration. Organizations pursuing service integration have many choices to make along the integration path. Service integration is not formulaic; it can be pursued in both incremental and large-scale initiatives.

Service integration can be viewed as a continuum of capabilities and choices. At one extreme, there is little or no integration (even within a single agency). Services are narrowly defined and offered in isolation, with people and systems focused on a single service.

At the other end is full integration within and among human service agencies and their external partners. In a fully integrated service model, citizens and families are managed as individual cases, with teams work-

Figure 1: Service Integration in 3-D

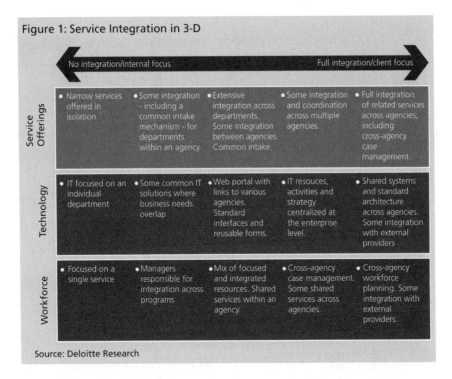

Source: Deloitte Research

ing across agencies—and often across sectors—to deliver all the appropriate services. Service providers are cross-trained to recognize and handle a wide range of related problems, and are supported by integrated systems that enable information sharing between departments, agencies, third-party providers and community partners. Systems and support are provided by shared service centers, maximizing coordination and eliminating duplication and waste between organizations.

Every agency in human services can benefit from some level of integration. But, depending on where you are starting from, full integration can be overkill in some situations.

The service integration roadmap for human services (see figure 1) describes the range of integration capabilities on each of the three key dimensions: *service offerings*, *technology* and *workforce*. It is designed to help agencies assess their current capabilities—and to help them decide where they want to go.

Choosing the Right Destination

The service integration roadmap reflects a range of capabilities along three key dimensions. However, the ideal mix varies from one organization to the next.

As *service offerings* move toward full integration, they are increasingly organized around a citizen's specific needs, with services from various departments and agencies combined to address problems from every angle. New York City's online portal, NYC.gov, for example, is organized from the citizen's perspective. Citizens access services based on their "intentions"—rather than having to locate the specific department or agency that administers the particular program or service they are trying to find. The portal is organized by categories (employment, insurance, and children, for example) that are understandable to the average New Yorker, not just those in the bureaucracy.[18] That is a fundamental shift in the way citizens access services.

As *technology* moves toward full integration, it generally migrates toward shared services, integrated systems, shared applications and shared databases—enabling business processes to be more flexible and making it easier for people to collaborate across different departments and agencies. Analytical capabilities are also more advanced, with data warehouses and business intelligence tools giving managers the insight they need to allocate resources effectively—and to detect fraud and waste across boundaries.

As the *workforce* moves toward full integration, people are increasingly organized into multidisciplinary teams and cross-trained to address a wider range of program areas. Shared services and collaboration across organizational boundaries is common. Workers tend to have diverse program knowledge and technical skills. And the work itself tends to be more satisfying because there are more successful outcomes—making it easier to attract and retain top-quality staff.

Different organizations combine these three dimensions in different ways. In some cases, the cost of full integration outweighs the benefits—at least in the near term. In other cases, lack of support from the public or key government leaders makes full integration impossible, at least initially.

Wisconsin, for example, has achieved a high level of integration across all three dimensions. Texas is striving for full integration across all three dimensions—and has the funding and mandate to do so. Massachusetts, in contrast, is striving for a high level of integration in service offerings and technology, but a medium level of integration for its workforce. As these examples show, the "right" destination depends on a government agency's vision and objectives.

Here are some things governments need to keep in mind when devising their integration strategies.

- *Focus on stakeholders.* Look at the problem from the perspective of the major stakeholders (agency workers, third-party providers, advocacy groups and, most important, citizens). Successful integration strategies generate meaningful benefits for all key players.

- *Identify points of diminishing returns.* Service integration can generate significant value, but at some point the costs begin to outweigh the benefits. Go beyond that, and integration is pursued for its own sake.

- *Mix and match.* Many organizations will find their best option is a hybrid of integration and specialization. Some issues such as unemployment or family services will lend themselves to an integrated approach—using integrated services, systems and workers. Others such as disease detection and surveillance may continue to be delivered using specialized resources and a highly focused approach.

Getting from Here to There

Service integration is a major undertaking, rife with potential pitfalls. Here we examine the most common roadblocks and provide guidance on how to avoid them.

How Fast and How Far?

There are countless ways to implement service integration, but most organizations gravitate to one of two approaches. They either launch a massive transformation program that tries to implement the entire integration as one huge project—typically over a period of three to five years. Or they launch smaller, focused initiatives that each address part of the service integration challenge, gradually transforming the organization through a series of individual projects.

A few states are currently pursuing or considering a comprehensive, multi-year transformation—revamping their systems, developing new, integrated services and processes and adding new systems to support the new processes—all while shifting their workforces to more of an outsourced model. Texas, for example, is in the process of transforming all of these things at the same time—and discovering that trying to accomplish too much, too quickly can create unanticipated challenges.

Pennsylvania's Incremental Approach to Service Integration

In 1999 when initial plans were drawn up to create a simple on-line portal for health care applications that later became known as the Commonwealth of Pennsylvania Access to Social Services (COMPASS), no one in the state Department of Public Welfare could have foreseen the far-reaching implications of these integration efforts. As a pioneer in providing online access to services applications, Pennsylvania's trail-blazing effort has not been without its challenges. The process has been slow and a great deal of work has yet to be done. But the state's one-project-at-a-time strategy created an admirable long-term track record of consolidated, efficient, and easily accessible services.

Pre-COMPASS

As late as 1999, service delivery for all of Pennsylvania social services was paper-based and depended on face-to-face interactions. Like many other states, Pennsylvania citizens had to fill out separate applications in several different government departments and programs. TANF, Food Stamps, and Medicaid were found in the Department of Public Welfare (DPW). The National School Lunch Program applications were administered by the Pennsylvania Department of Education. And health care for pregnant women and children was administered by the Pennsylvania Insurance Department (PID).

Other inefficiencies existed as well. For example, welfare recipients who had to work a certain number of hours had difficulty going to a government office during the day. Michael Coulson, director of program support in the DPW, describes the problem: "With the regulations that require welfare recipients to work a certain amount of hours, we felt a need to expand the number of hours our services were available. That wasn't easy, because we needed the evening hours to run batch processes on the mainframe. We can't have our client information system up and available to caseworkers during that time. Also, with unions, there was reluctance for people to work evening hours."[19]

Many citizens who simply wanted to know if they were eligible for a certain service had to spend 20 to 30 minutes to fill out an application and then wait for a response. And particularly with application procedures that demanded cross-department communications, the turnaround time was long and unpredictable. In response to these and other issues, Pennsylvania devised a strategy to improve social services.

Strategy

In 1999, the DPW set out to make citizen access to government services more readily available. The first partnership, between DPW and PID, was established to allow citizens to apply online for limited health care programs for pregnant women and children. Medicaid, cash assistance, and food stamps were later added to COMPASS. Long-term care and home and community services came next. The strategy was simple: integrate each social service program into COMPASS one project at a time.

The main reason for this "incremental renewal strategy" was lack of funding for large-scale transformation all at once. Yet the strategy proved to have its own advantages. For example, the naturally evolving process encouraged cross-program funding. When a social services government program saw the positive citizen response from one project, it expressed interest and provided some of its own funds to become part of the integrated system. Another advantage of the incremental renewal strategy was the ability to make on-going adjustments. Input from advocates and local agencies was used to continually hone the operation, ensuring that end users were satisfied that the system worked well.

Results

The response of citizens is reflected in the rate of applications per month. In April 2003, COMPASS received roughly 2,000 applications per month. By April 2006, that rate increased to 9,000 applications. Nearly 50 percent of all COMPASS applications are now received outside the hours of 9 to 5.

Another important aspect of COMPASS, and Pennsylvania's integrated services in general, is the bolstered relationship between government and community partners. COMPASS allows community partners to access protected citizen information to aid citizens and provide them with other services. Case in point: the National School Lunch Program. In early 2005, the federal government changed the process by requiring school districts to provide free school lunches for any student who claimed eligibility for TANF and food stamps. The federal laws also required that school districts verify citizen eligibility, an inherently arduous process because the school districts lacked access to that sort of information. Fortunately, COMPASS electronic interfaces were already built into the DPW eligibility system. The built-in interface was simply expanded to provide school districts with secure access to the data they needed.

The integrated project is on-going, and given both the successful history and the number of programs yet to be integrated, it will not be finished anytime soon. The gradual addition of new programs is likely to create more successes like school lunch. Coulson, summarizing both the vision and the major challenge of the incremental strategy, said he did not "see an end to the possibilities. A lot will depend on the budget, so we may not be able to move as quickly as we want to. But until we get every social service program in Pennsylvania on there, we won't be satisfied that it's finished."

In May 2003, the Texas legislature mandated a complete overhaul of the state's Health and Human Services agencies. The state's transition plan called for the design, development and deployment of new technology and a new business model, along with a new workforce. Everything was legislated to be fully operational within just 15 months—an unprecedented speed with which to carry out such a massive transition.

The state's overhaul has not gone as smoothly as planners had hoped, with unanticipated problems arising since the plan went into effect. Some customers have experienced long wait times when they phone into the state's new call centers and have received incorrect information from inexperienced staff unfamiliar with the "ins" and "outs" of complex policies for Medicaid, food stamps and TANF. As a result, the state has had to revise its ambitious plan to take account of the lessons learned along the way, extending the implementation timeline to make it more realistic.

New Hampshire and Pennsylvania are taking things one step at time— developing basic capabilities in one or two areas, then gradually extending and refining those capabilities over time.

Large transformational projects such as the one under way in Texas and incremental approaches such as COMPASS in Pennsylvania have advantages and disadvantages—and the right choice varies from one situation to the next. Questions to consider include:

- Does the organization have the *appetite* for a major transformation? Or is it already exhausted by change?

- Are *financial resources* available for a long-term project? Or is a quick return on investment needed?

In the end, either a big bang or incremental approach can succeed—or fail. The key to success is striking the right balance. If an incremental approach is selected, it still pays to think about the overall process as a complete transformation. That big-picture perspective will help ensure the pieces fit together. Conversely, if a comprehensive approach is adopted, the overall effort should still be structured as a series of smaller initiatives that can deliver intermediate benefits and reduce risk. In other words, the best approach is often a hybrid—combining the broad strategic perspective of an all-out transformation with the quick-win benefits of an incremental approach.

The Cost Paradox

Service integration delivers services more efficiently, driving transaction costs down and improving longer-term outcomes for recipients. At the same time, efficient integration may increase the volume of services an agency delivers. If the increases in volume outweigh the efficiency savings, an agency's total costs might actually rise—particularly in the short term—which could be a deal breaker for cash-strapped state governments. In the past, bureaucratic silos and red tape effectively served to ration services. But now that service integration is eliminating those barriers, how can agencies prevent their costs from skyrocketing?

First, focus on longer-term costs and benefits. Because integrated services generally focus on the whole problem—rather than one small part—clients may become self-sufficient faster, reducing an agency's costs and volume in the long run. California's community mental health treatment program provides integrated service delivery to citizens with severe mental illness who are at risk of homelessness or incarceration. Bringing mental health, substance abuse, housing, outreach and employment services together has reduced recidivism among the program's population, in terms of hospitalization and incarceration. The integrated approach has delivered annual savings of $7 million to the state and the county.[20]

The goal is to move away from the old system, which rewarded people who were good at filling out forms, mastering complex rules and waiting in line, toward a fair process for allocating services based on actual need. That is a big responsibility, but it is an enviable one—giving agencies the opportunity to help those citizens who really need it.

Second, with a seamless view across organizational boundaries, governments can identify and eliminate avoidable costs such as fraud and waste. They can also allocate resources more effectively—increasing their investments in programs that are doing the most good. Utah's new integrated information system that allows greater information sharing among state agencies has cut caseload errors by half.[21]

Privacy Concerns

Integrated systems and shared information are inherently more efficient and effective than silo solutions. They eliminate overlapping forms and paperwork, reduce the cost of maintaining redundant systems and data, minimize the chances for data entry errors and conflicting data and thereby help agencies make more informed decisions.

Yet service integration also can raise concerns about privacy and confidentiality. Integrated service delivery requires collecting, managing and sharing information in digital form across a broad network of public, private and nonprofit providers—creating significant potential for misusing data. A well-designed system can minimize the problem, however, by establishing precise levels of access for every user. For example, a health care process could provide a limited level of access for agencies and administrators that process applications and a more in-depth level of access for physicians and nurses dealing with disease and diagnosis data, while still maintaining compliance with federally mandated privacy regulations.

An integrated system also allows agencies to adjust access rights as privacy policies change. That is particularly important in these fast-changing times, when many organizations are still learning what they can and cannot share. More often than not, policies about information sharing and privacy have evolved over decades, with each generation of management adding its own interpretation and restrictions. Yet when agencies refer back to the original legislation, they sometimes find they have more latitude than they thought—creating more flexibility to do what is best for the citizens and communities they serve.

Engage Users

Remembering the customer is critical to success. For example, to facilitate the state's efforts to integrate health care delivery, Massachusetts engaged hospitals—the ultimate customer of the system—early in the process and design stages. As a result, hospitals are using the system for 80 percent of their applications—a greater adoption than was anticipated for the system.

And do not forget staff. They are part of the overall solution. Service integration is a big organizational change. People hearing the words efficiency and decommissioning can naturally fear for their jobs. Without understanding the goals, they may even try to undermine the work. Keeping open communication lines about the objectives and outcomes of service integration efforts can help to ease concerns.

Overcoming Opposition from Within

State leaders must also consider certain internal structural obstacles to service integration from within. First, it is important to garner buy-in from the mid-level managers inside state government. Many of these managers have learned the unwritten rule that the more full-time employees and the bigger the budget a manager controls the more power and prestige that manager wields inside a state government. Because service integration projects might shrink staff and budgets for at least some mid-level managers, these managers might oppose change for parochial reasons. But their technical knowledge and day-to-day operational control of the very programs in need of reform make these mid-level managers essential allies in any big change. Experience shows that mid-level managers can be brought on board if given the proper incentives. Most important, state leadership must affirmatively communicate the reasons for the change and underscore the service improvements that are expected as a result. In addition, incentives such as cash bonuses for delivering services with fewer people or a smaller budget and new responsibilities for successful managers will also help counter initial resistance to change.

Second, many states have powerful labor unions that may view with skepticism any integration reforms that reduce staff, streamline the number of service delivery locations or change delegations of authority and reporting lines. Therefore, it is a good general policy to engage labor unions early in the process, hear the concerns of the workforce and take action to address reasonable concerns. In the event that a particular service integration project will result in downsizing a particular operation, a number of steps can be taken to ease labor's concerns. For example, preferential transfers into other high-priority state jobs, "early-out" compensation packages and training for new opportunities are just a few of the options available to ease the transition for workers.

Governing by Network

In recent years, government has seen a dramatic shift toward greater use of the private sector to deliver services. In a growing number of areas, many of the services are delivered through networks of private parties, nonprofit organizations, community partners and citizen self-service—rather than by the agencies themselves. Consider Florida's Department of Children and Families (DCF).

In 2003, the Florida State Legislature enacted budget cuts mandating that DCF develop an alternative service delivery model—one that better utilized technology to integrate the eligibility application process for major public benefits while simultaneously cutting the existing labor pool by 50 percent.[22] The following year hurricanes Charley, Frances, Ivan and Jean put tremendous pressure on Florida's public benefit system. Over 2 million disaster victims became eligible for food stamp benefits within a few short months, yet many of them did not have the capacity to drive to their local welfare office to undergo the benefit determination process.[23]

Leveraging the accessibility of the Internet, DCF created ACCESS Florida, an online portal that allows citizens to apply for benefits via the Web. For Florida, the increased accessibility provided by a Web-based application process allowed DCF to quickly change its business model. Now, greeters and helpers are posted in agency lobbies to assist clients in accessing self-service computer terminals. In addition, toll-free customer call centers have been created to assist clients in filling out forms over the Internet. These technologies have allowed DCF to restructure its workforce to enhance the integrated service design. Caseworkers who were once spread out across a myriad of agency locations are now centralized at regional call centers enabling the overall DCF workforce to be reduced by approximately 43 percent.

In addition to agency offices, more than 2,500 community partner sites—including hospitals, homeless shelters, health clinics, libraries, churches and workforce one-stops have committed to opening ACCESS Florida terminals for public use. Without the support of these partner organizations, the Florida DCF would not have been able to achieve such a dramatic reduction in its workforce.

With partnering on the rise, government agencies can no longer just mandate change. They have to *sell* it. Success requires effective marketing, managing and training.

When marketing the program, agencies need to target service providers and stakeholder groups with dedicated communication campaigns, highlighting the specific benefits and concerns—along with solutions for addressing those concerns—for each stakeholder group. Examples of marketing vehicles include posters in public places such as libraries and schools, informational inserts in gas and electric bills, press releases and local media coverage and quotes and testimonials from community partners and advocacy groups. But the government can not stop there. Government agencies also need to leverage community partners in order to spread the message. One way to do this is to engage them in pilot initiatives. Doing so can help identify problems early and also spread positive public relations.

Second, everyone needs to be involved in the transformation process in order to establish a sense of personal ownership. This can be accomplished by conducting interviews, focus groups and feedback sessions with stakeholder groups. Experienced people should also be recruited for the project team—including representatives from leading community partners and

Service Integration Self-Assessment

- Is there a clear understanding of customers' service expectations?
- Is the organization aligned to meet customer expectations?
- Are systematic processes in place for administrative and programmatic reviews?
- Is communication to customers and staff clear and consistent?
- Is access to client and program information timely and consistent?

third-party providers. Actively managing change also requires communicating with key stakeholders early and often.

Third, the shift to a "network" model of government naturally gives agencies more options for getting work done. However, to fully capitalize on that flexibility, agencies must continue to develop their ability to manage external providers—a challenge that is often very different from managing the work itself.

Last, selling change requires providing extensive training to everyone—from agency workers to external providers to clients. Training is a key investment for the transition to an integrated model to be successful.

Staying Flexible

Perhaps the greatest challenge of all is developing integrated systems and processes that will remain relevant and useful years in the future. The world is moving faster than ever—fueled by sweeping social and technical trends—and there's no way to know which way things will go. What services will people need? How will people want to access those services? What technologies will predominate?

A service integration strategy must be designed with an eye to the future. But even more important, solutions must be flexible enough to adjust to whatever the future holds. In these rapidly changing times, no agency can afford to be chained to rigid and inflexible systems, processes and organization models.

From a technology perspective, one way to achieve flexibility is through a server-based technology architecture, which is intrinsically more flexible and scalable than a mainframe platform. Another way is through reusable technology components. Reusable components speed up development by freeing programmers from constantly reinventing the wheel. Moreover, when changes are required, they only need to be made in one place—rather than in each separate application—making it easier to adapt a system to new and changing requirements.

Deploying the right processes, systems and organization models gives states and agencies tremendous flexibility in deciding which services to integrate—and how to deliver them. Agencies can quickly change the way they do business in response to changing needs. And constituents have many more options for how they access and consume services—instead of being locked into a single, rigid approach.

Staying on Course

Finally, success requires simply staying the course once set. Service integration is a significant undertaking that can take years to complete. Success requires a long-term commitment and a reliable source of funds—two requirements that can be hard to sustain through shifts in the political climate. It also requires cooperation and support from existing stakeholders—some who have a vested interest in the status quo, and others who are simply afraid of change. Here are some proven techniques to help build an enduring base of support and funding:

- *Focus on intrinsic benefits.* The efficiency and effectiveness of service integration are compelling—and transcend personal agendas. It's important to stay focused on these overall goals throughout the transformation process.

- *Strive for a broad base of support.* Avoid tying the integration effort to a particular leader, political party or isolated metric.

- *Break the project into manageable pieces.* Structure the work so it accomplishes a significant milestone and delivers tangible benefits on a regular basis. Continuous success helps build credibility and momentum—and gives current leaders something to crow about. For example, in Pennsylvania, the current administration has continued to refine and expand on service integration projects initiated by a previous administration—improvements the current leadership can rightfully claim as their own.

- *Set reasonable expectations.* Although service integration offers significant benefits, it's not an instant cure-all. Some benefits such as 24/7 access and worker productivity show up immediately. Others such as fraud detection can take longer to develop. A rigorous business case that articulates the expected benefits and timing helps avoid the pitfall of expecting too much, too soon. It also provides a baseline for tracking progress and success.

- *Plan the work and revisit the plan.* Once a plan is developed, it will need to be revisited periodically. An annual planning exercise seems to work best from the perspective of fiscal-year planning and by having tangible goals that can be accomplished within a reasonable timeframe. For example, the State of Wisconsin formulated a long-term strategic plan to expand access for services to its citizens for health and nutrition programs. This plan sets the agenda, business drivers and an implementation direction. It also set incremental goals along the way as measures of success as well as points of reevaluation.

Finding Your Bearings

The following assessment has been designed to assist government agencies in determining their readiness and need for service integration.

IS THERE A CLEAR UNDERSTANDING OF CUSTOMERS' SERVICE EXPECTATIONS? Customers now expect to interact with government much as they do with retail businesses, receiving information when they want it, not just when a government office is open. State government needs the infrastructure and workforce capabilities to handle these needs. Government agencies lacking these capabilities need to determine what it will take to obtain them.

IS THE ORGANIZATION ALIGNED TO MEET CUSTOMER EXPECTATIONS? For example, if services are being provided in an office, on the Internet and through a call center, do the organization's processes align efficiently across all three, or are duplicative processes created, making it easier from an administrative perspective but harder on the customer?

ARE THERE SYSTEMATIC PROCESSES IN PLACE FOR ADMINISTRATIVE AND PROGRAMMATIC REVIEWS? Are there effective procedures in place to ensure accountability across programs? What about changes in federal and state policy regulations occurring at varied times throughout the year? Are these changes handled with little disruption to ongoing business activities?

IS COMMUNICATION TO CUSTOMERS AND STAFF CLEAR AND CONSISTENT? While many may be tempted to immediately answer yes, consider the number of calls received about unclear mailings or about the instructions on application forms for services? Is it possible that communications could be improved? Have staff ever learned about a new initiative or program from the newspaper, or an outside source, or even worse, been surprised when a client called with a question on a new program they were not familiar with or didn't know had started yet?

IS ACCESS TO CLIENT AND PROGRAM INFORMATION TIMELY AND CONSISTENT? Managing information and access to that information is a common denominator across public and private sector businesses alike. The ability to quickly obtain and synthesize this information is not, however. Service integration provides the ability for data to be integrated across service areas and combined in ways that allow business decisions to be made using data, not speculation. In trying budgetary times, legislators and budget officials need to make tough decisions on allocating limited funds. Information drives these decisions, and health and human services organizations are often left behind because they lack ready access to meaningful and reliable data. The last time program or client information was needed for decision-making, how many people and ad hoc reporting requests had to be made to get the data? How long did it take?

After answering these questions, government agencies will be in a better position to determine their needs and their path for service integration. However, part of that determination has to come in the form of a cost-benefit analysis of service integration practices.

Conclusion

Service integration presents significant opportunities as well as challenges. Many government organizations pursue service integration in the wrong way. More often than not, they focus on one narrow aspect of the problem—usually technology—without developing the necessary capabilities in other areas. Then they are disappointed when the results fall short of expectations.

Successful service integration requires a mix of capabilities across three key dimensions: service offerings, technology and workforce.

Chapter 6: The Final Word

THE CHALLENGE

• Governors and state and local health and human services officials are under tremendous pressure from politicians and the public to improve service delivery systems for citizens in need of public assistance.

• Citizens in need of social services face a number of challenges, including a bureaucratic maze that can make it hard to get the assistance they need.

• While states are working to integrate siloed HHS agencies, there is a disconnect between what service integration means conceptually and how it actually gets operationalized.

REFORM STRATEGIES

• *Adopt a comprehensive approach.* Service integration requires a mix of capabilities across three key dimensions: service offerings, technology and workforce. The ideal mix varies from one organization to the next.

• *Focus on stakeholders.* Look at the problem from the perspective of your major stakeholders (agency workers, third-party providers, advocacy groups and, most important, citizens). Successful integration strategies generate meaningful benefits for all key players.

• *Mix and match.* Many organizations will find their best option is a hybrid of integration and specialization.

EXAMPLES

• *Massachusetts' Virtual Gateway* is an online portal that serves as a single front door for health and human services programs. The gateway streamlines the application procedure and reduces the time and effort required to access services.

• *Pennsylvania's COMPASS* started as a simple online portal for health care applications. It has grown incrementally to a one-stop shop for multiple health and human services programs.

• *ACCESS Florida* is a Web-based application designed to meet the increased demand for public benefits following the 2004 and 2005 hurricane seasons while simultaneously cutting the state's HHS workforce in half. Call centers were set up and community partnerships across the state were leveraged to assist citizens with the new online process for applying for benefits.

NEXT STEPS

• *Conduct a self-assessment.* This analysis determines the organization's readiness and need for service integration.

• *Draw up a roadmap.* The roadmap is the optimal plan for service integration.

• *Perform a cost/benefit analysis.* Such an analysis helps determine the point at which the cost of full integration outweighs the benefits.

• *Remember that the customer is critical to success.* If the needs of the ultimate customer of the integrated system are not included in the initial process and design stages, the effort is likely to fail.

{ 7 } *William D. Eggers and Merrill Douglas*

Upgrading Emergency Preparedness and Response

Soon after Hurricane Katrina hit the Gulf Coast on August 29, 2005, the *Washington Post* threw a spotlight on three individuals who would never see the storm fade away. For Louisiana governor Kathleen Blanco, Mississippi governor Haley Barbour and, to a lesser extent, Alabama governor Bob Riley, Katrina "will define and dominate their public lives for the duration of their time in office," said a *Post* reporter on Sept. 1, 2005.[1]

A public executive's leadership in a disaster could well become his or her most important legacy. New York mayor Rudolph Giuliani's performance in the days after the September 11 terrorist attacks—his strong management, effective coordination of emergency response and frequent appearances on radio and TV—made him a national figure. Some believe it could one day make him president.

In a similar way, a governor's performance in an emergency—and what that performance says about his or her ability to manage—may well shape that governor's future career.

Hurricane Katrina was one of the most devastating natural disasters to hit the United States. Largely due to the failures of government at all levels to plan, prepare for and respond aggressively to the storm, emergency preparedness policies are being redrawn at the federal level of government. The focus will necessarily be on building capabilities, improving communication and coordination and managing risk at all levels of government. But even as capabilities are built and new, more efficient interfaces with the federal government developed, the long-standing principle that emergency preparedness begins at the lowest possible jurisdictional level probably won't change. Local and state governments are still "on the hook" for all phases of emergency management—from preparing and planning to response to recovery.

The list of emergencies for which states need to prepare is daunting in size and variety. In the 10 years from 1996 through 2005, a total of 82 hurricanes, 40 of them considered major, swept through the Atlantic basin.[2] While not every hurricane makes landfall in the United States, state and local officials in storm-prone regions must prepare as though each of them will.

In some parts of the United States, tornadoes often threaten property and lives. The National Weather Service reported 1,376 tornadoes in 2003, 1,819 in 2004 and 1,264 in 2005.[3] Wildfires also tax the resources of emergency responders year after year. From January 1, 2000, through May 24, 2006, such fires burned a total of more than 6 million acres across the country.[4]

Along with disasters that recur many times in a season, governors must prepare for the kinds of events that, although rare, exact terrible costs. In 1993 widespread flooding on the Mississippi River killed 52 people, damaged or destroyed nearly 50,000 homes and made more than 12,000 square miles of farmland useless. Losses from the flood were estimated at $15 billion to $20 billion.[5]

The Northridge Earthquake of 1994 killed 51 people and injured more than 9,000, left 22,000 people homeless, forced portions of 11 major roadways in the Los Angeles area to close and caused $44 billion in damage.[6]

The power outage that darkened the northeastern United States and Ontario, Canada, in 2003 became a nightmare for many states and cities. In Cleveland, for example, it caused the public water system to fail, depriving tens of thousands of people of safe drinking water. Also, as Ohio governor Bob Taft explained to the U.S. House Committee on Energy and Commerce, "the interruption of business activity resulted in the loss of millions of dollars of economic activity that will not be fully recouped through private insurance and state or federal programs."[7]

Major disasters, those we have endured and those we will face in the future, loom large in the American imagination. The release of recordings of phone calls from the World Trade Center to 911 operators, and the recent movies *World Trade Center* and *United 93*, have reawakened memories of September 11, 2001. Even as the Gulf region braced for the 2006 hurricane season, evacuees from Hurricane Katrina still lived scattered across the United

States, wondering if and when they would ever be able to go home. Public safety agencies scramble to deploy new technologies to detect and prevent attacks by explosive or biological agent, or to save lives if terrorists should slip through their safeguards. Health officials lay plans for managing an avian flu pandemic. Meanwhile, citizens and first responders struggle with the yearly round of floods, tornadoes, ice storms, mud slides and wildfires.

Emergency management, of course, demands networked collaboration. Planners and responders on the federal, state and local levels, and from the not-for-profit and private sectors, all make vital contributions. But in a major disaster, the state plays a pivotal role, communicating needs to partners above and below and making sure the right resources flow to the right places at the right times.

When Hurricane Andrew crashed through parts of southern Florida in 1992, frightened residents sat in the rubble of their homes for days, waiting for food and water, while looters emptied stores. Part of the problem, reported Kate Hale, director of emergency management for Miami-Dade County at the time, was that federal agencies somehow came to believe that local officials didn't want the aid they stood ready to provide. "The state was unable to coordinate effectively with the federal government," she said. And when state officials, arriving in Homestead by helicopter, saw the devastation all around them, they initially committed most of the state's relief resources to that city, "which was only a small part of the area of impact," she said.[8]

In the 14 years since Andrew, Florida has overhauled its emergency management strategies, under the leadership of its governors. Now it sets the standard for emergency planning and response. "One of the biggest differences between how Florida and other states handle natural disasters lies in the degree of cooperation between cities, counties and the state," said a story in the *Palm Beach Post* in September, 2005. "In Florida, they are in constant communication with one another as storms and advance during the recovery phase."[9]

Having honed its emergency management capabilities through numerous hurricanes over the years, Florida can now move quickly when disaster strikes, either inside its own borders or in neighboring states. "Within hours of Katrina's landfall, Florida began deploying more than 3,700 first responders to Mississippi and Louisiana," Governor Jeb Bush wrote in an op-ed piece in the *Washington Post* in September 2005.[10]

Florida's emergency management plan depends on effective coordination among numerous local and state officials, volunteer organizations,

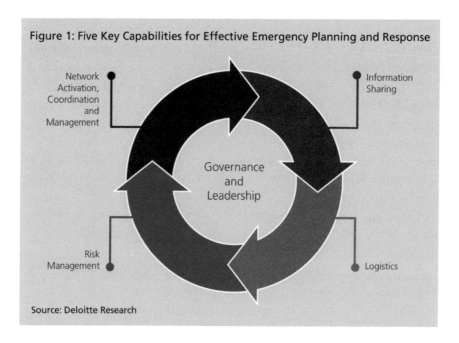

Figure 1: Five Key Capabilities for Effective Emergency Planning and Response

Network Activation, Coordination and Management

Information Sharing

Governance and Leadership

Risk Management

Logistics

Source: Deloitte Research

public and private health care organizations and utility companies. As governors plan for future disasters, they will find it critical to create similar networks of organizations, each with well-rehearsed tactics they can deploy as soon as needed.

A governor who excels in emergency planning and response is one who has mastered these five key areas (see figure 1):

- Network activation, coordination and management
- Information sharing
- Logistics
- Risk management
- Governance and leadership

Designing, Integrating and Activating Emergency Response Networks

Emergency management and response is first and foremost about integrating a disparate array of organizations—FEMA (Federal Emergency Management Agency), first responders, local governments, Red Cross, nonprofits, private companies—into functioning networks that share information, coordinate activities and synchronize responses to prepare for widespread emergencies and respond to them when they occur. To be sure, one element of the National Response Plan is the mandated Incident Command System, a command and control structure. However, without augmenting this with effective network coordination and management, the response to a disaster, public health epidemic or terrorism incident will likely not be timely or effective. Organizations with the best of intentions end up duplicating one another's efforts in some areas, while other vital needs fall through the cracks. Lack of knowledge of assigned roles in the network prevents these organizations from performing their duties. Lack of coordination means affected areas have to wait days for FEMA to deliver various goods and services, while officials at FEMA wait for affected states to issue formal requests. Lack of interoperable database systems means organizations can't effectively track requests for assistance. In short, the lack of a networked approach typically means a slow, uncoordinated, overly rigid, procedure-bound response.

The realization that we are vulnerable to terrorist acts on American soil makes a well-integrated network response more critical today than ever. The emergency management network, no longer focused only on natural disasters, now includes many local, state and federal agencies with investigatory responsibilities. These are loosely tied to legacy emergency management agencies through an existing emergency management function or new state office of homeland security. Many traditional emergency management personnel, however, lack access to material aimed at prevention and detection simply because they don't meet the "need to know" criteria. Fusing groups that have not worked together in the past creates a tremendous potential for conflict. The situation demands leadership and clearly defined roles.

So what should a state government do to ensure an integrated, networked response? The most important principle to bear in mind is that the role of state government is not necessarily always to stand in the center, shoulder the main burden and call upon partners to supplement its efforts here and there. Instead, state government's role is to coordinate a network of networks.

Public officials need to identify effective emergency response networks that already exist, allow each of them to do the work they do best and encourage these groups to multiply their power by working together. For example, a pandemic flu outbreak would mean coordinating networks across state and local public health and safety services; federal emergency management, health, and homeland security agencies; relevant international agen-

The Evolving Federal, State, Local Relationship in Emergency Planning

In the wake of 9/11, the federal government moved to provide billions of dollars of aid to local, state and tribal governments to enhance preparedness levels, or "capabilities." The "carrot"—federal funding—is tied to a plethora of "sticks"—grant compliance requirements and mandated activities. Most notable among the requirements is the National Incident Management System (NIMS) implementation timeline. Starting in FY 2007 full compliance with NIMS implementation guidelines is required in order to be considered for all federal preparedness funds. In subsequent years, state and local governments must continue to meet evolving requirements identified by the NIMS Integration Center as a prerequisite to receiving federal preparedness funding. This places states in a unique position of promoting a federal ideal to local units of government as a condition of receiving federal homeland security funding.

Another notable feature of federal homeland security and the Centers for Disease Control and Prevention funding is the requirement that 80 percent of the funds be passed through to local units of government. That means only 20 percent may be retained by the states to fund competing priorities across state agencies with commensurate responsibilities. This requirement, and a plethora of others, demands a review of governance, accountability, transparency in decision-making and robust strategic planning.

Capabilities-Based Planning

Recognizing that always being prepared for every possible event is simply not feasible in a world of finite resources, the U.S. Department of Homeland Security (DHS) issued the Interim National Preparedness Goal calling for risk-based target levels of capability—the idea being that federal funds should be allocated on the basis of risk. Capabilities-based planning (see figure 2) requires all levels of government to identify a plausible range of threats and hazards, to determine the tasks necessary at each event phase (prevention, protection, response and recovery) and to articulate the capability needed to minimize the impact on lives, property and the economy. Through this process, federal, state, local and tribal governments are able to prioritize their needs and tailor their strategies accordingly.

State Homeland Security and Emergency Management Responsibilities

Emergency preparedness is a task for all levels of government, as well as all agencies within government. Given their proximity to incidents, government agencies in communities are the first to provide aid. Hurricane Katrina demonstrated that for at least the first 72 hours, local agencies

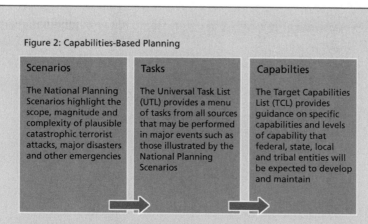

Figure 2: Capabilities-Based Planning

Scenarios	Tasks	Capabilties
The National Planning Scenarios highlight the scope, magnitude and complexity of plausible catastrophic terrorist attacks, major disasters and other emergencies	The Universal Task List (UTL) provides a menu of tasks from all sources that may be performed in major events such as those illustrated by the National Planning Scenarios	The Target Capabilities List (TCL) provides guidance on specific capabilities and levels of capability that federal, state, local and tribal entities will be expected to develop and maintain

Source: U.S. Department of Homeland Security

must be self-reliant to lead recovery efforts as well as sustain critical government services and public infrastructure. Yet, most states and state agencies still do not have plans and even fewer have operationalized their plans. To be self-sufficient, each state and local agency must develop its own comprehensive emergency response plan. But it's not enough to plan. Plans need to be operationalized in order to be effective. This requires figuring out who within your extended delivery network (federal, state, local, private sector, NGOs, citizens) does what and what services each partner might provide in an emergency situation, simulating response scenarios to identify issues and practicing to develop familiarity.

cies; and the health care industry, among others (see figure 3). Key resources would include hospitals, clinics, inpatient and outpatient facilities, health care personnel, emergency medical staff, first responders, police, security enforcement, fire departments, and the National Guard. Supporting entities to deliver public health and safety services include ambulances, helicopters, vehicles, other transportation, other privately held infrastructure deemed critical, mortuary and funeral services, and veterinary services.

State governments can also identify needs not being met by any existing organization and devise ways to fill those gaps. The networked model of emergency response augments the command-and-control model the United States has traditionally employed to manage disasters. The question for a governor should be: How do I bring together the resources necessary to execute our shared mission as well as possible? Key steps in developing a networked emergency management response include

- Convening and activating the network

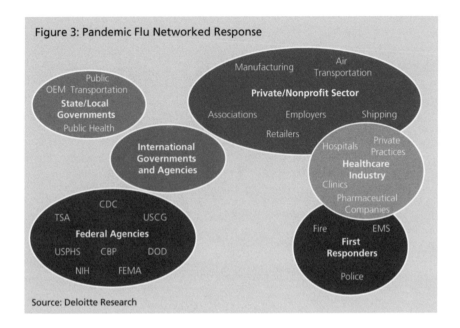

Figure 3: Pandemic Flu Networked Response

Source: Deloitte Research

- Creating the networked governance structure

- Coordinating activities and synchronizing response

- Realigning the state's organizational structure and governance

Convening and Activating the Network

Creative public officials possess a variety of assets they can deploy to bring together existing emergency management networks and provide for capabilities they do not already possess (see figure 4). A government can bring together parties whose intense yet narrow knowledge will provoke valuable insights when deployed in conjunction with others. Often nonprofit organizations are so overwhelmed with demands for their core services that they lack the time or the resources to find and interact with others even in the same sphere. Using their convening authority as a catalyst, an official can provide a venue for organizations and individuals with similar goals to meet, find common ground and perhaps even find ways to divide labor and share resources, making each more effective and efficient than before.

Arkansas governor Mike Huckabee demonstrated exactly this kind of leadership when the White House asked his state to house evacuees after Hurricane Katrina. Huckabee, a former Baptist minister, met with church

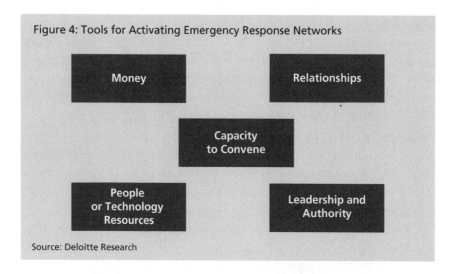

Figure 4: Tools for Activating Emergency Response Networks

Money

Relationships

Capacity to Convene

People or Technology Resources

Leadership and Authority

Source: Deloitte Research

leaders to arrange for 8,000 to 9,000 evacuees from the New Orleans Superdome to stay at church camps throughout his state.

Without Huckabee's actions, the church network would not have come into existence. While the churches had their own networks within the community, their leaders rarely communicated with one another. Since church leaders serve as community leaders, their influence led to an outpouring of volunteers to attend to the evacuees.[11]

In addition, public officials can add resources, in the form of people or technology, to help activate a network. The Department of Homeland Security (DHS) created the Office of the Private Sector (Office) to reach out to the roughly 25 million businesses in the United States. The Office provides the business community with a direct line of communication to DHS, and it works to build partnerships and relationships with the private sector.[12]

In addition to working with businesses, the Office worked with nonprofits during the Katrina response.[13] Craig Nemitz of Second Harvest noted the importance of the DHS Private Sector Office in helping his organization obtain warehouse space in Louisiana and housing for volunteers. Second Harvest was able to utilize this resource—without going through FEMA—because it had the contact information for the right person in DHS.[14]

Creating the Networked Governance Structure

Taking a group of organizations with substantial professional differences and tacking them together at the top level can be a recipe for failure. To be sure, leaders of organizations must set the stage for a successful multiparty partnership. They won't succeed, however, unless people throughout their organizations see the benefits of the network.

The first step is to set up an effective network governance structure. The more points of contact among the players, the more likely trust and communication will flourish. Success depends on quickly identifying and resolving any friction points. Joint governance structures that address strategy, management and organizational activities can frame a successful network by setting out the overall vision and strategy of the network, bringing areas of contention between members of the network to the forefront early on, anticipating problem areas and establishing a way of handling them.

Governance structures also must incorporate procedures for promoting innovation and managing change. Governments need to create at the outset a streamlined way to capture innovative ideas and suggestions from their partners. Since many citizens clearly wish to help in any way they can during an emergency, governments would also do well to leverage that spirit. Individuals accomplish amazing things during an emergency. Governments can provide the leadership and tools to turn independent gestures into organized efforts and accomplish much more.

Coordinating Activities and Synchronizing Responses

Along with designing a network structure that enables collaboration, government can provide the infrastructure that allows organizations to share information. Take a city facing a terrorist threat to its water system. The group of individuals charged with responding to such a threat might include FEMA representatives, state environment officials, local hospitals, environmental groups, public utility executives, local law enforcement officers and building inspectors.[15]

Some states and regions have established fusion centers to collaborate on emergency planning and management. While these were initially formed to bring together law enforcement agencies from multiple jurisdictions and layers of governments, there is a trend to include representatives from the private sector as well as personnel responsible for health surveillance, agriculture surveillance and transportation infrastructure.

A basic requirement for any of these networks to function would be some kind of electronic coordination mechanism that allows disparate groups to share information in real time and synchronize their response.

Pennsylvania's National Electronic Disease Surveillance System (PA-NEDSS) offers one model. In February 2002 Pennsylvania became the first state to introduce a fully integrated disease surveillance system that allows participants to share information quickly so that they can identify, track, predict and contain the spread of disease. More than 130 hospitals, 120 labs, 450 public health staff and 475 physicians are connected to PA-NEDSS. Public health officials can communicate public health alerts and advisories immediately and collect patient case data on a continuing basis over a secure system.

Thanks to the enhanced coordination and information-sharing capabilities, the reporting cycle of each patient case in Pennsylvania dropped from three weeks to fewer than 24 hours, enabling a more rapid and effective response.

During the Katrina response, corporations, countries and individuals wishing to contribute to the relief effort found themselves frustrated because agencies like the Red Cross and FEMA could not handle the thousands of offers and requests they received.[16] The overwhelming public response prompted the Private Sector Office of DHS to activate the National Emergency Resource Registry (NERR), which had been in place for more than a year but had not been used.[17] NERR, an online database characterized as "eBay for the government," provided a place for companies to register resources available for sale or donation and allowed those involved in the relief effort to register their needs.[18]

While technology is critical, some of the most important work a state performs in creating an emergency management network involves building strong relationships. Successful networks rely, at least partly, on trust. Without trust, network participants shy away from sharing knowledge, hindering coordination among them. Networks operating with a high level of trust, in contrast, lower the costs associated with interorganizational exchanges.

Realigning the State's Organizational Structure and Governance

Many states rely on emergency management organizational structures established years ago, based upon strict hierarchies and administrative silos. The existing chain of command, the established work flow, the criteria for hiring and the system of rewards may inhibit, rather than encourage, an effective networked response. A government working to create an integrated emergency management network needs to take a long, hard look at its structure, its organizational culture and its information architecture. Once officials understand the current situation, they can determine what changes are needed to encourage better information sharing, collaborative activity and flexibility.

The Transportation Security Administration (TSA) made a transition

Types of Networks Operating in Emergency Response

The public sector, private sector and nonprofit organizations that already perform aspects of disaster response in states provide the most valuable resources for building an integrated emergency management network. Few of these entities act alone; many have already formed relationships that allow them to collaborate in times of needs.

A first step in building a statewide emergency response network is to take stock of the organizations and networks involved in emergency response. These generally fall into four categories, and it is important to understand where each existing cluster of organizations fits in this scheme. Knowing this, one can conduct a full assessment and inventory of available assets.

Formal, Hierarchical Networks

A hierarchical network is created before an emergency event or disaster happens. Members within the network are legally or financially bound to perform established roles. Within the hierarchical network, official documentation identifies a clear path of authority, delineates decision-making and dictates the roles and responsibilities of network entities. Hierarchical networks generally have detailed procedures that limit the flexibility of the members, as they are bound to operate according to regulation and face enforceable repercussions if they do not. The American Red Cross stands at the center of a hierarchical network. It has a congressional charter and a specific role in the federal government's National Response Plan.

Contractual Networks

Formed from contractual relationships with key suppliers, these networks are critical to emergency response, covering everything from ice shipments to temporary housing to construction. Contracts negotiated in advance for basic supplies and services are needed in most every kind of emergency.

Relational Networks

Formed through agreements between independent organizations, these are created in advance and designed to facilitate cooperation over the course of multiple emergencies. The agreements may be formal (legally or financially binding) or informal. One example of a formal relational network is the National Voluntary Organizations Active in Disaster (NVOAD), a group of 40 organizations that coordinate a unified response to disasters based on strong partnerships between nonprofit and faith-based organizations. State VOADs help to coordinate nonprofits at the state level.

The Partnership for Disaster Relief is an informal relational network. Formed after the 2004 tsunami in Asia, this group's mission is to bring together the resources and expertise of U.S. businesses to improve recovery efforts for natural disasters. The Business Roundtable, an association of 160 CEOs of U.S. companies, founded the network and facilitates these partnerships by working with nonprofits and agencies to match them with U.S. companies. During Katrina, the Partnership became a central repository of information and needs, a guide for those wishing to contribute in-kind donations and a media source. Moreover, Roundtable member companies contributed $362 million in funding, services, supplies and equipment to support the Katrina relief effort.

Spontaneous Networks

Spontaneous networks arise suddenly and are cultivated by the interactions among people and organizations. They typically form out of necessity to solve a specific problem. Immediately after the terrorist attacks of September 11, for example, numerous individuals who owned boats used them, on their own initiative, to evacuate people from Lower Manhattan.

Witness accounts of those left in New Orleans in the wake of Katrina demonstrated the innovative and immediate response of citizens trying to help each other. These people used their skills and talents to help where possible: maintenance workers used forklifts to carry the sick and disabled, engineers started generators and kept them running and nurses manually ventilated patients when the power failed. "Stolen" boats and hotwired cars rescued people in need.

Sources: "Roundtable on Answering the Call: The Response of Community-Based Organizations to the 2005 Gulf Coast Hurricanes," Ande Miller, Testimony before the Committee on Health, Education, Labor, and Pensions, March 7, 2006; NVOAD, "Organizing Protocols for Community Disaster Recovery Mechanisms, National Volunteer Organizations Active in Disaster," (www.nvoad.org/articles/recovery.php), accessed on April 20, 2006; Business Roundtable (www.businessroundtable.org/taskforces); and L. Bradshaw and L. B. Slonsky, "Trapped in New Orleans by the flood—and martial law," Socialist Worker Online, September 9, 2005 (http://www.socialistworker.org/2005-2/556/556_04_RealHeroes.html), accessed on April 19, 2006.

to a networked organizational model when it established the Transportation Sector Network Management (TSNM), an office within TSA. The office is divided into eleven divisions. Ten encompass modes of transportation such as rail and mass transit, and the eleventh works as an integration unit facilitating collaboration across the modes (see figure 5). TSNM's organizational structure includes staff devoted to stakeholder relations that focus exclusively on external collaboration and partnership with the transportation industry and transportation associations.

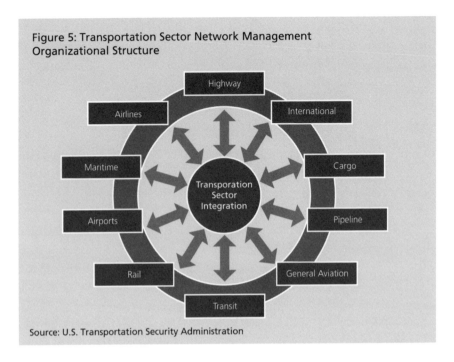

Figure 5: Transportation Sector Network Management Organizational Structure

Source: U.S. Transportation Security Administration

To encourage collaboration, TSNM has structured itself to mirror the current organizational structure of private industry. For example, the aviation industry is split into three passenger modes—commercial airports, commercial airlines and general aviation—plus cargo, because this division best reflects how the commercial arena makes distinctions in this area. By mimicking these divisions, TSNM hopes to maximize the information flow between government and the private sector. Knowledge is both power and the key to stopping the next terrorist attack, which links directly back to the TSA mission.

The U.S. Coast Guard's performance in the Katrina response provides another good example of an organizational structure that matches the needs of emergency response. During the storm, the Coast Guard rescued 33,000 people, reconstituted waterways, conducted environmental assessments and restored buoys and channel markers.[19]

Critical to the Coast Guard's success was the flexibility in the command structure that allowed those in the field to exercise their own discretion.[20] Captain Frank Paskewich, commanding officer of Sector New Orleans, describes the Coast Guard model as one that has commanding officers setting "broad-based objectives" for a mission, which frees them from micromanagement since the Coast Guard member on the scene is the one making the judgment calls. Coast Guard members are trained to carry out a mission in the safest way possible and given the latitude to do what is needed to fulfill the mission.[21] This type of flexibility helps overcome the bureaucratic hurdles that delay response.

Information Sharing

One of the most critical elements of a networked emergency response is the ability to share information. Many of the failures that occurred on September 11, 2001, and in the response to Hurricane Katrina were, at bottom, failures to communicate.

The statewide public safety networks established or planned in several states provide a common infrastructure for coordinating a state and local response. But as the nation saw in the 9/11 attacks and after Hurricane Katrina, a disaster may topple radio antennas and knock out communications centers. Or technical obstacles, such as incompatible computer and communications systems, may keep information from flowing to people who need it.

While technology is important, governance structures that support effective information flows are even more so. In the 9/11 and Katrina disasters, institutional impediments within agencies and turf-minded cultures were responsible for many problems. In New Orleans, poor communications channels made it hard for federal, state and local agencies to coordinate their post-Katrina rescue and relief efforts. Many government officials remained ignorant of the enormity of the situation for too long, delaying aid and prolonging the suffering.

Actions a government can take to improve information sharing include making specific plans that spell out the types of information that need to be collected; the organizations responsible for collections; data-sharing uses; guidelines and standards for shared information; and technology tools for information management and collection, including databases, accountability systems, logistics systems and approaches to track injuries or illness among responders. All in all, there are seven principles for creating an effective information-sharing plan.[22]

Set Clear Goals

All the partners collaborating in an emergency management network should outline what they hope to achieve by sharing information.[23] Top officials working for government, nonprofit and private organizations must define what kinds of information they need from partners and how quickly they need it.

Get Buy-In at the Top

Because information sharing represents a fundamental shift for a government organization, it must be driven by someone with the authority and influence to make decisions and get people in line. In most cases, only the head of the agency (or perhaps a top deputy) has that kind of clout. Leaders must be directly involved in making things happen, sitting down with counterparts from other agencies and organizations to hammer through the details.

Many agencies view information sharing as a technology issue and assign it to the IT group. This is a mistake. In most cases, the real issue is getting people to change their behavior. Dumping the problem on IT won't get the hard work done.

Create a Culture of Sharing

September 11 has entirely changed the way public agencies view information. Before 9/11, agencies designed their policies and approval processes with the goal of keeping information from leaking out. They shared only on a "need to know" basis. Today, government's philosophy has generally shifted to a "need to share." But in many cases, the restrictive practices and policies of the past live on, hampering collaboration.

To create a culture of sharing, government leaders must analyze their policies and, where necessary, establish new ones. But that's only the start. It's important to give those policies teeth, reinforcing them with performance measures, incentives, training programs and job definitions that will change the way people think and act. Leaders should also streamline and automate approval processes to make sharing information just as easy as not sharing. In short, make sharing the rule, not the exception.

The most important part of TSA's new network organizational design is that it stimulates the greatest possible information exchange by focusing on communication and information sharing as core competencies. Each mode has been authorized to focus on threat vulnerabilities, policy and stakeholder relations so that each network sector has the necessary skills and capabilities to carry out its respective goals and objectives.

This does not mean government agencies should share everything. Pri-

Principles for Developing Effective Information Sharing

- Set clear goals
- Get buy-in at the top
- Create a culture of sharing
- Create a governance model
- Establish communication protocols
- Implement appropriate technology
- Mitigate risks

vacy laws and other legal requirements dictate that some information may circulate only to a limited number of people. Some information simply isn't mission critical. But the process of sharing becomes easier if partners assume that they will make visible most of the information relevant to an emergency response, and then create mechanisms for controlling the smaller volume of information that needs to be restricted.

Establish Communication Protocols

It is difficult to route the right information to the right parties unless it has been properly classified and organized. Government agencies need to create guidelines defining what information should be produced as part of an emergency response, with whom it should be shared and how that sharing should be accomplished.[24]

One step in creating the necessary protocols is to sit down with partners and walk through all the scenarios that could occur in a variety of disasters. Through such exercises, along with actual emergency drills, it will soon become clear where you already have clear information pipelines, and where there are bottlenecks and dead ends you can rectify by establishing clear rules for information sharing.

Implement Appropriate Technology

As in just about any complex enterprise today, information sharing for an emergency response depends on effective use of digital technologies.

Steps taken by the Kaiser Permanente health group of the mid-Atlantic states during the anthrax attacks of 2001 illustrate how one private sector organization has already harnessed information technology to try to contain a health crisis. The company used e-mail and phone messages twice each day to provide new guidelines for treating the disease. It also conducted an electronic search of patient records to identify hundreds of patients who were postal workers and might be at risk of infection, and it contacted them to suggest possible treatments.[25]

FEMA has developed an information system that contains documentation on millions of police, firefighters and other first responders. The aim of the National Emergency Responder Credentialing System is to identify those emergency personnel that should be allowed to enter the scene of a disaster or terrorist attack.

Several states have implemented statewide radio systems, which provide a shared communications pipeline for all of their own agencies. Local governments that want to join the network can buy new equipment based on the same standards as the state's system, or they can implement "gateway" technologies to connect their existing systems to the state's.[26]

A state's emergency plan should also include a communications system that doesn't require land-based infrastructure and that will continue to operate if towers and base stations are destroyed. A satellite-based network is one possibility. Another is an ad-hoc mesh network, in which a collection of mobile communications devices relay signals among one another without the need for base stations or fixed Wi-Fi access points.

Along with implementing new systems, governments need to evaluate their legacy systems to find out whether they already promote information sharing, or whether the emergency management network suffers from a proliferation of information silos.

Tearing down impediments to sharing requires first creating an electronic gateway that allows the transfer of important information to partners in a timely fashion. The TSA did this soon after it opened for business in 2002, when it built a collaboration platform to support rapid and secure communications across federal, state and local governments, as well as with its priority partners—air carriers, airport operators, external law enforcement, vendors, travel partners and contractors.[27]

Mitigate Risks

Public and private sector partners must understand how the information they provide to one another might be used outside the context of emergency management. They might need to create legal contracts that spell out how different classifications of information may be used by the different partners.[28]

Governments creating emergency response plans also must anticipate how they will accommodate laws that protect citizens' privacy. In July 2006 the U.S. Department of Health and Human Services (HHS) introduced a Web-based, interactive decision tool with this end in mind. Emergency planners can use the tool to learn how they may obtain health information about individuals with disabilities, for use in an emergency response or recovery plan, while meeting the provisions of the Health Insurance Portability and Privacy Act (HIPPA) of 1996.[29]

Logistics

While difficulties during a disaster may provoke blame and finger pointing, one group often finds itself singled out for praise. Those are the major U.S. retailers—the Wal-Marts, Home Depots and other big box stores. News reports after Hurricane Katrina, and after the hurricanes that washed over Florida in 2004, tell the story: how fast the trucks started rolling; how soon the stores reopened to meet demand for plywood, mops, bleach, generators, food and water; how quickly the corporations also came through with donated goods.[30] Transportation and logistics firms such as DHL Corp., UPS and FedEx are also known for contributing manpower, equipment and much-needed expertise to disaster relief around the world.

One lesson that states and their relief agency partners should learn from the private sector is the importance of logistics. This is the science of moving the right goods to the right place at the right time, and leading corporations long ago stopped treating logistics as an afterthought. Companies recognize that logistics is a core function that requires strategic planning and a serious investment of time and resources. Done right, it cuts costs, improves service and boosts the bottom line.

In emergency management, getting the right goods to the right place at the right time is also vital. Long before a need emerges for emergency equipment and supplies, leaders must develop strategies for procurement, transportation and distribution. Without such strategies, other aspects of the emergency plan will fall apart. Evacuation centers, for example, serve no purpose if they aren't stocked with enough food, water, bedding, toilet paper and other supplies to meet the needs of the people who shelter there. Depending on the emergency, the ability to quickly bring in sandbags, firefighting equipment, sump pumps, medication or a host of other vital supplies can mean the difference between success and failure. A well-conceived logistics program saves effort, money and lives.

The Wal-Mart Model

Wal-Mart's performance in the summer of 2005 offers a model for logistics in emergency management. Six days before Hurricane Katrina hit New Orleans, Jason Jackson, Wal-Mart's director of business continuity, started tracking what was then a tropical depression as it made its way across Florida. The company began staging items it knew customers would need after a big storm—mops, chain saws and the like—at distribution centers in the areas most likely to be hit.[31]

Wal-Mart could anticipate customer demand because it keeps data on purchases after storms and analyzes those patterns, even to the point of discovering that a hurricane triggers big sales of Strawberry Pop Tarts. The company also prepares store managers with lists of procedures to follow after a hurricane.[32]

When the storm landed in Louisiana on August 29, Jackson set plans in motion to replenish high-demand merchandise and deliver generators and dry ice to stores that had lost power. Katrina initially closed 126 Wal-Mart stores; by September 9, the company had reopened all but 15 of them.[33]

Besides positioning itself to sell products to storm victims and serve its communities, Wal-Mart lent its distribution muscle to relief agencies, providing goods both for sale and free of charge. Of the 2,500 truckloads of supplies the company dispatched to states ravaged by Katrina, 100 were donations.[34] In Union Parish, Louisiana, law enforcement officers called Wal-Mart the day after the storm; two days later, Wal-Mart delivered two truckloads of flashlights, batteries, meals ready to eat, protective clothing and ammunition.[35]

Wal-Mart's recovery and relief efforts, however, weren't entirely problem-free. "The company sometimes struggled to coordinate with the Louisiana National Guard and other government agencies about what to send, how to dispense it, and what to charge," writes Sydney Freedberg, Jr. in the *National Journal*. "Shipments were held up needlessly, turned back at checkpoints or delivered without clear agreement on whether the supplies were to be given away or sold." These difficulties arose because Wal-Mart and the National Guard hadn't worked out beforehand exactly how to cooperate in a disaster.[36]

Four Principles of Logistics for Emergency Management

Experience in disasters and other emergencies suggests four lessons for effective logistics operations.

1. PREPARE IN ADVANCE. Wal-Mart's challenges and its successes after Hurricane Katrina point to one of the basic principles of logistics for emergency management—prepare in advance.

Wal-Mart was able to get goods moving to its stores almost immediately after Katrina hit because it routinely tracks hurricanes and puts merchandise in strategic locations before the winds and rain arrive.

Home Depot, too, has a detailed logistics strategy for dealing with major emergencies. In 2005, it went so far as to reorganize its geographical divisions to correspond with the types of disasters they deal with most often, so that managers in the West can specialize in earthquakes and wildfires, those in the North in blizzards, and those in the South in hurricanes.[37]

2. INTEGRATE THE PRIVATE SECTOR INTO THE LOGISTICS PLAN. Along with the desire to act as good citizens, corporations feel another powerful motive to help in emergency planning and response. The sooner roads are cleared and residents feel safe and comfortable, the sooner companies can get back to making money. Governors should understand that the private sector wants to help and, as part of the state emergency plan, establish mechanisms for collaboration.

Some government organizations have done an excellent job of this. The sheriff of Orange County, California, has a full-time staff member devoted to coordinating the efforts of public and private organizations. In New Jersey, Massachusetts and the Kansas City metropolitan area, chapters of the organization Business Executives for National Security have built databases of resources they can offer in a crisis, with information about whom to contact to obtain help and how equipment will be delivered and set up. The companies develop their offers based on state officials' prioritized wish lists.[38]

Governments may even want to consider partnering with the private sector to operate all or part of the state's emergency logistics management effort. This is a common solution in the private sector, where many companies outsource supply chain activities to third-party logistics providers.

Outsourcing logistics brings many advantages. Clients benefit from the expertise of logistics powerhouses such as UPS Supply Chain Solutions and FedEx Supply Chain Services. They can harness sophisticated information

Common Logistics Management Mistakes Made in Emergencies

- Storing equipment and supplies where they cannot be easily transported to the scene of an emergency.
- Reinventing the wheel, rather than partnering with organizations and businesses with proven logistics expertise.
- Allowing in-kind donations to flow in at random, rather than publicizing exactly what is needed and creating a mechanism for accepting and storing it.
- Failing to plan for how an emergency might disrupt the transportation network.
- Relying on outdated manual processes rather than harnessing advanced supply chain management technologies.

systems without having to build or buy their own. They gain economies of scale as the logistics providers leverage the large volumes of freight they move for multiple customers to obtain better rates.

3. TAKE CONTROL OF THE FLOW OF DONATIONS AND VOLUNTEERS. After the earthquake in Bam, Iran, in 2003, that country had to turn away many humanitarian aid flights because the runways were clogged with relief supplies and blocked by partially unloaded planes. Sri Lanka suffered similar bottlenecks after the tsunami of 2004. Companies and individuals may respond generously to a disaster, but without a solid plan for unloading, moving and storing in-kind donations, piles of food, blankets and other vital supplies may go to waste while victims languish without them.[39]

One solution is to bring in logistics experts who know how to manage large shipments efficiently. In Sri Lanka, Chris Weeks, a DHL executive who often helps with disaster relief, took over the operation at the airport. Instead of unloading on the runways, he had pilots shift the planes to a quieter location. Then workers moved supplies to holding areas for sorting and orderly distribution.[40]

Even before the goods arrive, though, a government can stave off chaos with a simple technique: tell the world what you need and ask donors to hold off on the rest. Sometimes, organizations and individuals with the best of intentions respond to a disaster by shipping truckloads of goods that victims simply can't use. Clothing, for example, is just about never needed.[41]

In many cases, donors would do better to contribute cash rather than

Logistics and Relief Aid Organizations

Why is the Wal-Mart model for disaster response rare among humanitarian aid agencies? Private businesses live and die by metrics and performance measurements, according to Steve Leventhal of the Fritz Institute, which brings private sector expertise to address complex challenges in delivering humanitarian relief, but few humanitarian aid organizations do the same. This results in the following core challenges for these organizations:

• Failure to recognize the importance of logistics

• A lack of professional staff

• Inadequate use of technology

• Lack of institutional learning

• Limited collaboration

Together with the International Federation of Red Cross and Red Crescent Societies, the Fritz Institute developed "Humanitarian Logistics Software" to meet the specific supply chain needs of humanitarian aid agencies. The software addresses the lack of institutional learning, inadequate use of technology in the humanitarian sector and measurement of several of the performance indicators emphasized by the institute by allowing agencies to track their input, output and delivery accuracy in real time. Key performance indicators include appeal coverage (or return on donation), donation-to-delivery time (also known as "supply chain velocity"), financial efficiency and accuracy of information for decision-makers at headquarters and in the field.

Source: Interview with Steve Leventhal, Director of External Relations, Fritz Institute, April 17, 2006.

goods. Governments need to get that message out to the public. "In a similar vein," advises a handout developed by the Partnership for Disaster Relief, the initiative of the Washington, D.C.-based Business Roundtable, "it's not usually a good idea to have a lot of volunteers streaming in. They tie up transportation and other services." [42]

Of course, that is not always the case. Volunteers with specialized skills, and goods that local authorities specifically request, are important resources. The point is that government leaders must determine the kind of help they will need and control the influx to keep misdirected kindness from undermining the relief infrastructure.

4. IMPLEMENT TECHNOLOGY TO SUPPORT EMERGENCY MANAGEMENT LOGISTICS. Corporations rely on sophisticated computer systems to run their supply chains. Governments also should take advantage of technology to manage the flow of relief supplies. In Alabama, the Governor's Office of Faith-Based and Community Initiatives operates the Alabama Volunteer and Donations Database System (AVADDS) to match offers of goods, money and services with areas where they are needed most.[43]

Although developed at the last minute for Katrina relief, AVADDS now positions Alabama to deal more efficiently with future emergencies. Governors of other states should not wait until the next disaster strikes to develop systems of their own for managing the emergency relief supply chain.

Managing Risk

Understanding the different kinds of risk a state may face, and developing appropriate strategies to manage each kind, is a vital part of emergency planning. Given infinite resources, it might be possible to reduce many risks nearly to zero. But, of course, resources are always limited. How do we set priorities? That's where risk management comes in.

To manage risk means to assess the dangers posed by various threats that might occur, weigh each threat against the chances that it *will* occur, and then prepare for the full spectrum of risks to protect life and property as effectively as is feasible. "Feasible" is a key word. A solid risk management plan doesn't assume that all disasters are created equal, nor does it expect to avoid all harm. Instead, it aims to do the best job possible with the resources available.

Risk management consists of all the planning and preparation leaders must accomplish long before they find themselves in the chaos of a major catastrophe, so that when disaster does strike, responders can operate effectively. Once they have conducted a risk management process, state and local executives can make informed decisions about engineering robust and resilient emergency management networks.

A rigorous risk governance model incorporates five different elements: pre-assessment, assessment, an evaluation of risk appetite, risk management and risk communication.

Pre-assessment

Pre-assessment frames the issues and develops a common understanding and vocabulary. To be successful, the process should identify and bring together all the organizations that might be involved in emergency planning and response so they can define the issues that need to be discussed, establish ground rules for the response and identify roles and responsibilities. [44]

Assessment

The first step is to understand the nature of, and interrelationships among, key variables that make up the risk. The assessment addresses these questions:

- What could go wrong (threat)?
- What could cause it to go wrong (drivers)?
- How likely is it to go wrong (probability)?
- What are the consequences?
- How vulnerable are we?

The results of a risk assessment can be mapped to a graphic that depicts the relative position of risks across a consequence vs. vulnerability land-scape (see figure 6). Exact probabilities may be hard to estimate accurately, so order-of-magnitude assessments can be used. The objective is not to develop rigorous estimates so much as it is to develop understanding and provide a framework for developing risk management options.

The real killers (often, unfortunately, in the literal sense of the word) are risks that carry very serious consequences but happen rarely. Until recently, most managers didn't pay much attention to these risks because the odds against them happening "on their watch" were pretty low. But in the rare event that they do occur, the harm they cause is so extreme that neglecting to plan for them leaves the public dangerously vulnerable. Virtually all ter-rorist actions fall into this category. The chance that terrorists will strike most locations is small. But as most locations have no particular safeguards against terrorists, they are highly vulnerable, and a successful attack on them would cause tremendous damage. The aftermath of Hurricane Katrina certainly fell into this category, as did the school siege in Beslan, Russia, and the Asian tsunami of 2004. The risk of an avian flu pandemic, a "dirty" bomb attack or (at the extreme) a collision between an asteroid and the earth all fall into this quadrant as well.

Evaluating Risk Appetite

Since it's impossible to make the world 100 percent danger free, it's neces-

A Framework for Risk Assessment

Figure 6: A Framework for Risk Assessment

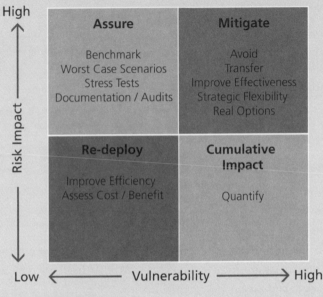

Source: Deloitte Research

The four quadrants of the figure can be interpreted as follows:

LOW CONSEQUENCE—LOW VULNERABILITY (BOTTOM LEFT QUADRANT: SAFE). Risks that fall into this area probably don't require a large infusion of resources. For example, on certain highways, when the sun is low during the evening rush hour, glare in drivers' eyes could cause accidents. Compared with many other risks, the dangers this situation poses and the chances that it will cause widespread harm are small. More good probably can be gained by deploying money, personnel and other resources in more critical areas.

LOW CONSEQUENCE—HIGH VULNERABILITY (BOTTOM RIGHT QUADRANT: CAUTION). Residential fires could fall into this category. The consequences, at least from a societal point of view, are relatively low. The key here is to measure the cumulative impact: Is there a pattern of fires, perhaps indicating arson? Are certain types of fires more likely than others, perhaps indicating a needed change in building codes?

HIGH CONSEQUENCE—LOW VULNERABILITY (UPPER RIGHT QUADRANT: CAUTION). Risks in this quadrant could pose great danger, but because we have implemented the necessary policies and plans and allocated the necessary resources, we live comfortably with the knowledge that they could occur. Florida, for example, faces the prospect of one or more destructive hurricanes every year. But the state has become reasonably good at mitigating the results of such disasters, so people continue to move to and invest in Florida despite the risk. For risks in this zone, the best strategy is to evaluate continuously and audit the emergency management plan to make sure it remains viable as conditions change over the years.

HIGH CONSEQUENCE—HIGH VULNERABILITY (UPPER LEFT QUADRANT: TAKE ACTION). If a risk carries serious consequences and is very likely to occur, then everyone focuses on it with laser-like intensity. Much time and many resources are devoted to moving this risk out of the red zone. Government leaders in the northern United States know their areas will endure major snowstorms practically every winter, posing a serious danger to motorists and vulnerable residents. Since there's no way to change the weather, they invest heavily in snowplows and road salt.

sary to negotiate priorities, defining those risks that the community can live with and those that are intolerable. Then, for each risk, one can decide on the appropriate strategy:

- RISK ACCEPTANCE. The risks may be negligible, and risk reduction may not be worth the effort or is perhaps not feasible

- RISK AVOIDANCE. Take a path that avoids the risk. For example, if a particular technology poses significant risk, abandon research on it.

- RISK TRANSFER. Transfer the risk to insurance or a third party.

- RISK REDUCTION. Change policies and processes, get supporting infrastructure tuned up, set up training, define organizational roles and responsibilities and wrap all these activities in a "quality" and continuous improvement envelope[45]

Evaluating risk appetite sets the overall priorities for developing emergency response capabilities—both those that would apply to a broad range of emergencies and those tailored to specific risks.

Figure 7: Risk Management Process Capability Maturity Model

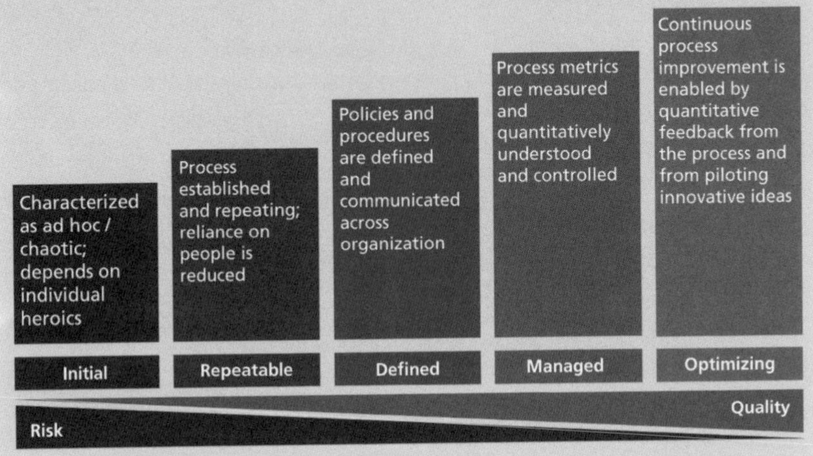

Initial	Repeatable	Defined	Managed	Optimizing
Characterized as ad hoc / chaotic; depends on individual heroics	Process established and repeating; reliance on people is reduced	Policies and procedures are defined and communicated across organization	Process metrics are measured and quantitatively understood and controlled	Continuous process improvement is enabled by quantitative feedback from the process and from piloting innovative ideas

Risk → Quality

Source: Deloitte Research

Risk Management

In this stage, government officials develop risk-specific policies, organizational roles and responsibilities and training. Risk management involves building and sustaining capabilities to support the plans and priorities developed during the risk assessment process. These capabilities include:

- Policies—strategy, operations, finance

- Organizational and people strategies

- Support infrastructure including technologies

- Processes for assessment and continuous improvement

Each organization responsible for emergency management should assess its capabilities to manage risk, starting with a "gap analysis" to illuminate any shortcomings in the management process—as aligned with the organization's risk appetite. A gap analysis begins with describing the *process* for responding to a crisis or catastrophe. By describing the process, and surfacing and reconciling conflicting points of view, government agencies can better explain, predict and prescribe improvements in policies, organization, infrastructure and technology for emergency response.

Policies should provide unambiguous direction about roles, responsibilities and standard operating procedures to follow as a catastrophe unfolds.

Organizational and people strategies should clearly delineate responsibilities within and among organizations. One useful tool is a memorandum of understanding that defines the role of each state and local agency, nonprofit and private sector partner expected to respond in an emergency. Partners should conduct training to make sure everyone understands the command, control and communications protocols; knows how to use the necessary technology; and can step into his or her role as soon as it's time to implement an emergency plan. Also needed are well-defined procedures for interfacing with stakeholders—citizens groups, utility and transportation companies and health care organizations—as well as with the media. Support infrastructure includes communication technology and processes to keep all levels of government connected, from first responders to executive management.

Assessment and continuous improvement recognizes that perfection won't come easily or immediately. Governments need to develop controls to ensure that everyone understands expectations and that participants continuously measure their progress toward the goal. The goal is to move to a capability maturity model, in which the response to risk is no longer an ad hoc exercise, but rather a well-managed process, if not an entirely "optimized" one (see figure 7). If such a model had been applied in New Orleans at the time of Hurricane Katrina, for example, none of the first responders would have needed to strike deals on the spot with retail managers to obtain food, water, ammunition, flashlights and other goods, or commandeer those goods first and make deals later. There would have been plans in place to equip responders for their jobs, with clear backup plans in case they couldn't obtain supplies and equipment from the expected sources.

Governance and Leadership

How a state rises to the challenge of emergency management depends very much on the leadership shown by its governor. The state's chief executive should be the chief evangelist for a networked emergency response. He or she should understand the risks facing the state, put mechanisms in place to answer each of those risks, promote mitigation strategies and lead the charge to restructure government in ways that encourage collaboration.

States have developed several strategies for organizing their homeland security and emergency management infrastructures. Popular approaches include:

- Creating a homeland security department whose director coordinates emergency management, law enforcement, fire and rescue, public health, National Guard, transportation, public works and information technology activities related to homeland security, and also advises the governor.

- Appointing the Adjutant General, head of the state's National Guard, as homeland security advisor.

- Forming a homeland security task force, comprised of executive office staff and agency heads from areas such as law enforcement, fire and rescue, public health, the National Guard, transportation, public works and information technology.[46]

The first governance model appears to work best for ensuring high-level attention to emergency response and a single individual who can be held accountable by the governor.

Examples of Creative Leadership

Oklahoma offers several examples of creative leadership in emergency planning. Since 1999 the state's Office of Emergency Management has provided an emergency preparedness curriculum to public and private schools, colleges and vocational-technical schools. This curriculum incorporates lessons learned in the Oklahoma City bombing, the tornado outbreak of May 3, 1999, and the December 1999 shooting at Fort Gibson Middle School.[47]

In 2003 the state launched OK-WARN (Weather Alert Remote Notification), a program that transmits hazardous weather information via pagers to residents who are deaf or hard of hearing.[48] In 2004 Governor Brad Henry announced McReady Oklahoma, a statewide campaign to educate families about how to prepare for floods, tornadoes, lighting and other weather hazards. The state created this program together with McDonald's, Oklahoma Gas and Electric, the American Red Cross, the National Weather Service, the Salvation Army, the Tulsa Mayor's Citizen Corps/Tulsa Partners, Inc. and several other partners.[49]

In Florida, Governor Jeb Bush used his 2006 state of the state address to call for a multimillion dollar initiative encouraging residents to prepare for hurricanes. Soon afterward, the state launched its "GET A PLAN!" campaign, which includes television and radio ads, billboards and a Web-based, interactive tool that families and businesses can use to develop disaster plans.[50]

When an emergency occurs, a governor who remains visibly in charge sets the tone for the entire network of responders and for the public. During the immediate crisis, a strong leader coordinates an effective response while keeping the public informed and calm. Over the long term, this leader gets everyone pulling together to restore life to normal and apply lessons learned to make the state even better prepared for the next emergency.

As Elizabeth McNie, a fellow at the Center for Science and Technology Policy Research at the University of Colorado, Boulder, observes, decision-making in an emergency is different from the formal process government agencies use in the course of ordinary business. " [The] decision making process becomes truncated, intelligence may be incomplete, and multiple problems demand solutions almost simultaneously," she says. "Effective leadership in a 'crisis' situation often requires years of training and experience to hone those qualities that separate capable leaders from those who are out of their league."[51]

Former New York mayor Rudolph Giuliani was a model of executive leadership during a crisis. As the consultant A. J. Schuler remarks, in the wake of the 9/11 attacks, Giuliani not only guided New York through an unimaginable catastrophe, he also pointed the city toward a better future. Among Giuliani's exemplary leadership moves, Schuler says, were the following: he articulated a positive vision for the future; he stayed visible, calm and always prepared to share critical information; he challenged individuals to serve others; he set clear limits on what people could do and gave clear choices about how they should respond to those rules; he offered lavish praise to those who made positive contributions; and he kept public attention focused on critical issues.[52]

Beyond the initial response to an emergency, a governor's leadership plays an important role in recovery. When the Northridge earthquake shook Los Angeles in 1994, it destroyed the overpass bridges of Interstate 10 in the city, shutting down one of the most heavily used roadways in the world. Experts said it would take more than two years to get traffic flowing again, making life difficult for masses of commuters and disrupting the region's economy. But using the emergency powers conferred on him by state law, Governor Pete Wilson helped get the freeway rebuilt in virtually no time. He suspended the operation of statutes and regulations that mandated lengthy hearings and reports before construction could begin. When the state went out for bids, it required contractors to specify the date they would complete the project, levying a $200,000 penalty for each day the project ran late and offering a $200,000 bonus for each day it was early. California reopened the freeway to normal traffic flow in 66 days.[53]

The list of emergencies that might challenge a state administration is a formidable one. But a robust emergency management strategy can help avert a great deal of suffering. By coordinating and managing an efficient networked response, establishing structures for effective information sharing, implementing state-of-the-art logistics practices and wisely managing risk and exercising creative leadership, state government can protect its citizens and smooth the path to recovery.

Chapter 7: The Final Word

THE CHALLENGE

• The list of emergencies for which states need to prepare is daunting in size and variety, ranging from floods, tornados, hurricanes and earthquakes to pandemics and potential terrorist attacks.

• Enhanced federal funding for emergency response and preparedness is tied to a plethora of "sticks"—grant compliance requirements and mandated activities. Most notable among the requirements is the National Incident Management System (NIMS) implementation timeline, which requires by FY 2007, full compliance with NIMS guidelines in order to be considered for all federal preparedness funds.

REFORM STRATEGIES

• *Emergency response networks*. Effective emergency management and response involves integrating a disparate array of organizations into functioning networks that share information, coordinate activities and synchronize responses.

• *State-of-the-art logistics*. Long before a need emerges for emergency equipment and supplies, leaders must develop strategies for getting the right goods to the right place at the right time.

• *Creative leadership*. This includes being visible and calm, keeping public attention focused on critical issues and articulating a positive vision for the future.

EXAMPLES

• *Florida's* emergency management plan depends on effective coordination among numerous local and state officials, volunteer organizations, public and private health care organizations and utility companies.

• *Pennsylvania's* National Electronic Disease Surveillance System (PA-NEDSS) connects more than 130 hospitals, 120 labs, 450 public health staff and 475 physicians. As a result, public health officials can communicate public health alerts and advisories immediately and collect patient case data on a continuing basis over a secure system.

NEXT STEPS

• *Integrate existing networks*. Identify effective emergency response networks that already exist as well as needs not being met by any existing organization, then devise ways to fill those gaps.

• *Improve information sharing*. Set clear goals, create a culture of sharing and establish a governance model for information sharing.

• *Incorporate the private sector into logistics plans*. Private firms can contribute manpower, equipment and much-needed logistics expertise to disaster relief. Establish mechanisms for collaboration to take advantage of this expertise.

• *Develop a risk governance model*. Assess risks in terms of likelihood and vulnerability, determine how much risk can be tolerated and then develop strategies for managing risk according to that assessment.

{8} *William D. Eggers, Robert Wavra, Lisa Snell and Adrian Moore*

Driving More Money into the Classroom
The Promise of Shared Services

Education spending constitutes a big chunk of most state budgets. Spending on elementary and secondary education represents a little more than a fifth of total state spending.[1] Ranging from teachers' salaries to building costs, these budget dollars have in the past mostly escaped the chopping block of the yearly budget cutting process. In recent years, however, states and school districts are under increasing pressure to reduce education costs, particularly of noninstructional services. The 65 percent solution—requiring 65 cents of every educational dollar to be spent on instruction—is now under consideration in numerous legislatures across the country.

Perhaps nowhere is the fiscal squeeze more evident than in California where scores of school districts have faced severe deficits in recent years. The school board in San Diego had to cut between $60 million and $84 million for the 2004–05 academic year—even after saving $14 million in 2003–04.[2] The Legislative Analysts' office in California reports that in 2005–06, school districts continue to face revenue and cost pressures.[3] Declining enrollment continues to affect some districts, reducing district revenues and requiring budget cuts at the local level.

The fiscal pressures on education budgets don't stop in California, however; they stretch across the nation.[4]

- The *Akron Beacon Journal* reported that many northeast Ohio districts face budget cuts for the 2005–06 school year and that the Ohio State Senate projects cuts in education funding through 2005–07.[5]

- The *Duluth News Tribune* reported that the Duluth, Minnesota, school district faced more than a $3 million shortfall for the 2005–06 school year.

Even in states with budget surpluses, money for education is always limited and rarely keeps pace with costs. Several factors are driving these educational cost pressures.

SURGING ENROLLMENT. Surges in the number of school-age children are overwhelming some school infrastructures. In Temecula, California, the school district must raise class sizes for the 2005–06 school year to meet the district's budget shortfall. Meanwhile, school districts in Texas, Louisiana and elsewhere that have enrolled significant number of Hurricane Katrina evacuees are grappling with large increases in student populations.

DECLINING ENROLLMENT. Many rural school districts and some inner city schools face the opposite problem of their fast-growing counterparts: declining enrollment. This often creates severe cost strain because it typically means budget cuts. The *Sacramento Bee* reported in 2005 that school districts across the state were canceling bus service and laying off bus drivers to save money.[6] Such cuts present a challenge because it is difficult to shed fixed costs—at least in the short term.

COURT RULINGS. States are also under financial pressure to direct more resources to the classroom as a result of school finance litigation. Lawsuits against state funding systems have been brought in 44 of the 50 states. Adequacy lawsuits are based on the notion that states are not providing enough funding for all students to meet state and federal academic expectations. According to the Education Commission of the States, adequacy lawsuits have been filed in 32 states. In 14 cases, the courts found that the school funding system, in part or in whole, violated the state's constitution.[7]

These lawsuits can compel states to invest significant new resources in primary and secondary (K-12) education.[8] For example, in February 2005, after the state of New York missed a deadline to revamp the state's school finance system, state Supreme Court Justice Leland De Grasse ordered the state to pay $5.6 billion in new aid to New York City schools. School adequacy lawsuits offer another compelling reason for states to encourage school districts to direct more resources into student funding rather than administrative services.

BALLOONING MEDICAID COSTS. Indirectly, escalating Medicaid costs, which now account for nearly one-third of some state budgets, put serious cost pressure on education spending and all other areas of state government. Medicaid cost increases, coupled with longer life spans, says former Virginia governor Mark Warner, are eating into state education budgets and will soon put the "needs of grandma over the grandkids" if something is not done.[9]

How can states and school districts respond to these fiscal pressures without adversely affecting educational performance? One promising approach is by reducing noninstructional spending costs through shared services. Whether a district has a surplus or deficit, a budgetary feast or famine, arrangements with other school districts, within large school districts or with outside entities to share services such as transportation, food services, human resources, finances and purchasing can help realize significant cost reductions without negatively affecting student outcomes. In this chapter we explain the concept of shared services, show where it has been successfully applied in the public and private sector, detail the best opportunities for shared services in education and provide guidelines for successful implementation.

Relationships between School District Size, Costs and Educational Performance

In most states, anywhere from one-third to one-half of every dollar spent on education never makes it into a classroom. The money goes to administration, support services, and operations. Lacking economies of scale—and often sufficient managerial expertise—many small and medium-size districts find it extraordinarily expensive to provide the full array of support and administrative services in-house. At the same time, many large districts suffer from duplicative or inefficient administrative systems due to layer upon layer of bureaucracy grown over time. For example, in many states, teachers make up a little more than half of all school district staff.[10] In contrast, teachers account for between 60 and 80 percent of all school staffing in Europe.[11] The bottom line: not enough funding allocated to education is getting into U.S. classrooms.

The U.S. Department of Education has found that approximately 39 percent of state education budgets are used for noninstructional purposes. More detailed analyses at the state level suggest that the federal statistics may understate the actual amount going to noninstructional costs. Texas

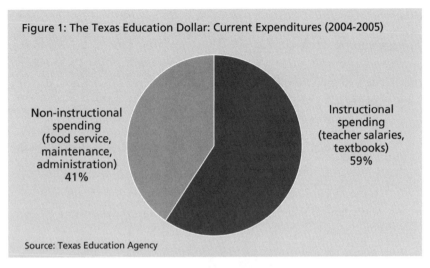

Figure 1: The Texas Education Dollar: Current Expenditures (2004-2005)

Non-instructional spending (food service, maintenance, administration) 41%

Instructional spending (teacher salaries, textbooks) 59%

Source: Texas Education Agency

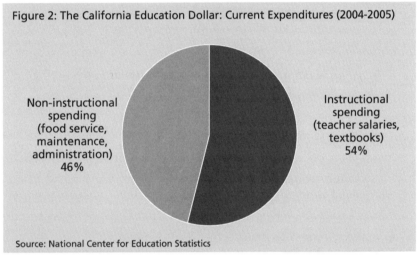

Figure 2: The California Education Dollar: Current Expenditures (2004-2005)

Non-instructional spending (food service, maintenance, administration) 46%

Instructional spending (teacher salaries, textbooks) 54%

Source: National Center for Education Statistics

has one of the most detailed systems of school cost accountability. It offers an instructive example for taking a closer look at education spending. Data from the Texas Education Agency (TEA) show that during 2004–05, Texas school districts devoted only 59 cents of every tax dollar to classroom instruction (see figure 1). The remaining 41 cents went to support functions such as student transportation, food services, facilities maintenance and operations and general administration.[12] Meanwhile, in California, only 54 percent of per-pupil spending goes to instruction costs (see figure 2), while in Illinois classroom expenditures represent only 56 percent of the budget, compared with 44 percent for support services.[13]

Pressures to Get Bigger—and Smaller

The growing recognition that something must be done to drive a higher percentage of school funding into the classroom has prompted a number of state leaders to propose the wholesale consolidation of small school districts into larger regional or citywide districts. Consider the following:

- In Arkansas, the legislature approved a plan in 2004 to consolidate small school districts with less than 350 students.[14]

- In Marin County, California (where 20,000 students are enrolled in 19 school districts), County Schools Superintendent Mary Jane Burke has explored district consolidation to conserve resources in the face of state budget cuts.[15]

- The Arizona legislature debated school district consolidation after a state auditor general's report found that small school districts spend far more on administrative functions than do large districts.[16]

- In Michigan a number of school districts are considering consolidation in order to take advantage of a state financial incentive that gives them an extra $50 per pupil for consolidating.

- Several small schools and districts in Maine have been consolidated. For example, Portland, Maine, residents voted in November 2003 to close some elementary schools and create a network of medium-size schools to serve students.[17] Sanford school district, in a rural part of the state, has closed two schools and consolidated students into five remaining facilities. Many other rural school districts are considering consolidation.[18]

Reason for Caution

Despite the growing interest in school consolidation there is ample reason for caution. A substantial body of research has questioned both the educational and cost savings benefits of school district consolidation. In 2002 a research team led by William Ouchi, a professor at UCLA's Anderson School of Management, examined nine different school systems, including the country's three largest school districts. The team found that the centralized management of schools brought about by consolidation actually led to higher spend-

Decentralized Management, Local Control and Educational Performance

School principals need to maintain local control of school budgets to manage the unique needs of their school population and improve outcomes for students. Yet, schools also need scale to purchase outside services efficiently. UCLA management professor William Ouchi's work on decentralized schools offers insight into how a school can benefit simultaneously from both local control of resources and scale. Ouchi and a team of 12 researchers found—after studying a variety of public and Catholic school systems in North America—that decentralized school systems run more efficiently and produce better student achievement.

Ouchi included three types of large North American school systems in his research sample:

- Three very centralized public school districts: New York City, Los Angeles and Chicago

- Three very decentralized public school districts: Seattle, Houston and Edmonton, Canada

- Three very decentralized Catholic school districts: Chicago, New York City, and Los Angeles.

The research team visited 223 schools, representing at least 5 percent of the schools in each system. For each school system, the team gathered data about student performance, school centralization and the amount of money that reaches the classroom. The team focused on school budgets, accountability systems and student achievement.

They found that how a school is managed matters. Schools perform better on fiscal and academic outcomes when there is local control of school budgets by principals and when there is open enrollment, which allows per pupil funding to follow the child.[a]

Overall, the decentralized public school districts and Catholic schools had significantly less fraud, less centralized bureaucracy and staff, a greater percentage of money going to the classroom and higher student achievement.

The research also found a lower achievement gap between white and minority students at decentralized public school districts. For example, at John Hay Elementary School in Seattle, the principal controlled approximately $25,000 before the change to decentralization and now controls about $2,000,000 per year, which is virtually the entire school budget. After the change, the principal, in consultation with her teachers, decided to throw out the standard schedule of six periods per day and instead adopted an innovative schedule that made more efficient use of teacher time. The principal also used her new freedom to hire 12 part-time reading and math coaches and set up a tutoring station outside of every classroom with another station in a wide hallway for "turbo-tutor-ing" the gifted children. Now reading in that school is taught in groups of five to seven students. Other classes are in larger sections, and every student who is behind grade level receives one-on-one tutoring.

Over a four-year period following the change, the school's standard-ized math scores rose from the 36th percentile to the 62nd, while read-ing scores rose from the 72nd percentile to the 76th. Black and white students in third grade now have identical reading scores and all are at or above grade level.[b]

Dr. Ouchi describes what happens in school districts that practice decentralized management and attach school funding to the backs of children (this novel funding approach is termed "weighted student fund-ing formula"):

"Each school in these districts controls most of its instructional decisions. Each school must attract its own students—no students are 'assigned' to any school. However, certain important functions, such as administrative computing, auditing of schools, bus transpor-tation, food preparation, payroll and pension and new school con-struction, are carried out by the central office."[c]

The bottom line: decentralized management allows schools to have local control while still taking advantage of scale and purchasing power for outside services from a central district office. This is important be-cause schools can then take advantage of shared services that are man-aged at the district level and still maintain control over the bulk of their budgets. This allows principals to direct resources into improving student outcomes at the school level.

a. The decentralized public school districts all used the "weighted student funding for-mula" pioneered by Edmonton school superintendent Michael Strembitsky. The formula links specific school funding to each child and in so doing gives budgetary control to each school principal.

b. William G. Ouchi, "Power to the Principals: Decentralization in three large school districts," *Organization Science*, March/April 2006.

c. Ibid.

ing on administrative staff and an increased number of administrators per student. In the huge Los Angeles Unified School District, for example, only 45 percent of education dollars were spent in the classroom, according to Ouchi. The district spends only $84 per pupil on textbooks (or 90 percent of the state average) but spends $107 per student on supervisors' salaries (which is 191 percent of the state average and does not include principals or other school-level administrators). The trend holds true among all of California's large school districts. In fact, while Los Angeles spent $710 per student on "other services," San Francisco Unified spent $1,004 and Oakland spent $1,254 per student. The state average for all districts is $644 per pupil.[19]

In another study, education researcher Vicki Murray analyzed Arizona's 209 school districts. Her finding: medium size districts tend to have the lowest administrative spending.[20]

In very large districts of 10,000 or more students, bureaucracy, approval bottlenecks and supervisory problems proliferate and lower the value of each administrative dollar spent. A Cato Institute study, for example, found that between 1960 and 1984, the number of school districts nationwide fell more than 60 percent, from 40,520 to 15,747. During this time school administration grew by 500 percent, while the number of teachers and principals rose by only 57 and 79 percent, respectively.[21] The implication is clear: rather than large cost savings, the end result of consolidation often has been higher administrative costs.

Small Schools Movement

On the flip side of pressures to consolidate is the growing trend toward smaller schools. Schools that are strategically designed to have no more than 400 students represent the small schools movement. These schools are in place or starting up in at least 41 states. Some urban districts like Sacramento and Los Angeles have converted or are planning to convert all large high schools to small high schools. The schools are either new or created by subdividing large high schools and having several schools share one building.

In the past decade, the Bill and Melinda Gates Foundation has invested $745 million in grant money into promoting small schools. In addition, the federal government is operating a $142 million grant program for subdividing larger high schools in order to give students more individual attention.[22] These smaller school units have a financial incentive to share services to avoid high noninstructional and administrative costs and to drive more money into the classroom.

Can We All Be Small?

With large districts generating high overhead and instructional spending, does this mean that small districts and small schools are the answer? From an education quality perspective, a strong case certainly can be made for smaller schools. The American Legislative Exchange Council's 2002 Report Card on American Education found that fewer students per school and fewer schools

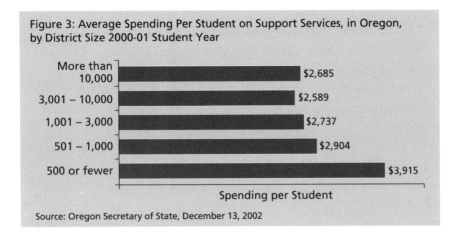

Figure 3: Average Spending Per Student on Support Services, in Oregon, by District Size 2000-01 Student Year

More than 10,000 — $2,685
3,001 – 10,000 — $2,589
1,001 – 3,000 — $2,737
501 – 1,000 — $2,904
500 or fewer — $3,915

Spending per Student

Source: Oregon Secretary of State, December 13, 2002

per district (which means more and smaller districts) are associated with higher SAT, ACT, and National Assessment of Educational Progress scores.[23]

In addition, research by Harvard economist Caroline Hoxby has demonstrated that smaller and more numerous school districts are linked to higher student achievement.[24] Her study, which analyzed the effects of competition among school districts, found higher student performance in metropolitan areas with many school districts such as Boston, than in a single large school district, such as Miami. While Hoxby did not analyze the effects of district size per se, her results suggest that the consolidation of smaller districts into larger districts could weaken school performance by reducing competition among them.

There is a major problem, however, with small school districts. According to a substantial body of research, they tend to have comparatively high noninstructional costs:

- *California.* The ten smallest school districts in California had average spending on "other services" 578 percent higher than the state average for all districts.[25]

- *Oregon.* A 2002 audit conducted by the Oregon secretary of state's office found large discrepancies in average per student spending on support services depending on the size of the school district. School districts with 500 or fewer students spent 34 percent more per student on support services than medium districts with 3,000–10,000 students ($3,915 per student compared with only $2,589 per student in the larger school districts; see figure 3).[26]

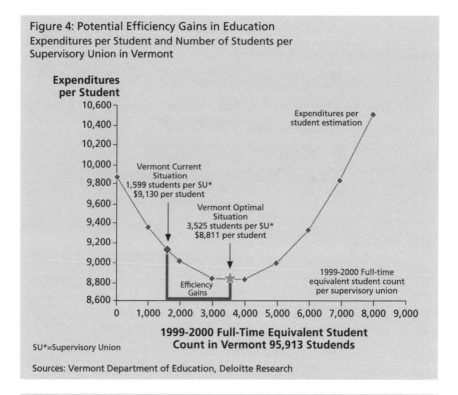

Figure 4: Potential Efficiency Gains in Education
Expenditures per Student and Number of Students per
Supervisory Union in Vermont

SU*=Supervisory Union

Sources: Vermont Department of Education, Deloitte Research

Table 1: School District Size and Per Pupil Spending in California (2001)

Sample Category	Per-Pupil Spending on "Other Services" (state average $644)	Percent of state average for all school districts
Ten smallest districts	$3,724	578%
Ten largest districts	$784	121%
Ten mid-sized districts (all with 6,000 students)	$584	90%

Source: Reason Foundation

- *Maine.* All but one of the state's 25 highest-cost districts have fewer than 300 students, according to research conducted by Phillip Trostel of the Margaret Smith Center for Public Policy at the University of Maine.[27] Maine's per pupil costs are 10 percent higher than the national average, a difference Trostel attributes almost entirely to the disproportionate number of very small school districts in the state.

- *Iowa.* A January 2003 Iowa State University study found that Iowa school districts with fewer than 750 students spent larger proportions of their funds on administrative services.[28]

The Size Paradox

Thus, while being very small often improves educational outcomes, it can also result in higher per-pupil costs. Consolidating into very large districts, in contrast, may create economies of scale for purchasing but may also drive up administrative costs, increase bureaucracy and adversely affect student learning. An examination of school spending patterns across states and in other countries shows a strong correlation between district size and per-pupil costs. As a general rule, the very small and the very large school districts tend to spend the most per capita on noninstructional services. Mid-size districts seem best able to find the "sweet spot"—delivering quality education while keeping costs under control.

Three Syracuse University policy researchers surveyed more than three decades of research on school size and school consolidation. Their finding: the optimal number of students in a district for total cost effectiveness was 6,000. Costs begin to rise when districts grow larger than 6,000 students, and "sizable" per-pupil funding discrepancies "may begin to emerge for districts above 15,000 students."[29]

This finding is supported by a Deloitte Research analysis of Vermont's school spending. Comparing educational costs in Vermont with other northeastern states, the optimal school district size strictly from a cost perspective was 3,525 students per school district. When the results of that study are depicted graphically, a clear savings per pupil is achieved in mid-size districts (see figure 4).

In California, Reason Foundation's snapshot of school district size shows that small districts spend the most per capita on noninstructional costs, large districts spend above the state average even with their large economies of scale and districts with about 6,000 pupils spend less than the state average (see table 1).[30]

Beyond Consolidation: The Shared Services Alternative

Recognizing that not every district or school in the country can or should become mid-size overnight, how can schools still control their noninstructional costs?

The way the consolidation debate is often framed, parents and school districts are left with the false choice of keeping school districts small with strong local control but with high per-student costs or potentially lowering per-pupil costs but having to give up local control through school district consolidation. It need not be one or the other.

It is possible to educate students as if they were in a small school district and still have the economies and buying power of a large district. How? By implementing shared services. Small districts can band together to share everything from purchasing materials to gymnasiums. These agreements can create the same effect as medium-size districts, retaining the educational benefits of small schools while expanding purchasing power. Large districts can organize their individual schools into smaller units and clusters and still achieve economies of scale by sharing services *internally*. Districts of all sizes can participate in shared services to improve the quality of their staff and internal capacities.

Shared services is a technique both the private and public sectors have employed for decades. Since the late 1990s, for example, large-scale shared services have become commonplace in the private sector. Companies such as Ford, General Electric, Hewlett Packard, Pfizer and British Petroleum now have company-wide shared services groups performing certain centralized services once performed at each individual plant, saving money and gaining efficiency.

Shared services have also become commonplace in government. The U.S. Postal Service saves $25 million a year by using shared services for accounting. Work that had been performed by 1,100 employees at 85 unique district accounting offices has been consolidated and standardized and is now being performed by 350 employees at three accounting service centers.[31]

Local governments also have extensive experience with shared services. In New Jersey and Michigan, many municipal governments have engaged in shared services approaches.[32] A study of local government shared services in Wisconsin found many long-running case examples across a range of services, from police and fire to wastewater treatment and economic development.[33]

The most basic form of shared services in the public sector is mutual aid agreements that allow rural communities to share public safety assets across a region, avoiding costly duplication of equipment and specialized training. Another common example is found in water supply. Communities of widely

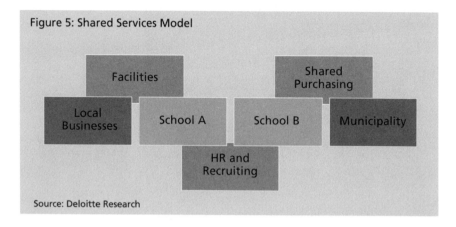

Figure 5: Shared Services Model

Facilities

Shared Purchasing

Local Businesses

School A

School B

Municipality

HR and Recruiting

Source: Deloitte Research

varying sizes enter into joint-powers agreements to operate reservoirs, aqueducts, water treatment plants and distributions systems.

Similar situations exist in solid waste disposal when local governments join together to provide regional solid waste services in landfills or waste-to-energy plants. In Taylor County, Wisconsin, 15 towns and 2 villages combined with the county government to share recycling services. Under a joint agreement each municipality is responsible for its own solid waste contract with the county and must provide a collection site and attendants during operating hours. The county provides a recycling trailer at each site and administers the state grant, the budget and accounting.[34]

Within education, service sharing is also becoming more commonplace. In 2002, the two largest school districts in Texas, Houston and Dallas, entered into a five-year partnership to increase their buying power for health insurance and reduce duplicative administration by pooling their assets to procure employee health benefits. Similarly, two small districts in Wisconsin joined together to share a superintendent, splitting her $120,000 salary.[35]

A shared services center is typically an independent unit created to provide services to client groups within an organization. The services offered are usually based on common needs or operations that are shared by two or more units. The overall aim of a shared service center is to optimize the available resources for the benefit of the participants. It can be as simple as a single administrator overseeing a shared busing system or as complex as an office housing multiple school districts' human resources, information technology (IT), purchasing staff and systems (see figure 5).

Shared services can be based on formal or informal agreements to share nearly anything. In Michigan, Northville Public Schools, Northville Township and the city of Northville have a long history of coordinated efforts. The

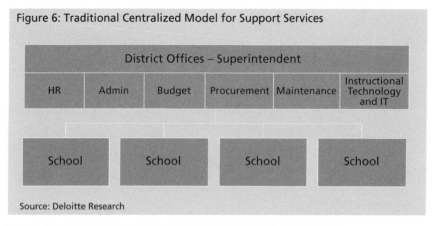

Figure 6: Traditional Centralized Model for Support Services

Source: Deloitte Research

Figure 7: Independent Business Unit Model

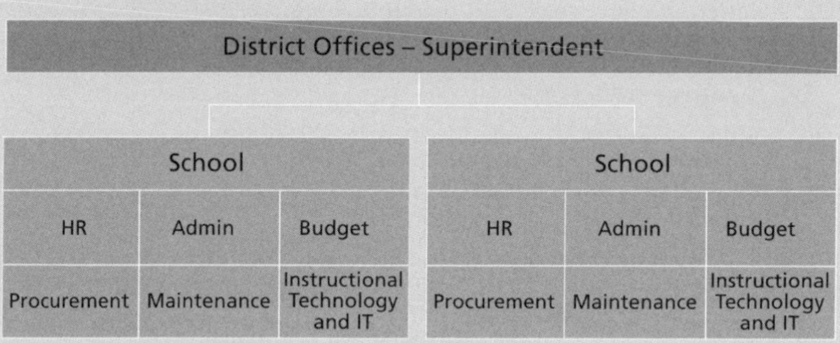

Source: Deloitte Research

Northville Parks and Recreation Department was started in 1980 with the signing of a joint services contract between the municipalities that created a joint recreation authority. The department oversees a substantial recreation program, a youth services organization and a senior citizens program. The township and city have a formula for funding contributions, and the school district has provided facility assistance and commission members.[36]

The idea of sharing services evolved from a number of traditional organizational structures. One common approach featured a centralized structure where administrative expertise was heavily relied upon for smooth functioning. In the case of education, the administrative functions were typically concentrated at the headquarters of large school districts and sometimes inattentive central support agencies (see figure 6).

In an effort to improve responsiveness and make each unit responsible for its share of administrative dollars, the "independent business unit" approach later developed. Each school created its own set of administrative and

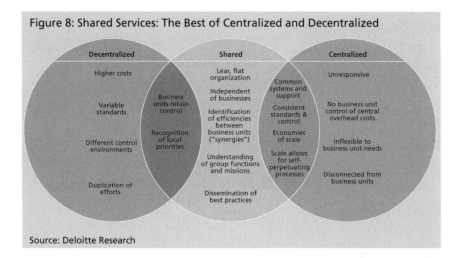

Figure 8: Shared Services: The Best of Centralized and Decentralized

Source: Deloitte Research

support functions (see figure 7). This structure was helpful to customize the competencies and resources to the specific requirements of the school and community. The principal was responsible for the core instructional operations as well as the administrative functions. This structure, however, led to massive duplication of activities, with every school and district procuring its own infrastructure, administration and IT systems.

Both the centralized and the independent business unit support models provide a mix of benefits and drawbacks. Highly centralized administration can be disconnected from its customers. Decentralizing support services provides "in-the-trenches" knowledge and personal service, but makes the use of consistent processes and management controls more difficult.

Shared services allows for the best of both worlds, creating lean, flat organizations that share processes and provide consistent service (see figure 8). Sharing services creates the economies of scale, consistency of process and results that come with centralized models. It also allows districts to maintain the benefits of decentralized control, giving individual administrators oversight of curriculum, education, and other aspects of nonshared processes. By sharing processes that aren't mission critical while still retaining local control of the most important aspects of education, shared services combines the best of big and small.

Opportunities for Sharing Services in Education

While it sounds complex, sharing services is actually a fairly simple concept. Organizations in both the public and private sectors have long rec-

Table 2: School Functions Amenable to Shared Services

Capability	Fit for Shared Service	Savings Potential (Comparative)
Direct (Services to Students)		
Transportation	●	●
Food Service and Nutrition	◑	◑
Instructional	◑	◑
Safety and Security	◑	◑
Health Services	◑	○
Indirect (Services to Staff or Infrastructure)		
Purchasing	●	●
Finance and Payroll	●	◑
Facilities & Real Estate	●	●
Human Resources	●	◑
Technology Services	◑	●
Administration	◑	◑

○ ◑ ●
Low ──→ High

Source: Deloitte Research

ognized that they have activities, business processes, services and physical plant maintenance that can be shared effectively with others. These elements can be as simple as sharing a printer between two offices or as complicated as sharing a common payroll system across a global organization spanning multiple continents. Such sharing, with its shared responsibility and shared benefit, is fast becoming standard practice.

Shared services can yield very real operational efficiencies around facilities, transportation, food service, real estate management, procurement, human resources, information technology, security and even instruction.

Specific shared service opportunities for schools can be divided into two general areas: direct services to students and indirect services to staff or infrastructure.

Direct Services

INSTRUCTIONAL. A number of creative approaches to applying shared services to instruction and content-related applications have been successful. In northeastern Ontario, for instance, all three French-language school boards belong to a regional consortium for teacher training. It has yielded sizable savings in instructional costs per student and curriculum development costs for the districts.

In the Greater Lawrence area of Massachusetts, ten school districts have banded together to provide special education services. This sharing will save them approximately $13 million over the next two decades.[37]

Another example of sharing instructional services is in Minnesota, where two rural school districts joined together to provide instruction. One district instructs grades K–3 and 7–9 while the other teaches grades 4–6 and 10–12. Some teachers travel between schools and all activities are paired. Despite joint school board meetings, the school districts remain separate governmental units.[38]

TRANSPORTATION. Large districts have the flexibility to incorporate sharing in a number of creative ways. The simplest involve internally sharing resources, time, or space, such as when a handful of neighboring schools band together to host a recruiting fair. Even more interesting, though, are examples of well-planned formal shared services agreements. Two school boards in Ontario, Canada, have joined together to share bus transportation services and audio-visual (AV) resources. By creating a single bus system, the two boards will save $8 million in administrative, capital, and fuel costs over three years. The boards' shared AV library serves classrooms in both districts, saving $300,000 annually.

Indirect Services

PURCHASING. Municipalities in Middlesex County, New Jersey, have set up the Shared Services Program that helps each town reduce daily operating expenses through cooperative purchasing. The program began in 1998 by offering towns aggregate natural gas purchasing, resulting in a 5 percent savings on electricity for public buildings during the first year of the program. Currently the municipalities share services for water and wastewater programs and the purchasing of natural gas, electricity, equipment, services and supplies.[39]

ADMINISTRATION. Seven school districts in Connecticut have a shared services arrangement for administrative services that includes the superintendent, director of instruction, federal programs, special education directors and a legal agent.[40] Meanwhile, in west Texas, the Region 17 regional service center located in Lubbock, which serves an area encompassing about 19,000 square miles (close to the size of Pennsylvania), provides payroll and account-

Food Services Sharing in Pennsylvania

Cornwall-Lebanon School District and Northern Lebanon School District in Pennsylvania entered into an agreement to share the services of a food service director. After the first year of operation, the arrangement netted a savings of $100,000, compared with a previous year combined loss of $20,000. The financial success created a more stable working environment for all the food service employees, resulting in a lower employee turnover rate. The combined volume increased the districts' purchasing power, resulting in lower food costs.

The districts benefited from the shared services by hiring an individual who possessed in-depth knowledge of nutrition, food preparation, marketing, fiscal management and interpersonal skills. Both districts have been able to combine efforts in areas such as purchasing, in-service programs, safety issues, collaboration of ideas for marketing products and the substitute food service workers labor pool. The supervisor of food and nutrition services has been able to take advantage of combined purchasing by buying skids of food items rather than cases, a practice that has saved money for both districts.

The shared food service programs have saved time and expense. By combining the programs for the two districts, costs are basically reduced in half and a common day or days can be scheduled for training in both districts. This allows for discussion and sharing of information between two districts and the in-service consultant. Because kitchens are subject to many safety and health issues, both districts can benefit from ideas that each district may have experienced and allow the supervisor to initiate common safety and health practices in all of the kitchens.

Another benefit of sharing is the opportunity to increase the substitute food service employee pool. Because the supervisor is performing the interview process, an individual may apply at one of the districts and be considered for employment at both districts pending individual district policies and paperwork and the job candidate's availability to work for both districts.

Menu planning has been another area that the two districts share. Because the supervisor can coordinate purchases for both districts, daily menus can be planned based on the purchases for both districts. Collaboration on menus has helped to increase sales and improve quality of food items that are offered to students in both districts.

Source: Benchmarking Project, Center for Total Quality Schools, Pennsylvania State University (http://www.ed.psu.edu/benchmarking_sbm/taxonomymain.htm).

Potential Partners for Shared Services

- Other school districts
- Other schools (especially for large school districts)
- Universities and colleges
- Businesses
- Municipalities
- Nonprofits
- Community health and service centers

ing services for a number of rural school districts, saving each more than 50 percent a year and some up to 88 percent annually. The service center has also established an insurance co-op, which allows about 20 rural districts to purchase optional health services plans, such as dental insurance, at a much lower rate with better coverage than they could obtain on their own.

Human resources represents another good opportunity for shared provision of administrative services. In 2004, the Massachusetts Human Resources Division (HRD) implemented shared services to streamline human resource services for all state agencies. The HRD allowed government agencies to reduce staffing and save the commonwealth millions of dollars. The HRD reduced its own staffing by 50 percent even while handling more complex responsibilities and offering more innovative services to state agencies. For example, the state agencies devised a new shared recruitment process that reduced the time to fill a position from four months to five weeks.[41]

TECHNOLOGY. Districts have vast opportunities to share technology, ranging from shared systems and applications to shared helpdesk and onsite IT support. Districts across the country have found creative ways to develop payroll and human resources systems with municipalities and neighboring schools, to share the cost of software licensing and purchasing applications, and even to share chief information officers. Sarasota County, New York, and the local school district created a shared services partnership for information technology that cut personnel and software costs for the school district.[42]

FACILITIES AND REAL ESTATE. A new frontier for educators is combining forces with the private sector. Examples of successful pairings abound, often where the schedule or needs of a school nicely balance those of a local business or

Shared Services and Charter Schools

The approximately 3,400 charter schools in the United States are also good candidates for shared service arrangements. Shared services can help charter schools uphold the integrity of their individual school missions while sharing the cost of administrative services and other general operating costs. The California Charter Schools Association (CCSA), for example, has helped its members enter into shared service agreements to purchase goods and services. The CCSA Joint Powers Authority was created to save charter schools significant costs in mandatory workers' compensation insurance and liability insurance—saving the typical charter school over $20,000 per year on workers' compensation insurance alone.

Similarly, CCSA has created CharterBuy—a program that taps California charter schools' collective buying power and assembles a team of experts in purchasing to provide charter schools the best deals on supplies and equipment. The CharterBuy program has been saving charter schools as much as 50 percent of a school's expected costs on various goods and services.

Charter schools can also combine resources to share instructional services such as special education. For example, the Redding School of the Arts (RSA) charter school in Redding, California, formed a Charter Schools Special Education Consortium open to charter schools in Shasta County. The consortium currently serves six charter schools. The schools pool their special education dollars into a central fund, and the consortium coordinates all special education services.

corporation. The Lincoln Unified School district in Stockton, California, negotiated with a private fitness center operator to build a facility on site at a newly planned school. The district will provide the land, and the fitness center operator will pay to build the facility. Once operational, private fitness center clients will use the facility in the morning before school and in the evening, while students will use it during the school day.

Seven Benefits of Sharing Services

So while shared services can take many forms, and look different from application to application, sharing offers the best of both worlds—the benefits of common systems, support and process, with the priorities of local control. Seven benefits to implementing this approach stand out.

Benefit 1: Save Money

For most school officials, the primary impetus for moving to shared services is the ability to reduce business costs and channel the savings into the classroom or address budget shortfalls. Studies of private firms find that nearly 90 percent of shared services agreements lead to cost reductions, with the majority experiencing cost savings greater than 20 percent.[43] When Bristol-Myers Squibb created a global business services division for financial transaction processing, it was able to eliminate 85 worldwide invoice-processing locations, saving $1.5 billion per year.[44] Similarly, the Dow Chemical Co. replaced 400 financial service centers around the world with four global centers in 1994, eliminating 70 percent of finance positions. The result: a 50 percent reduction in costs.[45]

Public sector shared services arrangements also produce significant cost savings, especially in the long run.[46] Through the New Jersey Regional Efficiency Aid Program (REAP), 31 Somerset County municipalities and school districts have saved nearly $10 million over the past five years by sharing services with each other, according to the Somerset County Business Partnership.

The cost savings from shared services typically fall into these categories:

- *Lower capital costs.* School districts can reduce the capital costs of facilities and equipment by sharing with other districts and municipalities. For example, the Mount Olive School District in New Jersey reduced its transportation costs by establishing transportation partnerships with other districts to transport their special education students. Mount Olive's transportation agreements bring in $200,000 in revenue a year.[47]

  In South Lyon, Michigan, the city and school district built the first combined administration building in the state.[48] The school district provided the land and the city financed the building. The building saved the school district the costs of a bond issue and the city was spared the expense and effort of purchasing land.

- *Diminished administrative and development costs.* The Midwestern Higher Education Commission worked with external vendors to create the Academic Scheduling and Management Software program. Colleges and secondary schools across states in the Midwest, including Illinois, Indiana, Kansas, Michigan, Minnesota, Missouri, Nebraska, Ohio, and Wisconsin, share this software package. By sharing the administrative and de-

Potential Magnitude of Cost Savings

California schools spend about 46 percent of their budgets on noninstructional services (including administration, operation and maintenance, transportation and food service). This amounts to $23 billion in state education dollars flowing to noninstructional services in the 2005–06 California budget. Various studies and literature reviews have identified cost savings of anywhere from 20 to 40 percent from using shared services arrangements. Assuming a very conservative 20 percent cost savings rate, shifting only one-quarter of the $23 billion in California's noninstructional school costs to shared service arrangements could potentially save California school districts more than $1 billion annually.

Using similarly conservative numbers, cost savings to public schools in the United States as a whole from shifting just a quarter of noninstructional services to shared services could potentially yield savings in the range of $9 billion. To put this number in perspective, it is the equivalent to 900 new schools or more than 150,000 additional school teachers. In other words, it could have a significant impact on education funding.

These numbers, of course, are only rough estimates. Nevertheless, they demonstrate that the potential savings from moving to shared services approaches are great enough to warrant considerably more attention than they are currently receiving from most school districts.

velopment costs of the package, member institutions saved $800,000 as a result of the lower purchase price.

• *Reduced redundancy.* Shared services also help organizations shave costs by reducing redundancy in activities, processes, employees and IT systems. School districts have been innovative in using shared services to reduce the high costs of special education. Since small districts may have very few students with a specific type of disability, school districts have often banded together to share staff and facilities that serve students with specific disabilities. For example, the Northern Valley Regional High School District in Bergen County, New Jersey, shares special education services, staff training, and curriculum development with the seven elementary school districts whose students attend its two high schools. The district also operates a preschool program for autistic children, which according to district officials, offers significant savings to the 22 participating districts.

- *Lower personnel costs.* Administrative and support functions consume nearly 50 percent of the budget in most school districts. Shared services allow school districts to capture economies of scale in staffing these functions.[49] Small districts can share specialized staff for such areas as legal services, maintenance, payroll, transportation and food services. In Illinois, Bloom Township operates back-office services for 13 local districts with four to six "support personnel" in a central office location. Similar sized school districts require one or two support personnel within each district. The center provides a full range of budget, payroll, audit, reporting, grant administration and similar services. Each of the districts pays a pro rata amount for these shared services. The smallest of the 13 districts pays approximately $12,000 per year for all of these services, which likely equates to less than one-quarter of a full-time employee.

  In Salem County, New Jersey, a single school business administrator with a staff of 10 provides business services to 14 districts in four adjoining counties, saving each district about half of what it would spend to employ a full-time business administrator with benefits.[50]

- *Revenue from sales of surplus assets.* Shared services can reduce costs in other ways as well. For example, shared service agreements can create surplus assets and potential revenue from selling them.[51]

Benefit 2: Gain Economies of Scale

Shared service agreements can enhance purchasing power and the ability to buy more products at a lower price. For example, in 2003 the Desert Sands and Coachella Valley unified school districts in California created the Coachella Valley Alliance, a purchasing cooperative aimed at buying in volume at a substantial discount.[52] In southeast Texas, 14 small school districts pool their money for school violence and substance abuse programs, allowing them to buy more and higher-quality programs.[53]

Benefit 3: Standardize Processes

The shared services model helps districts and schools standardize approaches to problems across the organization. When processes are consistent, performance is more likely to be predictable and improvements easier to implement. Moreover, when processes are transparent, staff and stakeholders have more realistic expectations. For example, when the Cornwall-Lebanon and Northern Lebanon school districts in Lebanon, Pennsylvania, shared food services, the partnership allowed them to standardize common safety and health practices in all of the schools' kitchens.

When Deloitte Consulting LLP reviewed student transportation costs for the Illinois Board of Education, it found huge disparities in cost per student ($319 a year vs. $2,006 a year) and cost per mile ($2.61 a mile vs. $5.21 a mile) among districts across the state.[54] Standardizing how schools approach key challenges can help all districts benefit from the practices of their most innovative peers.

Benefit 4: Attract More Highly Qualified Staff

The shared services model allows districts that are often unable to match the salaries of larger districts to pool resources and attract more highly qualified personnel. In 2002 David Freeman, the superintendent of the Placerville Union School District in California was approached by the superintendent of the one-school Camino Union School District, who asked if the two districts could work together to share a transportation director. Camino offered to pay Placerville Union approximately $15,000 a year to administer Camino's bus service. "That offset our costs, and the benefit to them was they got a full-time quality (transportation) person," Freeman said.[55]

Benefit 5: Retain Local Control and Achieve Scale

Shared services provide a mechanism to allow schools to maintain control over their instructional budgets, yet still benefit from cost savings for non-instructional services. Schools and school districts can take advantage of shared services that are organized across districts while still maintaining control over the majority of their budgets and direct resources into improving student outcomes at the school level.

Benefit 6: Flatten Out Peaks and Troughs

There are regular variations in needs for certain types of services as well as unexpected spikes and dips. Shared services help spread out such risk and variability. For example, fluctuating enrollment averages can sometimes lead to annual personnel shortages or surpluses, especially for special education

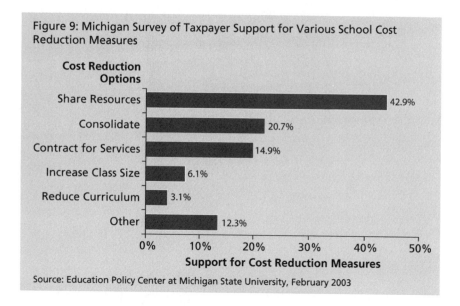

Figure 9: Michigan Survey of Taxpayer Support for Various School Cost Reduction Measures

Source: Education Policy Center at Michigan State University, February 2003

and similar services, but these variations in personnel needs are much less likely across several districts sharing such services. Shared services also tend to smooth out spending and thus make budgeting and planning easier.[56]

Benefit 7: Less Political Opposition

For taxpayers, sharing services is a much more popular cost-cutting option than political consolidation. A 2002 survey by Michigan State University found that about 43 percent of Michigan residents favored sharing resources as the best way to reduce school district costs and spending, double the share of those who favored consolidation (see figure 9).[57]

State Government's Role in Advancing Shared Services

Shared services can help address many of the management challenges faced by school districts. While superintendents and administrators at the local level must identify performance gaps, design the shared service systems and sell the change to the community, state legislators, governor's offices and state education officials can all also play a critical role. States that desire to reduce overall education costs by promoting the greater use of shared services in local school districts have three levers they can pull—budget pressure, financial incentives and technical assistance.

One Model for Sharing Services

The Educational Services Commission (ESC) of Morris County, New Jersey, offers one well-tested model for sharing services. A publicly managed cooperative program, the ESC is overseen by a board of directors consisting of a representative board of education member from each Morris County school district. This structure enables districts to share ideas for ways to pool services and save money. The commission offers school districts opportunities to share bus routes, special education consultants and purchasing contracts for supplies. The commission also runs two schools for students with special education needs. All its services are aimed at allowing local districts to use centralized services to hold local costs down.

Created in 1970, the ESC employs 300 people and is run like a business. It operates solely on tuition and funding from local school districts and does not receive state aid. Its largest service is transportation, coordinating $14.3 million in contracts for school bus routes for more than 50 school districts in the Morris County area. The commission has grown from a $7.5 million operation in 1992 to $25.5 million in 2003.

Morris County school districts largely take advantage of the ESC's offerings. Local public school business administrators say the ESC saves them time and money, especially when it comes to finding a bus route for one or two students attending a special education school. In addition to the ESC's busing program, the commission's two schools and a cadre of special education consultants and specialists, such as physical therapists, are among the most popular services.

Small districts like Mount Arlington find the ESC is the antidote to local staffing difficulties, said business administrator Elizabeth George. The K-8 district with roughly 650 students can neither afford a transportation director nor full-time physical or speech therapists. Depending on who moves in and out of town, the need for such therapists can change from one year to the next, George said. Rather than hiring and firing people each year, the ESC can fill in with one of its professionals, she said.

One long-standing program that 17 districts are drawn to is the insurance pool, which allows districts to pool their fees to pay claims for employees hurt on the job. The program includes coverage of medical expenses and lost salary, as well as mandatory safety training seminars. Although the fund had a few years where full premiums had to be paid, James From, Washington Township's business administrator, said districts often get a refund from the pool.

Budget Pressure

As the funder of a large percentage of local school district spending, states can use their budget leverage to encourage or require school districts to share services. This is now difficult to do for a variety of reasons, one of which is that state officials have little information on how much schools spend on support services.

The first step therefore is to make noninstructional school spending more transparent. One way to do this is to divide the education budget into instructional and noninstructional categories, forcing more detailed explanations of expenditures. The state of Idaho, for example, separates its education budget into five categories: instruction, support services (such as guidance counselors and librarians), noninstructional services (food services, for example), facility acquisition services (such as additions or new facilities), and other services (such as debt servicing and contingency reserves).[58] Texas is considering establishing spending targets for instruction, central administration and district operations. If the new rules are adopted, school boards that exceed the targets will be responsible for defending their spending decisions to the public.[59] This type of partitioning allows state legislators and state departments of education to dig deeper into the actual ways education dollars are being spent and reduce state contributions in areas shown to be inefficient.

Second, states can put school management practices under a microscope. In Florida each school district must undergo a best financial management practices review every five years. The reviews are conducted by the state legislature's Office of Program Policy Analysis and Government Accountability with the help of outside consultants. Meanwhile, the Texas School Performance Review, operated out of the State Legislative Budget Board, has conducted more than 75 audits of Texas school district business practices. The reviews have identified hundreds of millions of dollars in savings through better business practices. Typically nine of every ten suggestions made by the school performance review team are ultimately adopted by the school districts.

Once states have a better handle on noninstructional school district costs and practices, they can allocate a certain percentage of state appropriations (10 percent, for example) depending on the degree to which districts implement shared services and achieve greater efficiencies. Such an approach would complement efforts under way to make educational achievement at individual schools more transparent and funding based more closely on improvement.

Alternately, school districts can be required to devote a certain minimum percentage of their spending to the classroom. The Louisiana legislature passed a resolution in 2005 encouraging state officials to require local school districts to limit spending on nonclassroom activities to 35 percent of their budgets. Texas governor Rick Perry went one step further and issued an executive order in August 2005 requiring Texas schools to limit such spending. Districts that fail to boost classroom spending to 65 percent of total spending will eventually face sanctions, according to the Texas Education Agency. Perry's proposal has encountered strong opposition from some local school officials who argue that the order infringes on local control.[60]

Financial Incentives

Some states have laws and regulations that limit the ability of districts to share resources or to engage in partnerships with municipalities and the private sector. Eliminating these types of barriers can greatly enhance the chance that shared services will be considered.

States can also make shared services a more attractive option for communities by providing incentives and inducements to school districts, including financial assistance for study and start-up of shared services agreements. In 2004 the Wisconsin legislature budgeted $45 million in incentive payments for local government entities that demonstrate cost savings in the first year of a shared services arrangement.[61] Similarly, in 1998 New York provided more than $700,000 in grants to help establish shared services between school districts and municipalities.[62] Such incentives can make the task of "selling" the idea of shared services to the community, local board or parents much easier.

Several states have enacted legislation and set up financial incentives to encourage shared services.

NEW YORK STATE. Boards of Cooperative Educational Services, also known as BOCES, have been a cornerstone of the state's educational system since 1948 when they were first created by the state legislature.[63] Each of the 38 BOCES regions is referred to as a supervisory district under the leadership of a district superintendent. The district superintendent serves as the representative of the commissioner of education and as the chief executive officer of the BOCES program. BOCES services are created when two or more school districts decide they have similar needs that can be met by a shared program or service.

BOCES helps school districts save money by providing opportunities to pool resources and share costs of programs and services that they might not be able to afford otherwise. It is more efficient and less costly to operate one central service than it is to have separate programs in each school district. However, BOCES services are often customized, offering districts the flexibility to meet their individual needs. The decision to participate in BOCES services is based on the unique needs of each district. If the district doesn't need a BOCES service, it does not request it and does not have to pay for it. The state of New York offers aid for BOCES-provided services. Each spring the local district's board of education selects BOCES services for the upcoming year. In the following year, a portion of the cost of BOCES services is returned to the district by the state. The amount returned is based on a formula that takes into account the district's financial resources and needs. Money returned to the district is used as unrestricted revenue.

The BOCES program is governed by a board of education just like local districts are governed. The BOCES Board of Education is composed of representatives from local (component) school districts who are responsible for curricular, financial and other policy decisions, just as boards are at the local level. Except for an administrative charge that is based on each school district's size, districts pay only for those BOCES services they use.

NEW JERSEY. In 1999 New Jersey developed an incentive-based system to encourage shared services. The state's REDI program (Regional Efficiency Development Incentive) provided financial support to local government in order to get shared services programs started with neighboring school districts, towns or counties. Before a fiscal crisis forced the program to be cut, school districts received nearly $2.2 million from the REDI program.[64]

Another New Jersey incentive program, REAP (Regional Efficiency Aid Program), publicly rewards school districts and municipalities for sharing services by giving homeowners tax credits. In 2001 taxpayers in 249 communities had their property tax bills lowered through REAP.[65]

CALIFORNIA. The state of California created a shared service partnership agreement with the University of California library system.[66] Since 1998 the state has provided close to $12 million in funding to encourage a shared digital library across all UC campuses. In addition, each individual UC campus contributes a portion of its discretionary funding to maintain the shared collection. If campus libraries were to independently negotiate for the same rights to use the 8,000 titles and 250 databases in the systemwide digital library, the UC library system would have to spend an additional $34 million per year.

INDIANA. Indiana recently enacted shared services legislation giving broad authority to school administrators to make decisions that will save their districts money. School districts can consolidate their purchasing authority to buy insurance, supplies, buses and services. In addition to greater ac-

quisition authority, school corporations can access technical assistance from
the state's Department of Education's Division of Finance and the Office of
Management and Budget. The legislation uses both carrot—recognition and
reward for reducing costs—and stick—annual reporting requirements—to
rein in overhead costs and drive a greater percentage of each education dollar
into the classroom.

Technical Assistance

Implementing shared services requires a number of sophisticated management and contracting competencies rarely available at local levels. Schools
and smaller districts often have limited capacities in the realm of contract
development, process improvement and management design, large-scale
business proposals, contract management and performance measurement.
States typically have more well-developed networks of vendors who can provide support for designing and implementing shared services systems and
processes, frequently deal with proposals from technology and consulting
firms and have more sophisticated performance measurement capabilities.
They therefore are well positioned to provide some of these complex technical services, either directly or through training and education for staff. The
state can also provide a repository of research, case studies and models that
school districts can use in analyzing their own shared services prospects.[67]

At the federal level, the U.S. Office of Personnel Management (OPM)
is managing and evaluating a large-scale human resources shared services
project across 22 federal agencies.[68] Shared service centers will be key components of the federal government's human-capital management structure.
OPM will take prequalified candidate agencies and conduct a rigorous qualification and selection process with the assistance of employees from the
agencies participating in the human resources task force. At the end of the
process, OPM's director will announce the first group of centers.

Six Steps for Getting It Right

Success in reducing education costs through shared services depends on savvy
politics, accurate assessment, public consultation, planning, advocacy and
implementation. It also depends on the prudent boldness of good leadership.

Like many other business transformation approaches, shared services
agreements sometimes fail. Such failures typically occur because of the lack

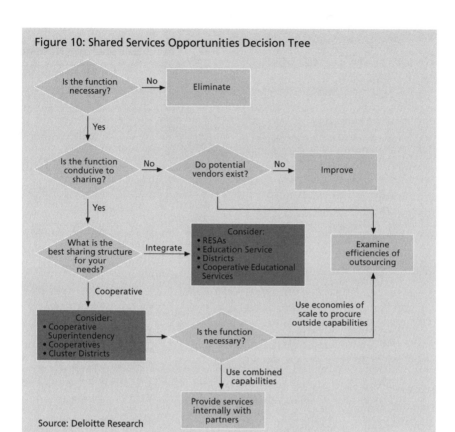

Figure 10: Shared Services Opportunities Decision Tree

Source: Deloitte Research

of a coherent vision for change, weak business cases, inadequate attention to managing the change, poorly trained staff or ill-defined contracts and service levels. These missteps can be avoided by following these six guidelines when transitioning to a shared services model.

Conduct an Assessment and Develop a Business Case for Change

First, a political champion and overarching government authority must articulate support and a vision for the creative delivery of services. Then school officials need to conduct an assessment to be certain that sharing services makes economic sense. Sometimes this model won't fit local needs and circumstances. A careful business case that weighs costs and benefits will make this clear.

Potential partners must then start the sharing process with the joint planning, development and evaluation of the shared service plan. A shared service agreement might be as simple as two school districts exploring over-

Bringing it All Together

STRUCTURES FOR SHARED SERVICES

A variety of different models for shared services in education have emerged in the United States and throughout the world. Each model has certain strengths and may be the most appropriate solution to a school district's challenges, whether applied to small schools or large districts. In 1995 the New Jersey School Boards Association developed a definition of shared services in education as "Any voluntary formal or informal agreement between two or more entities that enhances educational opportunities for students and/or demonstrates cost effectiveness and accountability."[a] That leaves room for a lot of different opportunities to share, ranging from different legal structures of sharing to different shared functions, like transportation and safety.

COOPERATIVES

Specific-function cooperatives are the most common form of shared services. They are formed among multiple school districts to share functions and provide economies of scale. While not every cost center or responsibility of a district fits ideally with a shared services model, many functions and services are appropriate for shared services.

Example: In Texas, three transportation cooperatives provide bus services for multiple school districts. One of these, the Bowie County Transportation cooperative, provides bus services for 13 districts in Bowie County through interlocal agreements with each district. The cooperative is run by a board, composed of superintendents for each of the districts, which establishes policy and operational procedures. The cost-per-mile achieved by the Bowie County cooperative is far lower than the state average for bus transportation.

COOPERATIVE SUPERINTENDENCY

Commonly used in many states with small districts in sparsely settled regions, two or more local school boards enter into an interlocal agreement to retain a single superintendent who serves both boards. Sharing superintendents can be thought of as the sharing of administrative capabilities. The agreement specifies the terms of employment and the sharing of expenses for maintaining a single office.

Example: In New Hampshire, the state has created School Administrative Units, each one directed by a superintendent of schools and one or more school boards.

REGIONAL EDUCATIONAL SERVICE AGENCIES

In this arrangement regional cooperatives, governed by separate boards, collaborate with local member school districts to serve and support them. Membership in regional service centers is typically voluntary, and fees for services rendered by the regional agency may be assessed in a variety of ways.

Example: In West Virginia the state Board of Education established regional agencies that provide basic computer skills support, cooperative purchasing, feasibility studies, instructional models, legislative evaluation reports and similar services.

EDUCATIONAL SERVICE DISTRICTS

This is a special purpose school district that consists of member local school districts within a specific geographic area. These public entities typically operate in a highly entrepreneurial fashion, deriving their funding from grants, cooperatives and other self-directed initiatives. "Membership" or participation is likely to be required of local districts. The educational service district board is appointed by the member districts and it operates a central office providing shared services to local districts.

Example: In Washington State, Education Service District 105 was created to provide cooperative and informational services to local districts.

COOPERATIVE EDUCATIONAL SERVICES (CES)

When two or more school districts decide they have similar needs that can be met by a shared program or service, they can create a Cooperative Educational Service region. Each CES is referred to as a supervisory district under the leadership of a district superintendent who serves as the representative of the Commissioner of Education and as the chief executive officer of the CES. The CES Board of Education is composed of representatives from local (component) school districts, and these board members are responsible for curricular, financial and other policy decisions, just as school boards are at the local level. Except for an administrative charge that is based on each school district's size, districts pay only for the CES services they use. State aid helps to offset some of the expenses, while others are directly funded by the state or federal government. CES entities have no taxing authority.

CLUSTER DISTRICTS

Cluster or union districts are initiated by local school boards and involve sharing services with neighboring school districts, with certain academic programs being made accessible to the students of different schools. The local boards may, for example, select a superintendent who spends some time in one district and some time in another. Students from one district may be sent temporarily to another school for specific activities. Clusters have been formed around science programs and materials, computers, staff development and in-service training for administrators.

Example: Smithville Independent School District in Texas kicked off a staff development initiative, called Eastern Cluster Districts, whose purpose was to use shared instructional specialists to provide staff development in a location convenient to the districts on the eastern edge of Region 13 in Texas. The goal was to reduce travel time and costs and encourage greater participation in staff development by the participating districts.

a. Zenaida Mendez, "Shared Services like in Parsippany Trim School Costs," *Daily Record* (Morris County, New Jersey), December 20, 2003.

lap in food or transportation service or as complex as several school districts forming an independent board to oversee and manage several types of service agreements.

This initial stage also consists of researching what each partner has to offer and establishing the formal structure to support the shared service agreement, whether it's a written contract or a structured cooperative. During this phase, the following questions should be addressed:

- Do shared services make sense given local circumstances?

- What processes are the best candidates for shared services?

- What legal structures best match our needs?

- What is a realistic time frame for integrating the service?

Figure 10 provides a simple decision-making process to evaluate which services and business activities would be most appropriate to include in a shared services approach.

Communicate to Staff and Stakeholders—Early and Often

Shared services cannot be implemented top-down or in a bubble. Change management is a critical component of all successful shared services projects. Moving from multiple processes, delivered by disparate staffs in multiple locations in many systems, to a complete regime of shared, rationalized services can be difficult for all stakeholders. The transition often involves the dissolution of authority and power that may threaten individuals' conceptions of certain roles and responsibilities (such as individual school control of payroll) and lead to discomfort, suspicion and entrenchment. During each of the shifts involved in the implementation of shared services, staff, teachers, administrators and parents must feel they are involved and have a substantive role in how the final sharing solution will function. Ensuring this involvement entails documenting successes and seeking continual feedback.

Consider Shared Services if...

- Diverse, hard-to-find or expensive skills are required to provide a service

- Peer or neighboring districts provide the service better or cheaper than you currently can

- Multiple outsourcing or potential private sector partners exist

- Needed outputs or services are clearly defined and can be packaged

- Shared services supports financial incentives or mandates from state or local government

- Partnering will give you greater reach or credibility (certified staff, for example, broader pools of resources)

- Third parties can deliver service or achieve goals at lower cost than government can

- High barriers to entry or best-in-class performance make economies of scale desirable

Carefully Design the Requirements

All parties will benefit from the rigors of the requirements definition process—the act of spelling out each party's needs and expectations in a clear, detailed way. Schools that are the most successful with shared services view the process of setting service-level agreements as more than a legal step—it helps them understand what it is about each process or operational responsibility they consider critical to their district's own success. Each party must also have the technical and staff capacities to develop these kinds of agreements (if they don't, they should seek out such capabilities from the marketplace).

Baselines should be documented to avoid entering into arrangements with false expectations. Other issues that should be addressed in the service-level agreements include risk-sharing mechanisms and incentives to create alignment.

Create a Governance Board

Where pairing occurs, the two school boards usually act as the governing board with each board approving any service agreements. If more school districts are involved, a representative board member from each participating school district may be elected or appointed to the governing board.

As the cooperative relationship becomes more formal and provides a variety of services, the board of directors may be elected from a broader community base. Advisory committees also may exist. In such cases it's important to involve local school board and community members, teachers and administrators regularly to achieve buy-in and understanding. Working with teachers, staff and administrators from the beginning and making their opinions an important part of the implementation approach can create strong support for and promotion of shared services programs within participating schools or districts. The governing board can also help to create cultural alignment in the new, shared services organization.

Achieve the Right Balance between Accountability and Flexibility

Clear performance criteria and measures, explicit sanctions for nonperformance, an open monitoring scheme and frequent performance reviews are essential components of a shared services approach. At the same time, interagency agreements and contracts with providers must evolve as the sharing matures. Targets and performance indicators should be reevaluated if it becomes apparent that they are unhelpful, unattainable or create incentives that don't match with the district's goals. This kind of review should be frequent, data-driven, collaborative and friendly. Partners must always be able to withdraw from the arrangement—given appropriate lead time and transition.

Conclusion

In this era of tight budgets and loud calls for results and accountability, schools need to identify every means of saving money while improving classroom learning. Shared services provide one answer: a way to improve the ability to procure services, better use facilities and classrooms and educate students without greater spending.

As school board officials, superintendents and state legislators consider shared services, they will soon discover that politics is by far their greatest challenge: good old-fashioned turf protection, more than anything else, has caused schools to lag behind the private sector in adopting shared services. The processes are obviously important. The technology has to work. The design has to fit local circumstances. Due attention must be paid to managing change. But it is usually policy issues, or politics, that will make or break shared services.

While the politics of shared services is daunting, this cost reduction strategy can be presented as one of the least painful ways to pare educational costs. It doesn't pit education against administration or dollars against test scores or result in any loss of local control over schooling. It's a proven way to move more tax dollars into the classroom, an objective few educators would find unworthy of pursuing.

Chapter 8: The Final Word

THE CHALLENGE
• Tight state budgets, surging school enrollment in many districts (and falling enrollment in others), executive mandates and court rulings put increasing pressure on states and school districts to reduce education costs, particularly for non-instructional services.
• Lacking economies of scale—and often sufficient managerial expertise—many districts find it extraordinarily expensive to provide a full array of support and administrative services in-house.
• While district consolidation is one option for achieving economies of scale to reduce costs, it can have serious downsides including a negative impact on educational outcomes.

REFORM STRATEGIES
• *Functional sharing.* Shared services agreements can be used for services across a range of school functions: transportation, food service and nutrition, instruction, safety and security, health services, purchasing, finance and payroll, facilities and real estate, human resources, technology services and administration.
• *Cooperative purchasing.* Pooling purchasing power can yield substantial savings for school districts and their partners by reducing operating expenses for such items as utilities, equipment, services and supplies.
• *Tapping underutilized assets.* Partnering with businesses can help school districts tap into underutilized assets such as land. For example, in exchange for land, private partners may provide school facilities with fitness centers that can be used by students during the day and by private clients outside school hours.

EXAMPLES
• In the greater *Lawrence, Massachusetts,* area 10 school districts banded together to provide special education services, saving them approximately $13 million over the next two decades.
• In *Pennsylvania,* Cornwall-Lebanon and Northern Lebanon School Districts share the services of a food service director. By sharing the director and increasing the districts' purchasing power, the agreement has saved both districts time and money.

NEXT STEPS
• *Make noninstructional school spending more transparent.* Dividing the budget into instructional and noninstructional categories forces more detailed explanations of expenditures.
• *Eliminate the barriers to shared services.* Examine and, if need be, amend state laws and regulations that limit the ability of school districts to share resources or to engage in partnerships with municipalities and the private sector.
• *Encourage school districts to share services.* Make shared services more attractive by providing incentives and financial and technical support.

{9} *William D. Eggers and Tiffany Dovey*

Closing the Infrastructure Gap

Back in the 1960s, California was known for more than just Hollywood, the Beach Boys and some of the most beautiful scenery in the country. The state was also famous for its unparalleled infrastructure building. Led by Governor Pat Brown, California had one of the world's most extensive transportation infrastructure programs in the late 1950s and early 1960s, paving the way for much of the state's subsequent economic prosperity.

Those times seem like ancient history. These days, annualized state transportation needs amount to around $16 billion, but California currently funds only about one-quarter of that. The result is a huge and growing backlog of projects—$100 billion at last count.[1] It is no wonder that traffic problems are huge in many of the state's metropolitan areas. Los Angeles and San Francisco–Oakland are the two most congested metropolitan areas in the country.[2]

Most of California's fuel tax money is now used to maintain existing infrastructure, but even these annual revenues—about $2 billion—fall short of the $3 billion a year that's needed to maintain existing highways. The result: substantial deferred maintenance and reduced road quality.[3] Thanks to the poor quality of their roads, San Jose, Los Angeles and the San Francisco–Oakland area have the dubious distinction of being among the highest cost vehicle maintenance areas in the country.[4]

While the magnitude of the problem may be bigger in California than elsewhere, the state is not alone in facing a widening gap between infrastructure needs and current spending.

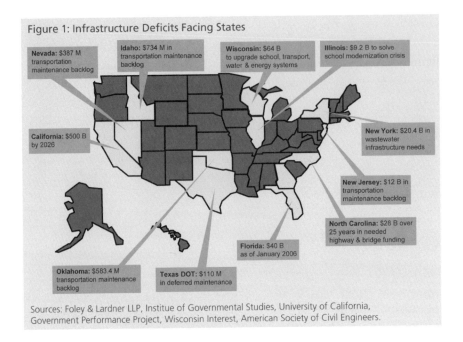

Figure 1: Infrastructure Deficits Facing States

Nevada: $387 M transportation maintenance backlog

Idaho: $734 M in transportation maintenance backlog

Wisconsin: $64 B to upgrade school, transport, water & energy systems

Illinois: $9.2 B to solve school modernization crisis

California: $500 B by 2026

New York: $20.4 B in wastewater infrastructure needs

New Jersey: $12 B in transportation maintenance backlog

North Carolina: $28 B over 25 years in needed highway & bridge funding

Florida: $40 B as of January 2006

Oklahoma: $583.4 M transportation maintenance backlog

Texas DOT: $110 M in deferred maintenance

Sources: Foley & Lardner LLP, Institue of Governmental Studies, University of California, Government Performance Project, Wisconsin Interest, American Society of Civil Engineers.

Across the nation, crowded schools, traffic-choked roads, corroding bridges and aged and overused water and sewer treatment facilities erode the quality of American life.

Nearly three-fourths of major roads in Massachusetts are in poor or mediocre condition, while more than half the bridges in Rhode Island are structurally deficient or functionally obsolete.[5] Recently, the American Society of Civil Engineers (ASCE) graded the overall condition of the nation's infrastructure a "D" and recommended investing $1.6 trillion in infrastructure over the next five years.[6]

Roads, dams, wastewater, drinking water and navigable waterways top the list of infrastructure concerns. Since 1990, the total vehicle miles traveled on the nation's highways has jumped by more than 35 percent. Growing transportation needs require major investment: $40 billion annually for roads alone. The bill for public transit, where demand has increased by 23 percent over the past decade, is also steep. According to the U.S. Department of Transportation, $20.6 billion in capital investment is needed annually just to improve current facilities without adding any new capacity.[7]

Meanwhile, the U.S. Environmental Protection Agency estimates that local water and sewer infrastructure will need investments of $300–$500 billion over the next 20 years.[8]

Yet the ability of government to properly maintain and invest in new public infrastructure is constrained. Many states confront huge gaps between their infrastructure needs and their current rate of investment (see figure 1). North Carolina, for example, faces a projected shortfall of $28 billion over the next 25 years in highway and bridge funding.[9] In Wisconsin, more than $64 billion is needed to upgrade the state's school, transport, water and energy systems, with another $26 billion required for road safety and traffic improvements.[10] U.S. Secretary of Transportation Mary Peters recently warned Arizona that, given its rapid population growth, it would soon have to turn to nontraditional revenue sources for new highway construction and maintenance.[11]

These infrastructure deficits impose huge costs on society, from lower productivity and reduced competitiveness to an increased number of accidents. The Federal Reserve Bank of Chicago estimates that more than half of the decline in labor productivity growth rates in the United States during the 1970s and early 1980s resulted from infrastructure neglect.[12] Today, driving on roads in need of repair costs U.S. motorists $54 billion every year in extra vehicle repairs and operating costs. This works out to an average of $275 per motorist each year. Moreover, this cost does not include the economic loss that occurs when productive workers are stuck in traffic rather than on the job. According to the U.S. Federal Highway Administration, outdated and substandard road and bridge design, pavement conditions and safety features are contributing factors in one-third of the more than 43,000 highway fatalities that occur each year.

How Did We Get Here?

Few governors, state legislators or members of Congress would question the economic importance of having a strong infrastructure. Nevertheless, it is an area where governments perennially underinvest. Why?

For transportation infrastructure, the funding shortfall results from the inability of traditional highway transportation funding sources to keep pace with increased demand. Since the inception of the Federal Highway Trust Fund in 1957, the country's highway system has been funded in part through fuel taxes. In the 1980s, however, expenditures began to fall relative to revenues.[13] Voter concerns about high fuel prices and taxes limited gas tax increases (the federal gas tax has been level at 18.4 cents a gallon since 1994). Without being indexed to inflation or the direct cost of fuel, the buying power of the 18.4 cents has declined, effectively dropping 8 percent in the last seven years.[14] Also, with the increase in the number of

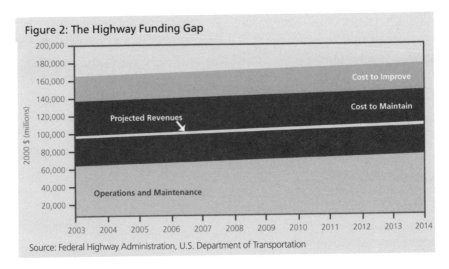

Figure 2: The Highway Funding Gap

Source: Federal Highway Administration, U.S. Department of Transportation

more fuel-efficient vehicles, which reduce fuel consumption and thus gas tax revenue, state transportation departments have less money to use for maintenance and new construction than they need (see figure 2).

Federal law also encourages financially constrained planning because projects generally cannot be pursued unless and until federal funding is available. States are constrained by this "pay-as-you-go" approach; it hampers their ability to do effective long-term planning for new projects.

For states with budget pressures, funding for new projects may also fall to the bottom of the priority list. New projects often require funding from multiple authorizing authorities, each of which may be dealing with a different political situation. For example, existing funding for the Bay Area Rapid Transit (BART) connection to the Oakland airport comes from five sources.[15]

Budget shortfalls also undermine the ability of states to maintain existing facilities properly, leading to deferred maintenance. This shortens the useful lifespan of roads, bridges, ports and other infrastructure, necessitating expenditures of 6 to 20 times the maintenance costs for rehabilitation or reconstruction. Chronic deferred maintenance also results in reduced quality of services and generally worse financial outcomes.

Options for Closing the Gap

Given these constraints, how can states close their infrastructure gaps? New construction generally involves substantial up-front costs. Traditionally, government agencies have had two main options for financing their infrastructure needs: pay-as-you-go financing and debt financing (also known as public

Table 1: Pay-As-You-Go versus Debt-Financing

Financing method	Pros	Cons
Pay-as-you-go (or PAYGO	•Future funds are not tied up in servicing debt payments •Interest savings can be put toward other projects •Greater budget transparency •Avoid risk of default	•Long wait time for new infrastructure •Major projects may exhaust an agency's entire budget for capital projects •Risk of inflation
Debt-financing (or public bonding)	•Infrastructure is delivered when it's needed •Spreads cost over the useful life of the asset •Increases capacity to invest •Projects are paid for by the beneficiaries of the capital investment	•Potentially high borrowing rate •Debt payments limit future budget flexibility •Diminishes the choice of future generations forced to service debt requirements

Source: Transportation Research Board

bonding). With pay-as-you-go financing, government accumulates revenues sufficient to pay for the new infrastructure before beginning construction or as construction occurs, thereby lengthening the construction period. Given the challenges associated with generating such savings and securing approvals from the multiple authorizing bodies, there can be considerable lag time between when an infrastructure need arises and when it actually gets met.

Public bonding (that is, obtaining a loan to pay for infrastructure), on the other hand, allows infrastructure needs to be met when sufficient public funds aren't immediately available. Each option comes with its own set of pros and cons (see table 1).

Closing state infrastructure gaps requires raising additional revenue, reducing costs or finding new financing sources. Given government restrictions on tax exempt bonds and the political difficulty of raising taxes to secure new revenue, the most viable options for governments may be to lower costs and to draw upon private financing for new projects or concession revenues through long-term leases of existing assets, where appropriate.

Cost reductions can be achieved by curbing inefficiencies associated with the traditional way governments deliver and maintain infrastructure. One kind of inefficiency often occurs because governments currently have little political incentive to invest in proper maintenance. As a result, some

Choosing the Right Financing Model

Several criteria should be considered when determining how to finance new infrastructure projects. Two key factors are the level of urgency and current availability of funds. For example, if the infrastructure needs are not immediate and funds are available over time to make a new capital investment, then pay-as-you-go may be a good option. Key questions policymakers should consider include:

• Is there an immediate need for the asset?

• What is the expected useful life of the asset?

• What is the current availability of funds relative to the size of the project?

• Are there multiple projects that need to be completed simultaneously?

• Is inflation expected to increase?

• Is the borrowing rate expected to increase?

Source: Transportation Research Board

assets end up costing substantially more than they would have if they were properly maintained.

Take roads for example. Early repairs cost about 20 percent less than maintenance conducted in the last quarter of a road's life. Even in cases in which user fees generate funds to maintain roads, states often can't raise enough revenues to offset maintenance costs. Consider Indiana. It cost the state about 34 cents to collect a 15 cent toll paid on the Indiana Toll Road. Upon learning this, Governor Mitch Daniels remarked, "We'd be better off going to the honor system."[16]

One avenue for achieving greater efficiency from infrastructure investments is to utilize innovative procurement models. A survey of managers conducted by the Federal Highway Administration estimates that design-build project delivery, which combines the design and construction phases of a project into one contract, reduces project duration by 14 percent and cost by 3 percent, compared to the traditional design-bid-build approach.[17]

Given the potential of design-build and other innovative models to reduce project costs and deliver higher quality transportation projects more quickly than with traditional financing and contracting methods, governments in the United States and around the world are increasingly turning

Figure 3: Potential Sources of Efficiencies from PPPs

Type	Definition	Examples
Resource Allocation Efficiencies	• Efficiencies are gained from the private sector's ability to allocate resources more effectively	• The private sector's motivation is on the completion of the project to a set of performance standards. Conversely, the public sector will have competing interests for operating resources, which may reduce the performance of the project over its lifecycle
Production Efficiencies	• Resources for a specific application can also be used more effectively • The ability to be more productive is developed during the private sector organization's years of practice delivering similar projects	• The construction and operation of infrastructure may be completed in less time and / or lower overall cost by using market tested techniques and incentives for innovation
Economic and Social Efficiencies	• Access to more capital allows more projects to be funded on a fixed capital budget • Social benefits of infrastructure accrue faster as infrastructure is built sooner	• More efficient movement of goods and people • Improved quality of life resulting from increased access to infrastructure

Source: Deloitte Research

Figure 4: State PPP Legislation and Activity

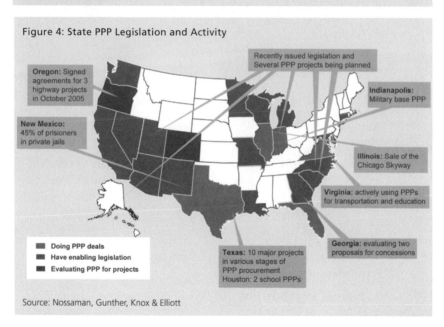

Oregon: Signed agreements for 3 highway projects in October 2005

Recently issued legislation and Several PPP projects being planned

Indianapolis: Military base PPP

New Mexico: 45% of prisioners in private jails

Illinois: Sale of the Chicago Skyway

Virginia: actively using PPPs for transportation and education

■ Doing PPP deals
■ Have enabling legislation
■ Evaluating PPP for projects

Texas: 10 major projects in various stages of PPP procurement
Houston: 2 school PPPs

Georgia: evaluating two proposals for concessions

Source: Nossaman, Gunther, Knox & Elliott

to private sector financing, design, build and operation to meet their infrastructure objectives. These public-private partnerships (PPPs) typically rely on long-term contractual relationships between government agencies and their private sector partners for the provision and operation of an infrastructure asset. Once employed in only a handful of countries and in limited settings, these public-private partnerships are now being used to deliver new

Public Private Partnerships 101

A public-private partnership, or PPP, refers to a contractual agreement between a government agency and a private sector entity that allows for greater private sector participation in the delivery of public infrastructure projects. Compared with traditional procurement models, the private sector assumes a greater role in the planning, financing, design, construction, operation and maintenance of public facilities. Project risk is transferred to the party best positioned to manage it. Some of the most common PPP models are described below.

BUILD-TRANSFER (BT): Under this model, the government contracts with a private partner to design and build a facility in accordance with the requirements set by the government. Upon completion, the government assumes responsibility for operating and maintaining the facility. This method of procurement is sometimes called Design-Build (DB).

BUILD-LEASE-TRANSFER (BLT): This model is similar to Build-Transfer, except that after the facility is completed it is leased to the public sector until the lease is fully paid, at which time the asset is transferred to the public sector at no additional cost. The public sector retains responsibility for operations during the lease period.

BUILD-TRANSFER-OPERATE (BTO): Under this model, the private sector designs and builds a facility. Once the facility is completed, the title for the new facility is transferred to the public sector, while the private sector operates the facility for a specified period. This procurement model is also known as Design-Build-Operate (DBO).

BUILD-OPERATE-TRANSFER (BOT): This model combines the responsibilities of Build-Transfer with those of facility operations and maintenance by a private sector partner for a specified period. At the end of the period, the public sector assumes operating responsibility. This method of procurement is also referred to as Design-Build-Operate-Maintain (DBOM).

BUILD-OWN-OPERATE-TRANSFER (BOOT): Here the government grants a private partner a franchise to finance, design, build and operate a facility for a specific period of time. Ownership of the facility goes back to the public sector at the end of that period.

BUILD-OWN-OPERATE (BOO): In this model, the government grants a private entity the right to finance, design, build, operate and maintain a project. This entity retains ownership of the project.

DESIGN-BUILD-FINANCE-OPERATE/MAINTAIN (DBFO, DBFM OR DBFO/M): Under this model, the private sector designs, builds, finances, operates and/or maintains a new facility under a long-term lease. At the end of the lease term, the facility is transferred to the public sector.

In addition to being used for new projects, PPPs can also be used for existing services and facilities. Some of these models are described below.

Lease: The government grants a private entity a leasehold interest in an asset. The private partner operates and maintains the asset in accordance with the terms of the lease.

Concession: The government grants a private entity exclusive rights to provide, operate and maintain an asset over a long period in accordance with performance requirements set out by the government. The public sector retains ownership of the asset, but the private operator retains ownership over any improvements made during the concession period.

Divestiture: The government transfers all or part of an asset to the private sector. Generally, the government includes certain conditions on the sale to require that the asset be improved and services be continued.

Source: Adapted from the National Council for Public-Private Partnerships

and refurbished roads, bridges, tunnels, water systems, airports, schools, hospitals, social housing and prisons.

The United Kingdom pioneered this approach to infrastructure development. The UK government draws on partnership models to develop and deliver all manner of infrastructure, from schools to defense facilities.[18] PPP projects now represent between 10 and 13 percent of all UK investment in public infrastructure.[19] Meanwhile, in continental Europe, the volume of PPP deals is doubling, tripling, and even quadrupling year to year in many countries. And in Canada, 20 percent of all new infrastructure in British Columbia is now designed, built and operated by the private sector.

The United States has been slower to adopt this trend. However, this is rapidly changing. More than half the states now have PPP-enabling legislation on their books.[20] Texas, Virginia and Florida have been especially active in using PPPs. Texas, for example, is relying on the PPP approach to develop the Trans Texas Corridor, a massive new statewide transportation network that includes roads, commuter and freight rail and utilities infrastructure. Virginia, for its part, is negotiating PPPs for several new projects, including the Dulles Rail Corridor, high occupancy toll lanes and reconstruction of tolled truck lanes. Across the country, PPPs are now being considered for an increasing number of projects (see figure 4).

Benefits of Public-Private Partnership Models

PPPs are just one tool among many; they won't replace traditional infrastructure financing and development any time soon. Governments typically have a number of objectives when building infrastructure: acquiring needed assets, getting good value for money, timely delivery, meeting public needs and so on. The procurement model selected for a particular project should be the one that best addresses these objectives.

PPPs, however, have shown significant promise in helping governments address infrastructure shortages. To begin with, they provide new sources of capital for public infrastructure projects. Private equity, pension funds and other sources of private financing must still be repaid, but shifting the financing and delivery responsibility to the private partner can help improve infrastructure in settings where public entities are unwilling or unable to shoulder the debt or the associated risk. Additional benefits include:

On-Time and Within-Budget Delivery

With payments better aligned to the delivery of project objectives, public-private partnerships also have a solid track record of completing construction on time or even ahead of schedule. In Canada, for example, Terminal 3 at the Toronto Pearson Airport was completed 18 months ahead of schedule under a PPP contract.[21]

The United Kingdom's National Audit Office reported in 2003 that 73 percent of non-PPP (Private Finance Initiative) construction projects were over budget and 70 percent were delivered late. In contrast, only 22 percent of the PFI projects came in over budget and 24 percent were late.[22]

Shifting Construction and Maintenance Risk to the Private Sector

Politics and budget pressures play havoc with proper maintenance of existing infrastructure. There always seems to be another higher priority: a program or crisis requires more urgent funding. Or a budget deficit pushes funding for infrastructure maintenance further down the priority list. The effect of reducing spending on maintenance is rarely immediate; long before the public complains about crumbling roadbeds or overburdened electricity networks, the elected officials have moved on.

Well-designed PPPs can ameliorate this problem by transferring maintenance responsibility and risk to the private partner. Contract structures require that the assets be available and properly maintained over time. The public sector thereby gains greater confidence in the level of its spending commitments over the lifetime of the asset. Greater cost transparency, in turn, supports better planning and helps to avoid cuts in other service areas as a result of unexpected infrastructure costs.[23]

Cost Savings

Cost savings from PPPs typically materialize in several different forms: lower construction costs, reduced life-cycle maintenance costs and lower costs of associated risks.

CONSTRUCTION SAVINGS. Experience from several countries has demonstrated that PPPs cost comparatively less during the construction phase of the contract. The savings typically result from innovation in design and better defined asset requirements. A 2000 UK Treasury report found that among a sample of 29 PPP projects for which public sector comparisons were available, the average savings were close to 17 percent.[24]

In Colorado, the costs of completing construction for segments of the Denver E-470 Toll Road that used a PPP approach came in $189 million below the original cost estimate of $597 million. Through the use of an innovative design-build-finance contract, the Virginia Pocahontas Parkway (Route 895) project came in $10 million below the original $324 million estimated cost of the project.

Meanwhile, the construction costs of a primary school constructed through a public-private partnership in Pembroke Pines, Florida, was 22 to 34 percent lower than comparable primary schools.[25]

REDUCED LIFECYCLE COSTS. In traditional contracting, the private sector's role is typically limited to immediate construction. This can create a perverse incentive to economize on elements of construction today even though maintenance costs might be higher in the long run. Shifting long-term operation and maintenance responsibilities to the construction organization creates a stronger incentive to ensure long-term construction quality because the firm will be responsible for maintenance costs many years down the road. It also encourages more preventative maintenance and reduces the risk of future fluctuations in operations costs. The public benefits from this life-cycle efficiency.

Addressing the Variable Cost of Capital Issue

A common objection to private financing of infrastructure is that the private sector's cost of debt is higher, making it appear to be a bad deal for taxpayers and users. That is, given its tax-exempt status, government-issued debt is cheaper than the private sector, making private financing and development more costly than traditional procurement models. While this argument contains a kernel of truth, it overlooks several important points.

DIFFERENCE BETWEEN COST OF CAPITAL AND COST OF DEBT. First, it assumes that the cost of capital and the cost of debt are one and the same. However, a government's risk-adjusted cost of capital typically exceeds its cost of debt because the public sector takes on project-specific risks (such as cost overruns and delays) that need to be factored into the cost. Moreover, even though the private sector assumes some of the risks of construction, time overruns and project performance, it can control its capital costs by making efficient use of resources. Rather than comparing nominal borrowing costs, a more appropriate comparison is between the public sector's cost of capital (to which a risk premium must be added) and the private sector's cost of capital (which amounts to a weighted average of its cost of debt and equity).[26] In many cases, the benefits of superior service delivery are often worth the extra costs.

GAP NARROWING. Second, as the private infrastructure market has grown and financing mechanisms have become more sophisticated, the gap between the public and the private sector's cost of debt has narrowed. With the maturing of the private finance market in the United Kingdom, for example, the cost differential between private capital and public borrowing is now in the range of only one to three percentage points. Provided the private sector is able to deliver savings in other aspects of the project, the higher borrowing costs should not be a determining factor.[27]

CREATIVE FINANCING MODELS. Last, a variety of financing approaches enables governments to combine their ability to obtain lower interest rates with the benefits of private financing and development. The U.S. Department of Transportation has allocated $15 billion in tax-exempt private activity bonds for qualifying PPP highway and intermodal freight facilities. This approach lowers the cost of capital significantly, enhancing investment prospects. Likewise, some school districts have set up nonprofit corporations (often in partnership with a developer) that can use tax-exempt bonds to finance the school construction. The district then leases the building from the nonprofit.

Accelerating Infrastructure Construction

Conventional pay-as-you-go infrastructure procurement requires the public sector to provide significant up-front capital even though the benefits of the project may be delayed or uncertain. As with public bonding, most PPPs enable governments to spread the public's share of the infrastructure investment over the lifetime of the asset, much the way homeowners do with a home mortgage. As a result, infrastructure projects can be brought forward by years, allowing users to benefit much sooner than is typical under pay-as-you-go financing. For example, the creative financing approach used for the Virginia Pocahontas Parkway PPP project eliminated what might have been a 15-year delay in construction while financing was assembled.[28] Similarly, private financing accelerated South Carolina's Eastern Toll Corridor by 20 to 30 years.[29] In many cases, the private contractor also has a strong incentive to complete the project as quickly as possible because it needs the stream of revenues to repay the capital costs.

Many jurisdictions also face limits on the amount of debt they can incur. Debt limits are not applicable to some forms of PPPs because the private sector assumes the risk. Hence PPPs can enable more infrastructure to move forward earlier than might otherwise have been possible in the face of debt limits.

Facilitating a Strong Customer Service Orientation

Private sector infrastructure providers, often relying on user fees from customers for revenue, also have strong incentives to focus on providing superior customer service.[30] Moreover, since the asset is no longer managed by the public sector, government managers are freer to concentrate more heavily on ensuring the provider meets desired customer service levels. For example, in school or defense facility PPP projects, customer satisfaction metrics can be built into the contract.

In the United Kingdom, more than three-quarters of end users reported that their public-private partnership projects were performing as expected or better than expected; one-quarter said that the facilities were "far surpassing" expectations.[31]

Innovation in customer service delivery helps to account for these high satisfaction levels. Motorists using the private sector–operated I-Pass Illinois Tollway, for instance, can receive traffic alerts on current travel times and incident and event information directly on their wireless devices, thereby allowing them to make more educated driving decisions. In addition, the I-PASS Gift Card provides low-income users with an alternative to credit cards.[32]

Enabling the Public Sector to Focus on Outcomes and Core Business

When properly structured, public-private partnerships enable governments to focus on outcomes instead of inputs. Governments can focus leadership attention on the outcome-based public value they are trying to create. This is an important shift for most agencies as they begin to focus on the levels of service, performance and benefits they hope to achieve. The destination, not the path, becomes the organizing theme around which the project is built. Working with their private partners, departments can establish performance metrics to monitor the partners and demonstrate that the intended benefits are being achieved.

School construction PPPs provide a powerful example of how partnerships enable school officials to shift their focus to outcomes and the core business of learning. When the Montaigne secondary school near The Hague in the Netherlands needed additional school capacity, school officials could have just chosen the usual route of getting bids from several contractors to build a school. Instead, they concluded that what they really wanted to buy was a quality learning environment and not just a physical asset—in this case a school building.[33] To that end, they entered a PPP with a consortium of private firms that provide cleaning, caretaking, security, grounds maintenance and information technology, leaving school teachers and officials free to spend all their time on the core mission, teaching children.

Private partners not only help reduce the construction and maintenance costs (thereby reducing the overall cost of the building), they also negotiate other uses for the building after hours. Involvement of the private partner may also help avoid some of the conflicts regarding acceptable after-school and nonacademic use of the facilities.[34]

Infrastructure Sector Opportunities

While much of the public-private partnership activity in the United States has focused on the transportation arena, other sectors with pressing infrastructure needs—water and wastewater systems, schools, military base conversions and prisons—also serve as strong candidates for PPPs.

Each sector carries different challenges. Partnership policies, approaches and political strategies therefore must be tailored to the unique characteristics of each individual sector.

Transportation

Internationally, transportation has been the largest area of PPP investment. Public-private partnerships have begun to play a central role in answering the pressing need for new and well-maintained roads, tunnels, bridges, airports, ports, railways and other forms of transportation infrastructure.[35]

Several factors make transportation infrastructure well suited for PPPs. First, the strong emphasis on the role of cost and efficiency helps to align private and public interests. Second, the growing (but by no means universal) public acceptance of user fees for assets such as roads and bridges makes private financing easier here. (In other sectors fees often come from the government.) The ability to limit participation to actual paying customers, in the form of train tickets or road or bridge tolls, ensures a revenue stream that can offset some or all of the cost of service—a format readily understood by the public. In cases where direct user fees are not desirable, politically or otherwise, fees can be levied indirectly (see Port of Miami Tunnel sidebar). Third, the scale and long-term nature of these projects are well served by PPPs.

To date, nearly $21 billion has been invested in 43 highway facilities in the United States using various public-private partnership models during the last 12 years.[36] California, Florida, Texas and Virginia are leaders in this field, having accounted for 50 percent of the total dollar volume ($10.6 billion) through 18 major highway PPP projects.[37]

State Highway 130 in central Texas is the state's first highway developed under a Comprehensive Development Agreement which allows property acquisition, design and building to proceed simultaneously.[38] The project costs around $3.66 billion and is being sponsored by the Texas DOT and Texas Turnpike Authority.[39]

To the West, the state of California has partnered with the San Diego Expressway, LP, to develop the SR 125 Toll Road San Miguel Mountain Parkway in San Diego County. The new highway will be built and financed by the private partner. Upon completion, ownership will be transferred to the state. Through a leaseback, the private partner will operate and maintain the new facility for a 35-year period, after which control reverts to the public sector.[40]

PPP models are not only being applied to new projects, they are also being used for operating and maintaining existing assets. The City of Chicago

Table 2: New Federal Tools for Innovative Partnerships

The Transportation Infrastructure Financing Innovation Act (TIFIA)	Provides federal credit assistance to nationally or regionally significant surface transportation projects. In 2005 the program was broadened. The qualifying project cost threshold was reduced to $50 million, or $15 million for Intelligent Transportation Systems projects, and program eligibility was extended to more projects including private facilities deemed publicly beneficial for highway users.
Private Activity Bonds (PABs)	Provides private developers and operators access to tax-exempt interest rates for highway and surface freight transfer projects, significantly lowering the cost of capital. Highway facilities and surface freight transfer facilities are eligible for up to $15 billion in tax-exempt facility bonds.
Special Experimental Project 15 (SEP-15)	Enables states to obtain federal waivers to experiment with new public-private partnership approaches in four major areas of project delivery: contracting, right-of-way acquisition, project finance and compliance with the National Environmental Policy Act and other environmental requirements.
Toll Credits	Allows states to collect tolls on federally funded Interstate highways for the purpose of improving Interstate highway corridors.

Source: U.S. Department of Transportation

struck a landmark long-term toll road lease with the Skyway Concession Company, a joint venture between Spanish toll road operator Cintra Concesiones de Infraestructuras de Transporte and the Australian Macquarie Infrastructure Group —the first of its kind in the United States—that brought in $1.83 billion to cash-strapped city coffers. In return for operating and maintaining the tollway for the next 99 years, the Skyway Company will collect toll and concession revenues. Subsequently, the Cintra-Macquerie venture partnered with the Indiana Department of Transportation to operate and maintain the Indiana Toll Road, paying the state $3.8 billion to lease the toll road over the next 35 years—a windfall of cash that's being reinvested in the state's 10-year "Major Moves" transportation plan.

An ardent supporter of "21st century solutions for 21st century transportation challenges," U.S. Secretary of Transportation Mary Peters explains that, "We can't assume that the methods of the past will work for the future."[41] The federal government is actively encouraging states to experiment with PPPs by providing new federal tools to make private sector participation in transportation infrastructure projects easier and more attractive (see table 2).

Port of Miami

The Port of Miami is actually an island off the coast of Florida, currently connected with the city of Miami by a highway that goes through the central downtown area. The port generates a tremendous amount of cargo and passenger traffic, causing substantial congestion in downtown Miami. The state's Department of Transportation has proposed construction of a $1 billion tunnel to bypass the downtown area and allow highway traffic direct access to the port.

Because it lacked experience in either designing or constructing tunnels, as well as the desire to build such expertise internally, the state transportation department initially decided on a design-build partnership. Quick construction was essential because of public concern regarding the congestion, so choosing a private firm made sense. The department also decided against imposing tolls on the use of the tunnel because it wanted to encourage users of the port to use the tunnel. Instead, the state would indirectly capture user fees through container and passenger fees on docking ships. Additional funds would come from Dade County and the city of Miami in return for the congestion relief.

After determining the sources of revenue, the department considered a large revenue bond, but decided against it because it would be tied to a 30-year repayment schedule. The agency finally settled on a DBFO/M for the tunnel proposal, with the private financing being repaid by the department through revenue raised on the container and passenger fees. The payments would be tied to the availability of the tunnel for public use and to quality measures, but they wouldn't be tied to the specific levels of traffic passing through unless traffic exceeded certain threshold levels, in which case, the private partner would receive more to cover increased maintenance costs.

The private partner in this arrangement does not bear any risk for demand management: if traffic falls below projections, the private partner would still receive the same payment, assuming it met quality measures. The state agency decided to retain the demand risk because it felt it had better control of that risk. The agency was relatively confident about the continued long-term growth of both the city and the port and did not believe that demand risk would pose a significant problem.

The Port of Miami project illustrates some interesting options. The use of availability payments could sidestep some of the political concerns regarding tolls. Just as important, the use of container and passenger fees in lieu of tolls could potentially streamline both traffic and collection issues.

While the reauthorization of the federal surface transportation program provides for modest increases in the share of federal funds states receive for transportation, states will continue to face a considerable funding shortfall absent the use of innovative approaches to close the gap. The significance of this shortfall extends far beyond the immediate mobility crisis. As Texas learned—the hard way—inadequate infrastructure can be a deal breaker for economic expansion. When PC maker Dell decided to locate its next expansion in Nashville rather than in Austin, the company's headquarters—given the mediocre condition of Austin's roads—the city lost out on 10,000 new jobs. As a result, the state is stepping up its efforts to close its transportation gap to regain competitive advantage. The good news for states willing to learn from Texas's experience is that by taking advantage of increased federal latitude, new financing and available delivery tools, as well as capital markets eager to invest in the transportation sector, states can get a handle on their own transportation backlogs.

Water and Wastewater

Water and wastewater management represents another fast-growing area for PPPs. In the United States, private operation of water and wastewater systems rose 84 percent during the 1990s and 13 percent in 2001 alone. As of 2003, more than 25,000 drinking water systems were managed by the private sector.

Outside the United States, many governments are engaging the private sector to design, build, finance and operate new water and wastewater facilities. For example, the total value of water and wastewater PPP projects in the Australian states of Victoria and New South Wales is approximately $131.5 million.[42] With aging water and wastewater systems demanding more than $28 billion for renewal, many Canadian municipal governments have also begun to consider alternative financing mechanisms to deliver water service.[43]

Helping to meet the huge and rising needs for new and refurbished treatment facilities could well be the biggest potential impact of PPPs in this sector in the United States. The estimated $300-500 billion in water and sewer infrastructure investment needed over the next 20 years is likely to be beyond the ability of the state and local governments to fund on their own.

IRS rule changes promulgated in 1997 allow governments to enter into long-term contracts of up to 20 years with private firms to operate infrastructure facilities without losing their tax-exempt bond status. The longer-term contracts give the private operators more time to recoup their investments in infrastructure improvements, making such investment far more attractive than before. Since the rule change, more than 100 municipalities have entered into long-term contracts for operations and maintenance of their water or wastewater systems.

Schools

The majority of public schools in America were built to accommodate the Baby Boomers—meaning these facilities, on average, are now more than 40 years old.[44] The investment required to bring the nation's schools up to good condition is estimated to run between $19.7 billion and $28.6 billion.[45] Public-private partnerships could potentially help make up the funding shortfall and meet growing near term enrollment demands.

While there are variations, the private sector typically finances, designs, constructs and operates a public school facility under a contract with the government for a given time period, for example, 20 to 30 years. At the end of that concession period, ownership of the facility transfers to the government. The private sector often also provides related noncore services (school transport, food services, cleaning and so on) under contract, while the government continues to provide core services, namely, teaching.

Sale-leaseback and lease-leaseback arrangements represent two other common PPP models used for schools. The school district typically either sells or leases surplus land to a developer who builds a school on the land and leases it back to the school district on favorable terms—or in some cases provides the facility free of charge to the school district in exchange for development rights on this land or other surplus property. In 1996, the Houston Independent School District used a lease-leaseback arrangement with a private developer to obtain two new schools $20 million under budget and a year earlier than originally planned.[46]

The United Kingdom is home to the world's largest and most sophisticated PPP schools program. Most new schools are built using some variant of PPP model. All in all, nearly 100 education PPP deals have been signed, with a value of £3.6 billion. The next frontier: using PPPs to refurbish and modernize every school in the country. Over the next 10–15 years, every school in Britain will be brought up to 21st century standards through a program called Building Schools for the Future.

Compared with those in the United Kingdom, school PPPs in the United States are still in their infancy. Several factors, however, point to continued growth here. First, the 2001 Economic Growth and Reconciliation Act passed by Congress allowed, for the first time, private developers to finance new school building with tax-exempt private activity bonds, providing them access to preferred borrowing rates.

Second, several states in recent years have passed laws explicitly authorizing and encouraging school PPPs. In 2002, for example, Virginia passed

Potential Benefits of School PPPs

- Faster construction

- Shift expenses from capital to operating budgets

- Focus attention on core educational goals and away from facilities management

- Innovative designs resulting in built-to-suit schools

- Enhanced community use from multi-use facilities

the Public-Private Education Facilities Act, enabling the public sector to enter into public-private partnerships for infrastructure projects. Stafford County was the first to take advantage of the new authority. The county partnered with a private developer to build two new elementary schools, a high school and several revenue-producing community facilities. Other cities and counties in Virginia have followed suit, allowing both solicited and unsolicited proposals for design-build schools. Maryland passed similar legislation authorizing alternative financing methods.[47] The absence of authorizing legislation in a state could potentially significantly delay school PPP projects.

Despite the potential benefits of using PPPs for school projects, Nova Scotia, Canada, which used PPPs to build 39 schools in the late 1990s, provides a cautionary tale. Originally, the government had planned to build 55 schools, but the number was scaled back when the initiative was beset by a variety of political and other problems, including cost overruns, weak government management and problems with the contract terms.[49] Today privately operated schools represent approximately 14 percent of the square footage in the province's schools.

Military Base Conversion

Base closures are a significant economic development issue in many states, involving the potential loss of thousands of local jobs. In certain instances, however, properly constructed PPPs may offer an innovative alternative to closure and the resulting local job loss.

Consider the example of the Indianapolis Naval Air Warfare Center. City officials, working with the Navy, rejected a simplistic view of base closure to ask a fundamental question: "What is the best possible way to maxi-

Using Partnerships to Overcome School Overcrowding

Several years ago, the Natomas Unified School District in Sacramento employed a public-private partnership to help address the problem of overcrowding in its high schools. Using a lease-leaseback model, the district leased part of its land to a private developer that financed and built a new school on the leased land. The school district makes payments to the developer until the end of the lease period, at which time the school will be transferred to the school district. The result: a state-of-the-art facility equipped with solar skylights, clerestory windows and glass walls to cut back on electricity costs, and an energy-saving system that earned the school district a $2 million rebate on its utility bill from the Sacramento Municipal Utility District. The new high school also features a geothermal heating and cooling system expected to last 35 years longer than a conventional system, making the school less expensive to operate and maintain over the life of the facility. The school was completed $2.5 million under budget and a month and a half ahead of schedule.[48]

mize defense of the country with the dollars available?" Instead of framing the question as whether to transfer government jobs from one place to another, city officials asked whether a public-private partnership could take over the installation and deliver the Navy's work at a lower cost.[50] The city of Indianapolis and the Navy issued a formal request to the private sector for ideas about how to use the naval facility to produce important engineering components for less while also spurring local economic growth. The result: the country's largest base privatization.

The joint effort saved more than 2,000 jobs and allowed the Navy to downsize its infrastructure while preserving needed services. By keeping the facility open, the parties avoided closure costs of $200 million and maintained access to a skilled workforce.

Other defense PPP opportunities exist in military housing redevelopment and privatization. For example, the Army's Hawaii Family Housing project, a joint venture between the Army and Actus Lend Lease, involves construction of 7,894 new military housing units at seven Army installations on Oahu over a 10-year period. Under a 50-year lease, $1.6 billion in privately financed housing will be furnished to the Army.

Prisons

Close to 7 percent of inmates in state and federal prisons in the United States are in private facilities, the highest number of prisons in any country in the world. As many as 34 states and the federal government have contracted with the private sector to provide prison services. In New Mexico, for example, around 45 percent of prisoners were in private prisons as of 2001. As public service contracting expert Gary Sturgess points out:

> The US prisons market is extraordinarily complex, with some facilities that are publicly owned but managed by the private sector under contract; some that are privately designed, built and operated under long-term contract to government; some that are privately-owned but leased to other private (or public) providers; and a number that have been constructed by private companies (or by public-private joint ventures) on a speculative basis and offered through a spot market to governments with overcrowding problems.[51]

All in all, the number of prisoners in private prisons is increasing at four times the rate of growth of inmates in public sector prisons. Six states now hold at least one-quarter of their prisoners in private facilities.[52] Texas, which has the largest number of prisoners in private prisons, compares its public and private prisons on a biannual basis and mandates that private prisons provide at least 10 percent more savings than publicly maintained prisons.[53]

Getting it Right

PPPs have generally proven an effective infrastructure financing and delivery tool, but a number of projects nevertheless have failed to live up to their advance billing. As states make increasing use of this tool, it's important for them to understand criteria for success and improve their capacity to execute and manage innovative partnerships. Some common pitfalls generally fall into these categories:

- *Lack of clarity about project objectives.* Sponsors sometimes lack consensus about the purpose of and expected outcomes for the project. Government officials then often try to compensate for this failure by overspecifying inputs.

- *Poor setup.* The success or failure of PPPs can often be traced back to the initial design of PPP policies, legislation and guidance. A common mistake is placing so many restrictions, conditions and expectations of risk transfer on the private sector partner and agencies involved that a financially feasible deal becomes impossible to structure. Another is having unrealistic expectations for PPPs—thinking that they provide "free money" or that they're the solution to all problems.

- *Too much focus on the transaction.* The government may view PPPs merely as financing instruments when in fact they represent a very different way of working. This leads to poor operational focus.

- *Inappropriate PPP model applied to project.* Much of what differentiates the various PPP models is the level of risk shifted to the private sector. A common mistake is transferring demand risk, the amount of use the infrastructure will receive, to the private sector when the private contractor has no control over demand factors.

- *Lack of internal management capacity.* Even when the government is supported by external advisers, many tasks cannot be outsourced, and often the agency does not have the skill sets internally to manage complex PPPs.

- *Failure to realize value for money.* This failure occurs when the borrowing and tendering costs associated with PPPs are not sufficiently offset by efficiency gains or when government officials don't have a real understanding of how to test value for money.

- *Inadequate planning.* Without taking proper account of the market in the planning phase, governments may come out with more projects than bidders which creates a noncompetitive environment. On the flipside, too few projects may result in industry moving on to a more active jurisdiction.

While a step-by-step how-to guide to PPPs is beyond the scope of this chapter, some key strategies are outlined here.

First, governments need a full life-cycle approach to PPP planning that confers adequate attention to all phases of a PPP—from policy and planning, to the transaction phase, and then to managing the concession. Such an approach can help avoid problems of poor setup, lack of clarity about outcomes, inadequate internal capacity, and too narrow a focus on the transaction.

Second, a strong understanding of innovative PPP models available to address more complex issues can help governments achieve the proper allocation of risk—even in conditions of extreme uncertainty about future needs. Proper risk allocation allows governments to tailor PPP approaches to specific situations and infrastructure sectors.

The third strategy involves using PPP transactions to unlock the value from undervalued and underutilized assets, such as land and buildings, and using it to help pay for new infrastructure. This strategy gives taxpayers more value for their money. A closer look at each of these strategies follows.

Life-Cycle Perspective

A life-cycle approach best ensures the interest of the government agency that retains ownership and ultimate responsibility for the asset throughout its life. While many experts emphasize the transaction phase of PPP transactions, the success of the project depends heavily on a sound policy and legal framework, effective procurement and risk allocation process and close attention to the concession phase.

A life-cycle perspective helps governments understand how decisions made during different phases will affect the long-term success of the project. For example, the amount of risk transferred to the private sector up front will influence how a project is monitored. As shown in figure 5, there are three major phases for an infrastructure project under an innovative finance approach.

POLICY AND PLANNING PHASE. Activities performed in this phase should include: defining the jurisdiction's goals and objectives; issuing major guidelines for PPPs; developing the legal framework; defining requirements establishing processes for receiving and qualifying candidate projects; outlining the role PPPs will play in the larger infrastructure program; defining the procurement process; analyzing stakeholder interests; and communicating both internally and externally.

A key requirement is establishing the necessary legislative and regulatory framework to support the PPP program. With governments worldwide competing to attract investment capital, a poor legislative and statutory environment will stymie a state's efforts to engage private firms in planned PPPs.

The Oregon Legislative Assembly established the Oregon Innovative Partnerships Program within its Department of Transportation (ODOT) in

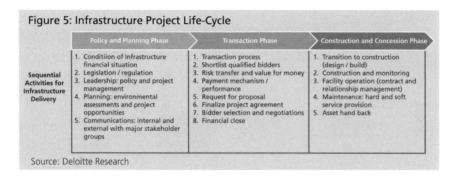

Figure 5: Infrastructure Project Life-Cycle

	Policy and Planning Phase	Transaction Phase	Construction and Concession Phase
Sequential Activities for Infrastructure Delivery	1. Conditiion of Infrastructure financial situation 2. Legislation / regulation 3. Leadership: policy and project management 4. Planning: environmental assessments and project opportunities 5. Communications: internal and external with major stakeholder groups	1. Transaction process 2. Shortlist qualified bidders 3. Risk transfer and value for money 4. Payment mechanism / performance 5. Request for proposal 6. Finalize project agreement 7. Bidder selection and negotiations 8. Financial close	1. Transition to construction (design / build) 2. Construction and monitoring 3. Facility operation (contract and relationship management) 4. Maintenance: hard and soft service provision 5. Asset hand back

Source: Deloitte Research

2003 to pave the way for accelerating important transportation projects by bringing in new funding, expertise and technology. The legislation gave the ODOT authority to form contractual relationships by entering into partnerships with private sector firms and units of government, and removed barriers to the formation of PPPs.[54] The program also allows for the fast-track study, design, funding and construction of state highway projects independent of the normal state procurement process. All in all, the Innovative Partnerships Program creates a platform for constructing new transportation infrastructure projects that might otherwise be decades away or might not be constructed at all.

TRANSACTION PHASE. The government needs to get a whole series of things right during the transaction phase (and subsequently during the concession phase) to ensure the success of the PPP approach. This includes: establishing clear and achievable performance standards; building in the right mixture of financial incentives for good performance and penalties for poor performance; and determining the optimal amount of risk to shift to the private sector.[55] The emphasis is on managing a competitive procurement that provides the best value for the state and meets the specific requirements of the project within defined procurement and contracting rules.

An important requirement of the transaction phase is to protect the public's interests. At every stage of the process, from initiation to the ongoing management of the partnership, government officials must ask key questions such as: What are the core values that the government must protect? How can public officials maintain these values under a contracted model? Answering these questions requires working through important issues, such as access to services, cost to citizens, fairness and equity, financial accountability, stability and quality.

Features of a Legislative Framework Conducive to PPPs

- Afford public entities considerable flexibility in the types of agreements they enter into and the specific procurement process.

- Allow contracts to be awarded according to best value, not just low price.

- Allow mix of public and private dollars.

- Allow "mixed concessions" (the reconstruction or expansion and long-term operation of existing facilities).

- Allow long-term leases of existing government assets.

- Authorize procedures to receive and consider unsolicited proposals.

- Avoid provisions that would require any further legislative act for a project to be authorized or financed, franchise agreement executed or toll rates changed.

Source: Nossaman, Gunther, Knox & Elliot.

CONSTRUCTION AND CONCESSION PHASE. Two major activities encompass this phase: construction, and maintenance and operation. While the issues involved in each activity are substantially different, in both cases careful attention to the terms and conditions of the contract and incentive methods will pay off. Public officials will want to form a close partnership with the infrastructure provider in order to achieve the goals and objectives for the project.

The key for ensuring that the private partner meets the project goals and objectives is to establish a series of performance measures as part of the concession agreement. These should be outcome-based and reflect the goals and objectives for the infrastructure facility. The British Columbia Ministry of Transportation, for example, divides requirements into these categories:

- *Key performance measures*, which focus on key objectives for asset and corridor management. These should help governments answer the question: "Is this facility meeting its transportation objective at multiple levels?"[56]

- *Asset Preservation Performance Measures*. Ensuring sound asset management takes place.

- *Operational performance measures*. These should focus on day-to-day serviceability.

It's important to recognize that asking private partners to provide government services places more—not less—responsibility on public officials. It demands that governments have a different set of abilities: managers skilled in negotiation, contract management and risk management who will focus on results rather than on defending bureaucratic turf.[57]

The presence of this cadre of managers with strong project management and change management skills will help to ensure that issues that arise in a long concession relationship can be addressed before litigation becomes necessary. When the Netherlands initiated its first highway PPP, for example, the government and the private partner held "alignment meetings" when they faced cooperation problems. These informal meetings, attended by the key team members of both sides, were aimed at de-escalating problems—or "working out conflicts for the benefit of the public."

Retain Flexibility: No One Size Fits All

You can't fit a square peg into a round hole. While standardization of PPP policies and practices is important, standard templates simply don't work in some situations and sectors. As with experimentation in any area, governments can learn from both the successes and failures of a particular method and adjust their approach accordingly. The same is true for PPP infrastructure development.

Officials need to be certain about the present and future infrastructure and service requirements before deciding on the right infrastructure approach. Without such certainty, achieving a fair contract price and ensuring that the infrastructure will continue to meet future demands can be difficult. Uncertainties might be present as a result of latent defects (flaws in the existing infrastructure that are not apparent until work begins), policy changes (implying a change in service requirements), demand risks (resulting from the introduction of user choice, for example), changes in public needs or rapid changes in technology. For projects that are especially vulnerable to these uncertainties, partnership models with increased flexibility and shorter contract periods can improve the likelihood of achieving infrastructure objectives.

Fortunately, recognition of these challenges has served to fuel innovation rather than frustrate further development. Between conventional procurement and full privatization, a wide range of financing options exist. To accommodate varying degrees of uncertainty about the future and to lower transaction costs, many different PPP approaches have been developed, thus expanding the options available for procurement.

Choosing the Right Delivery Model

Key Questions

- How confident are you now about the type of infrastructure and services that are needed over the next 5, 10, 15 or 20 years?

- How likely is it that the needs of citizens in this area will change?

- How likely is significant policy change?

- How easy is it to specify what will be needed?

- In which sector is the PPP approach going to be employed?

- How confident are you in the supplier of a service and how much control do you wish to retain?

- Can risks be transferred or would better outcomes be achieved through risk sharing?

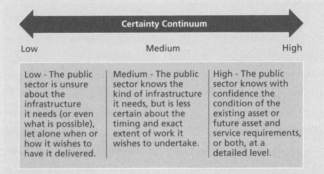

Certainty Continuum

Low	Medium	High
Low - The public sector is unsure about the infrastructure it needs (or even what is possible), let alone when or how it wishes to have it delivered.	Medium - The public sector knows the kind of infrastructure it needs, but is less certain about the timing and exact extent of work it wishes to undertake.	High - The public sector knows with confidence the condition of the existing asset or future asset and service requirements, or both, at a detailed level.

The level of certainty the public sector possesses about its infrastructure and service requirements should be a key determinant of the choice of model. A high level of certainty suggests that the government can shift substantial control and risk to the private sector. Where certainty is more limited, the public sector will likely need to retain some degree of control and risk associated with the project.

Source: *Building Flexibility: New Delivery Models for Public Infrastructure Projects,* Deloitte Research, 2005.

For example, for smaller projects, traditional PPP processes can be particularly costly when weighed against the project's modest revenue streams. This high cost can deter possible private partners from bidding if they feel future revenue is unlikely to outweigh transaction costs. Bidding on building individual hospitals, for example, requires substantial investment and may present relatively small returns compared to the expense of construction and maintenance.

One way to address this problem is by bundling together several projects. By contracting with just one partner to provide several small-scale projects, the public sector can reduce the length of the procurement process as well as transaction costs. In Australia, bundling sometimes takes the form of grouping hospital construction with ancillary structures and commercial activities, thereby generating enough revenue to balance against building and procurement costs.

Unlock Value from Underutilized Assets

Graduates of the internationally recognized James F. Oyster Bilingual Elementary School wouldn't recognize their old school today. Built back in the 1920s, the school was on its last legs in the early 1990s. Despite the school's strong academic record, leaking roofs, shutdowns due to building code violations, lack of computer hookups and limited space frequently disrupted the learning environment. Yet, the District of Columbia government didn't have anywhere near the $11 million budget required to build a new school befitting the nation's capital, nor did they have the borrowing power.[58]

What the city lacked in financial assets, however, it made up for in physical assets—the school sat on 1.67 acres of prime real estate within walking distance of the National Zoo. A fiscal crisis forced the city to make a hard decision: shut down the decrepit school building and relocate students or find another way to bring the school up to code. So the city decided to convert its underutilized physical assets into a financial asset by dividing the property in half to accommodate a new school and a new apartment building built by the private sector. In return for the sale of the land, the city got its first new school in 20 years—designed and built by a private developer—without spending a single public dollar.

Today, a visit to the old school grounds reveals a new state-of-the-art learning facility—nearly double the size of the old building—with long lines of parents eager to enroll their kids—a dramatic departure from the 70-year-old facility that once occupied the same space.

This example points to an important and growing strategy for getting the biggest bang from PPP projects: understanding and unlocking value from undervalued and underutilized assets. Savvy governments take a close look at their full portfolio of assets and determine how to release the maximum value from such assets by exchanging them for other assets or services that might serve more pressing needs. The state of Oregon, for example, is currently working on a swap of highway maintenance facilities in exchange for construction of new facilities.

These public assets tend to be sited in prime locations and often have excess land or control of adjacent properties. The government can use these as equity to partner with the private sector to create new facilities and develop the existing assets. This not only unlocks value from these assets but also helps to meet critical infrastructure needs.[59]

Conclusion

Looking at the infrastructure challenge facing state governments today may seem overwhelming. The historical boom-and-bust spending cycle in the states has created huge infrastructure deficits, the consequences of which are significant both for citizens who have to deal with decrepit facilities and for state governments fighting to stay competitive in today's flat world.

PPPs are not a panacea. Rather, they are *one tool* governments have at their disposal for infrastructure delivery; one that has produced several benefits: faster construction; big gains in on-time and within-budget delivery; reduced life-cycle costs; better value for money; a vastly improved overall investment climate for infrastructure; and economic stimulus. By making the best use of the delivery models that are available and by continuing to innovate, the public sector can confront the infrastructure challenges ahead.

Chapter 9: The Final Word

THE CHALLENGE
• The American Society of Civil Engineers (ASCE) graded the overall condition of the nation's infrastructure a D—recommending $1.6 trillion of investment in infrastructure over the next five years.
• Many states confront huge gaps between their infrastructure needs and their current rate of investment.
• The infrastructure deficits impose huge costs on society, ranging from lower productivity and reduced competitiveness to an increased number of accidents.

REFORM STRATEGIES
• *Make full use of the wide range of delivery options available.* Choosing an appropriate financing and delivery model requires first understanding the full range of delivery options available, including new innovative public-private partnership (PPP) models developed to address more complex issues such as proper risk allocation.
• *Adopt a full life-cycle perspective.* Governments need a full life-cycle approach (e.g., a clear framework) for infrastructure partnerships that confers adequate attention to all phases of the project—from policy and planning, to the transaction phase, and then to managing the concession.
• *Unlock value from underutilized assets.* Underutilized assets can be used as equity to partner with the private sector to create new facilities and develop the existing assets.

EXAMPLES
• *Focus on outcomes.* The Florida Department of Transportation opted to utilize an innovative PPP model to develop the Port of Miami Tunnel. The payments will be tied to the availability of the tunnel, in addition to quality measures. Supporting revenue will come from container and passenger fees in lieu of tolls.
• *Turn a physical asset into a financial asset.* A fiscal crisis forced the District of Columbia to make a hard decision: shut down the James F. Oyster Bilingual Elementary School or find another way to bring the decrepit old school building up to code. In response, the city divided the 1.67 acres of prime real estate in half to accommodate a new state-of-the-art learning facility and a new apartment building, built and paid for by the private sector—without spending a single public dollar.

NEXT STEPS
• *Assess the condition of the state's existing infrastructure.* Then determine the highest priority development needs.
• *Determine how innovative financing and delivery models can be used to supplement other delivery tools to help meet infrastructure needs.*
• *Establish the necessary legislative and regulatory framework to support a PPP program.* A poor legislative and statutory environment will stymie a government's efforts to engage in PPPs.

[10] *William D. Eggers, Christina Dorfhuber, Robert N. Campbell III and Steve Dahl*

Transforming State Government
Building New Business Models for a Changing Future

The bold and fundamental changes detailed throughout this book don't just happen. Even the best policy and management improvement ideas will fail without a sound understanding of current operations, a clear strategic imperative, a strong implementation capability and savvy political and people strategies. The public policy battlefield after all is filled with grand policy ideas that failed because of poor execution or a flawed political strategy. How then should a governor plan for transformational change?

In the past, most states equated transformation with more incremental change—the kind that could be solved by establishing a few broad goals that could then be assigned to individual agencies. That may sound logical and it may achieve incremental improvements, but it will not achieve sustained and lasting change and benefits. For one thing, an agency-led model perpetuates a siloed approach to governance and service delivery. The tremendous cost efficiencies and citizen service improvements made possible by implementing business process and program reforms that cross government agencies will not be realized.

For another, such an approach will inhibit governors from effectively tackling their greatest challenges, because very few of those challenges fit neatly into existing bureaucratic department silos. As we suggested in the introduction, from emergency response to health care, such challenges typically cross government departments as well as the public and private sectors.

If the historical model won't work, then what will?

Entering the reforms outlined in this book and transforming state government, first of all, requires a full understanding of the linkages and synergies between programs and functions of government. How will pension changes affect attempts to upgrade the government workforce? How will Medicaid reforms affect health and human services programs? How will transportation improvements affect economic development?

Second, state leaders need to be able to identify the duplication and overlap across programs, agencies and business processes in areas including financial management, procurement and human resource management. This is fertile ground for realizing cost efficiencies and service improvements through shared services, consolidation and other approaches.

In short, true transformation becomes possible only when government leaders view government as a single enterprise rather than as a series of discrete agencies performing individual functions and services. Such an enterprise approach enables governments to:

- Better see the linkages between programs and business processes;

- Impose uniform methodologies and frameworks across government processes as a whole in the search for greater efficiency and effectiveness;

- Organize services from the perspective of citizens and businesses rather than having the agency uppermost in mind.

Enterprise transformation spans political, legislative, department and program boundaries to deliver permanent cost reduction in the machinery of government. It begins by targeting areas where multiple state agencies or departments perform essentially the same task. Consolidating these functions—and automating them to the extent possible—saves money and improves satisfaction for citizens and businesses that use them. In the second stage of an enterprise transformation, top-to-bottom reviews of state programs, agencies, and departments are conducted and recommendations made to maintain, eliminate, redesign, or restructure.

Tackling the daily crises governments must address often doesn't allow much time for really looking beyond the horizon. Transformation initiatives provide an opportunity to think in new ways and exercise some muscles that aren't often used.

Thinking Differently

Not long ago, states across America faced major and unprecedented budget challenges, increased employment, and difficult federal regulations and relationships. For many states, the typical response was to raise taxes, slash budgets and reduce staff. But a few took a fundamentally different approach. One of those states was Minnesota.

Facing a sobering set of budget and workforce challenges, Minnesota governor Tim Pawlenty in late 2004 declared his intention to change state government radically. Six months later, he launched a package of reforms to overhaul many of the Minnesota government's most basic functions. The goal: to do a better job for state residents while saving an estimated $350 million over the next six years.

"One of our greatest opportunities for success lies in the alignment of the state's technology strategies with the Administration's business objectives," Pawlenty said in April 2004, announcing what became known as Minnesota's Drive to Excellence initiative. "Aggressive use of information technology will help allow us to achieve our business objectives and offer better services for Minnesota citizens."

Chief among those business objectives was keeping state operations afloat in the face of rising citizen expectations and a looming government workforce crisis. The Baby Boomers who made up the bulk of Minnesota's government workforce were poised to retire en masse over the next few years, taking with them vast experience and institutional knowledge. At the same time, Minnesota residents were demanding better performance and more convenience from state agencies. Citizens accustomed to performing nearly any type of consumer transaction online were losing patience with government services that were available only in person during normal business hours and frequently only after waiting in long lines.

The upcoming state staff exodus offered a chance to reduce the size of Minnesota's public workforce by automating routine tasks and focusing scarce labor where it could have the most impact. Success, however, would demand a cultural shift in how the state conducted business. Minnesota government needed to operate as a single enterprise, rather than a collection of individual agencies.

A core team of more than 200 state employees spent five months working with consultants to craft a transformation roadmap that laid out strategy, defined key projects, set timelines and identified expected results for the wide-ranging Drive to Excellence initiative. The roadmap identified numerous business areas ripe for reform from licensing, regulation and compliance to grants management.

Transforming these activities into true across-government business functions would produce dramatic operational improvement and measurable savings. Better business processes would enable state agencies to do the same work with fewer people and lower overhead. New technologies and techniques would help the state extract more revenue from existing sources. Consolidating statewide purchasing would allow Minnesota to buy the same goods at much lower prices.

Just as important, citizens would find it much easier to deal with their state government. The rethinking of traditional agency roles and divisions would facilitate expanded access to electronic services and the streamlining of processes such as professional licensing and business regulation. Before the Drive to Excellence plan, for example, 800 people operated more than 60 professional licensing systems in more than 40 agencies, completing more than 1 million business and professional licensing transactions each year. The new plan recommended making the process more convenient by providing one-stop access for business and professional licenses at a projected savings to the state of $12 million a year while redirecting significant numbers of employees to critical frontline service work.

First Steps in the Transformation Process

Minnesota is one of the more recent states to initiate enterprise transformation. While at least 20 states have undertaken some form of statewide efficiency and effectiveness review over the past five years, few achieved anything resembling true transformation from their efforts. Many states simply did not have the time or the expertise to understand how to "transform" their current operating models using the same or fewer resources into a more efficient and productive environment or to capitalize on some of the new technologies and business practices. They discovered that trying to make government run like a business in its purest sense does not work—the mission orientation of government and the politics do not support it. Similarly simply cutting budgets or raising taxes without a vision for long-term sustainable change also will not work.

Enterprise transformation pays much greater dividends than isolated, incremental reform. But it also demands sweeping organizational and business process change that can be challenging to implement in a political environment with often complex civil service rules. There are proven ap-

History Lesson

Enterprise transformation in government has its roots in corporate efficiency programs of the early 1990s. Multinational corporations, driven by global competitiveness concerns, launched a series of programs to cut costs and improve customer service.

These efforts often used technology—enterprise resource planning (ERP) systems, for example—to drive broad cultural and business process changes. ERP and other enterprise software applications were designed to provide core business functions—such as budgeting, procurement, payroll and human resources functions—for entire organizations. Tasks that once were performed on a department-by-department basis could be performed throughout the organization with a single application. As technology evolved to provide integrated enterprise capabilities, corporations restructured to eliminate redundant departments and positions.

Businesses also quickly learned to exploit the power of the Internet. Online merchants developed effective mechanisms for offering merchandise and accepting payment electronically. Shipping firms opened up internal systems, allowing customers to track their shipments via the Web. Online auctions changed the way many citizens shopped for everything from stuffed animals to airline tickets. Unlike many cost-cutting strategies, online transactions did not just save money, users often preferred them to traditional methods.

The significance of these trends was not lost on government, and state executives who had migrated from the private sector sought to bring similar reforms to their jurisdictions. Some of them failed because of their belief that the processes and approaches applied in business could be directly applied to government. Only in rare instances with particular agencies was that found to be true. For the most part, these tools and techniques needed to be tailored so as to be palatable and accepted by the major stakeholders who would be supporting the transformation effort.

Texas launched one of the first modern enterprise-wide efficiency initiatives in 1991 with its Texas Performance Review. The program—the brainchild of two venerable Texas Democrats, Comptroller John Sharp and Lieutenant Governor Bob Bullock—was launched to address huge financial problems created by economic recession and an oil-industry slump. In five months, the team came up with more than 1,000 recommendations and identified more than $2.4 billion in budget savings, ending the budget crisis and averting the need to impose a state income tax. The success of this initiative led to the biennial review of Texas government that has resulted in more than $15 billion in savings and gains to state funds since it was launched in 1991.

Since then, several more states have undertaken transformation initiatives, often to address budget shortfalls or to deliver the funds needed to meet critical policy objectives.

proaches, methodologies and best practices that help drive enterprise transformation efforts toward success. But ultimately, broad-based government reform demands deep commitment, courageous leadership, legislative support and appropriate resources. Answering a series of questions can help policy-makers determine whether their states can assemble the elements necessary for successful enterprise transformation.

1. Are You Ready?

Effective state transformations start at the top—with a visible, committed and involved governor. To effectively lead enterprise transformation, a public official must be willing to make tough decisions and withstand the potential political fallout. This type of effort takes courage. Entrenched interests, both inside and outside government, may vigorously oppose some changes. What will drive success is a governor's ability to accept the risk and confront opposition with an abiding belief that the benefits of reform far outweigh the personal sacrifice.

Effective government reform can boost political popularity, and the leaders of such efforts should proudly take credit for the results. But, ultimately, the decision to launch an enterprise transformation initiative should be driven by a genuine and deep-seated desire to improve government for the good of citizens. And reaching agreement on change almost always requires sharing the spotlight.

2. Are Your People Ready?

If you are ready, assess the people around you. Are members of your cabinet or leadership team committed to reform, and do they have the capabilities to pull it off? Obviously, you need to trust them professionally and personally. But you will be asking your team to do more than just run government; you need them to help you transform it and commit some of their staff to support that end. That demands both keen intelligence and a disposition toward change.

The right people for this job excel at critical thinking and questioning the status quo. They must be able to go beyond analyzing what is wrong, however. They need the ability to formulate bold solutions and put them into action.

In many cases, transformation requires pulling the best talent out of their line responsibilities. When Texas launched its first performance review, state leaders assembled more than 100 of the best budget analysts, auditors and number crunchers in Texas government and gave them a single mission: get us out of this budget crunch! Kentucky involved more than 300 state staff members in its Empower Kentucky transformation initiative. Furthermore, the governor personally held each cabinet member accountable for his or her progress toward the goal through the use of regular reports and scorecards.

Additionally, at the outset, a cultural or change assessment should be completed to measure the readiness of the organization to accept and drive meaningful change. The results of this assessment are critical to determining the level of change management and training support needed for success.

3. What Is Your Issue?

Successful transformation initiatives are driven by a compelling need. A desire for good government, by itself, generally is not enough. Several issues—or combinations of issues—have proven effective at galvanizing support for widespread reform. In Kentucky, for example, the state's transformation initiative was still on the drawing board when Governor Paul Patton announced that the first $50 million in annual savings would be redirected to upgrading education performance and preparing the workforce of the future. Kentucky at the time was ranked in the bottom five states for education results and workforce capabilities.

These drivers of change must be spelled out in a business case that is well documented, communicated and understood. Ultimately, this business case provides a strong measuring stick throughout the transformation and can be used as a tool to make the change stick once in place. Remember that people tend to revert back to previous ways when they don't understand why the change is needed and what the benefits of the change are to the organization and citizens.

Budget pressures often are the foremost driver. Texas, Virginia and Georgia, among other states, launched performance reviews and reform initiatives in the face of serious fiscal challenges. For example, former Virginia governor Mark Warner established the Governor's Commission on Efficiency and Effectiveness shortly after taking office in 2002. At the time, Virginia was contending with a budget shortfall estimated at as much as $500 million.

Potential government workforce shortages are a growing reason to initiate enterprise transformation. As mentioned earlier, the specter of a huge number of Baby Boomers retiring from their state government positions was a key reason behind Minnesota's Drive to Excellence.

Education is another extremely popular driver for reform. Governor Patton launched the wide-ranging Empower Kentucky initiative in 1996 after state schools scored poorly on national education report cards. The initiative proposed using business process changes and technology improvements to reduce the cost of operating government, allowing some of the savings to be plowed back into Kentucky schools. Improving education proved to be an issue that united political parties in the state's executive and legislative branches. Empower Kentucky has generated cumulative savings of more than $700 million, of which $300 million has gone toward education.

Other potential reasons for launching a performance review could include the need to finance infrastructure improvement, reduce taxes, modernize service delivery, improve child welfare or fund greater access to health care. The key point is to provide a compelling end benefit that justifies the difficult changes transformation entails.

4. Can You Engage Lawmakers?

Enterprise transformation initiatives must have legislative support to succeed. There is little point in creating committees and issuing recommendations if you have not first engaged legislative leaders and worked to find common ground. Furthermore, transformation programs require seed money to capitalize investments that can achieve longer-term transformation and savings. And seed money is possible only with legislative support. Securing this support can be challenging under good circumstances, and it becomes extremely difficult in politically polarized environments.

The Texas Performance Review offers a good model for involving state lawmakers in the transformation process. Typically, legislative language was drafted incorporating the review recommendations as soon as they were finalized. Performance review staff members then worked hand-in-hand with bill sponsors throughout the legislative session to get the measures enacted. Thanks largely to this approach, approximately 65 percent of the review's recommendations—more than 1,000 proposals—became law over the first decade of the performance review's existence.

Consistent methodologies, business cases and savings validation also are key to diffusing politics. The reasons for undertaking transformation must be clear and widely supported. Cost savings and service improvements must be measurable and credible. Having these facts at hand helps push the discussion away from ideology and toward good government. In the same vein, a careful balance of expanded citizen service with cost savings helps align support.

5. Can You Get the Resources?

Transformation will cost money, although those investments will be repaid many times over. Projects often involve deploying new technology, which requires upfront investments in advance of the much greater anticipated returns. State staff resources must be dedicated full-time to the initiative, and outside expertise is almost always a prerequisite to success.

Illinois governor Rod Blagojevich launched a transformation initiative in 2003, aimed at cutting costs, improving results, increasing the transparency of government and improving accountability. In 2005 the state worked with consultants to validate the savings achieved through the program. Among the findings:

- Illinois invested $42 million to achieve savings of $210 million in information technology and telecommunications.

- An investment of $15 million resulted in savings of $217 million in procurement, health care and employee benefits.

- An investment of $16 million yielded savings of $83 million in internal audit, legal and facilities management functions.

In Illinois, incremental investment costs generally were related to new equipment or software purchases, temporary outside contractor assistance or losses in federal funds resulting from program funding changes caused by the initiative. States launching enterprise transformation projects need to anticipate the need for similar investments. Identify funding sources early in the process—even if you do not know exactly how the money will be used. In order to institutionalize the concept, you will need to spend a little money to save a lot. There are many creative business models that states and other countries are adopting to help them with these investments, including performance-based incentives.

Organizing the Effort

States have used various models and combinations of models to transform the way they operate. Over time some approaches have proven more effective than others. What tends to work best is an approach that combines top-rate public sector staff (both borrowed and permanent), private sector business executives with relevant transformation experience serving in some

State Transformation Approaches

Transformation efforts and performance reviews can be approached in four different ways. In practice, many states use a combination of these approaches to suit their own requirements.

- **Functional:** This approach examines government operations by function, such as education, health and human services, public safety, employee benefits and strategic sourcing.

- **Organizational:** This approach focuses the review on individual departments.

- **Programmatic:** This strategy reviews specific programs within the organizations, usually those with large client populations. These efforts may be focused on programs experiencing significant problems. These reviews often flow into other organizations that are a part of the service delivery process. For example, to be meaningful a review of service delivery of a program provided in the Department of Education also needs to look at local school districts' role in the process.

- **Business Process:** This method reviews processes that cut across the entire enterprise, such as human resources, procurement and licensing.

kind of advisory role and outside third-party consultant assistance.

In this model, a state's internal review team works with an outside partner to evaluate current operations, identify targets for reform, develop implementation strategies and create mechanisms to capture and validate results. Each of these groups brings critical skills and capabilities to a transformation effort. Internal review teams benefit from the fact that participants have a deep understanding of government operations, which can result in practical and insightful reform suggestions. Internal teams can also conduct reviews without a lot of publicity, which can be advantageous, particularly in politically charged environments.

These initiatives must be staffed appropriately, and staffers must have the proper analytic expertise. One useful tactic is to start with employees loaned from various agencies. Then you can request permanent funding from the legislature once some success has been achieved. For many of these staffers, the transformation experience proves to be excellent professional preparation for assuming a leadership role over transformed business processes. Most states, however, have limitations in the numbers of skilled employees that can be assigned to large-scale transformation efforts, in which case they should consider supplementing state employees with third-party expertise.

Adding third-party expertise to the process delivers a range of benefits: The organization is under contract, so resources are committed full time and deadlines are clear. And you are presumably hiring an organization that has built a suite of methodologies and best practices in the government transformation area (reengineering methodologies, performance benchmarks, change methods), which should result in a structured and efficient program with clear and impartial results.

Third-party assistance also can be invaluable for confirming the validity of reform strategies, viability of business cases and the credibility of results achieved. After launching its initial effort, Illinois contracted with a consulting firm to impose clearer structure, processes and results validation on the project. Kentucky, Minnesota, Pennsylvania, Texas, Wisconsin and others also have used this hybrid model successfully. For example, a team of Minnesota state employees worked with consultants for five months to create the state's transformation roadmap. A core team of 200 state staff members was augmented by input from hundreds of additional employees and dozens of executive-level managers. The transformation roadmap focused on eight business areas that had proven targets for reform from other public and private sector organizations. The roadmap identified improvements for each area as well as methods for measuring cost savings and service delivery benefits.

Validating Benefits and Savings

Strong business cases for change as well as the validation of results are key to the sustainability and accountability of enterprise transformation initiatives. The transformation effort results need to be proven by official and verifiable financial documents. A benefits or savings validation is a structured and objective method for capturing and reporting these improvements, building on business cases previously developed and approved.

A well-designed benefits-savings validation also helps governments transfer successful reform tactics to other areas. Organizations—both public and private—often respond to crisis by taking decisive action, but they seldom analyze the individual impacts of their efforts. The validation process delivers insight into how well a particular reform activity worked, reveals why it was or wasn't fully effective and helps build momentum for continued improvement.

Just as important, a benefits-savings validation provides accountability to constituents. Citizens and other stakeholders will want to know how they benefit from disruptive and perhaps unpopular changes. A savings validation delivers concrete results, based on official records such as expenditure reports, vendor invoices, and wait times.

Targets for Transformation

Targets for transformation can vary widely based on individual circumstances. But there are a number of potential opportunity areas that typically offer "low-hanging" fruit. Some of these opportunities are relatively low-profile administrative functions, which make them a good place to start transformation efforts. Once a state builds a track record of success, it can take on more complex reforms.

A number of states already have instituted first-wave reforms and they are achieving results. These reforms, many of which were launched in response to the post-2000 fiscal downturn, have encompassed systems modernization and integration programs, shared services, benefits consolidation, strategic sourcing of some goods and services and initiatives standardizing information technology (IT). First-wave reforms represent the starting point for statewide transformation programs; states that have yet to initiate these measures can realize relatively quick efficiency gains by aggressively targeting these opportunities.

First-wave transformations occur at both the agency and enterprise levels, with each approach carrying benefits and drawbacks. Agency-specific reforms are easier and faster to implement, often show quicker results and may create less upheaval. Enterprise transformation—statewide or countywide efforts, for example—typically involve greater complexity and potential resistance. But the payoff generally is higher—greater savings, enhanced operational efficiency and higher citizen satisfaction with government.

Beyond these opportunity areas, a new class of reforms has emerged. Much of this second wave focuses on how to position the delivery of core government services for the future. These reforms rely heavily on new delivery models, innovative partnerships, shared services, advanced technology and related reforms of organizational structure and process design. The second wave of transformation can lead to government efforts to form "networked governance" or "extended enterprise" models involving multiple levels of government as well as private and nonprofit entities.

In some cases, this new way of thinking completely reworks traditional government business models. Ultimately, these changes benefit taxpayers through lower operating costs; state agencies through more efficient use of strained public workforces; and citizens in general through more effec-

Ten Steps for Conducting a Benefits-Savings Validation

1. Ensure that all individuals and departments involved in enterprise transformation, including the executive and legislative branches, understand the objectives of the validation.

2. Establish the scope of financial periods to study. The period of analysis should focus on two areas: a base period, and subsequent periods in which transformation changes occurred.

3. Decide how to count one-time savings versus savings that will recur from year to year. Recovery of overpayments or rebates on expenditures typically occur in only one financial year. Also consider how to address cost avoidance. Finally, define up front how to treat the value of balance sheet improvements, including working capital enhancements.

4. Support savings calculations with official and verifiable sources whenever possible. Examples include financial reports, expenditure reports from the general ledger system, contract and payment records and payroll records. Determine as part of this process how benefits and overhead will be considered, if at all.

5. Define savings categories for analysis and presentation. Examples include reduced budget allocations, rate reductions, new revenue and enhanced reimbursement.

6. Inventory all of the individual transformation projects and assess how savings were achieved.

7. Develop calculation models based on appropriate savings categories. Collect documentation to support assumptions and variables used in the savings calculations.

8. Perform financial analysis to determine savings amounts.

9. Capture any new spending that was required for the transformation effort. Examples include purchasing new equipment, contracting with consultants or creating new staff positions for a specific reform initiative.

10. Beyond financials and other metrics, capture intangible impacts—both positive and negative. Consider effects of the transformation on service quality, decision-making, business process management, and data quality and accessibility.

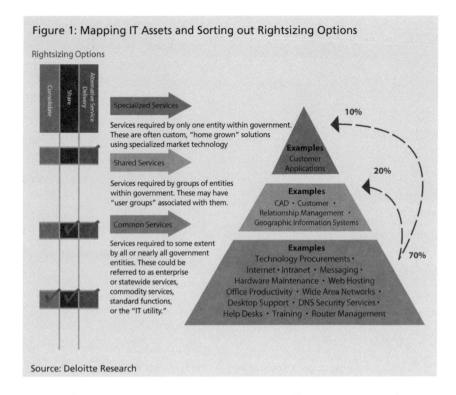

Figure 1: Mapping IT Assets and Sorting out Rightsizing Options

Rightsizing Options

Consolidate · Share · Alternative Service Delivery

Specialized Services
Services required by only one entity within government. These are often custom, "home grown" solutions using specialized market technology

10%

Examples
Customer Applications

Shared Services
Services required by groups of entities within government. These may have "user groups" associated with them.

20%

Examples
CAD · Customer · Relationship Management · Geographic Information Systems

Common Services
Services required to some extent by all or nearly all government entities. These could be referred to as enterprise or statewide services, commodity services, standard functions, or the "IT utility."

Examples
Technology Procurements · Internet · Intranet · Messaging · Hardware Maintenance · Web Hosting Office Productivity · Wide Area Networks · Desktop Support · DNS Security Services · Help Desks · Training · Router Management

70%

Source: Deloitte Research

tive, useful and convenient government service offerings. For example, state and local governments are exploring innovative arrangements that transfer operation of public assets such as toll roads, water systems, airports and lottery systems to private companies. These arrangements can generate revenue through the sale or lease of government assets and transfer operations to private enterprises that may do a more efficient job of running them.

Following is a more detailed discussion of first- and second-wave transformation opportunities across three main reform categories: administrative operations, client-facing programs and services and regulatory functions.

Administrative Operations

INFORMATION TECHNOLOGY. Information technology is a key enabler for enterprise transformation initiatives. But state IT operations and infrastructure often must be reviewed and reengineered to create the necessary foundation for delivering the desired performance and efficiency. Historically, states lacked coordination on IT spending; each agency bought its own expensive hardware and software systems and maintained its own services organization. States discovered this approach not only wasted money but typically resulted in islands of incompatible systems that could not communicate with each other.

Some states freed up specific funds for transformation simply by rationalizing and redirecting technology projects that were going on separately in agency silos (see figure 1). The goal: Move as many IT assets as possible into the common services category (utility services such as Internet, intranet, servers, routers and data storage, email, desktop configuration) where they can be consolidated across the enterprise by a process of relentless simplification and standardization. The resultant savings can then be invested in productivity-increasing shared and specialized applications. The key to realizing such benefits is a statewide systems plan and statewide technology architecture and standards.

Illinois, for example, implemented new IT governance procedures to better align technology investments with the state's business needs. The effort saved more than $8 million in spending on nonstrategic IT projects. In addition, a review of vendor billing practices revealed more than $1.4 million in billing errors, which the state recovered.

Similarly, under its Empower Kentucky initiative, that state realized $140 million a year in cost savings and revenue gains from using technology more strategically to reengineer the state's business processes. The savings drivers were common technology architecture and standards and common approaches to accounting procurement and human resources management across individual agencies.

Second-wave IT transformation will involve implementing enterprise-wide technology solutions, initiating tiered services, developing innovative networked government delivery options, outsourcing technology tasks historically performed by government agencies and developing regional initiatives that involve multiple governments.

For instance, Nevada officials recently announced the Nevada Shared Information Technologies Services project (NSITS), a move to transform the way state and local agencies protect critical applications from failure during a disaster. The NSITS would let government entities and agencies tap shared-use facilities to provide business continuity and disaster recovery capabilities if their own IT facilities are damaged. The initiative involves the Nevada Department of Information Technology, Clark County, the city of Las Vegas and the Las Vegas Metropolitan Police Department.

The plan, which envisions shared-use facilities located in Las Vegas and Carson City, would strengthen the ability of each partner jurisdiction to maintain vital services during a disaster. It also would be less expensive than creating separate disaster-recovery facilities for each jurisdiction.

BUDGET, ACCOUNTING AND FINANCE: ONE SOURCE OF THE TRUTH IN NUMBERS. Enterprise financial systems enable states to implement common business processes, streamline duplicative operations and obtain vital decision-making data. Many jurisdictions still rely on older, stand-alone systems that neither share data among themselves nor support users' reporting needs. Pennsylvania led the way with the first statewide enterprise resource plan for financial management, procurement and human resources management under then-Governor Tom Ridge. Other states have followed close behind, including Florida, Arkansas and South Carolina.

Minnesota is addressing these issues by creating a shared services organization to handle high-volume transaction-processing statewide. The organization will deploy new accounting and procurement applications to replace the aging Minnesota Accounting and Procurement Systems. These changes will eliminate redundant financial systems, improve financial planning and accountability, reduce costs and support better funding decisions, according to the state.

Another example comes from Texas, where the cities of Arlington, Grand Prairie and Carrollton intend to share a single enterprise financial system.[2] The North Central Texas Council of Governments will operate the shared system, and each participating city will pay the council for the services they need. The cities took a shared approach after confronting the staggering cost of deploying new financial systems individually.

The unified project cut initial procurement costs dramatically by requiring one Request for Proposal instead of three. It also will reduce expenses for deployment and operation. These savings are allowing the council to invest more money in the system itself, which will provide the cities with much better capabilities than they could have acquired separately.

Finance is also increasingly a catalyst for government reform. Sophisticated new tools allow policy-makers to develop fact-based business cases to inform decision-making; to provide analytical tools that offer quick "what-if" and scenario analysis and to measure results in government. The investments in these tools and related personnel training is made possible by even broader use of shared financial systems and services. This represents the next wave of transformation: transitioning from a focus in financial organizations on transaction processing to analytical functions.

MODERNIZING HUMAN RESOURCES. States often can reduce HR costs and improve services to employees by implementing self-service options for public workers. Minnesota is creating a shared services center for processing staff payroll and benefits. The goal: to reduce costs, increase employee self-service and establish centers of excellence to provide specialized HR functions for all state agencies. These reforms typically also evaluate contracting with private providers for payroll, benefits administration and other HR functions. Outsourcing these functions, if done well, eliminates the need to operate and maintain complex HR systems and reduces staffing needs for government HR departments. A note of caution is necessary here as states have found outsourcing HR processes to be complex and challenging to implement.

After implementing the basics, states can focus their time and attention on working on the critical areas of talent management: workforce transition and training and developing, recruiting and connecting employees (a subject discussed in full in chapter 3).

PROCUREMENT: MAKING IT STRATEGIC. Because purchasing often is scattered across multiple agencies that are buying the same types of goods and services, government procurement is a prime target for enterprise transformation. Consolidating and standardizing procurement gives states the buying power to negotiate much better terms on a wide range of transactions. For instance, under Empower Kentucky centralized procurement enabled the state to close several obsolete warehouses that it no longer needed. In another example, Texas expects to generate significant savings by requiring state agencies to acquire common computer hardware and software through central purchasing contracts negotiated by the state Department of Information Resources. In addition, the state will consolidate data center facilities and outsource their operation to a private vendor.

Regional purchasing initiatives enable groups of states and localities to combine their purchasing power to lower acquisition costs for products and services. The long-standing 15-state Western States Contracting Alliance develops cooperative contracts that are open to all members. In addition, the program is available to all cities, counties and schools located within those states.

Similarly, state and local governments are now able to buy directly from the federal government's General Services Administration schedule, which was opened to cooperative purchasing in 2003. This process allows states, cities and counties to take advantage of prenegotiated federal government procurement contracts.

REAL ESTATE. Looking beyond traditional office environments can produce significant savings by building on current commercial best practice and eliminating the need for costly real estate. A growing number of jurisdictions now encourage telecommuting arrangements that allow employees to work from home at least part of the time. Another promising technique is "hoteling," which provides office space to employees as needed, instead of assigning each worker a permanent desk. Both of these practices reduce the amount of space necessary to house government workforces.

States also may benefit from reevaluating their real estate and facilities management strategies. Illinois, for example, reviewed state-owned space for capital planning purposes and introduced new standards for facility utilization. The state also reduced property management expenses by $32 million through staff attrition and a hiring freeze.

One-stop centers where citizens can access a variety of government services represent a second-wave opportunity to rationalize real estate space. For example, Texas, Massachusetts and other states are consolidating field offices that each provide a different human service into single one-stop sites. This not only saves taxpayer dollars but means that program applicants, many of whom have multiple human service needs, aren't forced to trudge from one office to another.

Unlocking value from undervalued and underutilized assets represents another opportunity area. This entails conducting a thorough inventory of the full portfolio of assets and then determining how to release the maximum value from such assets by exchanging them for other assets or services that might serve more pressing needs. The state of Oregon, for example, is currently working on a swap of highway maintenance facilities in exchange for construction of new facilities.

RECEIVABLES MANAGEMENT AND COLLECTION. Many states have found that revenue generation can be a significant business case driver of statewide transformation efforts. In those states, receivables are housed in individual silo agencies that often lack core competency or technology support in revenue management. State overpayments that have not been recovered, outstanding tax liabilities and third-party liability for health care provided by the state all represent significant reform opportunities. A systematic review of existing receivables and other unrecognized revenue recovery opportunities can lead to significant one-time and recurring financial benefits.

In addition, several states have centralized or outsourced arrangements to pursue and manage receivables in the interest of maximizing the revenue available to the state.

Client-Facing Programs

HEALTH AND HUMAN SERVICES. As discussed in chapter six, integrating the provision of multiple health and human services programs offers an opportunity to save money and improve services to citizens who depend on these benefits (this is discussed in chapter 6). Government entities currently spend huge amounts of money determining eligibility for and operating stand-alone programs that provide food stamps, assistance payments, health care and other social services. And unfortunately, in many states those in need have to go numerous places to find answers to the same questions and provide the same documentation to receive services.

Shortly after taking office in 2003, Massachusetts governor Mitt Romney orchestrated the most significant reorganization of HHS in the state's history. A critical part of the reorganization effort is Virtual Gateway, an online Web portal that serves as a single front door for HHS services. What was once a complicated maze of different agencies—each operating independently with its own systems, processes and applications—no longer acts as a barrier to citizens trying to access services in a timely manner. Today, registered HHS providers can submit a single online application for up to 17 programs, including Medicaid, food stamps, and Women, Infants and Children nutrition programs. When low-income patients turn up in the emergency room, hospital staff can check to find out if the patient has any insurance. If the answer is no, they can immediately enter Medicaid application data into the system.

The next evolution for health and human services involves tighter integration of state and local programs, as well as integration between the human services system and education, criminal justice and mental health operators, which in many cases touch the same individuals.

MEDICAID MAKEOVER. Better management and closer oversight of Medicaid programs can be a valuable first step. In fiscal 2005, Illinois saved more than $10 million and avoided another $10 million in costs by improving methods for identifying Medicaid beneficiaries who also had private insurance coverage. Although the state Department of Health and Family Services had already recovered $180 million annually from private insurers for services provided to Medicaid recipients, Illinois tapped several new information sources to further improve its recovery efforts. Similar opportunities exist to ensure that services funded by the state are billed to Medicaid or Medicare where possible.

Beyond improvements in eligibility determination and oversight, meaningful Medicaid reform requires fundamentally restructuring the 40-year-old program, which has not seen much change despite radical shifts in the health care marketplace, in technology and in the population the program serves. (A more detailed look at what these reforms entail can be found in chapter 5).

TRANSFORMING JOB TRAINING. A thorough review and restructuring of job training programs can deliver dramatic improvement. Texas, for example, had two large job training programs located in separate agencies whose functions and clientele overlapped. In 2000 several independent performance evaluations of the programs demonstrated conclusively that one of them achieved much better results than the other, which was plagued with financial and operational problems. Rather than expend significant taxpayer resources trying to "fix" the poor performer, the legislature simply eliminated it, saving the state $25 million a year.

WorkInTexas.com—a Web portal created by the Texas Workforce Commission and the state's 28 local workforce development boards—offers a compelling example of second-wave transformation. The project uses advanced technology and innovative partnerships to improve services for jobseekers and employers. The site is designed to match companies of all sizes with qualified employees, at no cost to any of the users. Citizens can search job postings from more than 140,000 employers, which post approximately 1,000 new jobs every day. They also may seek advice online or though 284 local workforce centers across Texas. Employers have hired more than 500,000 people through the system since its launch in June 2004, and the system provided immediate support in managing the daunting challenge of job matching for relocated Hurricane Katrina victims.

TRANSPORTATION INNOVATIONS. Transportation transformation opportunities can be divided into two main categories: retooling business processes (financial management, HR, contracting, IT, procurement) and financing and delivery innovations such as innovative financing models, public-private partnerships, congestion pricing and pavement warranties (contractual guarantees that a road will function appropriately for a long period of time in which the contractor must replace or repair the road surface at no additional cost to the agency).

Intergovernmental partnerships can also play a growing role in making transportation more efficient and convenient for citizens. The multistate E-ZPass electronic toll collection system offers a well-established example. E-ZPass uses small electronic transponder devices attached to vehicles to eliminate cash collection for bridges, tunnels and toll roads. The system automatically calculates and deducts toll amounts from prepaid accounts as E-ZPass customers pass through toll lanes. Drivers may use a single E-ZPass account at participating facilities in Delaware, Maryland, Massachusetts, New Jersey, New York, Pennsylvania, and West Virginia. By creating an integrated, electronic toll system, these states radically transformed their interaction with citizens. Drivers receive much more convenience, and the states operate their toll systems more efficiently.

Other technological improvements also will be a significant part of second-wave transformation efforts. Digital technology will link transportation planners with emergency road crews and drivers, providing them with real-time information about accidents and congestion. Intelligent, Internet-connected vehicles could deliver data, navigation guidance, safety warnings and collision avoidance systems. Drivers would be armed with accurate, customized, real-time traffic guidance. With this information travelers could take alternative routes, delay departure or choose alternative transportation such as the bus, subway or train. These informed choices, in turn, would improve the overall system, reducing uncertainty and spreading out demand on the roads.

Regulatory Functions

REVENUE MANAGEMENT. The Florida Department of Revenue used enterprise resource planning (ERP) technology to integrate its state tax systems and boost tax collections dramatically. More than 90 percent of Florida's general revenue now is collected and distributed using the System for Unified Taxation (SUNTAX), which is based on integrated customer relationship management and ERP technology. These taxes formerly were administered using a collection of stand-alone systems.

Taking an enterprise approach to taxation paid off for Florida. As of June 2005, SUNTAX had cost $77.8 million to deploy and had generated $521.6 million in savings and increased tax collections, according to the state. The resulting return on taxpayers' investment is $6.70 for every $1 spent. The annual benefit now exceeds the agency's total spending.

Engaging third parties as partners in the provision of e-government services represents another transformation opportunity for revenue functions, as well as other regulatory areas. One of the best examples comes from the IRS, which partners with a host of companies—including H&R Block, Intuit (maker of TurboTax software) and TaxAct—that use software to simplify the complicated task of filing taxes. These firms compete intensely for market share and have strong incentives to make their programs as user-friendly and comprehensive as possible.[3]

LICENSING. A growing number of states view integrated licensing as a way to improve government efficiency and promote economic development. Consolidating licensing processes—which often are heavily fractured—shrinks overhead costs and cuts red tape involved in obtaining building permits and business and professional licenses. Minnesota, for instance, operates 60 different licensing systems that issue nearly 640 different types of licenses. A recent survey found that 70 percent of these licenses share common functionality—filling out an application and paying a fee—that could easily be integrated into an online process. The state's transformation roadmap recommends creating a "License Minnesota" portal—a Web-based, single point of contact for all state licenses.

Second-wave transformation extends the concept of one-stop state licensing portals to include local government resources. In other words, citizens would be able to carry out all necessary state and local licensing tasks through the same e-government site.

Increasingly, governments also must think beyond traditional government borders to deliver these services. Governments should think of themselves less as direct providers of e-government services and more as enablers of third-party integrators that tie together multiple agencies across multiple levels of government to package information, forms, regulations, and other government services and requirements in user-friendly ways.[4] Boat registration processes, for instance, vary widely among states, with some requiring an inspection and others requiring payment of local county tax and state registration fees. Some boats, depending on their size and use, also must be registered with the federal government. The process would be much easier if a national organization of boat owners developed a portal for boat registration.[5]

Lessons Learned

Based on a wide range of government transformation experience, here are some lessons that can help smooth the path toward government reform and transformation.

CONFIRM EXECUTIVE COMMITMENT. If you decide to launch a transformation initiative, throw the full weight of your leadership behind it. Ensure the effort has strong and consistent leadership, visible support and the resources it needs to succeed. Remember that these efforts require executive-level courage in execution to be successful. They also require talented and experienced full-time staff devoted to the effort.

KNOW YOUR GOVERNMENT'S STRUCTURE. Understand your sphere of control and design transformation initiatives that conform to that reality. Target opportunities that are directly under your authority, especially early in the process.

DO NOT BITE OFF TOO MUCH AT ONCE. Enterprise transformation involves big change, but there is a limit to how much change any state government and its stakeholders can absorb at any one time. Many of the California Performance Review's more uncontroversial recommendations failed to become law because the massive and highly controversial structural changes recommended by the review team ended up defining the whole review. Some leaders of the review acknowledged in retrospect that they might have had more success by first tackling the less controversial changes and then going after the more controversial structural changes.

PAY PROPER ATTENTION TO PROJECT MANAGEMENT. Something as complex as government transformation demands strong project management to keep work groups focused and projects on track. Invest time and resources in developing and implementing these structures before you begin. The job of the program management team (also known as a project management office, or PMO) is to develop detailed implementation plans, enforce a standard methodology on the review teams, coordinate activities across projects and organizational boundaries, eliminate gaps and overlap, track progress, hold the project teams accountable and resolve issues and conflicts. In addition the PMO should develop a standard process for reviewing and evaluating programs and business processes.

Tools and Methodologies to Support Transformation Reviews

- **Budget Driver Analysis:** This analysis examines the activities that drive state budgets over time. It aims to answer questions such as: What areas of state government have been growing the most over the past 10 years? What is driving the big increase in spending on the mentally ill? Why has prison spending doubled in the last 7 years? When conducting a budget driver analysis, it is critical to make sure that your data is as robust as possible. Some states have had to pull information from 15 or 20 different financial systems to find the data they are looking for and make some sense of it. The spending trend analysis over different agencies and across different functions helps ensure that your review focuses attention on the right areas.

- **Benchmarking Expenditure Analysis:** This analysis looks at spending patterns in key areas such as education, transportation and human services compared with other states. The benchmarking helps to illuminate areas to focus on in the review. In addition to providing a method to identify areas in need of improvement, benchmarking is a critical tool in measuring and sustaining government performance.

- **Business Process Breakdown of State Government:** Defining core processes for the enterprise and then mapping which departments currently have people, processes and systems that deliver those processes is an excellent way to find where duplications of people and processes exist within an organization and also the magnitude of and reasons for that duplication.

AVOID ANALYSIS PARALYSIS. Over-analysis can paralyze transformation efforts, causing them to lose critical support and momentum. At the same time, the history of government transformation is littered with failed projects that were started without sufficient forethought, coalition building and project management structure. Work to strike a balance between study and action.

WATCH FOR BARRIERS TO CHANGE. Look for statutes and policies that can hinder innovation and get them changed before they halt your progress. A few things to look for: accounting and procurement processes that preclude the use of performance- and savings-based contracts and restrictions on the use of digital signatures.

FOCUS ON THE PEOPLE ELEMENT. Pay particular attention to people change management. Without some degree of employee buy-in, the effort will likely fizzle out.

LOOK AT THE BIG PICTURE. Analyze the impact of transformation activity holistically to determine if reforms really make sense. For example, will workforce reductions that produce savings in one area boost unemployment expenses in another?

CELEBRATE QUICK WINS. You can achieve tremendous value from producing a series of early quick wins. Set up a formal process for capturing results from reforms that can be instituted quickly—those that deliver measurable improvement within 12 months. Sharing credible results from quick wins with stakeholders builds support for longer-term transformation projects. Quick wins improve the initiative's credibility, expand support within the state government and create positive momentum for the overall effort.

LIMIT THE POLITICS, SHARE THE SUCCESSES. Sustainable transformation can't be about one political party or another. Take credit for success, but share that credit with other stakeholders. Focus on a goal that is nonpartisan such as creating better value for taxpayers. Get buy-in from influential legislators from both sides of the aisle. Involve the most reform-minded legislators more deeply as advisory board members of the review.

BALANCE UNION INVOLVEMENT. Intense union involvement in transformation initiatives can result in the removal of many reform options from the table before the review is completed. But ignoring union input can jeopardize employee buy-in when reform proposals are released. Involve union leaders at appropriate levels early in the reform process and keep them informed as activities progress. You want them to support the process, but not drive it.

BALANCE THE LEVEL AND TIMING OF MEDIA INVOLVEMENT. The news media should be informed of transformation activities, but don't release details of everything being talked about. Transformation work groups should be forums for ideas, some of which may be unorthodox or controversial. A relatively confidential environment allows for discussion of these ideas, which can lead to more practical proposals.

COMMUNICATE AND TRAIN. Transformation efforts create unrest among stakeholder groups and require new skills for employees and managers to be successful in delivering services with new technology, new processes and new organizational models. Success depends on a thoughtful and well-executed communications and training plan.

USE YOUR BUSINESS CASE. A well-documented and understood business case is needed at the start of the transformation to communicate the need for change. Equally important, the business case should be updated periodically throughout the effort in order to track performance, measure results and adjust expectations based on new facts and circumstances learned during the course of the transformation.

Conclusion

State governments face competing pressures, financial and otherwise. Aging populations and workforces, rising unfunded pension liabilities, declining federal funds, growing desire for better customer service and scores of other issues all clamor for budgetary attention. Meeting these demands at a price that taxpayers can afford means changing the way governments do business. State enterprise transformation offers a method for permanently reducing the cost of government and improving the way public services operate.

Enterprise transformation implements reforms aimed at making governments act more like a single organization and less like a loose collection of independent agencies. It also opens the door to new and innovative ways of meeting the needs of citizens and businesses. These changes are not easy to implement, especially when deployed across entrenched bureaucracies and interest groups. But they are necessary.

By employing proven techniques, learning from the experiences of similar jurisdictions and using structured, repeatable processes, your state can confidently navigate the course toward state government transformation. The path is clear, and it is time to begin.

Chapter 10: The Final Word

THE CHALLENGE

• Enterprise transformation involves learning to think about government as a complete enterprise rather than as a series of discrete agencies performing individual functions and services. To do that, government leaders must first understand the linkages and synergies between programs and functions of government, identify any duplication and overlap across programs, agencies and business processes, and then reorganize government agencies, processes and functions to deliver improved services and lower costs.

REFORM STRATEGIES

• *Programmatic review.* Specific programs within the organizations are reviewed, usually those with large client populations, to determine how services can be produced and delivered more efficiently for the client and at less cost to the government and thus the taxpayer.

• *Business process review.* The goal: find where duplication of people and processes exist within an organization and also the magnitude of and reasons for that duplication.

• *Budget Driver Analysis.* An analysis should be conducted of the activities likely to drive state budget growth over time.

EXAMPLES

• *Minnesota's* Drive to Excellence initiative identified numerous business areas ripe for reform, from licensing, regulation and compliance to grants management. Estimated savings: $350 million over six years.

• The biennial performance review of Texas government has resulted in more than $15 billion in savings and gains to state funds since it was launched in 1991.

• *Illinois'* transformation initiative, launched in 2003, aimed at cutting costs, improving results, increasing the transparency of government and improving accountability. The state saved $500 million from an investment of $73 million.

NEXT STEPS

• *Garner executive support.* To be successful, a transformation initiative needs the full weight of the leadership behind it. Ensure that the effort has strong and consistent leadership as well as visible support and resources.

• *Organize the effort.* What tends to work best is an approach that combines top-rate public sector staff (both borrowed and permanent), private sector business executives with relevant transformation experience serving in some kind of advisory role and outside third-party consultant assistance.

• *Engage lawmakers.* Enterprise transformation initiatives must have legislative support to succeed. There is little point in creating committees and issuing recommendations if you haven't first engaged legislative leaders and worked with them to find common ground

• *Target transformation opportunities.* These can be divided into first-wave and second-wave opportunities. First-wave transformations occur at both the agency and enterprise levels, with each approach carrying benefits and drawbacks. Second-wave opportunities position the delivery of core government services for the future.

Endnotes

Chapter One: Window of Opportunity

1. Dan Yankelovich, "Accreditation in a More Demanding World," Presentation to CHEA Annual Conference, January 2006 (http://www.chea.org/Research/2006conf/Yankelovich_Accreditation_in_a_Demanding_World.pdf#search=%22yankelovich%20%20trust%20government%20watergate%202006%22).

2. Prior to the 2006 election, twenty-one of the nation's governors came from the political party that lost the state's presidential vote in 2004. See Josh Goodman, "Against the Grain," Governing.com, October 2006, (http://www.governing.com/articles/10govs.htm).

3. See Paul C. Light, *The New Public Service* (Washington: Brookings Institution Press, 1999). Coming after the recession of the 2001 and 2002, however, the numbers tended to rise. See Paul Light, "In Search of Public Service," Brookings Institution, June 2003 (http://www.brookings.edu/gs/cps/light20030603.htm).

4. "California's Population," Public Policy Institute of California, October 2004 (http://www.ppic.org/content/pubs/jtf/JTF_PopulationJTF.pdf).

5. Stephen Heffler and others, "U.S. Health Spending Projections for 2004–2014," *Health Affairs Web Exclusive*, February 23, 2005.

6. Mark Whitehouse, "Fed's Course Seen As Top Concern For U.S. Economy With Inflation Resurgent, Growth Easing, Forecasters Fear Rates Will Go Too High," *The Wall Street Journal*, July 5, 2006, A1.

7. "ACSI Overall Federal Government Scores with Historical Scores of Agencies Measured 1999–2005," American Customer Satisfaction Index, December 15, 2005. "Fourth Quarter Scores: Retail Trade; Finance & Insurance; E-Commerce," American Customer Satisfaction Index, February 21, 2006.

8. U.S. Bureau of Statistics, State Civilian Labor Force series, 2003.

9. Bill Testa, "Mid-Year Jobs Report," Federal Reserve Bank of Chicago, July 25, 2006 (http://midwest.chicagofedblogs.org/archives/michigan).

10. George Talbot, "Foreign Automakers Find Home in Alabama," Newhouse News Service, January 29, 2006.

11. Alisa Priddle, "Manufacturing: The Next Chapter," *Ward's Auto World,* August 1, 2005.

12. "Honda Motor Co., Ltd.'s Honda Manufacturing of Alabama, LLC Breaks Ground for New Auto and Engine Plant in Lincoln, Alabama," Reuters, September 10, 2002; "Toyota to spend US$20M to make V-6s in Alabama," Bloomberg News, July 15, 2003; "An Alabama

Industry Profile," Economic Development Partnership of Alabama (http://www.edpa.org/docs/automotive-industry-profile.pdf).

13. "Honda to Double Production Capacity in Alabama; Investment to Reach $1 Billion, Employment Increasing by 2,000," Automotive Intelligence News, July 10, 2002 (http://www.autointell.com/News-2002/July-2002/July-2002-2/July-10-02-p2.htm).

14. "Alabama's Automotive Manufacturing Industry Is Sizzling," Alabama Automotive Manufacturers Association, February 17, 2006 (http://www.aama.to/2005-survey-press.pdf).

15. "New Orleans Schools Before and After Katrina," Online NewsHour with Jim Lehrer, Public Broadcasting Service, November 1, 2005 (http://www.pbs.org/newshour/bb/education/july-dec05/neworleans_11-01.html).

16. (http://www.governing.com/articles/9schools.htm).

17. Ann Carrns, "Charting a New Course After Katrina: New Orleans's Troubled Educational System Banks on Charter Schools," Wall Street Journal Online, August 24, 2006 (http://online.wsj.com/public/article/SB115638176750244050-TTCHe63W9NuKkZm-HEwonG_D3OxU_20070824.html?mod=tff_main_tff_top).

18. Ibid.

19. Ibid.

20. National Center for Education Statistics, (http://nces.ed.gov/)

21. Mitt Romney, "Health Care for Everyone? We Found a Way," The Wall Street Journal, April 11, 2006.

22. Martha F. Juch, P.E., "Civil Engineers Give Texas Infrastructure A 'C-' in the 2004 Texas Infrastructure Report Card," 2004 Texas Infrastructure Report Card Committee. (http://www.austinasce.org/Misc/2004TexasReportCard.pdf#search=%22Texas%20infrastructure%22).

23. Mike Krusee, Speech delivered at IBTTA Transportation Improvement Forum, March 20, 2006, TOLLROADS News, April 23, 2006.

24. "State Boosts Tolls to Finance Highways," Focus Report, House Research Organization, Texas House of Representatives, November 12, 2004 (http://www.capitol.state.tx.us/hrofr/focus/tolls78-19.pdf#search=%22TxDOT%20said%20that%20all%20new%20roads%20through%20PPPs%22).

25. Robert Poole, "California Should Follow Texas' Lead for Financing Transportation Infrastructure," Keston Institute of Infrastructure, May 28, 2004 (http://www.usc.edu/schools/sppd/lusk/keston/news/item.php?id=451).

26. William D. Eggers, "Big, Bold Ideas and the Real World," Governing.com, September 2006.

27. Larry Bossidy and Ram Charan, Execution: The Discipline of Getting Things Done (New York: Crown Books, 2002), p. 19.

Chapter Two: Serving the Aging Citizen

1. The Baby Boom is generally defined as the generation born between 1946 and 1964.

2. "State of States 2006 Report" (www.Stateline.org).

3. Japan and the countries in the European Union are likely to be hardest hit. Japan's dependency ratio is expected to shoot up to 0.74 in 2030 and to 0.97 in 2050, meaning there will be almost one dependent for every worker.

4. The impact of the workforce decline on GDP could theoretically be overcome by a rise in productivity. But given the large scale of decline in labor supply in some countries, this would require a phenomenal growth in productivity. For instance, the German workforce is expected to decline by around 8 million by 2050. This would require a rise in productivity of close to 40 percent per annum, almost impossible to achieve given that the long-term annual productivity growth rate is close to 1.6 percent. The impact of these demographic changes on

per capita GDP is more difficult to predict, given a reduction in population accompanied by the reduction in labor force. See Axel Borsch-Supan, "Global Aging: Issues, Answers, More Questions," Working Paper WP 2004-084, Michigan Retirement Research Center, University of Michigan, 2004.

5. Ronald Lee and Ryan Edwards, "The Fiscal Effects of Population Aging in the US: Assessing the Uncertainties," *Tax Policy and Economy* vol. 16, (Cambridge, MA: MIT Press, 2002) p.154. Lee and Edwards have calculated the average government (federal, state and local) expenditure per U.S. individual, by benefit program and age; it shows that benefit programs for the elderly are by far the most costly on a per capita basis, followed by programs for children. The programs include 25 individual and or household benefits programs (school lunches, TANF, energy assistance, SSI) plus additional non-individual programs. Expenditures that do not accrue to individuals or households have been assigned on a per capita basis.

6. It should be noted that the number of survivors into old age is lower and so the per capita cost may be higher. A study by J. Gruber and D. A. Wise found that the expenditure per individual old person in OECD countries declined over time. Nevertheless, the total expenditure on the elderly increased. Further, they found that the total government expenditure as a share of GDP did not change with aging, mainly due to reduction in other areas. The conclusion is that the aging population will put pressure on government in terms of trade-offs and constraints, rather than in terms of level of expenditure. See J. Gruber and D. A. Wise, "An International Perspective on Policies for an Aging Society," NBER, Working Paper 8103, 2001.

7. Sonya M. Tafoya and Hans P. Johnson, "Graying in the Golden State: Demographic and Economic Trends of Older Californians," *California Counts,* 2(2), Public Policy Institute of California, November 2000.

8. Population Division of the Department of Economic and Social Affairs of the United Nations Secretariat, *World Population Prospects: The 2004 Revision. Highlights* (New York: United Nations, 2005).

9. The figures for the United States focus on legal migrants and therefore miss the large number of illegal immigrants, particularly from Mexico.

10. William H. Frey and Bill Abresch, "New State Demographic Divisions," *Spectrum: The Journal of State Government,* 75(3, summer 2002) and U.S. Census Bureau, "Table 4 - Cumulative Estimates of the Components of Population Change for the United States and States," December 22, 2004 (http://www.census.gov/popest/states/NST-comp-chg.html).

11. A majority still tends to stay in the gateways. A study for the Pew Hispanic Center showed that while 58 percent of the immigrants since 2000 settled in five gateway states, 11 percent went to states that had seen relatively little immigration before. See Rick Lyman, "The Bay Area's Minority Migration," *New York Times,* August 15, 2006 (http://www.sfgate.com/cgi-bin/article.cgi?file=/c/a/2006/08/15/MNG5KKIPQ71.DTL).

12. In the United States, the South witnessed an average net in-migration of 353,000 annually between 2000 and 2004. For more details on domestic migration in the United States, see United States Census Bureau, "Domestic Net Migration in the United States: 2000 to 2004," April 2006.

13. Douglas A. Wolf and Charles F. Longiono, "Our "Increasingly Mobile Society? The Curious Persistence of a False Belief," *Gerontologist*, February 25, 2005, p. 7.

14. See "Aging in Place: A Q&A with Fredda Vladeck," *Wall Street Journal*, May 5, 2006 (http://online.wsj.com/article_print/SB114685159631145074.html). Also see articles in "Graying Global Cities," *Forbes*, August 6, 2005, which point out that these are some of the attractions in the cities of London and Paris for senior citizens (http://www.forbes.com/2005/06/07/05graycitiesland.html?partner=daily_newsletter).

15. Lyman, "The Bay Area's Minority Migration."

16. The total fertility rate (or total period fertility rate) of a population is the average

number of children that would be born to a woman over her lifetime if she were to experience the current age-specific fertility rates through her lifetime. Age-specific fertility rate is the number of births to women in a particular age group, divided by the number of women in that age group.

17. Gary Becker, "Missing Children," *Wall Street Journal*, September 1, 2006.

18. Glenn Harlan Reynolds, "The Parent Trap: How Safety Fanatics Drive Down Birthrates," *TCS Daily*, May 24, 2006.

19. Joseph F. Quinn, "Has the Early Retirement Trend Reversed?" May 11, 1999 (http://fmwww.bc.edu/EC-P/wp424.pdf).

20. S. Blondal and S. Scarpetta, "The Retirement Decision in OECD Countries," OECD, Economics Department Working Paper Number 202, Organization for Economic Cooperation and Development, 1998. European Commission, *Employment in Europe 2005*, September 2005. Joseph F. Quinn and Garry Burtless, "Is Working Longer the Answer for an Aging Workforce," *Issues in Brief* 11, Center for Retirement Research, Boston College University, December 2002.

21. Daniel Gros and Nancy LeaMond, "A Balancing Act: Achieving Adequacy and Sustainability in Retirement Income Reform," Center for European Policy Studies, May 24, 2006 (http://www.ceps.be/Article.php?article_id=301).

22. "Canada's Demographic Revolution: Adjusting to an Aging Population," *Executive Action*, The Conference Board of Canada, March 2006, p 2.

23. David E. Bloom and David Canning, "The Effect of Improvements in Health and Longevity on Optimal Retirement and Saving," Working Paper 10919, National Bureau of Economic Research, November 2004 (papers.nber.org/papers/W10919).

24. Quinn, "Has the Early Retirement Trend Reversed?"

25. Robert B. Avery and Michael S. Rendall, "Estimating the Size and Distribution of the Baby Boomers' Prospective Inheritances," in the American Statistical Association's *1993 Proceedings of the Social Statistics Section*, 1999, pp. 11–19; and John J. Havens and Paul G. Schervish, "Why the $41 Trillion Wealth Transfer Estimate is Still Valid: A Review Of Challenges and Questions," *The Journal of Gift Planning* 7 (1, January 2003), pp. 11–15, 47–50. For a criticism of these large estimates, see Jagadeesh Gokhale and Laurence J. Kotlikoff, "The Baby Boomers' Mega-Inheritance—Myth or Reality," *Economic Commentary*, Federal Reserve Bank of Cleveland, October 1, 2000 (www.clev.frb.org/research/com2000/1001.htm).

26. Gokhale and Kotlikoff, "The Baby Boomers' Mega-Inheritance."

27. Suzanne Perry, "Baby Boomers Give More Than Older Americans," *Chronicle of Philanthropy*, September 1, 2005 (http://www.abagmd.org/info-url2446/info-url_show.htm?doc_id=294360).

28. "The Coming Flood: Philanthropy in the Decade," a GBN Report, GBN Global Business Network, May 2002.

29. Alan Johnson, "The Gray Vote," *Global Report on Aging*, AARP, Spring 2005 (http://www.aarp.org/research/international/gra/spring_2005/index.html).

30. John B. Horrigan, "How Americans Get in Touch with Government," Pew Internet & American Life Project, Washington, D.C., May 24, 2004, p. 9 (http://www.pewinternet.org).

31. For instance, in the United States, nearly 38 percent of the elderly respondents in a study conducted by the National Council on the Aging (NCOA) stated that being involved in the community contributes to a meaningful, vital life. See "American Perceptions of Aging in the 21st Century: The Myths and Realities of Aging," The National Council on the Aging, 2002.

32. (http://www.getinvolved.gov/newsroom/press/factsheet_boomers.asp).

33. (http://www.ncoa.org/content.cfm?sectionID=105&detail=499).

34. This is what Ronald Lee and Ryan Edwards call the Fiscal Support Ratio. Tax revenues

are not expected to decline in absolute terms but increase at a slower pace than expenditures. The result will also vary with the tax policy, which tends to change with expenditure needs. The impact of aging on revenue is expected to be felt more at the federal level than at the state and local level. But it will vary across states. States that are aging faster will feel the pinch more deeply.

35. Michael T. Childress, "9/11: The Uncertain Implications for State and Local Governments," *Foresight*, 9 (3, 2002).

36. For a study on Canada, see Wen-Fong Lu, Wei Li and Earl Bailey, "The Impact of Canadian Population Aging on Federal Personal Income Tax: Microsimulation Results from 2000 to 2026," Canada Customs and Revenue Agency, August 2003.

37. "Minnesota's State and Local Tax System," *Minnesota—Revenue*, January 2005, (http://www.taxes.state.mn.us/legal_policy/other_supporting_content/tax_system_overview.pdf).

38. Patrik Jonsson, "High Property Taxes Driving a New Revolt," *Christian Science Monitor*, March 8, 2006 (http://www.csmonitor.com/2006/0308/p01s02-usec.html).

39. William Saletan, "The New 65: Biology Can Solve the Social Security Debate," *Slate*, February 22, 2005 (http://www.slate.com/id/2113883).

40. For details, see Jeremy J. Siegel, *The Future for Investors: Why the Tried and True Triumphs over the Bold and New* (New York, Crown Business, 2005).

41. "When Boomers Cash Out," BusinessWeek Online, June 5, 2006, (http://www.businessweek.com/magazine/content/06_23/b3987073.htm).

42. Department for Work and Pensions, *Security in Retirement: Towards a New Pensions System*, May 2006 (www.dwp.gov.uk/welsh/pensionsreformA).

43. Saletan, "The New 65." Source is the Congressional Budget Office, "Budget Options," February 2005, Section 16 of 22. (http://www.cbo.gov/showdoc.cfm?index=6075&sequence=15)

44. Another obstacle is the cost of hiring older employees. Federal law establishes employer-sponsored health coverage as the primary payer for health care of employees aged 65 and older, and Medicare provides secondary care. This raises the cost of hiring older workers for employers. See Richard W. Johnson, Gordon Mermin and C. Eugene Steuerle, "Work Impediments at Older Ages," Discussion Paper 06-02, The Retirement Project, Urban Institute, May 2006.

45. There are a number of successful models of road pricing including that of California and London. For details on this, see William D. Eggers, Peter Samuel and Rune Monk, "Combating Gridlock: How Pricing Road Use Can Ease Congestion," Deloitte Research, November 4, 2003. For examples of the growth in park user fees, see Adam B. Summers, "Funding the National Park System: Improving Services and Accountability with User Fees," Policy Summary of Study 325, Reason Foundation (www.rppi.org/ps325.pdf). For wireless, see Robert L Bland, *A Revenue Guide for Local Government* 2d ed., (Washintgon D.C.: International City/County Management Association, 2005).

46. See data on County Governments—Service and Utility Charges as a Percentage of General Revenues in Bland, *A Revenue Guide for Local Government*.

47. Commission on Public Private Partnerships, *Building Better Partnerships: The Final Report of the Commission on Public Private Partnerships*, The Institute for Public Policy Research, London, 2001, p. 70.

48. See Stephen Goldsmith, *Putting Faith in Neighborhoods: Making Cities Work through Grassroots Citizenship*, (New York: Hudson Institute, 2002); and Lester M. Salamon, *Partners in Public Service: Government-Nonprofit Cooperation in the Modern Welfare State* (Baltimore: Johns Hopkins University Press, 1995).

49. Amy Joyce, "Snowbirds Take Their Jobs with Them," *Washington Post*, July 31, 2006 (http://www.post-gazette.com/pg/06212/709494-28.stm).

50. (http://www.aoa.gov/eldfam/Elder_Rights/Preventing_Fraud/Preventing_Fraud.asp).

51. *Trends in Health and Aging*, National Center for Health Statistics, Centers for Disease Control and Prevention, U.S. Department of Health and Human Services (http://209.217.72.34/aging/TableViewer/tableView.aspx).

52. Ibid.

53. In the past, mortality rates have declined much faster for the 70+ age group than was predicted on the basis of historical trends. See James W. Vaupel, "Demographic Analysis of Aging and Longevity," *American Economic Review* 88, (2, May 1998), pp. 242–47. Most of the rise in the old-age population will depend on the absolute decline in mortality rates, and these are declining faster for females who have a lower mortality rate than males.

54. *Trends in Health and Aging*, National Center for Health Statistics, Centers for Disease Control and Prevention, U.S. Department of Health and Human Services.

55. For an interesting discussion, see Carol Lewis, "Emerging Trends in Medical Device Technology: Home Is Where the Heart Monitor Is," *FDA Consumer*, May-June 2001 (http://www.fda.gov/fdac/301_toc.html).

56. "Shared Ambition: Peter Gilroy, Departing Kent Social Services to Take the Council's Helm, Tells Peter Hetherington About His Vision of a Brave New World for County Hall," *Guardian*, April 6, 2005.

57. Darran Simon, "A Generation of Caregivers: 20 Million U.S. Adults, Mostly Baby Boomers, Are Caring for Aging Parents," *Miami Herald*, May 21, 2006.

58. Richard J. Zaino, "Caregivers: Who Cares?" *Contexts: A Forum for Medical Humanities,* fall 2000, p. 8. In 1990 there were 11 potential caregivers for each person needing care. In 2050 that ratio will be 4:1.2, meaning four caregivers for every 1.2 people needing care.

59. Alice Dembner, "Program Pays Families to House Seniors," *Boston Globe*, July 8, 2005 (http://www.boston.com/news/local/massachusetts/articles/2005/07/08/program_pays_families_to_house_seniors?mode=PF).

60. AARP, "Looking Forward: Caring for South Dakota's Aging Population" (http://www.aarp.org/states/sd/sd-news/looking_forward_caring_for_south_dakotas_aging_pop.html).

61. "Nursing Homes in Need,"ArgusLeader.com, August 3, 2006 (http://www.argusleader.com/apps/pbcs.dll/article?AID=/20060803/OPINION01/608030351/1052&template).

62. See Colin Angel, "Safe as Houses: Long-term Care at Home," a talk given to the All Party Parliamentary Group for Patient Safety at Westminster, United Kingdom Homecare Association Ltd. (www.ukhca.co.uk).

63. AARP, *Enhancing Mobility Options for Older Americans*, January 2005, p. 7.

64. Linda Bailey, "Aging Americans: Stranded Without Options," Surface Transportation Policy Project, April 2004.

65. Free public transport is one of the great perks of being an older person in London. See Paul Maidment, "London: Free Ride," in "Graying Global Cities," *Forbes,* June 8, 2005 (http://www.forbes.com/2005/06/08/cx_pm_0608london.html).

66. See OECD, *Ageing and Transport: Mobility Needs and Safety Issues*, November 22, 2001. Data from the United Kingdom show that only 6 of every 1,000 male drivers in the 65–74 age group were involved in a crash in 1998 compared with 21 per 1,000 for drivers in the 25–34 age group. Data from the United States shows that number of road deaths among motorists aged 65 or more in 1997 was 12.7 per 100,000 people in this age group compared to 10.3 for 25–64 year-olds. See excerpt at (http://www.oecd.org/document/40/0,2340,en_2649_34351_2668191_1_1_1_1,00.html).

67. Robin Olson, "Senior Driver Issues: Upcoming Challenges and Solutions," International Risk Management Institute, 2004 (http://www.irmi.com/expert/Articles/2004/Olson10.pdf).

68. *Improving Transportation for a Maturing Society*, United States Department of Transportation, January, 1997.

69. Ford engineers have tried to address this issue by creating the Third Age Suit, which enables them to simulate mobility, strength and some of the vision limitations of seniors. See "Ford Research Benefits Senior Drivers," *Automotive Engineering International,* Tech Briefs, January 2001.

70. Interview with Nancy Naples, August 8, 2006.

71. *Project 2015: State Agencies Prepare for the Impact of An Aging New York,* New York Department of Motor Vehicles, 2006 <http://aging.state.ny.us/explore/project2015/report02/motor_vehicles.pdf).

72. Ibid.

73. Cabrini Pak and Ajit Kambil, "Wealth with Wisdom: Serving the Needs of Aging Customers," Deloitte Research, January 19, 2006.

74. Ibid.

75. See "The Utah Aging Initiative: Discovering and Identifying the Opportunities and Challenges of Our Aging Population," Utah Department of Human Services and Center for Public Policy and Administration, University of Utah, 2004-05.

76. John B Horrigan, "How Americans Get in Touch with Government."

77. Ibid. A recent study of FTSE 100 companies in the United Kingdom shows that by not making their Web sites accessible, British companies are forfeiting US$147 million a year in lost revenue. See "Improving IT Access for People with Disabilities Focus of 2006 International Day of the Disabled Persons," *Government Technology,* July 27, 2006 (http://www.govtech.net/magazine/channel_story.php/100331).

78. Hilary Browne, "Accessibility and Usability of Information Technology by the Elderly," *UUGuide,* University of Maryland, April 19, 2000 (http://www.otal.umd.edu/UUGuide/hbrowne/).

79. William D. Eggers, *Government 2.0: Using Technology to Improve Education, Cut Gridlock, Reduce Red Tape and Enhance Democracy* (Lanham, MD: Rowman and Littlefield, 2005), chapter 5.

80. *Project 2015.*

81. Interview with Nancy Naples, August 8, 2006.

82. Ibid.

83. Robert D. Atkinson, "Turbo-Charging E-Government," *Public CIO,* June 12, 2006 (http:www.public-cio.com/story.php?id=2006.06.12-99814).

Chapter Three: Bolstering Human Capital

1. "New York State Workforce Management Report, 2005," Department of Civil Services, New York State, 2005.

2. *Innovation and a Competitive U.S. Economy: The Case for Doubling the Number of STEM Graduates,* Information Technology Association of America, Arlington, Virginia, September 2005.

3. Jay Liebowitz, *Addressing the Human Capital Crisis in the Federal Government: A Knowledge Management Perspective* (New York: Butterworth-Heinemann, 2004).

4. Paul C. Light, *The New Public Service* (Washington: Brookings Institution Press, 1999), pp. 8–9.

5. "Federal Brain Drain," *Issue Brief,* Partnership for Public Service, November 21, 2005.

6. *Generation and Gender in the Workplace,* an Issue Brief by Families and Work Institute, The American Business Collaboration, 2002.

7. "The Future Workforce: Young People's Views on Career, Employers and Work," Institute for the Future, Palo Alto, California and Deloitte & Touche USA Youth Survey, January 2004.

8. Ibid.

9. Leigh Buchanan. "Forethought Demographics: The Young and the Restful," *Harvard*

Business Review, November 2004.

10. *Back to School: Rethinking Federal Recruiting on College Campuses*, Partnership for Public Service, May 2006, p.12.

11. Peter D. Hart Research Associates, Inc., "Survey of College Students," Panetta Institute for Public Policy, June 13, 2006, p.12.

12. Paul C Light, Testimony before the United States Senate Governmental Affairs Committee, June 4, 2003, p.6.

13. Rekha Sampath and Mark Robinson, "Talent Management in Upstream Oil & Gas: Strategies to Attract and Engage Generation Y," Deloitte Research, 2005.

14. *Government Executive,* September 1, 1996 (http://www.govexec.com/archdoc/0996/0996s4.htm).

15. U.S. Department of Labor (http://www.bls.gov/emp).

16. *Back to School,* Partnership for Public Service, p. 18.

17. Robin Athey, "It's 2008: Do You Know Where Your Talent Is?" Deloitte Research, 2005, p.1.

18. *Back to School*, Partnership for Public Service, p. 10.

19. Light, Testimony, p. 6.

20. *Asking the Wrong Questions: A Look at How the Federal Government Assesses and Selects Its Workforce*, Partnership for Public Service, October 2004, p.1.

21. Ibid, p. 4.

22. Ibid, p. 14.

23. Senate Hearing 106-547, *Managing Human Capital in the 21st Century*, United States Senate Committee on Governmental Affairs, March 9, 2000.

24. Joint Hearing 108-28, *The Human Capital Challenge: Offering Solutions and Delivering Results*, Senate Committee on Governmental Affairs and House Committee on Government Reform, April 8, 2003, pp. 53–57.

25. Five participants withdrew from the program.

26. In 2005, the Fast Stream Development Program attracted 12,957 applicants, up from 8,598 in 2004. Of these, 504 were recommended for appointment. A total of 94 percent of vacancies were filled, compared with 85 per cent in 2004. About half of these candidates came from the In-Service competition.

27. Katherine Barrett and Richard Greene, "When Boomers Retire," *Governing*, September 2006, p.76.

28. Ibid.

29. *Health Policy Research Bulletin*, Applied Research and Analysis Directorate, Health Canada (http://www.hc-sc.gc.ca/iacb-dgiac/arad-draa/english/rmdd/bulletin/ehuman.html).

30. *Innovation and a Competitive U.S. Economy,* Information Technology Association of America.

31. *Back to School,* Partnership for Public Service, p.18.

32. *Innovation and a Competitive U.S. Economy,* Information Technology Association of America.

33. Organizations should analyze these trends through a range of focused research activities, such as conducting one-, three- and five-year "look backs" at hires, terminations, transfers, and other aspects of internal transactions of various workforce segments. Organizations should also identify potential influences on the future supply of critical workforce talent, such as competition from nontraditional competitors. Last, organizations can employ "rapid response" techniques to address trends in the workforce that are not predictable but may have a significant impact.

34. William D. Eggers, "Show Me the Money: Budget-Cutting Strategies for Cash-Strapped States," American Legislative Exchange Council and The Manhattan Institute for Policy Research, 2002.

35. Ira Sager, "Big Blue Gets Wired" *BusinessWeek,* April 3, 2000. (http://www.business-week.com/2000/00_14/b3675050.htm).

36. Shawn Zeller, "Processing People" *Government Executive*, December 2004 (www.gov-exec.com/features/1204-01/1204-01s3.htm).

37. *FY 2003 Report to Congress on Implementation of the E-Government Act*, Office of Management and Budget, March 8, 2004, p. 44.

38. Ibid. pp.63–64.

39. Alfred Tat-Kei Ho, "Reinventing Local Governments and the E-Government Initiative" *Public Administration Review* (July/August 2002) p. 435.

Chapter Four: Solving the Pension Crisis

1. Tony Perry and Richard Marosi, "Under Fire, San Diego Mayor Quits," *Los Angeles Times,* April 26, 2005, p. A1.

2. Yamil Berard, "Underfunded Pensions May Put Cities in a Bind," *Fort Worth Star-Telegram,* February 13, 2005.

3. Dunstan McNichol, "N.J. Taxpayers Face a Pension Bill of $383 Million," *New Jersey Star-Ledger,* July 23, 2005.

4. Nanette Byrnes and Christopher Palmeri, "Sinkhole!" *Business Week,* June 13, 2005 (http://www.businessweek.com/magazine/content/ 05_24/b3937081 .htm).

5. Ibid.

6. Julia K. Bonafede, Stephen J. Foresti and John Dashtara, "2006 Wilshire Report on State Retirement Systems: Funding Levels and Asset Allocation," Santa Monica, CA, March 12, 2006.

7. George Passantino, "The Gathering Pension Storm: How Government Pension Plans Are Breaking the Bank and Strategies for Reform," Reason Foundation, June 2005 (www.reason.org).

8. Byrnes and Palmeri, "Sinkhole!"

9. "Before Congressional Panel, Witnesses Underscore Troubling Trend of Underfunded State and Local Pension Plans," *US Fed News,* August 30, 2006.

10. The cost estimated by Stephen T. McElhaney is quoted in Milt Freudenheim and Mary Williams Walsh, "The Next Retirement Time Bomb," *New York Times,* December 11, 2005.

11. Greg Toppo, "School Systems Face Health Care Squeeze," *USA Today,* February 6, 2006 (http://www.usatoday.com/news/health/2006-02-06-schools-health_x.htm).

12. Toppo, "School Systems Face Health Care Squeeze."

13. "State Faces $70B Health Care Liability," California Healthline, February 21, 2006.

14. Greg Wiles, "Retirees' Benefits Costs Mount," *Honolulu Advertiser,* March 19, 2006 (http://the.honoluluadvertiser.com/article/2006/ Mar/1 9/ln/FP603 1 90372.html).

15. "Retiree Health Benefits Contribute to Public Agencies' Projected Unfunded Liabilities," California Healthline, September 20, 2005 (http:// www.californiahealthline.org/index.cfm ?Action=dspItem&itemID=11 4807&classcd=CL3 50).

16. Dennis Cauchon, "Huge Bill for Public Retirees Hits Soon," *USA Today,* May 18, 2006.

17. Wiles, "Retirees' Benefits Costs Mount."

18. Jack Hoadley, "How States Are Responding to the Challenge of Financing Health Care for Retirees," Health Policy Institute, Georgetown University, September 2003, p. 33.

19. Cauchon, "Huge Bill for Public Retirees Hits Soon."

20. Wiles, "Retirees' Benefits Costs Mount."

21. Freudenheim and Walsh, "The Next Retirement Time Bomb."

22. Berard, "Underfunded Pensions May Put Cities in a Bind."

23. Ibid.

24. John Hill and Dorothy Korber, "Pension Jackpot: Many More Winning Safety-Worker Label," *Sacramento Bee*, May 9, 2004 (http://www.caltax.org/Hill-PensionJackpot5-9-04.pdf).

25. Passantino, "Gathering Pension Storm."

26. McNichol, "N.J. Taxpayers Face a Pension Bill of $383 Million."

27. Passantino, "Gathering Pension Storm."

28. This can occur directly by salary increase or more subtly by changes in job descriptions or special entitlements.

29. Nanette Byrnes, "How the Garden State Dug a Hole," *BusinessWeek*, June 13, 2005 (http://www.businessweek.com/magazine/content/05_24b3937088.htm?campaign_id=search).

30. Possible new benefit formulas include a reduced benefit accrual rate (such as 1.5 percent vs. 2 percent of pay); a flat benefit rate (such as $25 times years of service); and a career average formula (such as 2 percent of annual compensation for each year of service).

31. Kathleen Hunter, "Pensions Pose Time Bombs for Budgets," Stateline.org, September 23, 2005 (http://www.stateline.org/live/ ViewPage.action?siteNodeId=1 36&languageId=1 &contentId=55769).

32. Byrnes and Palmeri, "Sinkhole!"

33. Employee Benefits Research Institute, "Compensation Costs in the Private and State/Local Public Sectors," March 2005 (http://www.ebri.org/pdf/publications/facts/0305fact.pdf); Byrnes and Palmeri, "Sinkhole!"

Chapter Five: Fixing Medicaid

1. "Private Account Precedent," *Wall Street Journal*, August 30, 2005.

2. National Governor's Association (NGA) Center for Best Practices, "Managing Health Care Costs: Lessons from the Private Sector," October 2002.

3. Governor Dirk Kempthorne, Idaho State of the State Address, January 9, 2006 (http://www.stateline.org/live/ViewPage.action?siteNodeId=157&languageId=1&contentId=79991).

4. "Public Hospitals to Be Hit Hardest When TennCare Cuts Rolls," Associated Press, May 31, 2005.

5. Anna Sommers and Mindy Cohen, "Medicaid's High Cost Enrollees: How Much Do They Drive Program Spending?" Kaiser Commission on Medicaid and the Uninsured, March 2006.

6. State of Vermont, Summary Overview, Global Commitment to Health Medicaid 1115 Demonstration Waiver, November 3, 2005 (http://www.ahs.state.vt.us/OVHA/docs/Global-CommitOverviewNov2005.pdf).

7. "Public Hospitals to Be Hit Hardest When TennCare Cuts Rolls," Associated Press.

8. NGA Center for Best Practices, "Managing Health Care Costs," p.1. The extreme complexity of the system explains in large part the reactive manner in which most Medicaid programs are managed. Various care-delivery options, competing interest groups, beneficiaries with varying needs, and the program's own subeconomy contribute to that complexity, and program administrators are on their own to address the most urgent issues, primarily through a myriad of individual initiatives.

9. This array of beneficiaries and providers, not surprisingly, has spawned an equal number of advocacy groups. Any particular initiative or change that will improve one aspect of the program will affect another and irk at least one stakeholder group in the process. As a result, initiatives get stonewalled with regularity by stakeholders who feel threatened. The political power of particular stakeholder groups to stop state initiatives is exacerbated by most programs' relative lack of trustworthy information about the program and its performance.

Business case analyses that might serve to solidify and defend a particular proposal or program change are often impossible to create because of a lack of good data about the program.

10. Consider the Texas Medicaid program over the last year and a half. The legislature commissioned a study of the most effective method for expanding the managed care component of the state's Medicaid program. The state conducted the study, presented its most efficient model from both a cost and a quality of care perspective and made the decision to move toward that model. The state even went so far as to make arrangements with the dozens of health maintenance organizations that would deliver the care. At the eleventh hour, however, the legislature was lobbied aggressively by hospital and related provider groups who effectively killed the original plan.

11. The good news about these increasing expectations is that in addition to creating more satisfied customers, implementing such improvements also tends to reap large efficiencies in operations, reduce administrative costs and significantly reduce errors. The bad news is that such enhancements also require a higher level of staff and program performance, which in turn requires new business processes and technologies to support them.

12. "Empowered Care: A Proposed Concept for Florida Medicaid," Agency for Health Care Administration, State of Florida, March 14, 2005.

13. "The Healthy Economist," *University of Memphis Magazine*, Summer 2004.

14. "State Proceeds with TennCare Overhaul," *US Fed News*, January 10, 2005.

15. Pew Center on the States, *Special Report on Medicaid*, 2006.

16. Texas, for example, has frequently battled with its MMIS and claims administrator over alleged mismanagement, with at least one case ending up in the legal system. Similarly, Maine has had significant struggles with its MMIS systems vendor about delivering an on-time, functional system according to the terms of the state's contract.

17. "Georgia Department of Community Health 2002 Annual Report," Georgia Department of Community Health, State of Georgia.

18. "Governor Pawlenty Introduces Health Care Initiative to Improve Quality and Save Costs," Office of Governor Tim Pawlenty, State of Minnesota, July 31, 2006.

19. Pennsylvania Health Care Cost Containment Council, "Hospital-Acquired Infections in Pennsylvania," 5 PHC4 Research Briefs, 2005.

20. National Committee for Quality Assurance, *The State of Health Care Quality 2005: Industry Trends and Analysis* (Washington, D.C., 2005).

21. Centers for Medicare and Medicaid Services, *Premier Hospital Quality Incentive Demonstration* (http://www.cms.hhs.gov/HospitalQualityInits/35_HospitalPremier.asp).

22. Some states have had significant difficulties resulting from large technology projects to replace information systems—Maine's replacement efforts, for example, have lasted for more than four years, devouring critical state resources. To address these deficiencies, the federal Centers for Medicare and Medicaid Services is garnering support for the creation of a Medicaid Information Technology Architecture (MITA). MITA will combine effective business and technology strategies to provide common standards for a Web-based, patient-centric system for integrated public health data that is interoperable within and across states as well as within Medicaid and across other health care agencies. The information sharing enabled by MITA will enhance decision-making capabilities, reduce medical errors and paper costs and improve quality of care. MITA efforts also center on designing the information architecture and the business processes that allow states to be more integrated across functional domains and organizations. To spur this integration, MITA has offered 90–10 cost sharing between the federal government and state governments in funding MMIS solutions if the state adopts the common standards.

Chapter Six: Integrating Health and Human Services

1. Emily Gurnon, "A New Lease on Life: Hundreds of Evacuees-Turned-Adoptees Visit a Makeshift Aid Center Hoping to Start Anew," *St. Paul Pioneer Press*, September 16, 2005.

2. Salvation Army, "Salvation Army Uses Katrina Donations to Help Survivors in Twin Cities: State Aid Center Opens its Doors to Survivors Waiting for Assistance," September 16, 2005.

3. "Health and Human Services and Technology—Trends and Issues," presentation by Liz Wallendorf, Center for Digital Government, June 15, 2006.

4. Stephen Heffler, and others. "U.S. Health Spending Projections for 2004–2014," *Health Affairs Web Exclusive*, February 23, 2005.

5. INPUT, *INPUT Predicts $1.3 Billion in State Integrated Eligibility Spending by FY09*, August 23, 2006 (http://www.input.com/corp/press/detail.cfm?news=1277).

6. Pennsylvania Department of Health, "Governor Rendell Says PA's First-Ever Health & Human Services Guide Available to Public," April 19, 2006 (http://www.dsf.health.state.pa.us/health/cwp/view.asp?Q=244289&A=190).

7. Christy G. Black, "A New Frontier for Health and Human Services," Testimony prepared for the Texas House Committee on Government Reform, July 26, 2006 (http://www.ncpa.org/pub/speech/2006/20060727-sp.html).

8. The Commonwealth of Massachusetts Executive Department, "Romney Introduces State-of-the-Art Virtual Gateway: One-stop Portal Is Major New Feature of Last Year's HHS Reorganization," September 16, 2004. (http://www.mass.gov/?pageID=pressreleases&agID=Agov2&prModName=gov2pressrelease&prFile=gov_pr_040915_eohhs_gateway.xml).

9. "Technology Improves Access to Food Stamps," *States News Service*, March 23, 2006.

10. Gregory W. Sullivan, "The Virtual Gateway: MassHealth and Uncompensated Care Pool Web-based Data Intake and Eligibility Determination System: Review and Evaluation," Office of the Inspector General, Commonwealth of Massachusetts, March 2006.

11. "How Is the Virtual Gateway Working for Community-Based Enrollment? A Survey of Community-Oriented Organizations in Massachusetts that Help Residents Access Health Care Coverage," Community Partners, December 2005.

12. Mark Ragan, "Building Better Human Services Systems: Integrating Services for Income Support and Related Programs," Nelson A. Rockefeller Institute of Government, June 2003.

13. Statement of Don Winstead, deputy secretary, Florida Department of Children and Families, testimony before the Subcommittee on Human Resources of the House Committee on Ways and Means, April 5, 2006.

14. Statement of Don Winstead, April 5, 2006.

15. California Performance Review, "CPR Report, Issues and Recommendations: Transform Eligibility Processing," vol. 4, chapter 2, August 3, 2004 (http://cpr.ca.gov/report/cprrpt/issrec/hhs/hhs01.htm).

16. Texas Health and Human Services Commission, "Integrated Eligibility Determination, Phase II: Business Case Analysis," March 2004 (http://hhs.state.tx.us/consolidation/IE/BC_FinalReport.pdf).

17. Jerd Smith, "Improper Welfare Payments Add Up: State Audit Finds $90 Million Not Handled Correctly," *The Rocky Mountain News*, July 3, 2006.

18. William D. Eggers, *Government 2.0: Using Technology to Improve Education, Cut Red Tape, Reduce Gridlock, and Enhance Democracy* (Lanham, MD: Rowman and Littlefield, 2005), p. 18.

19. Justine Brown, "COMPASS Finds the Way," *Government Technology*, May 22, 2003.

20. Gray Davis, governor of California, Grantland Johnson, secretary of the California Health and Human Services Agency and Stephen W. Mayberg, Ph.D., director of the California

Department of Mental Health, "Effectiveness of Integrated Services for Homeless Adults with Serious Mental Illness," Report to the California Legislature as required by Assembly Bill (AB) 2034 Steinberg, Chapter 518, Statutes of 2000.

21. Dibya Sarkar, "Utah Takes and Integrated Approach to Human Services: Software Helps State Agencies Share Information and Provide Benefits," *Federal Computer Week*, April 17, 2006 (http://www.fcw.com/article94050-04-17-06-Print).

22. Statement of Don Winstead.

23. Ibid.

Chapter Seven: Upgrading Emergecy Preparedness and Response

1. Dan Balz, "A Defining Moment for State Leaders," *Washington Post,* September 1, 2005, p. A13.

2. Totals derived from figures in "Hurricanes," National Oceanic and Atmospheric Administration (NOAA) (http://hurricanes.noaa.gov).

3. "Storm Prediction Center," NOAA's National Weather Service (http://www.spc.noaa.gov/climo/torn/monthlytornstats.html).

4. "Wildland Fire Update," *National Fire News,* National Fire Information Center (http://www.nifc.gov/fireinfo/nfn.html).

5. "The Mississippi River Flood of 1993," Storm Encyclopedia, Weather.com (http://www.weather.com/encyclopedia/flood/miss93.html).

6. "Northridge Earthquake," from Web site of DIS, Inc. (http://www.dis-inc.com/northrid.htm).

7. Testimony by Governor Bob Taft of Ohio to the U.S. House of Representatives Committee on Energy and Commerce, September 3, 2003, (http://energycommerce.house.gov/108/Hearings/09032003hearing1061/Taft1669.htm).

8. Interview with Kate Hale, former director of emergency management for Miami-Dade County, February 23, 2006.

9. Dara Kam and Alan Gomez, "Lack of Plan Hurt Katrina-Hit States' Response," *Palm Beach Post,* September 10, 2005, (http://www.palmbeachpost.com/storm/content/state/epaper/2005/09/10/m1a_response_0910.html).

10. Jeb Bush, "Think Locally on Relief," *Washington Post,* Sept. 30, 2005, p. A19.

11. Dan Hopkins, Ph.D. Candidate, Department of Government, Harvard University, interview with Amy Petz, April 11, 2006.

12. Al Martinez-Fonts, testimony before the House Committee on the Judiciary Subcommittee on Immigration, Border Security and Claims. March 18, 2004.

13. Testimony of Craig Nemitz, Disaster Services Manager, America's Second Harvest, before the Senate Committee on Health, Education, Labor and Pensions, March 7, 2006.

14. Nemitz testimony, 2006.

15. M. Mitchell Waldrop, "Can Sense-Making Keep Us Safe?" *Technology Review,* March 2003, p. 45.

16. Peter Bailey, "Katrina's Aftermath: Willing Benefactors Hit Brick Wall of Bureaucracy," *Miami Herald.* September 6, 2005.

17. Zack Phillips, "DHS Launches Web Site for Katrina Response," *CQ Homeland Security,* September 7, 2005.

18. Sydney Freedberg, "Disaster, Inc," *National Journal,* December 17, 2005.

19. White House Report, *The Federal Response to Hurricane Katrina: Lessons Learned.* February 2006 (www.whitehouse.gov/reports/Katrina_lessons_learned).

20. Rear Admiral Thad Allen defined the Coast Guard's approach by identifying three critical elements to operations in the Gulf Region: use of resources, use of communications, and

use of command and control. He also stressed the importance of planning. Because the Coast Guard prepositioned resources and personnel, it could conduct a flexible and immediate search and rescue. These elements, combined with its adaptability, enabled the Coast Guard to produce a powerful result. See Thad Allen, "Katrina: It Reshaped the Gulf Coast—How Will It Reshape Washington, D.C.," remarks at The George Washington University, December 2, 2005.

21. Interview with Captain Frank Paskewich, Commanding Officer of Sector New Orleans, U.S. Coast Guard, April 17, 2006.

22. Brian Jackson. "Information Sharing and Emergency Responder Safety Management." Testimony before the House Committee on Government Reform. March 30, 2006

23. William D. Eggers, "Prospering in a Secure Economy, Deloitte Research, September 2004.

24. Ibid.

25. Marianne Kolbasuk McGee, "The Bioterrorism Threat Is Forcing Health Care to Lose Its Aversion to IT," *Information Week,* November 19, 2001, p. 52, quoted in Goldsmith and Eggers, 2004.

26. "State Strategies for Using IT for an All-Hazards Approach to Homeland Security," an Issue Brief from the National Governors Association Center for Best Practices, July 13, 2006.

27. "TSA: We Will Never Assume We've Got the Job Done," Deloitte Consulting, New York, 2002, p. 23.

28. Eggers, "Prospering in a Secure Economy."

29. "HHS Announces New HIPAA Privacy Decision Tool for Emergency Preparedness Planning," press release, U.S. Department of Health and Human Services, July 6, 2006.

30. Ann Zimmerman and Valerie Bauerlein, "At Wal-Mart, Emergency Plan Has Big Payoff," *The Wall Street Journal,* Sept. 12, 2005, B1.

31. Devin Leonard, "The Only Lifeline Was the Wal-Mart," *Fortune,* October 3, 2005, p. 74.

32. Freedberg "Disaster Inc."

33. Zimmerman and Bauerline, "At Wal-Mart, Emergency Plan Has Big Payoff."

34. Freedberg, "Disaster Inc."

35. Zimmerman and Bauerlein, "At Wal-Mart, Emergency Plan Has Big Payoff."

36. Freedberg, "Disaster Inc."

37. Justin Fox, "A Meditation on Risk," *Fortune,* October 3, 2005.

38. Freedberg, "Disaster Inc."

39. Glenn R. Simpson, "Just in Time: In Year of Disaster, Experts Bring Order to Chaos of Relief," *The Wall Street Journal,* November 22, 2005, p. A1.

40. Simpson, "Just in Time."

41. Interview with Lesli Remaly, a disaster response and recover liaison, Church World Service, March 30, 2006.

42. "Ten Myths of Disaster Relief," Partnership for Disaster Response, Business Roundtable (http://www.businessroundtable.org/pdf/20060327002Top10Myths.pdf).

43. Merrill Douglas, "Coordinated Aid," *Government Technology,* February 2006, pp. 44–45.

44. For a comprehensive discussion of the risk assessment/management process, see Ortwin Renn, *Risk Governance, Towards an Integrated Approach* (Geneva: The International Risk Governance Council, 2005).

45. Ibid, p. 42.

46. "Overview of States Homeland Security Governance," NGA Center for Best Practices, July, 2005.

47. "Safe Schools Program," Oklahoma Department of Emergency Management, Programs and Services (http://www.ok.gov/OEM/Programs_&_Services/Preparedness/Safe_Schools_Program/).

48. "OK-WARN for the Deaf and Hard-of-Hearing," Oklahoma Department of Emergency Management, Programs and Services (http://www.ok.gov/OEM/Programs_&_Services/Preparedness/OK-Warn_for_the_Deaf_and_Hard-of-Hearing/).

49. "McReady Oklahoma - Governor Helps Launch Tornado Preparedness Campaign," Oklahoma Department of Emergency Management, Programs and Services (http://www.ok.gov/OEM/News/2004_News/McReady_Oklahoma_-_Governor_Helps_Launch_Tornado_Preparedness_Campaign.html).

50. "State Launches Unprecedented, Multi-Million Dollar Public Education Campaign to Promote Hurricane Preparedness," Florida Division of Emergency Management (http://www.floridadisaster.org/GetAPlan.htm).

51. Elizabeth McNie, "What Kind of Leadership Does FEMA Need?" posting on Prometheus: The Science Policy Weblog, September 9, 2005 (http://sciencepolicy.colorado.edu/prometheus/archives/disasters/000564what_kind_of_leaders.html).

52. A. J. Schuler, "Change Management – Lessons of Rudy Giuliani, Post 9/11" (http://www.schulersolutions.com/html/change_leadership_lessons_of_r.html).

53. Pete Wilson, "The California Way," *The Wall Street Journal*, September 13, 2005.

Chapter Eight: Driving More Money into the Classroom

1. "2004 State Expenditure Report," National Association of State Budget Officers, January 2006.

2. Maureen Magee, "Some Consider It Passing the Buck," *San Diego Union Tribune*, January 8, 2004 (http://www.signonsandiego.com/news/metro/200401089999_1m8cuts.html).

3. California Legislative Analyst's Office, *Analyses of the 2005–2006 Budget Bill*, February 24, 2005 (http://www.lao.ca.gov/analysis.aspx?year=2005&chap=5&toc=1).

4. In 2004 in Kentucky, Governor Ernie Fletcher reduced education program funds by $6.9 million. Mark Pitsch, "Fletcher Defends Higher-Ed Cuts," *Louisville Courier-Journal*, January 13, 2004, p. 1A.

5. Ralph N. Paulk, "Manchester District Grappling with Budget Cuts," *Akron Beacon Journal*, May 26, 2005.

6. Elizabeth Hume, "School-Bus Budgets Are Braking," *Sacramento Bee*, May 19, 2005 (http://www.sactaqc.org/Resources/Literature/Funding/School_Bus_budgets.htm).

7. In seven cases the court ruled in favor of the state; four were settled out of court; six are still pending; and one case was withdrawn prior to being heard. See Michael Griffith and Molly Burke, "School Funding Adequacy Cases," Education Commission of the States, February 2005 (http://www.ecs.org/ecsmain.asp?page=/html/issue.asp?issueID=48).

8. A number of court case examples can be found on the ACCESS Website, a national initiative of the Campaign for Fiscal Equity, Inc. (http://www.schoolfunding.info/index.php3).

9. Bob Brewin, "Gov. Warner: IT Needed to Cut Medicaid Costs," *Government HealthIT*, Sept. 9, 2005 (http://www.govhealthit.com/article90703-09-09-05Web&newsletter%3Dyes).

10. In Texas, for example, teachers make up only 51 percent of all Texas school district staff.

11. Karen Hawley Miles and Linda Darling-Hammond, "Rethinking the Allocation of Teaching Resources: Some Lessons from High Performing Schools," (Philadelphia: Consortium for Policy Research in Education, 1997) p. 2.

12. "2004–2005 Budgeted Financial Data," Texas Education Agency, May 2005, budget report generated at (http://www.tea.state.tx.us/cgi/sas/broker).

13. Deloitte Consulting LLP analysis of Illinois State Board of Education, Fiscal Year 2002, Audited District Financial Statements.

14. Laura Kellams, "Wait on Consolidation," *Arkansas Democrat-Gazette*, July 12, 2005.

15. Nancy Isles Nation, "School Districts Consider Mergers," *Marin Independent Journal*

(California), March 2, 2003.

16. Elvia Diaz, "School District Consolidation Lacks Support," *Arizona Republic,* January 10, 2003, p. 9B.

17. "Portland Voters Endorse Course of City, Schools," *Portland Press Herald* (Maine), November 6, 2003, p. 12A.

18. Lee Burnett, "A New Wave of School Consolidation in Maine," *Maine Townsman,* April 2003.

19. Reason Foundation, "Spring 2004 School District Analyses." These data were compiled from the Ed-Data database at (http://www.cde.ca.gov/index.asp).

20. Vicki Murray and Ross Groen, "Competition or Consolidation? The School District Consolidation Debate Revisited," Policy Report 189, The Goldwater Institute, January 12, 2004.

21. David Boaz and R. Morris Barret, "What Would a School Voucher Buy? The Real Cost of Private Schools," Briefing Paper 25, Cato Institute, March 26, 1996, p.4.

22. "Can Small Schools Make a Big difference?" CNN, October 13, 2004 (http://www.cnn.com/2004/EDUCATION/10/13/small.schools.ap/).

23. American Legislative Exchange Council, "Report Card on American Education," 2002.

24. Caroline Hoxby, "Does Competition among Public Schools Benefit Students and Taxpayers?" *American Economic Review* 90 (5, December 2000), p. 1232.

25. Deloitte Consulting LLP analysis.

26. Secretary of State Audit Report, "Oregon Department of Education: Kindergarten through 12th Grade Cost Survey," Eugene, Oregon, December 13, 2002 (http://www.sos.state.or.us/audits/audreports/fullreports/200245.pdf).

27. Phillip A. Trostel, "Potential Efficiency Gains from Consolidation of Educational Resources in PV PILOT Communities," Margaret Chase Smith Center for Public Policy, University of Maine, October 6, 2002, p. 6.

28. Mark Imernan and Dan Otto, "A Preliminary Investigation of School District Expenditures with Respect to School District Size in Iowa," Department of Economics, Iowa State University, January 24, 2003 (http://www.econ.iastate.edu/research/webpapers/paper_10183.pdf).

29. Mathew Andrews, William Duncombe and John Yinger, "Revisiting Economies of Size in American Education," *Economics of Education Review 21*(3, March 2002) pp. 245–62 (http://www-cpr.maxwell.syr.edu/efap/publications/revisiting%20economics.pdf).

30. This analysis is not intended to provide a comprehensive look at school spending and school district size in California. It simply provides a snapshot of the 10 smallest, the 10 largest, and 10 school districts with approximately 6,000 students to look at their average "other services" spending.

31. United States Postal Service, Shared Services and Outsourcing network (http://www.iqpc.com/cgi-bin/templates/document.html?topic=240&document=41931).

32. Harriet Derman and Beth Gates, "Local Government Shared Services and Municipal Consolidation: A Report and an Agenda," New Jersey Department of Community Affairs, August 1995 (http://www.state.nj.us/dca/lgshar1.htm#toc); Timothy Davis, "Shared Services And The Economies Of Scale They Provide Local Governments," *Economic Development Handbook,* Taubman College of Architecture and Urban Planning, University of Michigan (http://www.umich.edu/~econdev/jointservice/).

33. Dan Elsass, "Merger of City-Village Services: Best Practices," University of Wisconsin-Extension Local Government Center (http://www.uwex.edu/lgc/intergov/pdf/bestpracticesbook.pdf).

34. Ibid.

35. "Agreement Provides for Shared Superintendent," *Milwaukee Journal Sentinel,* May 11, 2001, p. 2B.

36. Davis, "Shared Services And The Economies Of Scale They Provide."

37. Stephen J. Adams, "To Collaborate Is to Better Educate," *Boston Herald,* June 9, 2003.

38. Ibid.

39. Middlesex County, New Jersey Improvement Authority, Shared Services (http://www.mciauth.com/shared_services.htm).

40. Sarah Hanuske, "Shared Services for Rural and Small Schools," ERIC Clearinghouse on Rural Education and Small Schools (http://www.ericdigests.org/pre-922/shared.htm).

41. Shared Services and Outsourcing Network, The Human Resources Division for the Commonwealth of Massachusetts (http://www.iqpc.com/cgi-bin/templatesdocument.html?topic=240&document=54961&slauID=58&).

42. Patty Allen-Jones, "County, Schools Agree on Shared-Services Deal," *Sarasota Herald Tribune* (New York), December 2004 (http://www.findarticles.com/p/articles/mi_go1636/is_200412/ai_n9626932).

43. Hackett Group (https://portal.thehackettgroup.com/portal/index.jsp).

44. Ibid.

45. "Share Where?" *CFO Magazine,* September 2000, May 2005 (http://www.cfo.com/article.cfm,/2988006/1/c_3046527?f=magazine_featured).

46. Elsass, "Merger of City-Village Services," pp.10–11.

47. Zenaida Mendez, "Shared Services in Parsippany Trim School Costs," *Daily Record* (Morris County, New Jersey), December 20, 2003.

48. Davis, "Shared Services And The Economies Of Scale They Provide."

49. Personnel economies of scale lead to significant cost savings in most shared services arrangements. See Elsass, "Merger of City-Village Services," pp.10–11.

50. New Jersey School Board Administration (http:/www.njsba.org/press_releases/shared_services2.htm).

51. Ibid.

52. Mike Perrault, "Districts Form Purchasing Group," *Desert Sun,* July 9, 2003.

53. Region 5 Education Service Center, Safe and Drug Free Communities Shared Services Arrangement (SSA) (http://www.esc5.net/instructionalserv/is28.html).

54. "Illinois State Board of Education (ISBE) Budget Observations," Deloitte Consulting LLP presentation to Illinois State Board of Education Superintendent Schiller, August 2003.

55. Walter Yost, "Schools Cut Costs by Sharing," *Sacramento Bee,* November 3, 2003.

56. Elsass, "Merger of City-Village Services," provides a number of case studies of shared services by local governments that have reduced year-to-year variation in costs.

57. Lisa Ray and David N. Plank, "Consolidation of Michigan's Schools: Results from the 2002 State of the State Survey," Policy Report 14, Education Policy Center, Michigan State University, February 2003, p. 4.

58. "Annual Budget 2004-2005, Organizational Section," Independent School District of Boise City, Idaho, May 2005 (http://www.boiseschools.org/business/accounting/budget/budget_organiz.pdf).

59. Terrence Stutz, "School Reform in State's Hands: Education Chief Setting Rules for Local Districts on Spending, Test Scores," *Dallas Morning News,* July 10, 2006.

60 Jason Embry, "65% Order Fits First Class Education's Agenda," *Austin-American Statesman* (Texas), August 30, 2005.

61. Elsass, "Merger of City-Village Services," p. 4.

62. "Statewide Shared Services Program (SSSP)," Institute For Local Governance and Regional Growth, State University of New York (http://regional-institute.buffalo.edu/prog/sssp.html).

63. "BOCES and Your Local School," *Ithaca Journal* (New York), May 14, 2003.

64. "Schools Practice What They Teach: It's Good to Share," New Jersey School Boards Association, August 1, 2002 (http://www.njsba.org/press_releases/shared_services2.htm).

65. Ibid.

66. "University of California Systemwide Strategic Directions for Libraries and Scholarly Information, Perspectives on State Financing Issues," May 24, 2004 (http://libraries.universityofcalifornia.edu/planning/library_strategy_state_finance_issues.pdf).

67. A group of New Jersey local government officials, most of whom have experience with shared services, identified financial assistance and various forms of information and technical assistance as the most useful ways states can help local government bodies utilize shared services. Derman and Gates, "Local Government Shared Services and Municipal Consolidation."

68. "OPM Announces Human Resources Line of Business Shared Service Center Selection Process," Press Release, U.S. Office of Personnel Management, January 31, 2005 (http://www.opm.gov/viewDocument.aspx?q=801).

Chapter Nine: Closing the Infrastructure Gap

1. *California Transportation Commission Annual Report 1999*, California Transportation Commission, Sacramento, CA, 1999.

2. Texas Transportation Institute, *Texas Transportation Institute Mobility Report 2005* (tti.tamu.edu/documents/mobility_report_2005.pdf).

3. Interview with Andrew Fremier, deputy executive director, Bay Area Toll Authority, April 13, 2006.

4. TRIP (a national transportation research group), "Rough Ride Ahead: Metro Areas with the Roughest Rides and Strategies to Make Our Roads Smoother," May, 2005 (www.tripnet.org/national.htm).

5. American Society of Civil Engineers, "Massachusetts and Rhode Island State Infrastructure Report Cards," 2005 (http://www.asce.org/reportcard/2005/states.cfm).

6. American Society of Civil Engineers, "2005 Report Card for America's Infrastructure" (http://www.asce.org/reportcard/2005/index.cfm).

7. William W. Millar, "Statement on Texas Transportation Institute's (TTI) Annual Congestion Report," *Transit News*, American Public Transportation Association, May 9, 2005 (http://www.apta.com/media/releases/050509urban_mobility.cfm).

8. Kent Kirk, "Clean Water Threatened—As Federal Dollars Decline the Cost of Clean Rises," *Urban Water Council: Newsletter of the Urban Water Council of The United States Council of Mayors*, spring 2006 (http://www.usmayors.org/urbanwater/newsletters/spring06.pdf).

9. American Society of Civil Engineers, "States Report 2005" (http://www.asce.org/reportcard/2005/states.cfm).

10. Pete Millard, "The $64 Billion Question: Wisconsin's Looming Infrastructure Costs," *Wisconsin Interest* 13(2), spring 2004 (http://www.wpri.org/WIInterest/Vol13no2/Mil13.2.pdf).

11. Simon Ferrie, "New Head of USDOT Recommends Tolling," *America's News*, October 23, 2006, p. 3.

12. From an average of 2.8 percent between 1958 and 1969, to 1.4 percent between 1970 and 1986. See Robert Rider, "Maintaining Wisconsin's Competitiveness—Corridors 2020," Central Wisconsin Economic Research Bureau, 1ˢᵗ Quarter 1991 (http://www.uwsp.edu/business/CWERB/1stQtr91/SpecialReportQtr1_91.htm).

13. Scott M. Kozel, "Roads to the Future" (http://www.roadstothefuture.com/Road_Funding_US.html).

14. CA Legislative Analyst 2004, California Transportation Commission testimony 2005, Sacramento, CA, 2004.

15. The sources: $93.2 million from the California Transportation Commission; $76.3 million from the Alameda County Transportation Improvement Authority; $31.5 million from the Metropolitan Transportation Commission; $25 million from the Port of Oakland; and $30

million from SB 916 3rd Dollar Bridge Toll.

16. Governor Mitch Daniels, "Transforming Government Through Privatization," *Annual Privatization Report 2006,* Reason Foundation, April 2006.

17. "Design-Build Effectiveness Study," Federal Highway Administration, U.S. Department of Transportation, January 2006 (http://www.fhwa.dot.gov/reports/designbuild/designbuild.htm).

18. Grahame Allen, "The Private Finance Initiative (PFI)," Research Paper 01/117, House of Commons Library, December 18, 2001 (http://www.oldham.gov.uk/pfi_initiative.pdf).

19. Graham Beazley-Long and On-Yee Tai, "The United Kingdom Public-Private Partnerships Forum (established 2001)," presentation at *Transport Forum 2006: Infrastructure Governance Roundtable* held at World Bank, March 24, 2006. (http://www.worldbank.org/transport/learning/tf2006/Infrastructure%20Governance%20Roundtable/presentations/UK%20-%20PPP%20Beazley%20Long%20-%20On-YeeTai%20PRESENTATION.ppt#1).

20. Government Accountability Office, "Highway Finance: States' Expanding Use of Tolling Illustrates Diverse Challenges and Strategies," GAO-06-554, June 2006, pp.20-25.

21. Allison Padova, "Federal Commercialization in Canada," Parliamentary Research and Research Services, Library of Parliament, December 20, 2005 (http://www.parl.gc.ca/information/library/PRBpubs/prb0545-e.html).

22. "PFI: Construction Performance," National Audit Office, 2003. Note: Previous experience based on 1999 government survey. PFI experience is based on NAO survey of 37 projects.

23. Some of the risks that are transferred: meeting required standards of delivery; cost overrun risk during construction; timely completion of the facility; underlying costs to the operator of service delivery and the future costs associated with the asset; risk of industrial action or physical damage to the asset; and certain market risks associated with the project.

24. Allen, "The Private Finance Initiative (PFI)."

25. Cliff Woodruff, "Gross State Product, 2004," (data for 1997–2004), Bureau of Economic Analysis, U.S. Department of Commerce (www.bea.gov/bea/newsrel/gspnewsrelease.htm).

26. Public Private Partnership Forum (http://www.pppforum.com/faq.html#faqs).

27. Allen, "The Private Finance Initiative (PFI)."

28. Chapter 3 of "Report to Congress on Public Private Partnerships," U.S. Department of Transportation, December 2004, p. 51 (http://www.fhwa.dot.gov/reports/pppdec2004/pppdec2004.pdf).

29. Report to the Congress on PPPs, 2004 (http://www.fhwa.dot.gov/reports/pppdec2004/#ftnref65).

30. "A Study of Innovations in the Funding and Delivery of Transportation Infrastructure Using Tolls," Durbin Associates, November 14, 2005.

31. "PFI: Meeting the Investment Challenge," UK Treasury, July 2003 (http://www.hmtreasury.gov.uk/media//648B2/PFI_604a.pdf).

32. "Illinois Tollway Partners with Mobility Technologies to Help Chicago-Area Motorists Improve Travel Plans," *Company News,* December 15, 2003 (http://mobilitytechnologies.com/press/december_15_2003.html).

33. Stephen Goldsmith and William D. Eggers, *Governing by Network: The New Shape of the Public Sector,* (Washington, DC: Brookings Press, 2004) p.57.

34. Ronald D. Utt, "New Tax Law Boosts School Construction with Public-Private Partnerships," Heritage Foundation, August 8, 2001 (http://www.heritage.org/Research/Taxes/BG1463.cfm).

35. Doyin Abiola et al, "Solutions to International Challenges in PPP Model Selection: A Cross-Sectoral Analysis," paper prepared for Deloitte Research and the London School of Economics, March 13, 2006.

36. Bryan Grote, "Understanding Contemporary Public-Private Highway Transactions: The Future of Infrastructure Finance?," Testimony to Highways, Transit and Pipelines Subcommittee, Committee on Transportation and Infrastructure, U. S. House of Representatives, May 24, 2006 (http://www.house.gov/transportation/highway/06-05-24/Grote.pdf)

37. Nationwide, PPPs have accounted for more than one-quarter of the total user-backed private investment in U.S. highways (nearly $13 billion of the total $49 billion). See Grote, "Understanding Contemporary Public-Private Highway Transactions: The Future of Infrastructure Finance?"

38. To be considered a CDA, a project has to follow the characteristics of design-build (DB) contracting, defined as follows: "A comprehensive development agreement is an agreement with a private entity that, at a minimum, provides for the design and construction of a transportation project and may also provide for the financing, acquisition, maintenance, or operation of a transportation project."

39. "PPP Case Studies: Texas State Highway 130," Federal Highway Administration, U.S. Department of Transportation (http://www.fhwa.dot.gov/ppp/sh130.htm).

40. "PPP Case Studies: South Bay Expressway (SR 125)," Federal Highway Administration, U.S. Department of Transportation (www.fhwa.dot.gov/ppp/sr125.htm).

41. Ken Orski, "Beyond the Tipping Point VII," *Innovation Briefs*, November–December 2006.

42. Peter Fitzgerald, "Review of Partnerships Victoria Provided Infrastructure," January 2004 (http://www.gsg.com.au/pdf/PPPReview.pdf).

43. Elizabeth Brubaker, "Revisiting Water and Wastewater Utility Privatization," paper prepared for the Government of Ontario Panel on the Role of Government and presented at "Public Goals, Private Means," Research Colloquium Faculty of Law, University of Toronto, October 2003 (http://www.environmentprobe.org/enviroprobe/pubs/ev561.pdf).

44. U.S. Department of Education, "Conditions of America's Public School Facilities," Institute of Educational Sciences, National Center for Education Statistics, 1999 (http://nces.ed.gov/surveys/frss/publications/2000032).

45. American Society of Civil Engineers, "2005 Report Card for America's Infrastructure," March 2, 2005 (http://www.asce.org/reportcard/2005/page.cfm?id=31).

46. Evergreen Freedom Foundation, "School Construction: Building a Better Schoolhouse," *School Directors' Handbook*, 2003, p. SC-3 (http://www.effwa.org/pdfs/Construction.pdf).

47. "Need Space? School-Facility Public-Private Partnerships: An Assessment of Alternative Financing Arrangements," Appleseed Foundation, 2004, p.12 (http://www.edfacilities.org/pubs/appleseed.pdf).

48. Adrian Moore and Lisa Snell, forthcoming policy brief from the Reason Foundation, 2006. Also see: Jennifer Tell Wolter, "Lease-Leaseback Construction: The Sudden School," *Prosper, At Work, In Life*, May 2006 (http://www.prospermag.com/go/prosper/The_Magazine/may_2006/leaseleaseback_construction/index.cfm); Thomas York, "A Lesson in Saving Energy: Geothermal System at Inderkum High School, One of the Largest in Nation," *California Construction*, September 2004 (http://california.construction.com); and Mary Lynne Vellinga, "Old Is New Again," *Sacramento Bee*, May 16, 2004 (http://www.sacbee.com).

49. Jim Meek, "Schools' Out," *Summit* 4 (1), March 2001 (http://www.summitmagazine.com/Articles_Columns/Summit_Articles/2001/0301/0301_Schools_out.htm).

50. Stephen Goldsmith and William D. Eggers, *Governing by Network: The New Shape of the Public Sector*, (Washington, DC: Brookings Press, 2004), p.160.

51. Gary L. Sturgess and Briony Smith, "Designing Public Service Markets: The Custodial Sector as a Case Study," Policy Study 2, Serco Institute, 2006, p.8.

52. Bureau of Justice, "Prisoners in 2004," U.S. Department of Justice, Washington, DC, October 2005, p. 5.

53. Geoffrey F. Segal and Adrian T. Moore, "Weighing the Watchmen: Evaluating the Costs and Benefits of Outsourcing Correctional Services, Part II," Reason Public Policy Institute, January 2002 (http://www.rppi.org/ps290.pdf)

54. Office of the Innovative Partnerships and Alternative Funding, "Background of Innovative Partnerships Program," Oregon Department of Transportation (http://www.oregon.gov/ODOT/HWY/OIPP/background.shtml).

55. Goldsmith and Eggers, *Governing by Network*, chapter 5.

56. "Highway Asset Preservation Performance Measures for Highway Concessions," British Columbia Ministry of Transport, October 2004.

57. Goldsmith and Eggers, *Governing by Network*, chapter 7.

58. 21st Century School Fund, "Building Outside the Box: Public-Private Partnership—A Strategy for Improved Public School Buildings," 1999 (http://www.21csf.org/csf-home/Documents/Oyster/Building_Outside_Box.pdf).

59. John F. Williams, "Development Partnerships: Sharing Risk and Rewards on Publicly Sponsored Projects," National Council for Public Private Partnerships paper, June 2005 (http://ncppp.org/resources/papers/development_williams.pdf).

Chapter Ten: Transforming State Government

1. Shane Peterson, "Quid Pro Quo," *Government Technology*, July 2006.

2. Chad Vander Veen, "Breaking Barriers, *Government Technology*, October 2005.

3. Robert Atkinson, "Turbo-Charging E-Government," *Public CIO*, June 2006.

4. William D. Eggers, *Government 2.0: Using Technology to Improve Education, Cut Gridlock, Reduce Red Tape and Enhance Democracy* (Lanham, MD: Rowman and Littlefield Publishers, Inc., 2005).

5. Atkinson, "Turbo-charging E-Government."

Book Contributors

Robert N. Campbell III is Vice Chairman of Deloitte & Touche USA LLP and National Managing Director of Deloitte's U.S. Public Sector practice. Throughout his 33-year career with Deloitte & Touche USA, Bob has assisted government agencies at all levels with program planning and analysis, information systems planning, business process analysis, performance improvement and organizational transformation engagements. He has advised leaders in over 35 states.

Steve Dahl is a Firm Director leading the Midwest Regional and National Financial Management/Transformation Public Sector practice of Deloitte Consulting LLP. He has provided a leadership role in significant transformational efforts in the States of Minnesota, Illinois, Nebraska and the City of Minneapolis.

Rick Davenport is a Principal in the Total Rewards Group of the Human Capital practice in the Irving, Texas, office of Deloitte Consulting LLP.

Christina Dorfhuber leads Deloitte Consulting LLP's National Public Sector Strategy and Operations practice, a group of principals and directors with deep experience in the business of government. A graduate of Harvard's Kennedy School of Government, she has focused on helping government manage, deliver and improve services for most of her professional career, both in the United States and overseas.

Tiffany Dovey of Deloitte Services LP is a Research Associate with Deloitte Research-Public Sector. She is responsible for research and thought leadership for Deloitte's public-sector practice.

William D. Eggers of Deloitte Services LP is the Global Director for Deloitte

Research-Public Sector, where he is responsible for research and thought leadership for Deloitte's public-sector practice. Bill has authored numerous books on transforming government, including *Governing by Network: The New Shape of the Public Sector* (Brookings, 2004) and *Government 2.0: Using Technology to Improve Education, Cut Red Tape, Reduce Gridlock, and Enhance Democracy* (Rowman and Littlefield, 2005).

Kara Harris is a Senior Manager in Deloitte Consulting LLP's Public Sector practice. She practices in the Health and Human Services segment with a specialty in the strategy, design, and development of integrated eligibility solutions.

Matt Kouri is a Senior Manager in Deloitte Consulting LLP's Public Sector practice in Austin, Texas. He advises state and local government leaders on strategic, human capital and operational matters. He has recently led two state Medicaid programs through major transformations.

Greg Pellegrino of Deloitte Services LP is the Global Managing Director, Public Sector – Deloitte Touche Tohmatsu. He has assisted government organizations to improve performance and constituent service through the adoption of best practices and emerging technologies for more than 18 years. He is the Chairman of the Board of Directors for the Homeland Security and Defense Business Council in Washington, D.C., a nonprofit association of the leading companies focused on the homeland security market.

Mike Phelan of Deloitte Consulting LLP leads the delivery of workforce planning services for public sector clients of the firm. Mike has over 20 years of experience in leading organizations through the design and implementation of workforce planning solutions.

Tim Phoenix leads Deloitte's Public Sector Industry Group for the Deloitte Consulting LLP Human Capital practice. His principal areas of expertise are human resource strategy development, organizational performance, retirement and pension planning and executive compensation.

Rob Wavra of Deloitte Consulting LLP is a consultant in Deloitte's Federal Strategy and Operations practice, based in Washington, D.C. He serves U.S. government clients in a variety of engagements, with experience including process improvement, performance management, and e-Government.

Lance Weiss is a Senior Manager at Deloitte Consulting LLP in Chicago. Lance has over 30 years of experience in employee benefits and retirement planning.

Acknowledgments

With much of the media and public attention focused on the national stage since the events of September 11, 2001, states have taken something of a backseat to the federal government. However, few areas of government have as big an impact on our lives and are as complex to manage as are the states. We wrote this book for and about states because they have never been more important than they are now—and seldom have they faced the daunting challenges they do today.

Pulling this book together in an extremely compressed time period was a team effort in every sense of the word. Dozens of colleagues played a role in making *States of Transition* a reality, none more so than Deloitte Research Associate Tiffany Dovey of Deloitte Services LP. The co-author of several chapters in the book and a contributor to others, Tiffany also managed the book project from start to finish. Her diligence, tireless attention to detail and eternally positive attitude in the face of impossible deadlines made the final product possible.

Other Deloitte Services LP colleagues also played vital roles. Shalabh Singh's research and writing contributions to chapter 2 were substantial and invaluable. Analyst Venkataramana Yanamandra played a similarly important role in another chapter. Senior editor Jon Warshawsky, a gifted writer and book author in his own right, did a masterful job editing several chapters of the book, including the introduction. Ajit Kambil gave key support for the project, Robin Athey made significant intellectual contributions to the chapter on talent management and Ira Kalish provided helpful comments on the infrastructure issue.

Greg Pellegrino of Deloitte Services LP and Deloitte Consulting LLP colleagues Christina Dorfhuber, Steve Dahl, Kara Harris, Matt Kouri, Lance Weiss, Tim Phoenix, Mike Phelan, Rick Davenport and Robert Wavra contributed to the book as chapter co-authors. Other colleagues also made important contributions. John Marke of Deloitte & Touche USA LLP drafted the risk management framework in the chapter on upgrading emergency response. Dan Johnson, the former homeland security director of Minnesota, now with Deloitte Consulting LLP, also provided extensive comments and guidance for that chapter. Chetan Choudhury of Deloitte Consulting LLP made important contributions to the introductory chapter.

Jim Wetzler and Clint Stretch of Deloitte Tax LLP offered valuable input into the potential fiscal and tax policy implications of an aging population. Sean Fox, Gayatri Dornamraju and Praveena Rao of Deloitte Services LP contributed case studies on how the aging citizen was affecting individual states.

Drew Beckley of Deloitte Consulting LLP helped us to think through Medicaid issues, as did Shane Heiser, Patricia Zenner, Cindy Yang and Sheela Patil of Deloitte Consulting. Michael Adelberg, John Skowron, Sundhar Sekhar, Chip Blagg, Nicole Tichon, Don Hoag and Michael Britz, all of Deloitte Consulting LLP, made significant contributions to chapter 6. Deloitte Consulting LLP summer associates Jonathan Allen, John Kern and David Coombs also contributed to the integrated health and human services delivery chapter.

Deloitte Consulting LLP's Joanne Gallagher led the early research work for chapter 3. J.R. Ruiz of Deloitte Consulting LLP and intern Joy Jamir of Deloitte Services LP, a graduate student at Georgetown University, assembled the data on state workforce trends and contributed in other ways to the talent management chapter.

Charlie Thompson and Sukumar Kalmanje of Deloitte Consulting LLP, Saad Rafi of Deloitte Canada and Michael Flynn of Deloitte Ireland helped us develop our thinking on infrastructure issues.

Martha Gottron, who edited a previous book for us, did another first-rate job on this one. Aditi Rao of Deloitte Services LP proofed the pages and provided helpful editing assistance. Chris Ying did a yeoman's job typesetting the book and developing many of the graphics.

A number of other friends and colleagues played an important role in making the book a reality. Merrill Douglas, a free-lance writer specializing in information technology issues, helped write the chapter on emergency response. Lisa Snell and Adrian Moore of the Reason Foundation co-authored the chapter on driving more money into the classroom. Bruce Posner, Steve Towns and Shane Peterson also provided invaluable help and advice. Gary Sturgess and Vance McMahan, two good friends who also happen to be leading authorities on public policy issues, provided insightful comments that improved the book immensely. Graduate students from several graduate schools of public policy and administration also played important roles in the book. Students from The George Washington University looked at lessons learned from Hurricane Katrina in networked emergency response. At the Goldman School of Public Policy, graduate student David Kwok spent several months studying ways to close the infrastructure gap.

Last, we would like to thank the governors of our 50 states and other state government leaders and staffers for their public service to our country. Few industries are as challenging to manage as government, and only a handful of areas of government are more complex to manage than a state. As the CEOs of their states, governors have a range of responsibilities comparable to their corporate equivalents. But they must somehow manage without profitability or per-share value targets—not to mention working concurrently with numerous other statewide office holders. And it's all done in a fishbowl. It's an awesome responsibility—one we're grateful they've accepted amid the very difficult conditions facing states today.

Index

Note: *Italic* page numbers indicate figures and tables.

ACCESS Florida, 166

Accidents, 247

Accountability: in educational service sharing, 242; in educational standards, 17–18; in government transformation, 287–88

Accounting and Procurement Systems, Minnesota, 292

Accounting systems, 292

Actus Lend Lease, 265

Adequacy lawsuits, on education spending, 208

Adjutant General, 202

Administration: education spending on, 209–17; in educational service sharing, 220–21, 223–25, 229; in Medicaid reform, 133–35, 141, 142; of pension systems, 103–4; transformation of, 290–95

Administration on Aging, 41

Advocacy groups, in health and human services integration, 150, 153–54

Aging citizens, 25–56; changing service mix for, 41–47, *42*; civic engagement by, 34–36; delivery of services to, 28, 47–54; demographics of, 3–4, 25, *26*; in dependency ratios, 28–34, *29*; and financing for services, 36–41; health care for, 18, 42–44; innovating services for, 47–54; and need for reform, 3–4, 25; as percentage of population, 25, *26, 27*; philanthropy and, 34–35; transportation for, 41, 44–47, 49

Agreements, shared services, 218–20

Airline check-in kiosks, 52–53

Airport screening, 5

Akron Beacon Journal, 207–8

Alabama, 10–12, 196

Alabama Volunteer and Donations Database System (AVADDS), 196

Alaska, public pension system in, 106

American Customer Satisfaction Index, 8

American Federation of State, County and Municipal Employees, 75

American Legislative Exchange Council, 214–15

American Red Cross, 184

American Society of Civil Engineers (ASCE), 19, 246

Andrew, Hurricane *(1992),* 175

Anthrax attacks *(2001),* 190

Arizona: education reform in, 211; education spending in, 214; infrastructure gaps in, 247; old-age dependency ratios in, 29

Arkansas: education reform in, 211; emergency response in, 180–81

Arlington (Texas), 292

Army, U.S., 72, 265

Ashland Family Center (Oregon), 154

Assessment: in educational service sharing, 237–40; in government transformation, 283, 300; in health and human services integration, 167, 169–70; of Medicaid programs, 124, 136–41; of pension systems, 110; in public sector hiring, 71; in risk management, 196–97, *198, 198*–99

Assets, state: evaluation of, 15–16; in government transformation, 294; and public–private partnerships, 273–74; and service sharing, 229

Austin (Texas), 20, 262

Australia, 50, 54, 75, 262, 273

Automation, process: in public pension system, 104; and public workforce efficiency, 82–83

Automotive industry, 10–12

Avian flu, 175

Aviation industry, 186

Baby Boomers: and human capital shortage, 57–59; job satisfaction among, 62, 63; online services for, 51; philanthropy among, 34; retirement age of, 34; volunteering by, 35–36. See also Aging citizens

Balloon, Medicaid, 118–19

Bam (Iran), 194

Barbour, Haley, 173

BART. See Bay Area Rapid Transit

Base conversion, military, 264–65

Bay Area Rapid Transit (BART), 248

Benchmarking expenditure analysis, 300

Benefit plans, defined, 95–96, 106–7

Benefits: cost of, old-age dependency ratios and, 29–30, 30; employment, generational differences in, 62–63, 63. See also Pension benefits

Benefits-savings validation, in government transformation, 287–88, 289

Bergen County (New Jersey), 228

BHAGs (big, hairy audacious goals), 21

Bill and Melinda Gates Foundation, 17, 35, 214

Binghamton (New York), 88

Biometric data, 7

Bird flu, 175

Birth rates, 27

Blagojevich, Rod, 5, 108–9, 285

Blanco, Kathleen, 173

Bloom Township (Illinois), educational service sharing in, 229

Bloomberg, Michael, 92

Boards of Cooperative Educational Services (BOCES), 234–35

Boat registration, 298

Bonding, public, for infrastructure projects, 248–49, 249

Bonds: pension obligation, 101–3, 108; private activity, 260

Bossidy, Larry, 21

Boston (Massachusetts), 18, 215

Bowie County Transportation cooperative (Texas), 238

Brain drain, 79–80

Bredesen, Phil, 126

Bristol-Myers Squibb, 227

Britain. See United Kingdom

Brown, Pat, 245

Bucci, Richard, 88

Budget(s), state: aging citizens and, 3; in government transformation, 283–84, 300; legacy thinking in, 12; old-age dependency ratios and, 29–30; public pension systems and, 5, 88, 90, 97; during recession, 2, 6; threats to, 3–5; uncertainty and, 6. See also Education spending; Infrastructure gaps; Medicaid spending

Budget busters, 4–5

Buffett, Warren, 34

Build-lease-transfer (BLT) procurement model, 252

Build-operate-transfer (BOT) procurement model, 252

Build-own-operate (BOO) procurement model, 252

Build-own-operate-transfer (BOOT) procurement model, 252

Build-transfer-operate (BTO) procurement model, 252

Build-transfer (BT) procurement model, 252

Building Schools for the Future (UK), 263

Bullock, Bob, 281

Burke, Mary Jane, 211

Buses, school, sharing of, 223, 232, 238

Bush, Jeb, 175, 202

Bush (George W.) administration, No Child Left Behind initiative of, 7

Business Executives for National Security, 193

Business Roundtable, 185, 195

Business Week (magazine), 90–92, 113

Businesses. See Private sector

Cabinets: in government transformation, 282–83; recommendations on, ix

California: aging population in, 4, 30; demographic trends in, 30; education reform in, 18, 211, 214; education spending in, 207, 208, 210, *210,* 213–14, 215, *216,* 217, 228; educational service sharing in, 226, 228, 229, 230, 235; emergencies in, 174, 203; emergency response in, 193; government transformation in, 299; health and human services integration in, 155, 163; infrastructure in, 245, 259, 265; Medicaid spending in, 130; public pension system in, 87, 93, 106; state workforce in, 61, 73, 82

California Charter Schools Association (CCSA), 226

California Franchise Tax Board (FTB), 82

California Performance Review (CPR), 155, 299

California State Personnel Board, 61

Camino Union School District (California), 230

Campbell, Paul, 76

Canada: educational service sharing in, 222–23; emergencies in, 174; infrastructure in, 253, 254, 262, 264, 270; retirement age in, 33

Capabilities-based planning, for emergency response, 178, *179*

Capability maturity model, *200,* 200–201

Capability transfer, in state workforce, 78–80

Capital, cost of, 256

Car accidents, infrastructure gaps and, 247

Carcieri, Donald, 106

Career development: transformation of, 296; for young workers, 62–65

Carrollton (Texas), 292

Catholic schools, 212–13

Cato Institute, 214

CCSA. *See* California Charter Schools Association

Census Bureau, 71, 103

Centers for Medicare and Medicaid Services, 4, 139, 148

Centralization/decentralization: of emergency response, 7, 173–74; of school management, 211–13, 221; of school support services, *220,* 220–21; of state workforce recruitment and hiring, 71–72, 73; trends in, 7

Change: agency-led, 277–78; imperatives for, 2–12; marketing of, 166. *See also* Transformation

Change management: in educational service sharing, 240; in public–private partnerships, 271

Charan, Ram, 21

Charter schools: definition of, 15; experimentation with, 15, 17–18; after Hurricane Katrina, 15; shared services and, 226

Charter Schools Special Education Consortium, 226

CharterBuy program (California), 226

Chicago (Illinois), 259–60

Children and Families, Florida Department of (DCF), 155, 165–66

Choices, consumer, problems with, 21–22, 50

Churches, in emergency response networks, 181

Cintra Concesiones de Infraestructuras de Transporte, 260

Cintra-Zachry, 20

Civic engagement, by aging citizens, 34–36

Civic Ventures, 35–36

Clean slates, 14–21

Cleveland (Ohio), emergencies in, 174

"Clicks and mortars" services, 45, 52–53

Client-facing programs, transformation of, 295–97

Cluster districts, 239–40

Coachella Valley Alliance (California), 229

Coachella Valley Unified School District (California), 229

Coast Guard, U.S., 186–87

College-preparatory programs, 17–18

Colleges. *See* Higher education

Colorado: health and human services integration in, 155; infrastructure in, 255

Colorado Department of Health and Human Services, 155

Commission on Efficiency and Effectiveness, Governor's (Virginia), 283

Commission on the Future of Higher Education, 11

Commonwealth Care Exchange, 126

Commonwealth of Pennsylvania Access to Social Services. *See* COMPASS

Communication: in educational service sharing, 240; in government transformation, 301–2. *See also* Information sharing

Communities of Practice (CoPs), 76

Community Health, Georgia Department of, 135–36

Community partners, in health and human services integration, 150, 153–54, 161, 166

COMPASS (Pennsylvania), 150–52, 160–61

Complacency, recommendations on avoiding, viii

Computer scientists, in public workforce, 78

Concession phase, in infrastructure public–private partnerships, 270–71

Concession procurement model, 253

Confidentiality, in health and human services integration, 163–64

Connecticut, educational service sharing in, 223

"Connector" models for Medicaid, 115–16, 126, 127

Consolidation: of public pension systems, 103; of public workforce,

84–85; of school districts, 211–14, 217

Construction phase, in infrastructure public–private partnerships, 270–71

Consultants, third-party, in government transformation, 286–87

Consumers. *See* Customer(s)

Contract management: in educational service sharing, 236; in Medicaid reform, 133–35

Contractual emergency response networks, 184

Contribution plans, defined, 96, 106–7, 115

Contributions, pension: by employees, 94–95, 101; by government, 97, 97, 102

Cooperative educational services (CES), 239

Cooperatives, service sharing, 238–39

Coordination, of emergency response networks, 182–83

Coos County (Oregon), health and human services integration in, 154

CoPs. *See* Communities of Practice

Cornwall-Lebanon School District (Pennsylvania), 224, 230

Corzine, Jon, 87–88

Cost control strategies: educational service sharing as, 226–29; health and human services integration as, 154–55, 162–63; for Medicaid, 118–20, 130–33

Cost-of-living increases, in pensions, 107–9

Coulson, Michael, 160, 161

Court rulings, on education spending, 208

Credibility gap, 1

Crimes, against aging citizens, 41

Critical talent: fast tracking of, 72–74; identification of, 68; in talent-management strategy, 77–78

Critical workforce segments, 77–78

Critical workforce trends, 78

Culture, of information sharing, 188–89

Customer(s): choices given to, problems with, 21–22, 50; in Medicaid reform, 127–28; preferences of, 48–50; segmentation of, 48–49, 52

Customer service: with health and human services integration, 152–54; in infrastructure projects, 257–58; in private *vs.* public sector, 8; rising expectations for, 8–10; through self-service, 81–82

Customization, of services, 8

Customs and Border Protection Bureau, 82–83

CVS Pharmacy, 41

Dallas/Ft. Worth (Texas), 20, 219

Daniels, Mitch, 250

D'Arcy, Stephen, 113

De Grasse, Leland, 208

Debt: college, and hiring practices, 70–71; cost of, 256; and infrastructure projects, 256, 257; limits on, 257

Debt financing, for infrastructure projects, 248–49, 249

Decentralization. *See* Centralization

Decision making: automation of, 83; in educational service sharing, 237, 240; in emergency response, 203; government transformation and, 292; in Medicaid reform, 131–33, 144

Defense, U.S. Department of (DOD), 72

Deferred Retirement Option Plans (DROP), 110

Deficit Reduction Act (DRA, 2005), 116, 119

Defined benefit plans, in pension reform, 95–96, 106–7

Defined contribution plans: in Medicaid reform, 115; in pension reform, 96, 106–7

Delivery of services. *See* Service delivery

Dell, 20, 262

Democracy: aging citizen participation in, 35; states as laboratories of, 2

Demographics: of aging populations, 3–4, 25, 26; dependency ratios in, 28–34, 29; key trends in, 28–36; and need for reform, 3–4, 25

Denver E-470 Toll Road, 255

Dependency ratios, old-age, 28–34, 29

Desert Sands Unified School District (California), 229

Design-build-finance-operate/maintain (DBFO/M) procurement model, 252, 261

Design-build-operate-maintain (DBOM) procurement model, 252

Design-build-operate procurement model, 252

Design-build procurement model, 250–51, 252, 261

Develop-deploy-connect cycle, 74–76, 76

DHL Corp., 191, 194

DHS. *See* Homeland Security, U.S. Department of

Direct services, sharing of, 222–23

Disabilities, age-related, 51

Disaster Assistance, Office of, 84

Disaster Credit Management System, 84

Disaster response. *See* Emergency preparedness and response

Disease response: information sharing in, 190; networks in, 177–79, 182–83. *See also* Emergency preparedness and response

District of Columbia, infrastructure in, 273

Divestiture procurement model, 253

DMVs. *See* Motor vehicles, departments of

DOD. *See* Defense, U.S. Department of

DOL. *See* Labor, U.S. Department of

Donations, in emergency response logistics, 194–95

Donofrio, Nadine, 9

Dow Chemical Co., 227

DPW. *See* Pennsylvania Department of Public Welfare

Drive to Excellence program (Minnesota), 82, 279–80, 284

Drivers, older, 41, 45–47, 53
Drivers' licenses, Real ID bill on, 7
Dulles Rail Corridor (Virginia), 253
Duluth (Minnesota), education spending in, 208
Duluth News Tribune, 208

E-ZPass system, 297
Early college programs, 18
Early retirement, and public pension systems, 95, 109–10
Earth911.org, 54
Earthquakes, emergency response to, 174, 194
Eastern Cluster Districts (Texas), 239–40
EBRI. *See* Employee Benefits Research Institute
Economic Growth and Reconciliation Act *(2001),* 263
Economies of scale, in educational service sharing, 229
Economy: globalization of, 10–12; knowledge in, 11
Education: about emergency response, 202; government transformation and, 283–84; and human capital shortage, 67; legacy thinking in, 13; measuring outcomes in, 137–38; about Medicaid program, 133; about pension reform, 111; process automation in, 83. *See also* Higher education
Education, Louisiana Department of, 14–15
Education, Pennsylvania Department of, 160
Education, U.S. Department of, 83, 209
Education Commission of the States, 208
Education reform: through district consolidation, 211–14, 217; experimentation in, 17–18; failures of, 22; global knowledge economy and, 11; small schools movement in, 214–17; unfunded mandates in, 7; in urban areas, 14–15. *See also*

Educational service sharing
Education spending: court rulings on, 208; current status of, 207–9; district size and, 209–17; enrollment and, 208; local control of, 212–13; *vs.* Medicaid spending, 115, 209; noninstructional, 209–17, 233; pressure for cuts in, 207–9, 232–34; service sharing and, 226–29, 232–34; small schools movement and, 215–17; sources of funding for, 38–39
Educational performance: government transformation and, 283–84; measuring outcomes in, 137–38; school decentralization and, 212–13; small schools and, 214–15
Educational service districts, 239
Educational service sharing, 207–44; benefits of, 221, 226–31; concept of, 218–21; definition of, 218, 238; *vs.* district consolidation, 211–14, 217; fiscal pressures and, 207–9, 232–34; guidelines for success in, 236–42; models for, *219,* 219–21, *220, 221,* 232, 238–40; opportunities for, 221–26, *222;* potential partners for, 225; small schools movement and, 214–17; state government role in, 231–36
Educational Services Commission (ESC), 232
Efficiency: in health and human services integration, 154–55, 162–63; in infrastructure projects, 250–51; *vs.* legacy thinking, 12–13; in public workforce, technology and, 81–84; recommendations on, ix; of user fees, 40
Einstein, Albert, 15
Elder care, home-based, 42–44, 50
Elderly citizens. *See* Aging citizens
Elections, presidential, aging populations and, 35
Emergency Management, Oklahoma Office of, 202

Emergency preparedness and response, 173–205; centralization of, after Katrina, 7, 173–74; federal *vs.* state/local roles in, 174–75, 177–79; government transformation and, 291–92; information sharing in, 182–83, 187–91; key capabilities for, 176, *176*; leadership of, 188, 201–4; logistics of, 191–96; need for reform in, 6; networks in, 176–87; risk management in, 196–201, *200*; types of emergencies, 174

Employee Benefits Research Institute (EBRI), 106

Employee contributions, to pension systems, 94–95, 101

Employment, government. *See* Federal workforce; Human capital; Workforce

Employment benefits, generational differences in desired, 62–63, *63*

Employment Retirement Income Security Act (ERISA, *1974*), 93, 104

Employment Services Department (ESD), San Jose, 73

Empower Kentucky initiative, 283, 284, 291, 293

Empowered Care initiative (Florida), 124

Engineers, in public workforce, 78

Enrollment, school: and cost pressures, 208; and service sharing, 230–31

Enterprise resource planning (ERP) systems, 281, 297

Enterprise transformation. *See* Transformation

Environmental Protection Agency (EPA), U.S., 246

Europe: infrastructure development in, 253; retirement age in, 33

Execution, challenge of, 21–22

Execution (Bossidy and Charan), 21

Expectations: and customer segmentation, 48–49; for health and human services integration, 168–69; low, as opportunity, 1–2; for Medicaid reform, 122; for pension reform, 111; rising, and need for reform, 8–10

Experimentation: building foundations for, 15–17; challenges of, 15–16; in education, 17–18; examples of, 14–21; execution of results of, 21–22; federal encouragement of, 3, 6–7; in health care, 18–19; in infrastructure, 19–21; in Medicaid, 18–19, 115–17; states as laboratories for, 2; in transportation, 6–7, 19–21. *See also* Innovations

Facilities: in government transformation, 294; sharing of, 225–26

Family Caregivers Alliance, 43

Fast Stream Development Program, Civil Service (UK), 75

Fast tracking, of critical talent, 72–74

Feasibility, in risk management, 196

Federal Emergency Response Agency (FEMA), 7, 176–77, 190

Federal Highway Administration, U.S., 247, 250

Federal Highway Trust Fund, 247

Federal Reserve Bank of Chicago, 247

Federal workforce: age distribution in, 60, *60*; fast tracking in, 74; Gen Y in, 64; human capital shortage in, 60; IT initiative in, 79; retirement from, 60; service sharing in, 236

Federal–state relationship: in emergency preparedness and response, 174–75, 177–79; evolution of, 6–8

FedEx, 68, 191, 193

FEMA. *See* Federal Emergency Response Agency

Fertility rates, and old-age dependency ratios, 32–33, *33*

Fidelity Investments, 47

Financial systems, enterprise, 292

Financing. *See* Funding

Fires, emergency response to, 174

First-wave transformations, 288
Fiscal pressure: and educational service sharing, 207–9, 232–34; old-age dependency ratios and, 30
Flexibility: in educational service sharing, 242; in emergency response, 186–87; in health and human services integration, 167–68; in infrastructure public–private partnerships, 271–73
Flooding, emergency response to, 174
Florida: aging citizens in, 29, 41–42, 45; education reform in, 215; education spending in, 233; emergency response in, 175–76, 202; health and human services integration in, 155, 165–66; health care in, 45; infrastructure in, 261; Medicaid reform in, 120, 124–25, 132; Medicaid spending in, 4, 124; old-age dependency ratios in, 29; public pension system in, 90
Florida Commission for the Transportation-Disadvantaged, 41
Florida Department of Children and Families (DCF), 155, 165–66
Florida Department of Revenue, 297
Florida Department of Transportation, 261
Florida Senior Community Service Employment Program, 41
Flu: avian, 175; pandemic, 177–79, 180
Food services, sharing of, 224, 230
Ford, 10
Fortune 500 companies, vs. Medicaid programs, 4, 129, 130
Franchise Tax Board (FTB), California, 82
Fraud, in Medicaid programs, 129
Freedberg, Sydney, Jr., 192
Freeman, David, 230
Fritz Institute, 195
From, James, 232
FTB. See Franchise Tax Board
Fuel taxes, highway funding through, 247–48

Functional approach to transformation, 286
Funding sources: aging citizens and, 36–41; for emergency response, 178; in government transformation, 292; for infrastructure projects, 20, 247–53; for Medicaid, 120; nonprofit organizations and, 40–41; tax modernization and, 36–39; for transportation, 20, 245, 247–48, 248, 296–97; for unfunded mandates, 7; user fees as, 40

GAO. See Government Accountability Office
Gap analysis, in risk management, 200
Gas taxes, highway funding through, 247–48
Gates, Bill, 8, 34
General Motors, 10
General Services Administration (GSA), 293
Generation X (Gen X), 61–63, 63
Generation Y (Gen Y): attraction to nonprofit organizations, 65–66; attraction to public sector, 63–65, 65; definition of, 59; and human capital shortage, 59, 62–66; job satisfaction among, 62–63, 63; perception of public sector, 65–66
Generational convergence, and human capital shortage, 62–66
George, Elizabeth, 232
Georgia: government transformation in, 283; Medicaid reform in, 135–36
Georgia Department of Community Health, 135–36
Giuliani, Rudolph, 173, 203
Globalization, 10–12
Goals, viii, 21–22
Governance, state: in emergency response, 201–4; new approaches to, 16–17
Governance boards, 241–42
Governance structures, of emergency response networks, 181–82

Government Accountability Office (GAO), 64
Government employment. See Human capital; Workforce
Governors: in emergency response, 201–4; in government transformation, 282; recommendations to, viii–xi
Grand Prairie (Texas), 292
Granholm, Jennifer, 10
Great Britain. See United Kingdom
Greater Lawrence (Massachusetts), 223
GSA. See General Services Administration

Hague, The (Netherlands), 258
Hale, Kate, 175
Hawaii: infrastructure in, 265; retiree health care in, 91, 92
Hawaii Family Housing project, 265
Health and Human Services, Colorado Department of, 155
Health and Human Services, U.S. Department of (HHS), 6, 116, 191
Health and human services integration, 147–71; benefits of, 150–55, 156; definition of, 148–49; efficiency and costs in, 154–55, 162–63; in government transformation, 295; incremental vs. transformational approaches to, 159–62; overcoming barriers to, 159–70; privacy concerns with, 163–64; roadmap for, 156–59, 157; vs. traditional service delivery, 149–50, 151
Health Canada, 77
Health care: for aging citizens, 18, 42–44, 50; experimentation in, 18–19; quality of, in Medicaid reform, 136, 139; retiree, 5, 91, 91–92, 111–12; universal, through Medicaid expansion, 125–26; worker shortage in, 44. See also Medicaid
Health Insurance Portability and Accountability Act (HIPPA, 1996),
140, 191
Health outcomes, in Medicaid reform, 116, 136–40
Healthy Families (California), 155
Healy, Bernadine, 118
Henry, Brad, 202
Henry, Tom, 91
HHS. See Health and Human Services
Hierarchical emergency response networks, 184
Higher education: debt from, and hiring practices, 70–71; global knowledge economy and, 11; high school reform and, 18; and human capital shortage, 67; intellectual property in, 16; service sharing in, 227–28, 235
Highway systems: current status of, 245–47; destruction in earthquakes, 203; experimentation with, 19–21; funding for, 20, 245, 247–48, 248; maintenance of, 245, 248, 250; public–private partnerships in, 259–62; transformation of, 296–97
HIPPA. See Health Insurance Portability and Accountability Act
Hiring. See Recruitment
Hispanics, in public workforce, 67
Holcomb, Rick, 9
Home-based health care, for aging citizens, 42–44, 50
Home Depot, 41, 47, 191, 193
Homeland security, state departments of, 201–2
Homeland Security, U.S. Department of (DHS): on capabilities-based planning, 178; in Hurricane Katrina response, 181, 183; in network activation, 181; in network coordination, 183; process automation in, 82–83
Honda, 12
Hospitals: construction of, 272–73; in health and human services integration, 164
Hoteling, 294
Houston (Texas), 20, 219, 263

Houston Independent School District (Texas), 263

Hoxby, Caroline, 215

HR. *See* Human resources

Huckabee, Mike, 180–81

Human capital, public-sector, 57–86; age distribution in, 3, *60, 60*–62, *61*; critical talent in, 68, 72–74; decreasing demand for, strategies for, 58, *58, 80*–85, *81*; develop-deploy-connect cycle in, 74–76, *76*; fast tracking of, 72–74; future shortage in, 59–62; generational issues in, 62–66; and government transformation, 283–84, 296, 300–301; increasing supply of, strategies for, 58, *58, 68*–80, *69*; legacy thinking in, 14; in Medicaid reform, 134, 143; organizational restructuring and, 84–85; pension reform and, 111–12; retirement eligibility and, 57–62; service sharing in, 236; skill sets in, new, 67–68; succession gap in, 57–58, 67, 78–80; talent management in, 69–70, 74–78; technological advances and, 81–84; traditional approach to, 68–69, 70

Human resources: information technology and, 82, 85; online self-service in, 82, 293; service sharing in, 225, 236; traditional approach to, 68–69; transformation of, 293

Human Resources Division (HRD), Massachusetts, 225

Humanitarian aid organizations, in emergency response, 194–95

Hurricanes: emergency response to, 173–74, 175, 202; and health and human services integration, 147–48, 165. *See also* Katrina, Hurricane

Hyundai, 12

I-Pass Illinois Tollway, 257–58

IBM, 81

Idaho, 233

Illinois: education spending in, 210; educational service sharing in, 229, 230; government transformation in, 285, 287, 291, 294, 295; infrastructure in, 257–58, 259–60; Medicaid reform in, 295; state workforce in, 75–76

Illinois public pension system: administrative costs of, 103; approach to reform of, 5, 108–9; benefit expansions in, 93, 109; benefit formulas in, 100–101; closing loopholes of, 100, 108; defined contribution plans in, 106–7; early retirement and, 95; education about, 111; employee contributions to, 95; funding status of, 5, 108; new revenue sources for, 101, 102–3; repayment strategy of, 104, 108

Immigration, and old-age dependency ratios, 31–32

Incentives: for educational service sharing, 234–36; in Medicaid programs, 120, 136, 139

Incident Command System, 177

Income taxes, aging populations and, 4, 36, 39

Incremental approach: to government transformation, 277–78; to health and human services integration, 159–62

Independent business unit model, *220,* 220–21

Indiana: educational service sharing in, 235–36; infrastructure in, 250, 260, 264–65; position-based hiring in, 73

Indiana Toll Road, 250, 260

Indianapolis (Indiana): military base conversion in, 264–65; position-based hiring in, 73

Indianapolis Naval Air Warfare Center, 264–65

Indirect services, sharing of, 223–26

Inflation, and cost-of-living pension increases, 109
Information sharing: in emergency preparedness and response, 182–83, 187–91; in health and human services integration, 163–64; principles for, 187–91
Information technology (IT): brain drain and, 79; in emergency response, 188, 189–90, 196; in government transformation, 281, *290, 290,* 290–92; in human resources departments, 82, 85; in Medicaid reform, 117, 121–22, 132, 138–41, 143–44; in public pension systems, 104; reduced paperwork through, 83–84
Information Technology Association of America, 59
Information technology (IT) professionals, in public workforce, 78, 79, 84–85
Infrastructure: experimentation in, 19–21; procurement models for, 250–53; and public pension revenue, 101. *See also* Transportation
Infrastructure gaps, 245–53; current status of, 245–47, *246;* options for closing, 248–53; reasons for, 247–48
Infrastructure public–private partnerships, 251–74; benefits of, *251,* 254–58; federal support for, *260,* 260–62; guidelines for success in, 266–74; international use of, 251–53; legislation on, *251, 253, 260,* 264, 270; maintenance responsibility in, 254–55; models for, 20–21, 252–53, 267; opportunities for, 258–66
Innovations: in aging citizens' services, 47–54; federal encouragement of, 3, 6–7; federal waivers and, ix–x, 6–7; in Medicaid reform, 18–19, 115–17; states as laboratories for, 2. *See also* Experimentation
Instruction, service sharing in, 222–23

Intellectual property assets, 16
Internal Revenue Service (IRS), U.S., 262, 298
International Diesel, 12
International Federation of Red Cross, 195
Internet. *See* Online services
Internship programs, 64
Investment policies, for pension systems, 103
Iowa, 217
Iowa State University, 217
Iran, 194
IRS. *See* Internal Revenue Service
IT. *See* Information technology
IT Workforce initiative, 79

Jackson, Jason, 192
Jackson County (Oregon), health and human services integration in, 154
Jacobs, Leslie, 14
James F. Oyster Bilingual Elementary School (District of Columbia), 273
Jenison (Michigan), public pension system in, 92
Job satisfaction, generational differences in, 62
Job training programs, transformation of, 296
John Hay Elementary School (Seattle), 212–13

Kaiser Permanente, 189–90
Kansas, 136
Kansas City, emergency response logistics in, 193
Katie Beckett program, 130–31
Katrina, Hurricane: centralization of emergency response after, 7, 173–74; Coast Guard in response to, 186–87; education spending on evacuees from, 208; information sharing and, 187; integrated services for victims of, 147–48; logistics of response to, 191, 192; networks in response to, 180–81,

183, 185; public education after, 14–15; state and local responses to, 175, 180–81; Wal-Mart in response to, 191, 192
Kelly, Michelle, 147
Kempthorne, Dirk, 115
Kentucky: government transformation in, 283, 284, 291, 293; Medicaid reform in, 119–20
Kiosks, 53
KIPP Academy Charter Schools, 17–18
Kline, John, 92
Knowledge economy, global, 11

Labor, U.S. Department of (DOL), 11, 52
Labor productivity, infrastructure gaps and, 247
Labor Statistics, Bureau of, 59, 67
Labor supply, old-age dependency ratios and, 29
Labor unions: in auto industry, 12; in government transformation, 301; in health and human services integration, 165
Land, as underutilized asset, 16
Las Vegas (Nevada), government transformation in, 291–92
Law enforcement: aging citizens and, 41–42; public–private partnerships in, 265–66
Laws. See Legislation
Lawsuits, on education spending, 208
Leadership: in educational service sharing, 236–37; in emergency response, 188, 201–4; in government transformation, 282, 299; in information sharing, 188
Lease-leaseback arrangements, 263, 265
Lease procurement model, 253
Leavitt, Michael, 116
Lebanon (Pennsylvania), 230
Legacy thinking, 12–14; in education, 13; in government employment, 14; in health care, 18–19
Legislation: in government

transformation, 284–85, 301; on public–private partnerships, 251, 253, 260, 264, 270
Leventhal, Steve, 195
Licensing, 280, 298
Life-cycle approach, to public–private partnerships, 267–71, 269
Life-cycle costs, in infrastructure, 255
Life expectancies, and retirement ages, 34, 39
Light, Paul, 71
Lincoln United School District (California), 226
Litigation, on education spending, 208
Loans: college, and hiring practices, 70–71; disaster, for small business, 84
Local control, of schools, 212–13, 218, 230
Local governments: legacy thinking in, 13; shared services in, 218
Logistics, of emergency response, 191–96
Loopholes, in public pension systems, 100, 108
Los Angeles (California): education reform in, 214; education spending in, 213–14; emergencies in, 174, 203; infrastructure gap in, 245
Los Angeles Times (newspaper), 87
Lotteries, state, 27
Louisiana, education spending in, 208, 233. See also Katrina, Hurricane
Louisiana Department of Education, 14–15
Low-income students, 18
Lubbock (Texas), educational service sharing in, 223–25
Ludeman, Cal, 139

Macquarie Infrastructure Group, 260
Maine: education reform in, 211; education spending in, 216–17; old-age dependency ratios in, 29
Managerial/confidential (M/C) job classification, 57

Manchin, Joseph, III, 102
Mandates: health insurance coverage, 127; unfunded education, 7
Marin County (California), education reform in, 211
Maryland, 264
Massachusetts: education reform in, 18, 215; educational service sharing in, 223, 225; emergency response in, 193; government transformation in, 295; health and human services integration in, 153–54, 158, 164, 295; health care reform in, 19, 126, 127; home-based health care in, 43–44; infrastructure in, 246; Medicaid reform in, 126, 127; public pension system in, 106
Massachusetts Human Resources Division (HRD), 225
McNie, Elizabeth, 203
McReady Oklahoma, 202
Media coverage, of government transformation, 301
Medicaid Management Information Systems (MMIS), 133, *134,* 139–40
Medicaid reform, 115–46; assessment of status in, 124, 136–41, *138;* challenges of, 121–22; early cost control strategies in, 118–20; expansion of coverage, 125–26; experimentation with, 18–19, 115–17; failures in, 118–20; federal waivers in, 6–7, 116, 120; in government transformation, 295–96; health outcomes in, 116, 136–40; implementation of, 141–44; management choices in, *117,* 128–36; management problems in, 116–19; need for, 4–5; policy choices in, 119, 123–28, 130–32; recent trends in, *137;* strategic approach to, 119–23; technology in, 117, 121–22, 132, 138–41, 143–44; tough choices in, 120–23
Medicaid spending: as budget buster, 4–5; comparison by state, 130,

131; control strategies for, history of, 118–20; current status of, 115, 148; *vs.* education spending, 115, 209; federal funding and, 120; *vs.* Fortune *500* companies, 4, 129, 130; and integrated service delivery, 148; management choices about, 130–36; rising program costs and, 121
Medical care. *See* Health care
Medicare Prescription Drug Plan, problems with, 21–22, 50
Memoranda of understanding, 201
Mental health treatment programs, 163
Mentoring programs, capability transfer through, 80
Mercedes-Benz, 11–12
Merck, 130
Miami (Florida): education reform in, 215; infrastructure in, 261
Miami, Port of, 261
Michigan: education reform in, 211; educational service sharing in, 219–20, 227, 231; globalization in, 10–11, 12; public pension system in, 92; retiree health care in, 92; shared services in, 218; state workforce in, 60
Michigan State University, 231
Middlesex County (New Jersey), educational service sharing in, 223
Midwestern Higher Education Commission, 227–28
Migration, domestic, and old-age dependency ratios, 31–32
Military base conversion, 264–65
Minnesota: education spending in, 208; educational service sharing in, 223; government transformation in, 279–80, 284, 287, 292, 293, 298; Katrina victims in, services for, 147–48; Medicaid reform in, 139; state workforce in, 61, *62,* 82, 279, 293; taxation in, aging citizens and, 37, *38*
Minnesota Accounting and Procurement Systems, 292

Minnesota State Aid Center, 147–48
Mississippi River flooding, 174
MMIS. *See* Medicaid Management Information Systems
Mobile communications network, 190
Montana, old-age dependency ratios in, 29
Morris County (New Jersey), 232
Motor vehicles, departments of (DMVs): citizen expectations and, 9–10; delivery of services in, 53; older citizens and, 46–47, 53
Motor Vehicles, New York Department of, 46–47, 53
Motor Vehicles, Virginia Department of, 9–10
Mount Olive School District (New Jersey), 227
Murkowski, Frank, 106
Murphy, Dick, 87
Murray, Vicki, 214
Mutual aid agreements, 218–19
MyHealthyVet, 45

Naples, Nancy, 46
National Aeronautics and Space Administration (NASA), 59
National Assessment of Educational Programs, 17
National Association of State Retirement Administrators, 89
National Audit Office (UK), 254
National Committee for Quality Assurance, 139
National Council on Aging, 36
National Council on Teacher Retirement, 89
National Electronic Disease Surveillance System, Pennsylvania (PA-NEDSS), 182–83
National Emergency Resource Registry (NERR), 183
National Emergency Responder Credentialing System, 190
National Governors Association, 7
National Guard, 202

National Incident Management System (NIMS), 178
National Journal, 192
National Medicaid Pooling Initiative, 136
National Response Plan, 177
National School Lunch Program, 160, 161
National Voluntary Organizations Active in Disaster (NVOAD), 184
National Weather Service, 174
Natomas Unified School District (California), 265
Navy, U.S., 264–65
"Need to know" criteria: in emergency response, 177; in information sharing, 188
Nemitz, Craig, 181
Netherlands, 258, 271
Networks, emergency response, 176–87; activation of, 180–81, *181*; coordination of, 182–83; governance structure for, 181–82; identification of existing, 177–79; information sharing in, 187–91; need for, 176–77; organizational structures and, 183–87; types of, 184–85
Networks, private-sector, in health and human services integration, 165–67. *See also* Public–private partnerships
Nevada, government transformation in, 291–92
Nevada Shared Information Technologies Services (NSITS), 291–92
New Hampshire: educational service sharing in, 238; health and human services integration in, 162
New Jersey: educational service sharing in, 223, 227, 228, 229, 232, 235, 238; emergency response logistics in, 193; public pension system in, 87–88, 94, 96, 97, 101–2; shared services in, 218

New Jersey Regional Efficiency Aid Program (REAP), 227, 235

New Jersey Regional Efficiency Development Incentive (REDI), 235

New Jersey School Boards Association, 238

New Jersey Star-Ledger (newspaper), 88, 96

New Mexico, 29, 266

New Orleans, 14–15. *See also* Katrina, Hurricane

New South Wales (Australia), 262

New York (city): health and human services integration in, 158; retiree health care in, 92

New York (state): aging citizens in, 46–47, 53, 55; education spending in, 208; educational service sharing in, 225, 234–35; Medicaid reform in, 144; Medicaid spending in, 130; public pension system in, 88; state workforce in, 57, 60–61

New York Department of Motor Vehicles, 46–47, 53

Newark (New Jersey), public pension system in, 88

No Child Left Behind (NCLB) initiative, 7, 138

Nonprofit organizations: aging citizens and, 35–36, 53–54; delivery of services by, 53–54; in emergency response networks, 180, 181; financing of services through, 40–41; Gen Y workers at, 65–66; hiring practices of, 71; rise in philanthropy and, 16, 34–35; value of, 16

North Carolina: infrastructure gaps in, 247; public pension system in, 97, 110

North Central Texas Council of Governments, 292

North Dakota, old-age dependency ratios in, 29

Northern Lebanon School District (Pennsylvania), 224, 230

Northern Valley Regional High School District (New Jersey), 228

Northridge Earthquake *(1994)*, 174, 203

Northville (Michigan), 219–20

Northville Parks and Recreation (Michigan), 220

Northville Public Schools (Michigan), 219–20

Northville Township (Michigan), 219–20

Nova Scotia (Canada), infrastructure in, 264

Nursing homes, 42

NYC.gov, 158

Oakland (California): education spending in, 214; infrastructure gap in, 245

Occupational Safety and Health Agency (OSHA), 52

ODOT. *See* Oregon Department of Transportation

Ohio: education reform in, 18; education spending in, 207–8; emergencies in, 174

Oil and gas industry, Gen Y workers in, 66

OK-WARN program (Oklahoma), 202

Oklahoma, emergency response in, 202

Old-age dependency ratios, 28–34, *29*

Older citizens. *See* Aging citizens

One-stop centers, 294, 298

Online services: for aging citizens, 28, 50–52, 54; in enterprise transformation, 281; government transparency through, 8–10; in health and human services integration, 150–54, 158, 160–61, 166, 295; in Medicaid reform, 122; and public workforce efficiency, 81–82; for small businesses, 52; in taxation processes, 82

Ontario (Canada), educational service sharing in, 222–23

OPM. *See* Personnel Management, U.S. Office of

Orange County (California), emergency response logistics in, 193

Orbitz, 152

Oregon: education spending in, 215, *215*; government transformation in, 294; health and human services integration in, 154; infrastructure in, 268–69, 274

Oregon Department of Transportation (ODOT), 268–69

Oregon Innovative Partnerships Program, 268–69

Organizational approach, to transformation, 286

Organizational priorities, in talent-management strategy, 77

Organizational structures: and educational service sharing, *220*, 220–21; and emergency response networks, 183–87; legacy thinking in, 12; in public workforce, revision of, 84–85

OSHA. *See* Occupational Safety and Health Agency

Ouchi, William, 211, 212–13

Outcomes: in education, 137–38; in health and human services integration, 154; in infrastructure projects, 258; in Medicaid reform, 116, 136–40

Outsourcing: in government transformation, 293; in Medicaid reform, 133–35; in pension reform, 104

Overcrowding, school, 265

Oxo International, 47

PA-NEDSS. *See* Pennsylvania National Electronic Disease Surveillance System

Palm Beach Post (newspaper), 175

Paperwork reduction, through technology, 83–84

Partnership for Disaster Relief, 185, 195

Partnership for Public Service, 60, 70, 71

Paskewich, Frank, 186

Pastorek, Paul, 15

Patton, Paul, 283, 284

Pawlenty, Tim, 82, 279

"Pay-as-you-go" financing: in infrastructure projects, 248–49, *249, 250, 257*; in public pension system, 93; in retiree health care, 91

Payroll taxes, aging populations and, 4, 37

Pennsylvania: aging population in, 25–27; educational service sharing in, 224, 230; emergency response in, 182–83; government transformation in, 292; health and human services integration in, 150–52, 160–61, 162, 168; Medicaid reform in, 144; state workforce in, 61, *62*, 66, 112

Pennsylvania Department of Education, 160

Pennsylvania Department of Public Welfare (DPW), 160–61

Pennsylvania Insurance Department (PID), 160

Pennsylvania National Electronic Disease Surveillance System (PA-NEDSS), 182–83

Pension Benefit Guaranty Corp., 98

Pension benefits: adjusting formulas for, 100–101; in causes of crisis, 93–94, 95–96; closing loopholes in, 100, 108; cost-of-living increases in, 107–9; difficulty of modifying, 98; expansion of, 93–94; guaranteed, 95–96; medium- and long-term changes in, 105–10; public-safety, 93, 100, 108–9; restructuring of, 105–7; short-term changes in, 100–101; supplemental, 93–94; two-tiered, 105–7

Pension systems, public, 87–114; administrative costs of, 103–4;

basic math of, 94; as budget buster, 5; causes of crisis in, 92–98; current funding status of, 87–92, 88, 89; and human capital, 111–12; immediate fixes for, 99–104; implementation guidelines for, 110–12; medium- and long-term fixes for, 104–10; myths about reform of, 90; need for reform of, 5, 112–13; public officials affected by, 87–88, 92, 98, 112–13; revenue sources for, new, 101–3; roadmap to recovery of, 98–110

Performance, government: and Medicaid reform, 134–35; transparency in, 8–10

Performance-Based Data Management Initiative (Department of Education), 83

Performance measures, 270–71

Performance reviews, 281, 282–83, 284

Perry, Rick, 233–34

Personal health accounts, in Medicaid reform, 128

Personnel Management, U.S. Office of (OPM), 74, 79, 236

Peters, Mary, 247, 260

Phased Retirement Programs, 110

Philanthropy, rise in, 16, 34–35

Placerville Union School District (California), 230

Planning phase, in infrastructure public–private partnerships, 268–69

Policy choices, in Medicaid reform, 119, 123–28, 130–32

Policy phase, in infrastructure public–private partnerships, 268–69

Population. See Aging citizens; Demographics

Port of Miami, 261

Portland (Maine), education reform in, 211

Position-based hiring, 73

Postal Service, U.S., 218

Poverty: and delivery of services, 50;

Medicaid expansion and, 125–26, 127

Power outages, emergency response to, 174

PPPs. See Public–private partnerships

Pre-assessment, in risk management, 196–97

Prefunding requirements, for public pensions, 93, 104

Prescription drug costs, in Medicaid reform, 135–36

Presidential elections, aging populations and, 35

Presidential Management Fellows (PMF) program, 74

Principals, school, 212–13

Prisons: aging populations and, 41–42; public–private partnerships in, 265–66

Privacy: in health and human services integration, 163–64; and information sharing for emergency response, 188–89, 191

Private activity bonds (PABs), 260

Private sector: aging populations and, 3, 47; customer service in, 8; in emergency response logistics, 191–94; in emergency response networks, 181; enterprise transformation in, 281; infrastructure financing by, 249–53; pension systems of, 93, 96, 98, 106; shared services in, 218, 227; technology and efficiency in, 81. See also Public–private partnerships

Private Sector, Office of (DHS), 181, 183

Process automation: in public pension system, 104; and public workforce efficiency, 82–83

Procurement: infrastructure, 250–53; transformation of, 292, 293

Productivity: labor, infrastructure gaps and, 247; of public workforce, technology and, 83

Project management: in government

transformation, 299; in public–private partnerships, 271

Project management office (PMO), 299

Projects for Older Prisoners, 42

Property taxes: aging populations and, 4, 36–39; public pension systems and, 88

Protocols, for information sharing, 189

Public bonding, for infrastructure projects, 248–49, *249*

Public education. *See* Education

Public officials: emergency response affecting, 173; public pension systems affecting, 87–88, 92, 98, 112–13

Public opinion, 111, 231, *231*

Public-Private Education Facilities Act (Virginia), 264

Public–private partnerships (PPPs): for aging citizens' services, 28, 53–54; definition of, 252; delivery of services through, 53–54; in educational service sharing, 225–26; in emergency response logistics, 193–94; in health and human services integration, 165–67; in infrastructure projects, 20–21, 251–75; legislation on, *251, 253, 260, 264,* 270; in Medicaid reform, 132, 133–35; models for, 252–53

Public-safety pension, 93, 100, 108–9

Public transportation: for aging citizens, 44–46, 49; current status of, 246

Public Welfare, Pennsylvania Department of (DPW), 160–61

Purchasing pools: in education service sharing, 223; in government transformation, 293; in Medicaid reform, 135–36

Quality-of-care, in Medicaid reform, 136, 139

Quick wins, in government transformation, 301

Radio systems, in emergency response, 190

Ragan, Mark, 154

Raises, end-of-career, and public pension system, 100, 108

ReadyReturn initiative (California), 82

Real estate: in government transformation, 294; sharing of, 225–26

Real ID bill, 7

Reason Foundation, 89, 217

Receivables management and collection, transformation of, 294–95

Recession, 2, 6

Recovery, after emergency response, 203

Recruitment and hiring: assessment practices in, 71; decentralization of, 71–72, 73; of Gen Y workers, 63–66; position-based, 73; strategies for improving, 68–73; timeliness in, 70–71; traditional approach to, 68–69, 70

Recycling services, shared, 219

Red Crescent Societies, 195

Redding School of the Arts (RSA), 226

Reform, imperatives for, 2–12

Regional educational service agencies, 238–39

Regional Efficiency Aid Program (REAP), New Jersey, 227, 235

Regional Efficiency Development Incentive (REDI), New Jersey, 235

Regulatory functions, transformation of, 297–98

Relational emergency response networks, 184–85

Rendell, Edward, 148

Repayment strategies, for public pension systems, 104

Requests for Information (RFIs), 135

Retention: of critical talent, 72–74; develop-deploy-connect cycle in, 74–76, *76*; of Gen Y workers, 63–66; talent management in, 69–70, 74–78

Retiree health care: current funding

status of, *91,* 91–92; and human capital, 111–12; need for reform of, 5

Retirement: early, and pension systems, 95, 109–10; from federal workforce, 60; and human capital shortage, 57–62; from state workforce, 60–62, *62. See also* Pension systems

Retirement age: and old-age dependency ratios, 33–34; raising of, 39–40

Revenue, Florida Department of, 297

Revenue management, transformation of, 297–98

RFIs. *See* Requests for Information

Rhode Island: infrastructure gaps in, 246; public pension system in, 106

Ridge, Tom, vii–xi, 2, 292

Riley, Bob, 173

Risk allocation, in infrastructure public–private partnerships, 254–55, 267–68

Risk appetite, 197–99

Risk assessment, framework for, 197, *198,* 198–99

Risk management, in emergency preparedness and response, 196–201, *200*

Risk mitigation, in information sharing in emergency response, 190–91

Roads. *See* Highway systems; Transportation

Roman Catholic schools, 212–13

Romney, Mitt, 19, 106, 153, 295

Rural areas: education reform in, 211; education spending in, 208; health care in, 45; shared services in, 218

Ryan, Patricia, 45

Sacramento (California): education reform in, 214; infrastructure in, 265

Sacramento Bee (newspaper), 208

Safety Net Care, 126

Sale-leaseback arrangements, 263

Salem County (New Jersey), educational service sharing in, 229

Sales taxes, aging populations and, 4, 36–39

Salvation Army, 147–48

San Diego (California): education reform in, 18; education spending in, 207; infrastructure in, 259; public pension system in, 87

San Francisco (California): education spending in, 214; infrastructure gap in, 245

San Jose (California): infrastructure gap in, 245; position-based hiring in, 73

San Jose Employment Services Department (ESD), 73

San Miguel Mountain Parkway (California), 259

Sanford, Mark, 106

Santos, Aina, 10

Sarasota County (New York), educational service sharing in, 225

Satellite-based communications, 190

Scheduling, recommendations on, ix

School(s): Catholic, 212–13; charter, 15, 17–18, 226; small, 214–17. *See also* Education

School construction, through public–private partnerships, 255, 258, 263–64, 265

School districts and systems: consolidation of, 211–14, 217; decentralization of, 211–13; pension funds of, 92, 93, 100, 108; retiree health care in, 91, 92; size of, and education spending, 209–17; in small schools movement, 214–17. *See also* Educational service sharing

School Lunch Program, National, 160, 161

Schuler, A. J., 203

Schwarzenegger, Arnold, 106

Seattle (Washington): public workforce in, 80; school decentralization in, 212–13

Seattle Public Utilities, 80

Second Harvest, 181

Second-wave transformations, 288, 291, 294, 296, 297, 298

Self-service, online, and public workforce efficiency, 81–82, 293

SEP-15. *See* Special Experimental Project 15

September *11* terrorist attacks, 174; Giuliani's response to, 173, 203; information sharing and, 187, 188; networks in response to, 185

Service(s): customization of, 8; taxes on, 37–38; user fees for, 40. *See also* Customer service

Service delivery: to aging citizens, 28, 47–54; experimentation with, 16–17; legacy thinking in, 12–14; by private sector, 53–54; self-service, and public workforce efficiency, 81–82, 293; transformation of, 288

Service delivery channels: for aging citizens, 28, 47–54; multiple, management of, 50–51; partnerships among, 53–54

Service districts, educational, 239

Service integration, 147–52; critical elements of, 149; definition of, 148–49; for Katrina victims, 147–48. *See also* Health and human services integration

Service offerings, in health and human services integration, 149, 157–58

Service sharing: concept of, 218–21; in government transformation, 293; in public sector, 218–19. *See also* Educational service sharing

Sewer infrastructure: current status of, 246; public–private partnerships in, 262

Shared services. *See* Service sharing

Shared services centers, 219

Sharp, John, 281

Sick-leave policies, and public pension system, 100

Siegel, Jeremy J., 39

Sjögren, Rebecca, 147–48

Skill sets, in state workforce: in

Medicaid programs, 134, 143; new, 67–68

Skyway Concession Company, 260

Small Business Administration, 84

Small businesses, online services for, 52

Small schools movement, 214–17

Smithville Independent School District (Texas), 239–40

Social Security, retirement age and, 39

Solid waste services, shared, 219

Somerset County (New Jersey), 227

Somerset County Business Partnership, 227

South Carolina: infrastructure in, 257; Medicaid reform in, 18, 128; public pension system in, 106

South Dakota, health care workers in, 44

South Lyon (Michigan), 227

Special education, 228, 230–31

Special Experimental Project 15 (SEP-15), *260*

Spontaneous emergency response networks, 185

Sri Lanka, 194

Staff: in government transformation, 282–83; recommendations on, viii–ix

Stafford County (Virginia), infrastructure in, 264

Stakeholders: in educational service sharing, 240, 242; in government transformation, 300–301; in health and human services integration, 158–59, 164, 166; in Medicaid reform, 121; in pension reform, 111

Standardization, through educational service sharing, 229–30

Standards-driven accountability, in education, 17–18

State workforce. *See* Human capital; Workforce

STEM fields, 11

Stock market boom, and public pension system, 96–97

Stockton (California), educational service sharing in, 226
Streamlining, of operations, 84–85
Strembitsky, Michael, 213
Sturgess, Gary, 266
Succession gap, in state workforce, 57–58, 67; planning for, 78–80
Sullivan, Mark, 50
Sunbelt States, domestic migration in, 31
Sunshine Network Veterans Health Administration, 45
SUNTAX. *See* System for Unified Taxation
Superintendency, cooperative, 238
Surveys, on customer preferences, 50
Syracuse University, 217
System for Unified Taxation (SUNTAX), 297

Taft, Bob, 174
Talent. *See* Human capital
Tax preferences, 37
Taxation: aging populations and, 3–4, 28, 36–39; infrastructure funding through, 247–48; online initiatives for, 82; pension reform influencing, 112–13; restructuring and modernization of, 36–39; revenues from, by age, 37, *37*; of services, 37–38; state workforce efficiency and, 82; transformation of, 297–98
Taylor County (Wisconsin), shared services in, 219
TEA. *See* Texas Education Agency
Teachers: pension funds of, 92, 93, 100, 108; as percentage of school staff, 209; retiree health care for, 91, 92
Tech High School (San Diego), 18
TechBoston Academy, 18
Technology: in delivery of services, 52; in education, 18; in educational service sharing, 225; in emergency response, 189–90, 196; government transparency through, 8–10; in health and human services

integration, 149, 150–54, 157–58, 167–68; in Medicaid reform, 117, 121–22, 132, 138–41, 143–44; in public workforce, 81–85. *See also* Information technology; Online services
Tele-health program, 45
Telecommuting, 294
Temecula (California), education spending in, 208
TennCare, 125–26
Tennessee, Medicaid reform in, 125–26
Terrorism: in risk management, 197; uncertainties of, and need for reform, 5–6; war on, 7. *See also* September *11* terrorist attacks
Texas: education spending in, 208, 209–10, *210*, 233–34; educational service sharing in, 219, 223–25, 229, 238, 239–40; government transformation in, 281, 282–83, 284, 292, 293, 296; health and human services integration in, 155, 158, 159–62; infrastructure in, 20–21, 253, 259, 261–62, 263, 266; Medicaid reform in, 131, 133, 136; public pension system in, 87, 93, 103; state workforce in, 60, 82
Texas Department of Transportation (TxDOT), 20, 259
Texas Education Agency (TEA), 210
Texas Health and Human Services Commission, 155
Texas Performance Review, 281, 282–83, 284
Texas Transportation Institute (TTI) Urban Mobility Study, 20
Texas Turnpike Authority, 259
Texas Workforce Commission, 296
Third-party consultants, in government transformation, 286–87
Third-party providers, in health and human services integration, 150, 153–54, 166
Thompson, Tommy G., 116
TIFIA. *See* Transportation Infrastructure

Financing Innovation Act
Toll roads: in government
transformation, 297; infrastructure
financing through, 20, 250, 255,
260, *260*; and pension system, 101
Tornadoes, emergency response to, 174
Toronto Pearson Airport, 254
Toyota, 12
Traffic congestion, 20, 245
Training: in government transformation,
301–2; in health and human
services integration, 167. *See also*
Education
Trans Texas Corridor, 20, 253
Transaction phase, in infrastructure
public–private partnerships, 269
Transformation, state government, 277–
303; benefits-savings validation in,
287–88, 289; first steps in, 280–85;
incremental *vs.* enterprise approach
to, 277–78; issues driving, 283–84;
legislative support for, 284–85,
301; lessons learned from, 299–302;
organization of, 285–87; targets for,
288–98
Transformation Roadmap (Minnesota),
82
Transparency, citizen demand for, 8–10
Transportation: aging citizens and,
41, 44–47, 49; current status
of, 245–47; experimentation in,
6–7, 19–21; funding for, 20, 245,
247–48, *248,* 296–97; public–
private partnerships in, 259–62;
in recovery after emergencies, 203;
school, service sharing in, 223, 227,
230, 232, 238; transformation of,
296–97
Transportation, Florida Department of,
261
Transportation, Oregon Department of,
268–69
Transportation, Texas Department of,
20, 259
Transportation, U.S. Department of, 46,
246, 256

Transportation Infrastructure Financing
Innovation Act (TIFIA), *260*
Transportation Sector Network
Management (TSNM), 185–86,
186
Transportation Security Administration
(TSA): creation of, 5; information
sharing in, 188, 190; organizational
structure of, 183–86, *186,* 188
Trostel, Phillip, 216–17
Trust, in emergency response networks,
183
Tsunamis, 185, 194

Uncertainty, and need for reform, 5–6
Union districts, 239–40
Union Parish (Louisiana), 192
Unions. *See* Labor unions
United 93 (movie), 174
United Kingdom: aging voters in, 35;
cost of debt in, 256; infrastructure
in, 253, 254, 255, 257, 263;
nonprofit organizations in, 40–41;
public workforce in, 75; retirement
age in, 39
Universal health care, 125–26
University of California, 235
UPS, 191, 193
Upward Mobility program (Illinois),
75–76
Urban areas: education in, 14–15, 208;
renewal policies in, 21
User fees: for infrastructure, 250, 259;
services financed with, 40
Utah, 7, 163

VA. *See* Veterans Administration
Value creation, 16
Vance (Alabama), 11
Vermont: education spending in, *216,*
217; Medicaid reform in, 6–7, 120
Veterans: delivery of services to, 50;
health care for, 45
Veterans Administration (VA), 45
Viacom, 130
Victoria (Australia), 262

Video games, 72

Virginia: citizen expectations in, 8–10; government transformation in, 283; government transparency in, 8–10; infrastructure in, 253, 255, 257, 263–64

Virginia Department of Motor Vehicles (DMV), 9–10

Virginia Governor's Commission on Efficiency and Effectiveness, 283

Virginia Pocahontas Parkway, 255, 257

Virtual Gateway (Massachusetts), 153–54, 295

Volunteering: by aging citizens, 35–36; in emergency response logistics, 194–95

Voting, by aging citizens, 35

Wagner, John, 153

Waivers, federal: for Medicaid, 6–7, 116, 120; recommendations on using, ix–x

Wal-Mart, 191, 192, 193

War on terrorism, 7

Warner, Mark, 10, 209, 283

Washington (D.C.), infrastructure in, 273

Washington (state): educational service sharing in, 239; public workforce in, 80; school decentralization in, 212–13

Washington Post (newspaper), 173, 175

Wastewater infrastructure, 246, 262

Water infrastructure, 246, 262

Water supply, shared, 218–19

Wealth transfer, and rise in philanthropy, 34–35

Weather Alert Remote Notification. *See* OK-WARN

Weather emergencies, 174, 202. *See also* Hurricanes

Weeks, Chris, 194

Weighted student funding formula, 213

Welfare programs, in health and human services integration, 160–61

Welfare reform, 16–17

West Virginia: educational service sharing in, 239; Medicaid reform in, 120; public pension system in, 102

Western States Contracting Alliance, 293

Wildfires, emergency response to, 174

Wilshire Associates, 97

Wilshire Research, 89

Wilson, Pete, 203

Wisconsin: educational service sharing in, 219, 234; health and human services integration in, 158, 169; infrastructure in, 247; shared services in, 218, 219; state workforce in, 60, 72

Workforce, public: aging populations and, 3, 33–34, 41; defining critical segments of, 77–78; globalization and, 10–12; in health and human services integration, 149, 157–58, 164–65; knowledge economy and, 11; legacy thinking about, 14; and old-age dependency ratios, 33–34; validating critical trends in, 78. *See also* Federal workforce; Human capital

WorkInTexas.com, 296

World Bank, 76

World Trade Center (movie), 174

Wyoming, old-age dependency ratios in, 29